Reinventing the Good Life

Reinventing the Good Life

An empirical contribution to the philosophy of care

Jeannette Pols

First published in 2023 by
UCL Press
University College London
Gower Street
London WC1E 6BT

Available to download free: www.uclpress.co.uk

Text © Author, 2023

The author has asserted her rights under the Copyright, Designs and Patents Act 1988 to be identified as the author of this work.

A CIP catalogue record for this book is available from The British Library.

Any third-party material in this book is not covered by the book's Creative Commons licence. Details of the copyright ownership and permitted use of third-party material is given in the image (or extract) credit lines. If you would like to reuse any third-party material not covered by the book's Creative Commons licence, you will need to obtain permission directly from the copyright owner.

This book is published under a Creative Commons Attribution-Non-Commercial 4.0 International licence (CC BY-NC 4.0), https://creativecommons.org/licenses/by-nc/4.0/. This licence allows you to share and adapt the work for non-commercial use providing attribution is made to the author and publisher (but not in any way that suggests that they endorse you or your use of the work) and any changes are indicated. Attribution should include the following information:

Pols, J. 2023. *Reinventing the Good Life: An empirical contribution to the philosophy of care*. London: UCL Press. https://doi.org/10.14324/111.9781800086029

Further details about Creative Commons licences are available at https://creativecommons.org/licenses/

ISBN: 978-1-80008-604-3 (Hbk.)
ISBN: 978-1-80008-603-6 (Pbk.)
ISBN: 978-1-80008-602-9 (PDF)
ISBN: 978-1-80008-605-0 (epub)
DOI: https://doi.org/10.14324/111.9781800086029

For Anne and Ariane

Contents

List of tables ix
Preface xi

1 Introduction: on the shifting specificities of the good and the bad in everyday life 1

2 Folding words and practices: methodological notes on exploring the good life 29

Part I: Shaping the good life – and the end of its theorisation 59

3 Dignity in long-term psychiatry: principles and everyday values for caregivers 63

4 The end of morality: Adam Smith and the taming of the passions 89

5 Giving voice or making voice? The principle of autonomy and everyday patient values in care for people with learning disabilities 119

6 The particularity of universalism: life in the salons, or citizens against aesthetics 137

Part II: Reconceptualising the good life 161

7 Aesthetic values as social values: women losing their hair due to chemotherapy 165

8 Imperfect lives: Foucault's archaeological reading of the Cynics 189

9 The self as a practice of worth: on imminent aesthetic socialities 219

Part III: Researching the good life 237

10 'Quality of life' and everyday values: living with ALS and a feeding tube 241

11 Petrarch's practice of letter writing: the good life in research 265

12 Reinventing research practices for studying the values of everyday life 283

13 Conclusions: reinventing the good life, grasping specificities 309

Acknowledgements 341
Bibliography 349
Index 365

List of tables

3.1 Forms of dignity   75

Preface

Which stories can be told and which cannot? Are there particular times and places in which some stories can be told and others can't? Why is it that some things are impossible to talk about while tales of other things flow like rivers? How do words relate to worlds and vice versa? Where might such connections fail? This book is about folding together words and practices, the complex ways in which this may – or may not – be done, and to what new insights such foldings can lead. Not until very recently did I realise that the intricacies of storytelling practices and repertoires have fascinated me since I was young.

Ever since I can remember I have wanted to become a writer. But my first novel, about the adventures of two horses, could not be written. At the age of 10 or so, I was lacking the necessary skills. This was a story that remained untold. Before that were other stories that could not be told, but this time because they were too painful, such as the story about the death of my mother. I became very good at *not* telling this story.

When I was 12 or so, I encountered another kind of untellable story. The heroes of my favourite books were guys: great guys, young and courageous adventurers, who rode their giant black horses through dense forests and over mountains so high that it was difficult to breathe. But while Tiuri went out, Lavinia had to stay home, safe in her castle, if she did not want to be murdered or raped.

Why could girls in books not go on adventures? Of course, at that time I could not say something like '"The adventurous woman" was a subject-position that still had to be invented in literature.' This was another mystery about how some things could not be put into words.

My plan as a student was to learn about care practices, about how patients are positioned within them, and especially about the utterances and doings that are, or are considered to be, 'mad', enigmatic or irrelevant. During my training as a clinical psychologist, however, I quickly learned that there was a lack of academic tools for studying such particular concerns despite the multitude of tools and framings that *were* around. I remember attending a class on cognitive psychology where the professor casually stated that 'humans beings are, after all, integrated cognitive systems'. I gazed at the professor in astonishment. He was unperturbed and continued his lecture. His friendly face and posture were framed by schemes and tables with arrows in all directions that showed the various pathways of human thinking. But something was alarmingly wrong, I felt at the time, if scientific stories about humans ignore bodies and feelings.

I started my philosophy studies and a world of new stories opened up. I learned about the use of language and about different styles of doing philosophy. The Habermas–Foucault debates were raging at the time, which, on the one hand, claimed that the transparency and universality of language would eventually lead to a general consensus among humans. On the other hand, however, were claims about the situatedness and relationality of language and the importance of local use-practices in which words get their meaning, which demonstrated why such a general consensus could never be achieved. These stories evoked different realities that could not be reduced to one another.

Social theory at the time specialised in *critical* analysis, and this 'critical' style was to be taken quite literally. We students were taught how to tear things apart, however elegantly done. This approach, however, did not consider the question of how to construct *new* stories. But then my fellow philosophers and I read Donna Haraway's *Cyborg Manifesto* and Annemarie Mol's 'Who knows what a woman is' (in Dutch, 'Wie weet wat een vrouw is'). Annemarie was doing her PhD in the same philosophy department where I was a student. That paper provided several very convincing and appealing provocations. Medicine (anatomy, physiology and genetics) *did not know* and could not agree on what a woman is. Sex was not so easily quantified as statisticians thought it could be. Sex was underdetermined.

Imagine what possibilities this insight opened up for us! If nobody knew, then this gave 'us' (wink wink!) the possibility to create something new, an opportunity to escape existing and powerful categorisations. It created space for new stories and academic adventures to emerge.

Meanwhile, some of the older philosophy teachers were lamenting the death of the Subject (big S) and the loss of Grand Narratives, Theories that Comprehend Everything in a Coherent Way. Convincing arguments claimed that the modernist dream could not become reality, and these philosophers lamented the waning of such narratives.

We members of the women's studies group in philosophy had no patience for such nostalgia. We had work to do. As cyborgs, or as not so gender-determined researchers, or whatever, we were looking for narratives that could take us beyond the dead ends of critique and essentialism: these had to be stories that could acknowledge everyday care practices, articulate modest attempts at improving situations and highlight the relationality of identities. Rather than pointlessly criticising the doctors, nurses and patients we encountered in our research, we searched for new types of stories, stories that could include people who could not speak in understandable ways, let alone fill out questionnaires. We searched for different ways to care for people who could not be cured and to understand them better, while also joining forces with their caregivers in thinking about how these patients could live a better life.

And, slowly but surely, this became the narrative I started to work on in my research. In hindsight, I can see that these stories were about trying to make the best out of situations that were tragic and could never be 'fixed'. They were stories about situations in which there were no words yet to describe or interpret them, or when there *were* words that demanded further interpretation: the silences of the long-term psychiatry patients, the mundane talks about the weather in nursing homes, the invisible practices of nurses who always seemed to know what to do, or the plethora of words about the latest trends in care work that did not appear to refer to anything concrete ('We place the patient at the centre!'). And there were the dumb technologies that nudge people into doing things, intentional or not, good or less good. I had found my ocean of stories and silences and sought ways to navigate its waves and depths.

This book brings together and develops the multiple insights gathered over many years of research on different care practices in the Netherlands, and explores social theory to trace the history and fate of everyday life values. It seeks to develop academic approaches to learning from *specific* situations while simultaneously 'making a voice' for silent things. The book attempts to address these issues, which, as one might expect, open up yet more questions, such as the intriguing silence in academic studies about the *aesthetic* values of everyday life. In everyday language, we often praise the beauty, propriety and niceness of things, but in academic discourse we no longer theorise such qualifications and their social implications.

The stories in this book are complex. They explore how attempts to know something are as much ways to create something as they are courses for action. Look at this quote from the musician and Black civil rights activist Nina Simone: 'I tell you what freedom is to me . . . No fear!'[1] Where Western philosophy discusses freedom as the breaking down of barriers that limit individual autonomy, Simone redescribes freedom as a way for opening up entirely new modes of thinking. This form of freedom – having no fear – gives rise to fresh questions and radically different answers. Where does this fear come from? What is involved in inducing it? Can it be softened? Eradicated? Simone's quote is not there to represent a final truth but instead is an example of the strength and necessity of generating possibilities for embarking on new adventures in thinking, telling and doing.

Notes

1 From *Nina Simone: A historical perspective*, a documentary produced by Peter Rodis (1970).

1
Introduction: on the shifting specificities of the good and the bad in everyday life

> *The 'bathrobe trick' for people suffering from chronic obstructive pulmonary disease (COPD)*
> Mrs Jacobs: When you're done with the shower, well, you towel off [demonstrates drying her body and her hair], but she [her webcam friend] said: 'You can put on a bathrobe and wait till you're dry, you won't catch a cold.' That takes no energy but drying yourself does! You have to learn to think like this. What would *you* do? After a shower, you would grab a towel. But now I take 15 minutes. The walking frame is near the door, I bring my phone in case someone calls. I take it easy and recover with my bathrobe on. Dry up a little, then put on a little deodorant, pat a little cream on my face and then I dress. And I shower in the afternoons. I lie down for an hour or so, and shower after that.

The fieldnote above describes the everyday event of taking a shower and drying the body. To many of us, taking showers is one of the most mundane activities of everyday life. It is rarely worth discussing. But for people suffering from COPD, even mundane activities such as showering can be major obstacles because of the energy they require. People suffering from COPD are quickly out of breath due to this severe lung disease, which ruins the plasticity of the lungs and makes breathing – and the uptake of oxygen – difficult. Here, Mrs Jacobs discusses the suggestion of using a bathrobe to save energy. She has 'learned to think like this' – everyday activities use energy. But this lesson also opens possibilities for *saving* energy. Wearing a bathrobe to save energy sounds as trivial to many as it is important to Mrs Jacobs. It makes an important difference to the goodness of her life and the things she can do in her day. Wearing a bathrobe creates space for doing things that matter to her besides showering. It relieves suffering and makes the unavoidable activity of bathing a less stressful event. It is easy to see that 'the bathrobe trick' is a boon to Mrs Jacobs's life.

But where do suggestions like the bathrobe trick come from? Where can we find or learn them? For Mrs Jacobs this was a tip from a friend, a fellow COPD sufferer, whom she met at the Dutch national rehabilitation clinic for people with severe COPD and asthma. Mrs Jacobs's friend, in turn, learned the trick from her COPD nurse, a specialist who cares for some Dutch COPD patients, but not all: access to such a nurse depends on where you live and what care is available there. This makes the bathrobe trick a type of knowledge that is both very important yet hardly ready to hand for people suffering from COPD.[1]

Clearly, bathrobe tricks are not the object of medical research. Medical research examines the effectiveness of medications and other interventions in and on the body, but not of everyday activities such as bathrobe tricks. And this is for good reason: it is a harmless intervention that anyone can try out in order to see if it works in their situation. No harm done if it does not work, much gain if it does, and money for expensive clinical trials can be spent in better ways.

But the apparent simplicity is deceptive. Because where might one learn about bathrobe tricks? There is no systematic collection of these practical types of knowledge, which cost little and are easy to try for everyone who thinks they might benefit from them, and that may greatly improve the everyday life of people with chronic disease. These practical techniques are part of the knowledge of nurses, and they are transferred orally or by working with experienced colleagues and patients. But this knowledge runs the risk of being lost or of remaining only locally available. Why has there been no attempt to systematically collect the types of knowledge that are aimed at improving the everyday life of and care for people suffering from chronic disease?[2] In this book I use the term chronic diseases as a shorthand for multiple diseases, handicaps or problems that are persistent and that may even deteriorate rather than get better. As there is no cure for chronic diseases, one has to learn how to live with them as best as possible. Yet there are very few methods to create and gather knowledge about how to do this well. How may we understand a good life when health problems do not go away? And what can we do to improve such lives? These questions motivate my research and this book is one of my attempts at answering them.

What gave rise to the writing of this book

The book emerged from my puzzlement about the apparent lack of words for expressing – as well as academic tools for studying – the things that are of value to everyday life and to the care for or by people with chronic diseases in Dutch care practices and in the literature more generally: valuable things such as saving your breath by drying in a bathrobe.[3] The aim of the book is to learn about the values of everyday life, about the things that are important in daily practices. I want to reinvent repertoires for studying such 'values in practice'. The need for reinvention stems from a lack of *academic* repertoire to study everyday life values. There are two main academic discourses surrounding chronic diseases and treatments for people who suffer from them. The first is a medical discourse, which concerns itself with the underlying disease that should be treated and cured. The second is an ethical discourse that has emerged within medical institutions. This ethical discourse has placed much emphasis on safeguarding patients' autonomy, initially as a way to protect people from overly enthusiastic doctors and medical researchers, and later to include their voices in treatment. Alongside these academic discourses there are also more popular narratives of 'wellness', which have often emerged from the private sector. The term wellness denotes various approaches, aims and practices for making life better, even if there are no cures.

Wellness practices may resemble the everyday attempts of people with chronic diseases to improve the quality of their life. Wellness narratives often emphasise the role of feelings, beauty, health, wellbeing, fitness and so on. Yet some of these narratives have become almost completely individualised, psychologised and commercialised. The imperative of such narratives is that individuals 'have to feel good'. Yet wellness narratives rarely conceptualise life as being in relationship to other people, although I do notice the frequent use of the word 'love'; this, however, often refers to self-love. Rarely are their claims discussed and put to the test in academic research. There is work on wellbeing, even on happiness, and approaches such as mindfulness have become professionally accepted. Yet wellness narratives rarely raise questions about how to collect and share knowledge, partly due to an ill fit with state-of-the-art scientific methods.[4] One could also say that there are myriad forms of more or less inspiring and useful knowledge that inform practices of wellness.

So how can we learn about the values that make everyday life as good as possible? Everyday life is a theme in ethnographically oriented sociology, geography, science and care studies, and anthropology.[5] This book builds upon this work by studying the mundane practices that are involved in 'health care' or 'health science'. In this book I try to understand everyday life, roughly, as a sequence of concrete, often mundane and always specific, observable events that emerge from what people and things do *somewhere*. I juxtapose everyday doings with abstractions, generalisations or ideal types.[6] In the bathrobe trick example, I relate the observable event of taking a shower and drying the body in a bathrobe to more general observations about, say, how people with COPD quickly run out of breath due to a loss of lung elasticity. Everyday life is as important to every person as it is unheroic to write about. It concerns the hidden work of care.[7]

Not much has been written in present-day academic research about the *values* that are pertinent to everyday life and how to study them. A value signifies that something is important, and an everyday value signifies something that is, or is made to be, important in day-to-day activities within a particular setting. What makes everyday life 'good'? There are a number of approaches one might take to answer this question, such as the ethics of the good life. Such an ethics has things to say about the everyday, but its present-day understanding focuses on Aristotle's virtue ethics. This framework conceptualises care in prescriptive rather than descriptive ways ('This is what you should do to be a good caregiver'). Another approach is the organisation of moral debates, which stage discussions between professionals about matters of everyday life in medical and care practices. Such moral debates are indeed good examples of discussions of everyday life concerns. However, these discussions also tend to remain within the location or practice in which the debate took place. The participants rarely publish the things they discuss for others to learn from.

In contrast to wellness narratives, the relationship between readers and narrators on matters of everyday life is more obvious in the 'human interest' pages of journals and magazines. Here the emphasis is on the more difficult side of life. Such stories touch on having bad luck, living with disease, the occurrence of death and other difficult situations, but they also discuss matters of everyday morality and etiquette, such as friendship, sexuality, loneliness and common tensions in everyday life.[8] These stories provide an important repertoire for engaging in empathetic relationships with others because they provide language for describing everyday life concerns that are difficult to address otherwise.

The genre of problems addressed in these 'case histories' describing the situation of particular individuals rarely reaches academia. Exceptions are found in literary studies, where biographies are written and discussed, literary and cultural critique is practised, and sense is made of historical contexts and their impact on individuals, who are often the hero or heroine of the story. Biographies, however, often depict exceptional individuals. Yet another genre of writing about specific cases is the 'clinical case report' that describes individuals with exceptional diseases. This form has a long tradition in medicine but is waning now. Qualitative social science works with case histories in a different way, opening up the question of how to address specificities of events and situations rather than centring individuals. The book addresses how the study of specificities may be thought of as relevant to other situations than the ones researched.

Modes of generalising

One reason for the academic silence on everyday life is that the positivist sciences struggle to address specificities, or attempt to filter out specificities in their striving for generalisation.[9] Everyday life and its values are different for different people, and these may be seen as 'noise' in quantitative epidemiological studies looking for general trends. Epidemiology is the main approach in the social and medical sciences in the Netherlands. The positivist sciences study people and diseases by generalising across populations, not by considering particular situations or practices. The dominance of the epidemiological approach obscures approaches that seek to obtain knowledge about specificities and the important role they play.[10]

Another issue that contributes to the neglect of 'living with chronic disease' is that the dominant discourse within the medical sciences focuses predominantly on finding cures rather than understanding how to live with diseases that do not go away. At present, this curative model is strongly supported by medical research that emphasises effective treatments.[11] These effects are isolated by studying phenomena under controlled conditions and by using clearly defined methods and variables that erase 'noise', such as possible biases of the researcher or trivial differences between test subjects. This sits uneasily with the contingencies and specificities of everyday lives as well as clinical practices. Attempts are being made to include the values of patients in epidemiological research, particularly as outcome variables when testing medical interventions. Quality of life is probably the best-known example.[12]

In its current embrace with evidence-based medicine, epidemiological research has a lot to say about statistical generalisability. But it says almost nothing about how to use this generalisable knowledge in concrete cases of clinical practice. By adding things up and averaging, individual differences that are not deemed relevant are filtered out. Only relatively simple interventions with clear and pre-definable goals, such as medications, can be evaluated. But it is not always clear what such general guidelines can do for individual situations. What does it mean for a person that a certain intervention increases the quality of life for *many*? How does it do this, and under what conditions? The clinical question is always what a treatment might mean for *this* patient in *this* situation. But present-day medical science does not offer many answers to such questions,[13] other than invoking unspecified notions of 'professional expertise' and 'patient values'.[14] More helpful answers are, however, found in studies of clinical practice where knowledge is transferred 'by the bedside', taking the complexity and specificity of each particular case into account.

Modes of universalising

Philosophers and ethicists likewise tend to be silent about specificities and hence about the values pertinent to everyday life, which are always specific rather than abstract. They are interested in universal concepts, or in establishing general norms that can be useful for situations that are described abstractly. For example: Heinz is poor and cannot pay for the medications that his wife needs to stay alive. Is he morally allowed to steal them? The question is formulated as a general question about stealing. Other elements are left out. For instance, Heinz knows the pharmacist and may have a good chat with her about possible solutions.[15] Ways to make patients' concerns audible in ethics are often based on the principle of autonomy, a principle that serves as a procedural safeguard to allow patients to say what they have to say, and to grant them the formal right to decide for themselves if they want to accept treatment or not. Medical ethics is often about values, principles and norms that are valid for everybody, rather than about the values that are specific to certain everyday situations.[16] Moral case deliberations, in contrast, resonate with the concerns of philosophers who take philosophy as a way of living. These philosophers have studied everyday life practices and form an inspiration for this book.

Philosophy as the practice of a good life

Philosophy has not always been about abstract theory. Philosopher and historian Pierre Hadot shows how 'theorising' in philosophy started during the Middle Ages with the founding of universities.[17] This scholastic tradition came into being and created a 'professional' philosophy for specialised scholars, which served as an alternative to the classical philosophy that was first and foremost a practice of life aimed at achieving wisdom. Classical philosophy (and also later humanist interpretations of it),[18] Hadot shows, always started with the practice of examining questions. The theory would follow the practice, to reflect on problems and concerns and to find justifications on how to act. Philosophy, Hadot argues, despite present-day understandings of philosophy as the exegesis of texts or the analysis of concepts, was traditionally about the practice of living a good life and teaching this to others.[19] The specific aims varied for different schools, but Hadot shows that the general aim was to gain wisdom, or 'to feel united with others and with the universe', by changing the self for the better and by educating others. The primacy of living the good life over the development of theory was deemed so important by proponents of philosophy-as-practice that they valued doing things over writing things. An example is the ancient Roman senator Cato the Younger, who left behind nothing in writing – even if lots has been written about his ways of living a good life and educating others. The historical study of philosophical schools and practices also shows the importance of conversation and conversation partners. Philosophy as a way of living the good life was a relational thing: it was directed towards an audience. The aim of Hadot's book is to reconsider the importance of philosophy as a way of living – that is, as a practice of everyday life.

An important question for this book, which seeks to learn about the values of everyday life, is how to understand the *normativity* of writing about good lives. Here, normativity is not about general prescriptions for how one *should* live. The aim here is not to provide sets of rules on how to behave, such as, for example, all people should do X, or all people with COPD should wear bathrobes after a shower. These philosophers *examined* if something is true and good, and under which circumstances. This was a task they set themselves. The good-life-as-practice was informed by its relationship with concrete events and obstacles that needed to be overcome. These philosophers examined concrete events because they wanted to address questions about how to live well. The aim was not to present stringent doctrines. Theorising was contingent on the problems at hand and aimed to make sense of the things that happened. Wisdom was an ideal that might never be achieved, and would maybe even cause suffering for those pursuing it, but this did not lead to passivity. Rather, the good life was characterised by a persistent striving for the examination of good and the true in circumstances that one could not control. The resulting theory was hence not necessarily coherent, nor was it primarily a theory about the world. It was a theorising *in* the world. It was not a theory about how one should think but an exercise in good thinking. It was a set of contemplations on situations and themes, created in an active relation with the world and born from the desire to generate wisdom about how to live. It was a doing. General universal claims sit uneasily with this emphasis on improving concrete situations.[20]

Imperfect life as a good life

In this book, I will develop the consequences of such a 'theory of practising the good life'. I take the lessons of Hadot to heart by looking for inspiration in classical philosophy as well as in later humanist interpretations in order to think about the good-life-as-practice. I will analyse work from Hadot's student Michel Foucault, who developed the theme of the good-life-as-practice in his later work. Hadot points out the similarities between the various universal missions of the different schools of the good life. He even manages to interpret Kant's life and his categorical imperative as an example of a universal striving for wisdom and the good life ('act in the way you would want everybody to act'). By moving from exemplary lives to ordinary lives, however – as I attempt in this book – specificities, inconsistencies, contingencies and imperfections rather than theoretical coherence are foregrounded.

I will situate the difference between philosophical theory and philosophy-as-a-way-of-life as being part of the distinction between modern and pre-modern philosophy. Hadot argues that modern philosophers, such as Leibniz, Descartes and Spinoza, who worked outside the universities, were also practitioners of philosophy as a way of life. Rather than debating the exact distinctions, in this book, which seeks to learn from practices, I will instead make a distinction between philosophers who foreground practice – or theory about practice – and those who contribute to systematic (modernist) philosophical theory.

To do so, I will attend to the conceptual *forms* or ways of constructing the good life rather than to the substantive ideals of certain versions of the good life. I am not looking for doctrines, judgements or prescriptions on what it means to live well, but I do seek to understand attempts at living well, and find out how we may study these attempts. How do people pursue a good life? How may we study *ordinary* lives as oriented towards something good without a priori criteria for judging these lives as successful or not? What can we learn from pre-modern ideas about good-lives-as-practice and how might we apply these insights to present-day concerns about the everyday lives of people with chronic disease and their caregivers? What might those living with chronic disease learn from philosophy-as-practice? And vice versa, what may academic philosophers and social scientists learn from the lives of people with problems that do not go away?[21] The case of people with chronic disease is exemplary of a problem that cannot be solved or brought to a happy ending. Bathrobe tricks can help make life more bearable, but they will never cure a disease.

People and things

My study of the values of everyday life does not look solely at people but also focuses on materiality. Studies, theories or narratives about everyday life are often 'human-centred'. In these human-centred studies individual people, or representatives of groups of people, are put centre stage as the unit of analysis, even when their scores are aggregated or their claims are generalised. Stories and meanings are privileged over concrete things and practices. The different approach that I take comes from science studies, and its later-developed branch of care studies. Here, a turn to practice, and hence to the everyday, was made in the philosophy of knowledge. This (ethnographic) turn to practices focused on how scientists work in labs and with colleagues in their attempts to produce facts. This presented a shift in the theory of knowledge, because prior to this epistemology was a prescriptive, normative activity in which philosophers formulated criteria to demarcate good knowledge from error and belief.

Science and technology studies (STS) approaches the knowledge question differently. By ethnographically studying scientific practices, early STS scholars analysed how scientists produce knowledge with the help of literary techniques (styles of writing and publishing), social techniques (alliances with some, competitions with others) and material devices (such as the standardisation of research instruments).[22] Creating knowledge is hence studied as a practical activity by focusing on the everyday life of scientists or science-as-practice. People were not the only focal point of analysis: the relationships between them were also studied, as well as the relationships with words, things and social norms. The metaphor of the network was used to trace these relationships, and this technique eventually evolved into the material-semiotic approach used in this book.[23] Material semiotics analyses how entities obtain a certain identity through socio-material relationships. These identities are not stable but may shift over time as these relationships change.[24] The material-semiotic approach also studies *what types* of relationships are made, be they networks or other kinds, which I will elaborate in the next chapter.[25]

This book

This book grew out of the need for finding new registers to understand and write about the values of everyday life and their relationship to social and material practices. Such values emerge in specific situations and relationships and are informed by what counts as good there (in the case of the bathrobe trick, for example, accomplishing things that are important to you) and what counts as bad (the wasting of energy). I want to explore various ways of reinventing repertoires for attending to the values of everyday life in their specific contexts. Such an exploration, or so I argue in this book, requires an articulation – or reinvention – of the notions used to describe the aesthetic and moral values of everyday life. This endeavour, we will see, also comes with a particular understanding of what is *true* about everyday life. I want to reinvent a theoretically informed empirical approach for studying the values of everyday life and their specificity.

How may we learn more about the ways to address, think about and eventually also improve the day-to-day care practices and everyday lives of people with chronic disease or handicaps? This book will discuss people with learning disabilities, chronic mental health problems or amyotrophic lateral sclerosis (ALS), as well as the lives of women with cancer and other people with problems that are long-lasting or even permanent. These people live with their condition as best as they can, with the help and care of others. Their lives are profoundly influenced by the social and material environment and the numerous devices found therein. Their everyday is peppered with formal and informal conversations as well as tips and techniques such as the 'bathrobe trick'. These techniques each have their own different or shifting goals, demands and contingencies that are difficult to grasp when using current academic approaches.

So I ask in this book: what kind of object is everyday life, and what makes learning about it so hard? What are the values that are important to people's everyday lives, and how can they be approached in academic research?

What are values and how do aesthetics come into the story?

The embeddedness of values in practices and things does not rely on predetermined classes of values (for example, ethical, moral or juridical values). Instead, I will heuristically search for whatever 'goods' may be present in a practice, be this a healthy blood pressure, a fulfilling relationship or a precise instrument. Values may be present in warm fluffy bathrobes, in techniques for using one's energy wisely or in the methods of scientific research. Values, then, are not restricted to human motivations: they are also parts or products of as well as actors in material-semiotic practices. The next chapter will describe this in more depth.

The term 'values' is what I call an *open* concept: one that can be used to empirically examine things that are important in particular practices, such as certain ideals or notions of worth. There are different qualifications of values. In this book, I am particularly interested in what are commonly understood as moral or aesthetic values.[26] Making classifications of values in an everyday context – I will show later – is problematic when studying everyday life values. Any value may be used in a particular way, and the context of its use influences its functions. I use the qualifications 'moral' and 'aesthetic' as heuristic categories to explore the values pertinent to everyday life, but also to start my analysis from a common understanding for readers. Moral values generally refer to obligations, namely things that people 'ought' to or are allowed to (not) do, in relation to others, in order to do them justice. Morality is often related to ethics in times of modernity.[27] Modernist ethics is understood by its proponents as a systematic reflection on morality, which frames ethics as a task for professional ethicists who look for criteria to establish what 'good morality' might be. In this book I seek to understand the values of everyday life, or everyday morality, so I do not wish to draw a distinction between ethics and morality and instead seek to study how values emerge and function.

Aesthetic values of everyday life are usually conceptualised in relation to etiquette or social conventions about what counts as good manners in relations with others. It generally refers to taking notice of other people's sensitivities or how these might be breached. I understand the notion of aesthetic values more broadly as also being about things that are pleasurable and nice, as well as relevant to practices that strive to creatively reshape everyday life. As I will show in the chapter on dignity, in everyday life practices, the categorisation of values may shift and this shift is not trivial. Dignity functions either as a principle or as an aesthetic value, and this has great consequences for practices that involve dignity. As an aesthetic value, dignity is a matter of motivation for care workers, a desire for things to look right. As a principle, dignity functions as a matter that needs to be safeguarded through regulation. Again, context is crucial for seeing which classifications are relevant and what their effects are.[28]

Intriguingly, however, the good life was once theorised in terms of aesthetic values ('the art of living'). These modes of theorising have disappeared from academia or have otherwise taken on the shape of particular prescriptions on how to live a good life. The aim of this book is to see how a discourse on aesthetic, moral and other types of values in everyday life may be regained, and to learn what style of normativity is suitable for doing so.[29] To articulate varieties of thinking about everyday life is of vital importance to imagining what forms of everyday living and knowledge gathering are worth pursuing over others. Are there, for instance, options available, such as bathrobe tricks, or should people with severe lung disease accept that their day is over after having taken a shower? Or, as the chapter on 'quality of life' argues, when traditional academic methods cannot grasp the concerns of people with intestinal feeding tubes, is it not better to reinvent our methods and find out what these concerns might be? Moreover, when we do not understand how everyday values function and how we may study them, I claim, we know little about how societies arise nor about what holds them together.

A final contrast that is important to keep in mind when reading this book is that I analyse values of everyday life, in whichever way they may be categorised or qualified, as concrete and situated. This is in marked contrast to the abstract principles referred to in other theoretical frameworks. Justice, efficiency or appropriateness may be understood as general values, but these always take on a particular shape in concrete practices. It is this practical and material shaping of values that I am interested in exploring throughout this book and for which I wish to develop a methodological toolkit.

The aesthetics of everyday life

In addition to methodological issues with generalisation or universalisation, in this book I claim that the academic silence about everyday life values is due to the lack of a vocabulary for describing the moral, but also, and particularly, the *aesthetic* values of everyday life. Can one think of everyday life as an object of art or as containing things of beauty? Or, more modestly, as something that has a certain style or a particular element of niceness, appropriateness or goodness? In thinking about aesthetic values in this way, I broaden the notion of 'aesthetic' from 'things of beauty' to include everyday life concerns with etiquette and appropriateness.[30] What kinds of social conventions inform what we find pleasant, pretty or suitable?

Contemporary academic and philosophical traditions provide some ideas about morality, but very little on the aesthetics of everyday life. Can everyday life be analysed in terms of aesthetic practices or values? In the example of the bathrobe trick, how may creative use of clothing make everyday life a bit better when one runs out of breath quickly? And what exactly does 'better' mean if it is not a moral obligation or an effective treatment of a disease?

Everyday life aesthetics and morality, I will show, went 'underground', out of sight of academic study, even though such values are still present if only one makes an effort to see them. In everyday life as well as in care practices, aesthetic qualifications of our lives and the relationships we have with others or with objects are ubiquitous. We refer to a nice nurse, a trustworthy friend, a good death, a beautifully healing wound (in the eyes of the doctor) or a horrible scar (for the patient). We speak of an elegant design, an enjoyable companionship and a passion for music. I analyse these expressions as aesthetic qualifications that describe our relationships in terms of beauty, style or appropriateness rather than in terms of ethical or juridical principles. Systematic reflection on the aesthetic qualifications of everyday life is rare, however.[31] It remains unclear what the importance is of aesthetic values for our understanding of social life as well as for social theory.

Philosophers of aesthetics *do* theorise about beauty. They do this in the context of established art and skilled artists but not in the context of everyday life. Such discourses on aesthetics are often written in a normative style. They seek to formulate criteria for determining what makes a particular art form beautiful or for determining what beauty is more generally.[32] These are usually neither criteria that apply to everyday life nor prescriptions for how to live it well. Although it is often argued that Enlightenment and Romantic art forms, such as diaries and other 'individual expressions of individual emotions', had a great impact on how people learned to see themselves as individuals, the *variation* in available styles for creating everyday 'selves' is rarely acknowledged.

The relationship between everyday life as a good life under difficult circumstances and other 'higher' forms of art is interesting, but it is not an angle that I wish to explore in this book.[33] My focus is on the imperfect, ordinary lives of audiences rather than artists, on everyday life with disease, and on the attempts to live it well, while muddling through with always imperfect, tentative and shifting results.[34] I take what is good about this life to be an empirical question rather than a normative one. It is for this reason that I have an *everyday* rather than a *prescriptive* perspective on aesthetics in the study of the values of everyday life.

I use the concept of 'aesthetic values' in this book as a methodological tool to study everyday life and what is good (appropriate or beautiful) about it, but I also use the concept as an object of study that I hope to reinvent. The aesthetic values of everyday life have always been around, but there are no longer methods or concepts to study them. Aesthetic values in everyday life are an object of research that is fundamentally different from general principles or prescriptive norms, which are abstract concepts formulated to find alternative ways for addressing questions of the good life in academic contexts. Everyday aesthetic values are about people's appreciations and motivations rather than about rules. They are *concrete* values, because they always qualify a specific object or situation. As part of everyday life, such values are helpful for studying what is deemed good for whom in particular practices, even in bad situations. Everyday life values are grounded in conventions, and as such are not matters of individual preferences only. Aesthetic values, I will demonstrate, are social values.

Sociology and anthropology of the good

To study the values of everyday life, I build on the work of sociologists Boltanski and Thévenot, who together developed what Thévenot later called the 'sociology of the good'.[35] I explain this approach in greater depth in the next chapter. The work of Boltanski and Thévenot helps to *empirically* study how values are inscribed in things and how people juggle between different types of values belonging to different *genres* of activities (for example, justice, industry or commerce). Each of these genres also has a particular aesthetic style. One can think of the particular modes of writing in legal practice or of the use of clear, concise statistical tables that show *robust* results.

There are also genres in which aesthetic values are central to their organisation; this is the case for art and in aesthetic practices of 'enjoying something'.[36] The latter term is relevant to the work of Francophone pragmatic sociologists and anthropologists such as Antoine Hennion and Ariane d'Hoop on 'attachments'.[37] This research focuses on the importance of creativity and passion, and hence brings 'pleasure' and affect to the fore, both as the motivators for and as the results of social practices. In doing so, Hennion recuperates the concept of pleasure and its importance for social theory. Pleasure is an important recurrent theme in this book because it is theorised by philosophers of the good-life-as-practice not only as a reason for attempting to live life well and as a drive to pursue knowledge about life, but also as a gratifying result for achieving this knowledge.

Writings about individual aesthetic appreciation often contain a particular understanding of the social and how the two are linked. This is very clear in the work of Norbert Elias on the civilising process. Elias studied etiquette, which is an aesthetic code or style guide on how to behave in everyday life. Etiquette exemplified, as Elias showed in two voluminous books, the increasing interdependence of people and societies at large.[38] The social is reflected in individual behaviour by stipulating appropriate ways to sleep or eat. Everyday values and social conventions do not exist separately. Sociality resonates in specific situations. The question is *in what ways*?

Aesthetic values as social values

The history of aesthetic values in *art* shows that the values of everyday life became individualised in different ways, as I will discuss in this book. Everyday life values were important tools for ancient Greek and humanist philosophers, but in the shift to modernity these values were increasingly seen as whims and unruly passions that posed a danger for social stability rather than as a means to achieve order. Everyday life values were reduced to 'matters of taste' and as such became private concerns that were not open to debate or state intervention, unless they limited the freedom of others to enjoy their own specific tastes or forms of the good life. The modernist interpretation of artistic practices as evoking the most individual expression of the most individual emotion further contributed to the individualisation of art as taste. The individualisation of aesthetics in art, and, as I will show, also of the aesthetic values of everyday life, obscured how aesthetic values are part of practices and as such are *social* rather than individual values. The rehabilitation, reconstruction and renewed understanding of sociality in the study of the (aesthetic and moral) values of everyday life is crucial for the goals of this book.

An example of an attempt to theorise aesthetic values as social values is found in the work of Pierre Bourdieu.[39] Bourdieu shows how artistic preferences can be understood as unconsciously enacted matters of class. People enjoy art galleries or instead go to funfairs because of their class socialisation. Bourdieu uses the idea of 'the social' to explain how people's everyday doings reproduce their social positions. Categories of the social, such as class, exist before preferences of taste come into being, and therefore emerge in people's activities. Bourdieu turns class into a pre-given form of what the social looks like.

In this book I approach the social differently. Rather than starting from particular ways of 'knowing' the social – or taking these ways of knowing as a priori important or pre-existing – I analyse how the social emerges, what form it takes and what collectives it creates. It may very well be that class is an important category for understanding a certain practice. But then class would have to be the sensitising concept, and hence gain its meaning and relevance as a *result* of the analysis rather than the starting point. This makes sense when the aim is to study aesthetic values. Aesthetic values emerge, for instance, as particular ways of linking people through motivations, shared appreciations or traditions. This is very different from saying that social groups emerge through, say, governance, or from 'applying' the classic categories of social science (class, gender, age and so on) to one's materials, or a priori assuming that these are the most important categories. Rather than providing explanations using pre-given categories, I study when and where aesthetic values emerge in everyday lives and practices, and in what ways they are informed by – or generate – social orderings.

Anthropologists theorise how aesthetic values give rise to particular forms of the social. This is most explicit in existing studies on religion.[40] Everyday moral and aesthetic values orient practices in particular ways. Birgit Meyer calls these aesthetically organised practices 'aesthetic formations'.[41] Meyer uses the word 'formation' instead of 'community' to show that the creation of communities is a *process* in which particular subjects are formed through shared imaginations. These imaginations materialise as embodied aesthetic forms, such as modes of worshipping in religious practices. I employ the term *genres* rather than formations to stress that aesthetic genres may be formed through different media, objects, images, styles of clothing and so on, but also to highlight that these genres may also be shared by people who never meet.[42] The concept of the genre foregrounds the relationships between aesthetic values and practices and social conventions (imaginaries, stereotypes, habits) rather than the relationships between social groups.

Meyer and Verrips theorise local religious culture as a process of sharing certain ways of doing and appreciating things, and of using certain objects and modes of representation that create particular affects.[43] They illustrate this using the case of Pentecostal celebrations. The step from religious culture to wider popular culture is easy to make; people organise themselves through the aesthetic genres to which they feel attracted. They like particular kinds of music, engage in particular forms of celebration or enjoy particular types of food. Aesthetic values are hence linked to 'culture' and genres of social life as well as organisation that I will further explore in this book. By asking how aesthetic values are social – rather than either idiosyncratic or authentic *individual* values or socially determined ones – I aim to learn more about the ways in which aesthetic values contribute to the constitution of forms of 'living together' as well as how they organise forms of social life.[44]

My analysis of aesthetic values as social values shows how aesthetic sociality both emerges from and constitutes everyday lives, and vice versa, how people in their everyday life contribute to such forms of sociality through their own motivations, enjoyments or strivings for the good. I will refer to this process as 'motivated socialities'. Aesthetic appreciations, rather than being pre-given differences between social groups (such as gender, class and age), are spread across groups and individuals. You and I may share a love of books but we may heartily disagree about our preferences for certain colours or foods.[45] Therein lies our individuality, which is shaped in and through our different social connections and shared appreciations that together suggest what a life worth living might look like for us. Social organisation through aesthetic motivations is quite different from social organisation through state regulations. Regulation is not about motivation but about being governed. Aesthetic values can be subversive in the context of rules, as they are tacit and are not backed up by rational arguments.

The approach and structure of this book

One of the key themes of this book is that research methods actively and creatively shape the object that is being studied.[46] Methods are practical tools for shaping research objects and can therefore be seen as normative 're-scribers' of the world. I am confident that even the most positivist of scientists can agree to this – methods are tools for doing *good* science. But for these scientists this good means striving for objectivity. However, the creative power of methods and concepts is one of the reasons why everyday life values have disappeared from academic discourse; there is no longer a methodology to study them. The goal of rehabilitating everyday life values forces one to look for new concepts, methods and knowledge practices to articulate and study them.[47]

My study will combine an ethnographic approach to studying forms of the good in practice with a generative, interdisciplinary approach that folds together analyses of situations that were, before I wrote this book, unconnected in time and place but that are nonetheless capable of illuminating each other. I alternate between and fold together various empirical studies of contemporary care practices in the Netherlands, and combine these with social theories that I take liberally from the history of ideas. The metaphor of folding is perhaps most easily explained by comparing it to puff pastry. Different layers are folded on top of each other and rolled out again, but the structure of the layers remains present inside the dough. This illustrates how different parts of the dough become connected (here: different moments in history) as well as how different substances, such as the flour and the fat (here: concepts and situations) are put in dialogue. I will alternate between chapters containing empirical stories about present-day care practices and chapters containing historical social theories about everyday life values and how to understand and study such values. The latter type of chapter provides concepts for analysing and understanding what happens in care practices. The philosophical tradition of understanding and living the good-life-as-practice has disappeared in modernity, but it is important to remember that the values of everyday life were once seen as important and worth critically discussing. These historical debates in social theory provide keys for understanding the values of everyday life as well as the reasons why they are contested. I therefore explore how everyday life values either emerge or are marginalised in present-day care practices, as well as how historical social theorists interpreted such values.

The dual goal of examining how people shape the good life and its values while simultaneously asking what these values are and how they may be studied is the main line of inquiry of this book. People with chronic disease continuously reinvent what counts as a good life for them, and researchers and social theorists must reinvent concepts to research such processes. I will show that both types of reinvention are important for making sense of care practices as well as for understanding how different social forms emerge.

I work with the concept of 'foldedness' to draw connections between practical activities and their theoretical descriptions, which I will discuss at length in the next chapter. I foreground the linking of observed situations with words that describe them, in one way or another, to highlight the interwovenness of empirical and conceptual work. Everyday practices often confront us with certain situations that we may not be able to immediately understand or put into words. Concepts can help us articulate what is taking place in such situations, how they came into being and how one wants to relate to them. For example, the bathrobe trick is a concrete practice that I articulated both as a technique for improving the everyday life of people with COPD and as a form of knowledge that is conveyed orally. This is different from articulating the bathrobe trick as, say, 'an intervention that is backed up with evidence or not', or as something that needs justification by recourse to moral principles. I approach empirical-conceptual research as an alternating process between getting an intuitive grasp on the situation and patiently looking for concepts that may articulate this situation in a new and interesting way. Such an approach requires reflection on what concepts or methods might be *interesting* and for what reason. My use of the word 'interesting' suggests that there is more than one way of articulating a given situation. There are endless ways of doing so. My particular concerns in this book are to make a step towards articulating the values of everyday life with the help of empirical studies and social theory, and to generate concepts that can address contemporary problems. Hence, interesting articulations are interesting for this book if they do just that.

The implication of my approach is that in this book theory does not 'come first'.[48] If I had to say whether it was a theoretical or empirical question that led me to write this book, I would say that it was my general puzzlement about how to study practices. In my research I have studied many care practices, and I bring some of my thoughts on them together in this book. My observations of these practices form the starting point for a dialogue with theorists from different times and of different inclinations. This is the original meaning of folding.[49] Rather than placing historical events in a linear order, folding brings together texts from different times and places and makes them speak to one another. This allows for conversations with the ancient Greek or Renaissance humanists. Each part of the book forms a cluster of empirical and historical social theory chapters that resonate with each other. The stories on care practices in the Netherlands are not presented as exclusively relevant to the Dutch context. Moreover, I do not treat historical narratives as antique curiosities, as things that should remain in the past. I bring such narratives into dialogue with each other in a conversation about different *forms* of thinking about the values of everyday life. What ways of understanding everyday values can be excavated from such texts both present and past? By creating a dialogue between values in contemporary practices of care and conceptualisations of everyday-life values in the history of ideas, I seek to find the words for articulating this mundane, yet elusive object of research – the values of everyday life and care.

Aims and questions

The first aim of this book is to develop the conceptual grounds for making the values of everyday life an object of research and for developing knowledge about the specificity of situations. One aspect of this objective is to learn how to understand everyday life as a *good* life, even if it might be imperfect, and particularly how 'good life' might apply to care for people with chronic disease and those around them. These are lives that are far from seamless, and always involve good as well as less good things. I seek to develop concepts for studying these lives and for generating knowledge about them.

The second aim is to develop an understanding of aesthetic values, and particularly their role among the moral or other types of values that are also a part of everyday life. What aesthetic forms, motivations and creative practices are there, and how are they relevant to living with and caring for chronic disease as well to better understanding everyday social life?

The main questions in the different parts of the book are:

1. How are aesthetic, moral and other values of everyday life a part of care practices? How was the decline of aesthetic and moral values of everyday life conceptualised while these values disappeared from modernist social theory? What terms replaced them, and for what reasons? How does their disappearance affect present-day care practices? These questions are addressed in Part I, which contains the first cluster of four chapters.
2. How do aesthetic values emerge from or organise social forms, and particularly those of people with chronic disease? How are motivated socialities different from governed (formal) social forms? How may we conceptualise the good life in the context of chronic disease? These questions about the reconceptualisation of the good

life and its values, and how we may understand their social workings, are addressed in Part II, which contains the second cluster of three chapters.
3. How may practices of the good life in imperfect circumstances, specifically in the lives of people with chronic disease, be studied empirically and conceptually? What research practices are available to us and how can we generate new approaches to collecting knowledge about everyday life and its values, particular for living well with chronic disease? These questions are central to Part III of this book, which contains a last cluster of three chapters.

The chapters

The first part of the book examines how ethical principles affect care practices in which everyday values continue, stubbornly, to emerge. The historical chapters discuss how the aesthetic values of everyday life were previously understood, why they disappeared from social theory, and how aesthetic values were eventually displaced by modernist discourses about universal principles. Part I starts with a description of the care offered to people with severe and chronic mental health problems who are institutionalised either in psychiatric hospital wards or in residential homes for the elderly. Caregivers attempt to make their care as *dignified* as possible. The first chapter shows that dignity can take on different shapes, namely either as a principle or as a set of everyday aesthetic values. This chapter also shows that we cannot properly understand the practices of caregivers if we do not acknowledge that they strive for the good for their patients.

The second chapter, which concerns social theory, discusses how we came to disregard people's efforts towards finding 'the good' in their lives and work. In the writings of Adam Smith and his contemporaries we witness a shift towards modernity in social theory, which was 'on the ground' also a shift away from a feudal society towards more democratic forms of governance. In these shifts, aesthetic and moral values of the good life – as attempts of individuals to strive for the good – were increasingly seen as a threat to social stability. Aesthetic and moral values were devalued and replaced by economic, psychological and other narratives about the behaviour of people, and especially about society. Particular forms of social science hence prevailed over everyday ethics. The goal of safeguarding *self-interest* replaced, or rather privatised, all other values, which was deemed necessary for taming the capricious and unruly passions of individuals that could only lead to civil war. The notion of self-interest superseded any other values that an individual might have cherished. Self-interest hence created a single category for the passions and opened up one particular way to pursue them: earning money. Money could be spent on whatever one might fancy. The economisation of values signified the end of human morality as a variable of interest to the social sciences and to societies' rulers, and signalled the beginning of the 'universalist style' of modern ethics.

The third chapter is about caring for people with learning disabilities.[50] They live 'in the community' rather than in institutions, in accordance with contemporary policies. Care for people with learning disabilities centres on the abstract ethical principle of autonomy, which aims to give people the right to make their own decisions about their lives and therefore 'give them a voice'. My analysis shows that this principle has certain unforeseen effects and that it cannot replace the values of everyday life. The principle of autonomy, instead, makes it more difficult to articulate everyday values, particularly when they are in tension with caregivers' particular understandings of autonomy. As a consequence, everyday values go 'underground' and disappear from formal discourses about care, even if these values are still crucial for making care practices work and for allowing patients to 'make a voice' in specific socio-material contexts.

This chapter resonates with another chapter on social theory that analyses the work of Jürgen Habermas and Joan Landes.[51] My analysis shows that universal principles – a central characteristic of modernist ethics – arose in response to feudalism, and later, to the atrocities of the Second World War. However, the privileging of universal principles was eventually recognised as leading to the marginalisation of certain practices that are organised around everyday aesthetic particularities. The example Landes uses to argue this is life in the salons around the time of the French Revolution. Salons were dominated by women, or rather, rich ladies, and provided limited forms of social mobility through artistic merits, good manners and interesting conversation. Landes's analysis shows the importance of forms of social organisation that are aesthetically *motivated* rather than *governed* by principles of a singular and universal rationality. The latter would eradicate or bridle practices in which particulars are celebrated, such as happened in the salons.

Part II consists of three chapters and aims to reinvent concepts for articulating the values of everyday life in present-day discourse. The first chapter is about women undergoing chemotherapy for cancer, which is a condition that has become chronic for many patients. These women must deal with the loss of their hair, and I analyse how this aesthetic challenge unfolds as a serious social problem. Why is it so disruptive to women to have no hair? The chapter shows that the differences between aesthetic valuations of female baldness can best be understood through the lens of social values rather than through the modernist understanding of aesthetics as an individual expression of individual emotion. Women respond to their hair loss, and the reactions of others to this, in a pragmatic way, namely by modifying their appearance with wigs and scarves to avoid undesirable responses. Such responses arise from social and historical stereotypes about bald women. The modesty of these modifications may not change these women's everyday lives into works of art, but their lives are aesthetically and creatively shaped nevertheless. These responses are ways for maintaining a social life.

The next chapter speaks to the (later) work of Michel Foucault in which he made a start in conceptualising the good life.[52] He did this by examining forms of living the true life in ancient Greece. Foucault conceptualised the good and true life as a practice. His lifelong preoccupation with truth is apparent also in Foucault's later writings, but due to the Greek philosophical intertwinement of truth with the aesthetics and ethics of everyday life, his work also has a lot to say about the values of everyday life. The good life as conceptualised in ancient Greece suggests an inseparability between the good (the ethical relationships with others), the true (how to examine the good life and speak truthfully about it) and the aesthetic (a particular state of worth to strive for, as well as a technique for creatively giving shape to everyday life). I then shift my perspective from the exemplary life of Socrates and the Cynics towards the less-than-perfect citizens who muddled through life. I move away from philosophers and turn to citizens, or from the artists to the audiences, to people living imperfect rather than exemplary lives. These people are striving for the good, but they are often weak, hindered by difficult circumstances or simply failing in their attempt. I attempt to grasp the values of everyday life for ordinary people – or people with chronic disease.

It is clear that neither Foucault nor the ancient Greeks were, or could be, interested in the modernist notion of introspective individuality. In Chapter 9 I revisit the case of women losing their hair. I analyse how to think about 'individual lives' when considering everyday life. I show that when the good life is analysed as a practice, individuality emerges as a *value* rather than as a fixed or pre-given entity. People creatively attempt to shape their 'selves', often in conventional but sometimes also more original ways, with uncertain outcomes and informed by contingent cultural stereotypes. Achieving this is a process of trial and error. It becomes clear that subjects are motivated by the things they value, but they are also influenced by the socio-material circumstances in which they live. Individuals may want to change the aesthetic organisation of their social spaces, but my analysis shows that this is very difficult to achieve in practice. Social change seems to emerge through rather random combinations of people, things and conditions that can each motivate and incidentally create new practices.

The last part of the book concerns the good life as an everyday practice in *research*. How to study the good life in everyday practice? The first chapter shows how patients suffering from ALS anticipate and experience the use of a plastic feeding tube that is inserted into their stomach through their belly wall. Clinicians are well aware of patients' reluctance to have a feeding tube, but they remain bewildered by why patients resist such a clear solution to a life-threatening problem. For patients, however, feeding tubes evoke different considerations and values that shift over time, not the least of which is the aesthetic displeasure of having a plastic tube protruding from one's body. Rather than a mechanical problem, the tube can be a sensuous problem for patients. The tube disrupts the body as a sensual entity that relates to other bodies. I show how ethnographic methods succeed in making this value (and others) as well as their shifts visible, whereas quantitative studies on the 'quality of life' do not. Even if the term 'quality of life' was once invented to include the 'values of the patient' in the evaluation of possible treatments, I show how this methodology is unfit for revealing patients' concerns about the feeding tube.

The chapter on ALS patients and feeding tubes speaks to the next chapter on the Renaissance humanist Petrarch as seen through the eyes of philosopher Nancy Struever.[53] Struever points out that the most interesting aspect of Petrarch's work on the good life is that he provides a philosophical *practice* for addressing the good life rather than merely formulating doctrines about it. Petrarch's philosophical practice for addressing the good life is based on friendship and dialogue as well as on disciplined solitude. His inquiry about the good life took place through accessible forms of communication, such as letter writing and holding conversations. This chapter shows that practices of inquiry co-determine the object of knowledge as well as how everyday life can be such an object. Rather than producing grand philosophical doctrines, as was common at universities at that time, Renaissance humanists wanted to contribute to the good life of their contemporaries by providing them with accessible forms of wisdom. Through their practices of examining the good life, these humanists demonstrated that form and content are interdependent. They provided ideas for research practices that are better able to address everyday values.

I continue this discussion in the chapter that ends Part III by asking how ethnography can be further adapted for examining the values of everyday life for people with chronic diseases. This chapter explores participant observation as a form of 'generative hanging out'. When hanging out with one's research subjects in such a manner, the researcher cedes control of the research situation. Research subjects are given the space to optimally influence the situation even if they are not verbally fluent. To hang out together, both parties need to be able to set the terms. In this way, everyday life values can be studied by generating them *in the research practice itself*.

The book closes with concluding remarks on the study of the values of everyday life and on learning from specificities.

Notes

1. See Nunes and Fitzpatrick, 2018; Buse and Twigg, 2018; and Weisz, 2014.
2. I raised this question in Pols, 2014.
3. See also Kaufman, 2015.
4. But see Vogel, 2016 for an example of how this may be done with the more appropriate methods of ethnography.
5. See for classic texts, for instance, De Certeau, 2011; Lefebvre, 1991; Latour & Woolgar, 1979; Mol, 2002; Mol, Moser & Pols, 2010; for overviews: Sztompka, 2008; Adler et al., 1987; Back, 2015; Poster, 2002; and for methods: Ehn et al., 2015; Pink, 2012. See for care studies: Meyers, 1998; Mol et al., 2010; Moser 2008; Winance, 2007; 2010; Mol, 2010; Willems, 2010c; Wintthereik & Langstrup, 2010; Taylor, 2010; Pols, 2011; Van Hout et al., 2015.
6. The juxtaposition is not an opposition. Abstractions or 'theories' influence how everyday doings are interpreted (see Chapter 2).
7. But see Brodwin, 2013 and Banks, 2016 for examples of how to study 'everyday ethics'.
8. There are different genres here as well. There are narratives that expose things, bear witness, celebrate or mourn, and others that raise empathy. It would be a nice project to analyse the different genres of 'human interest' stories.
9. The clinical tradition of the case report went out of fashion when evidence-based medicine became dominant. See also Jonsen & Toulmin, 1988; Toulmin, 1976; Foucault, 1972; Osborne, 1992; Barry, 2002; Vos et al., 2005.
10. Timmermans & Berg, 2003.
11. Effects are constructed as generalisable over large groups of people (populations).
12. This makes different health care professionals – nurses, physiotherapists and other 'paramedics' – more important than specialist doctors. See Pols, 2013c.
13. I will back up this claim and further develop it using the example of quality of life in Chapter 12.
14. This is called 'evidence-based practice'.

15 The is a reference to the Kohlberg–Gilligan debate (Kohlberg, 1981; Gilligan, 1982). In Kohlberg's abstract version of the Heinz dilemma, boys who reasoned on the basis of ethical principles were seen as morally more mature. Gilligan countered by showing that girls in this test reasoned on the basis of contexts and relationships rather than principles, and argued that this was morally the more mature thing to do.
16 The moral case debates are the exception. Theoretical ethics of care also often use the style of formulating prescriptive principles. See Tronto, 1993; Walker, 1998; de la Bellacasa, 2011; 2017; Larrabee, 1993. The same is true for the anthropology of morality (Zigon, 2007; 2008; Faubion & Rabinow, 2000; Fassin, 2014; Mattingly, 2012). In science and technology studies, Latour (2004) put the question on the agenda 'how to be normative', by shifting his interest from matters of fact to matters of concern. In this field, valuation studies uses a framework of 'economies' to describe how an object gains (economic) value within certain (macro-economic) relationships (see Dussauge et al., 2015). Care studies and the 'sociology of the good' study 'normativity in action (see notes 5 and 35).
17 I use the Dutch translation of Hadot, 2004. See also Dohmen, 2003.
18 Though not all humanists were similarly oriented towards practice: see Nauta, 2009.
19 This primacy of the good life over good writing has also been used to explain the lack of original philosophical ideas provided by Renaissance humanists (Struever, 1992).
20 For this reason I am puzzled about the aim of Hadot's book. Could it be that Hadot, after all, aimed to uncover a general 'philosophy of the good life' when discussing the 'cosmic concept of philosophy that interests every man'? It is interesting that he notes overlaps between ancient Greek philosophy and old Chinese and Asian wisdom even though these traditions are unrelated. The turn to practice is not so easy to make when relying only on contemporary terminologies.
21 To 'find the good in the bad' was something Adorno and the Frankfurt School deemed impossible, and even undesirable, in relation to the post-Second World War situation. There could be no good in the bad because all forms of Nazism had to be categorically rejected. This is also relevant to wider 'wicked problems' that the world is currently facing, such as climate change, the so-called 'refugee crisis' and so on, which are problems that will not simply go away. See also Butler, 2012; 2015.
22 See Shapin & Schaffer, 1985; Latour & Woolgar, 1979.
23 See Mol, 2002; Law & Hassard, 1999; Haraway, 1988; and Mol & Law, 1994.
24 Law, 1999.
25 See also Pols, 2016.
26 See Pols, 2019a.
27 MacIntyre, 1969; see Searle, 1969 for a first empirical refutation of the is–ought opposition.
28 See Skeide, 2022 for an exploration of medical sounds as aesthetic forms.
29 See also Pols, 2019a.
30 Adam Smith uses the term 'propriety' to describe a morally good life, which is, as will become clear in Chapter 4, a clear aesthetic and convention-based qualification. This refers to conventions about what is appropriate rather than to abstract formulations of what is beautiful. In this book I will extensively analyse how aesthetic values are also social values. 'Goodness' is a term used by Martha Nussbaum (2001) and may also refer to ethics and justice. In Chapter 3 on dignity, I will show that it is difficult to distinguish between everyday morality and everyday aesthetics.
31 Pols, 2019a.
32 One could also say that it is an aesthetic theory from the point of view of the *artist* rather than *the audience*, which is a hierarchy that I aim to shift in this book (see Chapter 3, and D'Hoop & Pols, 2022). Note that art as 'expression' is here analysed from the perspective of the artist rather than the audience that is exposed to such artistic expressions. 'Artfulness' hence resides in the object of art and what it expresses, not in its reception. In this book I will shift the perspective to that of the spectators, namely those who are not necessarily skilled but who try to make sense of artistic expressions – for better or for worse. Philosophers like Kant have discussed 'the sublime' when speaking about uncontested notions of beauty for the arts and nature (see e.g. Kant, 2007; 2009).
33 But see DeNora, 2000.

34 This is also referred to as the difference between culture with a capital C versus a small c. See Nauta, 2009. The higher arts have, according to Nauta, a surplus value for which people are willing to pay. It is produced in a professional context. Culture has no such value or intentionality.
35 Boltanski & Thévenot, 2006; Thévenot et al., 2000; Thévenot, 2001; Lamont & Thévenot, 2010.
36 There is work on wine tasting, for instance (Shapin, 2016), or on the love of music (Hennion, 2003).
37 Freely translated, attachments are appreciations, or processes of *becoming attached* to something. Hennion (2003; 2007; Gomart & Hennion, 1999) address passions and subjectivities as well as how they come into being, for instance in the performance of music. D'Hoop (2023) explores the smaller attachments that emerge in everyday situations and in ways of arranging space.
38 Elias, 1978.
39 Bourdieu, 1984. With many thanks to Kristine Krause for teaching me about Bourdieu's position.
40 But see also the work on the arts or music by DeNora, 2000.
41 Meyer, 2009, defines aesthetics as 'aesthesis', which designates 'our corporeal capability on the basis of a power given in our psyche to perceive objects in the world via our five different sensorial modes'. (See also Meyer & Verrips 2008, 2; Meyer 2009, 6). This includes all sensory experiences but does not distinguish between truth, beauty and goodness.
42 See Moser, 2005, for modes of ordering as the smaller forms of Foucauldian discourses, based on Law, 1994. Pols, 2006b, describes the washing and showering of long-term mental illness patients as everyday-life practices or repertoires that enact different understandings of citizenship.
43 Meyer & Verrips, 2008.
44 See also my work on 'relational citizenship', which describes citizenship, or becoming part of a community, as a matter of building relationships with others. Hence there is no 'inside' or 'outside' to society, but rather more or less helpful relationships. Pols, 2006b; 2016. See for spatial metaphors in relation to the social also Muusse et al., 2020; Mol & Law, 1994.
45 STS research on taste often focuses on cultivated tastes, such as wine tasting and music. See for instance Shapin, 2011; 2016; and Phillips, 2016.
46 This is a classic lesson from science and technology studies, too, even if these generally foreground 'knowledge' rather than values. Fine examples of this claim are Shapin & Schaffer, 1985; Despret, 2015; Law, 2004; Law & Ruppert 2013; Ruppert et al., 2013; Law et al., 2011; Latour & Woolgar, 1979; Moser, 2010; Mol et al., 2010; Cohn, 2008; 2014; Rapp 2004; Dehue 1995; 2001; 2002.
47 In Pols, 2012 (last chapter) I suggest that we subvert the dichotomy between subjective and objective by asking in what sense a concept or way of knowing is *normative*. This normativity stems from the fact that concepts and methods reveal some things, but not others, and hence invite for certain sets of activities rather than others.
48 See Berg & Mol, 1998, in which they argue that theory is not the foundation of practice. The theoretical chapters of my book may be a bit difficult to read for readers with little background in philosophical or social theory. All the themes from the theoretical chapters, however, will be applied and hopefully become clearer in the chapters that discuss empirical care practices.
49 See Serres, 1995.
50 It is potentially problematic to liken learning disabilities to a chronic disease or handicap, but they are certainly problems that do not go away.
51 Habermas, 1962; Landes, 1988.
52 Foucault, 1983.
53 Struever, 1992.

＃ 2
Folding words and practices: methodological notes on exploring the good life

In this chapter I discuss the methodological and epistemological starting points that led to the research presented in this book. I describe the ways of practically achieving the task I set myself, namely, to articulate the values of everyday life and to develop ways for studying them. Crucial in this endeavour is *to connect words with situations*. Connecting words with situations is a way to *articulate* these situations, and hence to *interpret* these situations as objects of research.[1] The concepts and techniques one uses to articulate situations make a big difference. Is obesity a matter of individual responsibility, the consequence of a food industry that produces cheap and unhealthy food or the result of a lack of bicycle paths?[2] Is obesity a disease or is it a risk factor? Concepts shape how we understand certain phenomena, and this implies that concepts come with particular repertoires for approaching such phenomena.

The chapter emerges from my empirical work on care practices both in homes and in health care institutions. Care practices are layered. They contain various meanings, and they have a particular history that continues to resonate in the present. Think again of the puff pastry with its multiple layers on top of one another that only become visible after baking. Practices are also prone to change and subject to trends. To describe practices in a productive way means that a researcher *re-scribes* them, hence foregrounding and connecting some aspects while leaving others out. Research is *selective* about what it represents, and this selection is made with a particular aim.[3] In this book the aim is to generate concepts for articulating the values or forms of the good in everyday life. All scientific research has an objective that it seeks to accomplish, and therefore a good that it seeks to achieve. These outcomes can be as varied as learning about elementary particles or the justness of criminal law.[4] Hence, any form of research is a re-scription of the world. Concepts are folded into practices.

I then shift my attention to the repository of historical and philosophical concepts that researchers and philosophers have at their disposal. I show how practices and meanings are folded into theoretical concepts. Unfolding these various practices and meanings allows me to create a conversation between contemporary issues and ancient Greek or medieval philosophers. It is crucial, once again, to pay attention to specificities. Applying historical concepts to the present without further analysis or translation would be absurd. The meaning of the good life in ancient Greece was specific to that period. We would not want to think of re-establishing that particular interpretation in the present. Nevertheless, historical concepts may provide us with particular *forms* of thinking about certain questions. For example, uncovering the repository of concepts and practices pertaining to the good life in ancient Greece, as well as their later interpretations by humanists, provides us with forms of thinking that can be adapted by adding other approaches, changing accents or shifting perspectives. In this book, for instance, the good life is consistently conceptualised as a set of *practices* rather than as doctrines or prescriptions on how to live well.

Obviously, the possibilities for creatively recycling concepts are not endless. A concept cannot take on every possible meaning. The moon will never be made of green cheese. Both the historical and the contemporary uses of concepts need to be acknowledged. But I believe that much more is possible than present-day approaches to 'theory' in the sciences allow for, which often take theory to be static, fixed and predefined, something for *applying* rather than for generating interpretations of problems at hand.[5] In this book I use concepts, for hermeneutic reasons, as *generative concepts* or tools that may help us make sense of contemporary problems and to suggest different ways of looking at such problems. I want to highlight the generative use of concepts in this book by unfolding and refolding concepts in particular ways – a generative hermeneutics.

The chapter closes with an intermezzo, which is a demonstration of how to connect concepts and practices. This can be done by folding in meanings, or by unfolding meanings that have become part of a concept. Alternatively, when there are practices that one does not yet know how to put into words, one can also *point* to interpretative directions or to other situations that may be relevant. The technique of folding and pointing with the aim of (eventually) connecting words and practices is based on my work on the intricately layered concept of dignity and its relevance to care practices, philosophical theory and scientific research.

The empirical study of the good: open concepts

My chapters on care practices and on historical texts are both characterised by an empirical investigation of what Thévenot called 'forms of the good', and in particular of the goods or values, or what is important in everyday life.[6] 'Good', 'goods' or 'values' are so-called open or sensitising concepts that help focus one's observations and develop a sensitivity to situations while simultaneously leaving enough room for specifying their meaning in a particular practice. Is the aim of 'good care' to cure, to maintain independence or to learn how to live with disease as well as possible? 'Good care' means different things in different places. We can speak of good care as being effective, as just, as humane or as ethically sound or even dignified. All these forms of the good point to different ways of linking what is good to particular ways of understanding the world, as well as to particular ways of acting.

A loose or 'open concept' is relatively unburdened by theoretical baggage.[7] It obtains its meaning in a particular context and can therefore be used a tool to analyse empirical materials. 'Good' is a great example of an open concept, as it helps us to ask open rather than closed questions. It can be used to ask, what is good *here*, and what shape might this take? What 'good' means has to be specified in the context in which something is deemed good or is enacted as good. This means that 'good' is embedded in certain activities and arrangements.[8] 'Good' is an underdetermined concept that requires words to further articulate its meaning within a particular context. Yet it *does* direct the eye where to look. It provides access to what is deemed important *somewhere*.

Open concepts are thus heuristic concepts that can point us towards something. They are broad enough not to exclude potentially interesting findings but also narrow enough to provide analytical traction. Open concepts are tools to analyse fieldwork situations as well as texts. In the case studies in this book, I entered the field either with an open concept or with a 'big' concept. A big concept is a concept that already has many meanings folded into it. For example, I explored what the concepts of autonomy or dignity came to mean in practice and what we could learn about them. What does autonomy mean in professional care for people with learning disabilities, that is, in practices where it is used as an important orientation for caregivers' activities (Chapter 3)? What does this concept make visible and what does it hide? To what kind of care practices does it lead? Analysts may add or foreground meanings that stem from particular practices, or they may demonstrate the particular effects or outcomes of the use of certain concepts.

These are, roughly, my two approaches to empirically studying values or forms of the good: on the one hand, employing open concepts to explore what values are pertinent to particular practices, and on the other, reinterpreting concepts that already contain multiple folded meanings. The book will provide examples of both ways into a field or text. If one wishes to conduct empirical studies of the good, it is important not to predefine the concepts that one wishes to learn about, but instead to observe the various definitions and uses of the good that are already in circulation. Defining concepts in advance structures and limits one's view, and blinds one to alternative meanings. This flexible approach works for different kinds of studies. For my goal, which is to articulate an object of research (the values of everyday life), applying rigorous and inflexible concepts reduces the ability to ask questions that are conducive to good fieldwork as well as to generate insightful concepts.[9]

Empirically studying how caregivers do good

Open and big concepts are both indicators of how to analyse a practice. Since I pragmatically[10] understand care as a practice that is oriented towards improving or stabilising the situation of patients,[11] there is always a notion of 'good' within care practices.[12] With this analytical method I seek to learn more about what 'doing good' might entail when it is a practice, and hence is embedded in, striven for or achieved through activities and techniques rather than as a form of abstract reasoning.[13] My empirical approach is quite different from the approach that is dominant in academic ethics. Modernist forms of ethics use a form of abstract reasoning that is guided by norms and principles in order to reach a judgement about what is good in abstracted situations (say, at the end or beginning of life). Philosophers frequently claim that this involves *reasoning* rather than empirical research. An empirical study of values, however, zooms in on the specificities of practices and situations in which attempts at doing good are central. The aim is, first, not to *judge* whether these practices are good or not, but instead to unravel what notions of the good are present and to what kind of practices they lead. This approach is also different from that of the positivist sciences, which seek to achieve objectivity by treating values as subjective influences or interests that can and should be separated from facts.[14] The idea in these scientific approaches is that one should strive for objectivity by excluding the subjectivity of the researcher.[15] 'Good methods', it is thought, will achieve this objectivity.

The creativity of methods

My empirical approach to analysing forms of the good makes explicit the co-shaping of research methods and objects. I conceptualise this relationship as the normative and generative workings of research methods, as these help to shape the object of research. I see research methods not as a means for removing subjective influences or for preventing errors and beliefs from entering the practice of research. Rather, I see methods as a means for articulating certain kinds of objects rather than others. For example, wanting to know how *frequently* a certain phenomenon emerges requires very different methods from wanting to learn about the *different ways* in which such a phenomenon emerges.

My analysis of objects as they are co-shaped by research methods resonates with discussions in science and technology studies (STS) about research methods as interventions.[16] Rather than *representing* reality as if there is only one version that can be captured in a singular set of terms, we can analyse how our methods and concepts *re-scribe* reality in a particular way, and hence methods also intervene by generating certain versions of reality. The term re-scribing underscores the creative aspect of doing research.[17] Reality is not passively 'mirrored' by scientists.[18] Instead certain aspects are foregrounded and others left out. Different methods and concepts articulate different realities, all true yet all different, and all irreducible to one another.[19]

Acknowledging that methods and concepts are creative tools also suggests a shift in our understanding of the normative workings of the sciences. For example, the methods of evidence-based medicine (EBM) are supposed to keep 'external values' out of objective research in the medical sciences through the formulation of guidelines for conducting good research.[20] Such external values could be the special interests of a researcher, or an entire industry, who may find that earning money by selling drugs is more important than the health and wellbeing of patients and research subjects. The methods of EBM were designed to test the safety of new drugs and to determine an acceptable probability of effectiveness by calculating average results in specified populations. In contrast, I will unravel facts and values as they are brought together *within* the tools of science, hence analysing the normative working of the methods themselves. And there are quite a few of these types of normativity to be found in the example of EBM: there is the goal of objectivity through the exclusion of researcher bias; there is the belief in the separation of facts and values as well as the use of 'good methods' to uphold that distinction; there is the protection of the truth of science and of the safety of patients; and there is the aim of establishing efficacy by measuring individual outcomes, aggregating them across populations and establishing a statistical cut-off point to decide what effect or error margin is acceptable.

In contrast, the type of normativity that I am interested in understanding is the subtle shaping of the object of research that takes place well before the actual research has started. The techniques and concepts one choses determine for a large part what one will be able to learn from a particular study. This is not because EBM scientists are *subjective* but because, like all scientists, they are *normative* in their ways of designing and shaping what they think of as *good science*.[21] This is a normativity that is shared, actively promoted and developed in the community of EBM researchers under the heading of objectivity. The term 'objectivity' projects a prescriptive philosophy of what proper knowledge is and how to achieve it.

A variety of goods

An empirical study of what is good in practice starts by recognising that goods or values are not a priori part of a realm of moral reasoning. To study goods-in-practice means to make the various values embedded in technologies, methods and social norms or rules apparent.[22] A simple example of a device in which values are embedded is the thermometer. Not only does it measure one's body temperature but it also tells you whether the measured value is *good* or not, namely too high or too low. The use of this device is also embedded in norms about how to use it. When contacting a doctor about a sick child, one is supposed to have the child's temperature ready to hand. If you do not have this information, you will be asked to collect it first.

What is good, then, can mean many different things depending on the various modes of doing things. The meaning of good can range from 'good blood glucose levels' and 'good research methods' to helpful devices or particular expectations about appropriate behaviour. The wide variety of these forms of the good comes to the fore when empirically studying values *in practice*, when they are part of everyday activities and are embedded in rules and material objects. What counts as good may be as mundane as measuring body temperature or as complex as measuring quality of life. Values or forms of the good are embedded and enacted in everyday activities and doings. An empirical approach allows a researcher to capture forms of the good in all their breadth and variety. The aesthetic values present in everyday life are great examples of the merits of such an approach. Aesthetic values are omnipresent in our everyday practice and speech, but we lack an academic repertoire for studying and interpreting such values. Aesthetic values can be found in many, if not all, everyday practices, but these have barely been theorised. In this book I will show how aesthetic values disappeared as a topic of academic interest. One reason for this is that aesthetic values in everyday life are practical values that are dependent on specific contexts. They are particular and situated because they are always (sensuously) related to an empirical context. Such particulars are difficult to measure for quantitative social scientists, and similarly tricky for ethicists who seek to formulate general judgements.

Material semiotics

In the empirical approach taken in this book, values and goods are embedded in and shaped by a dynamic interaction between people's motivations, material objects and social regulations. People may express values verbally or may enact them in what they do, through rules or laws, in implicit conventions on 'how to behave' and in institutionalised research practices. Values may 'push' people's behaviour rather than motivate it, and this may have desirable or unexpected effects that people may or may not be aware of. Materialised values may become sedimented in habits or in routinely used objects that are taken for granted. The myriad values present in care practices compete for attention and lead to tensions that may never be resolved.[23] Technologies co-direct how things happen in practice; you cannot race over a speedbump but you may drive over it.[24]

An empirical study of forms of the good reveals, I argue, the 'everyday ethics' that are present in the day-to-day negotiation of values in practical situations.[25] These include, for example, considerations about what good care means for this patient, in these circumstances, now, or what good research might be if facing a particular obstacle. Here, values as diverse as clinical outcomes, aesthetic considerations and practical priorities may be studied together to articulate the relationships between them. In material-semiotic relationships, 'entities take their form and acquire their attributes as a result of their relations to other entities'.[26] Elements of these relationships are hence not studied as something solid in and of themselves. Identities come into being through connections between one another. Neither human nor non-human elements are privileged in this analysis because they are both actors that hold practices together.[27] This explains my preference for ethnographic methods; such methods allow one to see people and things 'in action', as *enacting* different forms of reality-and-goodness.[28]

Boltanski and Thévenot (2006) provide impressive examples of how a study of the good-in-practice may be done. By analysing how people justify their decisions and activities, they carefully formulated six worlds of justification that surround a particular value or 'state of worth'. For example, the economic world is oriented towards scarcity, the domestic world centres on familiarity and closeness, and in the industrial world the good is efficiency. In everyday talk people may use arguments from any of these six worlds to justify actions. This is why everyday practice and talk appear 'messy',[29] particularly when compared to the coherent theories that may be used within such worlds.

Boltanski and Thévenot present their worlds as being exhaustive, even though they are already more modest than, for instance, Foucault, whose discourses span centuries.[30] These discourses are built as comparable logics that relate facts and values, material things and concepts, within a single framework. But even smaller 'modes of ordering'[31] or even 'modes of doing good'[32] can be discerned by analysing ethnographic materials. My previous research on psychiatric nurses' approaches to washing patients, for instance, showed that no fewer than five repertoires exist for understanding what kind of activity washing is for patients, how one might go about this and what good this would do. For instance, if washing is seen as a private activity or as being at the discretion of individuals, caregivers will interfere as little as possible. But if they see it as a skill to be taught, they will train patients and show them how to do it well.

How good is the good? Comparing specificities

Articulating the good through empirical research does not necessarily mean *agreeing* with this good. This is an obvious assumption in historical studies, as historical contexts are so different from the present. But in empirical studies of care one should be even more cautious. For example, in the care practices in residential homes that I participated in, I discerned three approaches to good care that were all equally convincing. These approaches differed according to how different nurses understood the needs of their patients, whom they either called 'clients' (who needed to become citizens) or elderly patients (who need to be looked after because they can no longer do things independently), and how nurses understood what patients value (for instance, independence and training or supervised showering and other services). The different approaches were each good and coherent in themselves, but they were also in tension with each other. Care was approached differently by different sets of nurses, who each remained largely unaware of the tacit assumptions of other nurses. So even if practices are aimed at something good, their effects are not always good and their goals and effects are always relative to other ways of doing good.

Empirical study of the good articulates the various ways of striving for, enacting or embedding certain kinds of goodness as well as their effects. Articulating the good in such a manner requires comparative analysis and caution against taking normative standpoints before the empirical study is completed. Turning goods or values into objects of empirical work allows them to keep their value character but also causes them to lose their prescriptive power. There are always different values at stake, and the same value may mean different things in different contexts. It is not predetermined which values might have the best effect or what 'best' means. Establishing the effects of pursuing one good or another is, ideally, the result of the empirical study. Good intentions or seductive ideals may locally lead to bad consequences, while good consequences may only emerge under certain conditions that are difficult to replicate elsewhere. Some goods may suit certain patient populations, individuals or contexts and not others. Attention to specificities is crucial for transferring lessons learned from certain good practices to other practices.[33] What works well *here* but also *there*? And how might we qualify the differences between these two (or more) places?

Ethnographic studies of care practices can learn about 'the good of the good' by making contrasts within and between practices, and by comparing ideals and how they operate in specific circumstances. How may the 'goods' that caregivers strive to achieve be different from other practices in which, for instance, people use different technologies? Is it better to take over tasks from people with chronic diseases if they have difficulty performing them, or should they be encouraged to remain as independent as possible? When and where might one ideal or another be better? It is often interesting to compare the values *enacted* in local care practices with the values *proclaimed* by organisational policies. In their practical embeddedness, goods are rarely ever 'just' good. How our understanding of the good changes in and across different contexts needs to be considered if one wants to achieve good practices or improve them further.[34]

A wild goods chase: where to start?

How might we identify the goods that different social and material actors cherish, enact or embed within themselves? One way to locate goods in the empirical study of contemporary care practices is to *ask* human participants what they find important. The difficulty with such a strategy is that there is usually a 'fashionable discourse' that provides participants with certain popular terms. These terms may sound impressive, but how they are applied in actual care practices can be difficult to grasp. 'Our care places the client at the centre!' or 'We provide care "on demand" so that people can manage themselves.' And 'We stand next to our clients rather than above them.' But what one actually *does* on a day-to-day basis in the enactment of care for real people and how this is informed by particular values remains obscure.

To circumvent this problem, it can be useful to employ a strategy of participant observation in combination with conversations or interviews about what happens in such settings and the extent to which these are perceived as good or not so good. In short, an ethnographic strategy combines observations of situations with conversations about these situations. Caregivers are great evaluators of their own work. They can easily evaluate concrete activities as good or not so good ('I was stressed that day, because I had so many house calls to make. What I preferred to do in this case is . . .'). Combining observations and conversations brings out what caregivers try to achieve in their everyday practice and how they reflect on this. Doing so directs the conversation towards everyday events.

The same goes for the patients. If they 'cannot speak', or at least not in terms that are directly comprehensible to the researcher, one can still learn about their likes and dislikes by getting to know them and by observing what appeals to them or not. This form of listening is what formal and informal caregivers do all the time. They have learned to recognise important signs and 'know' how to relate to their patients.[35] Simultaneously, observers may articulate effects of which actors are not consciously aware.

Objects, such as care technologies, can be a bit more difficult to decipher than people. 'Opening up' the various forms of the good inscribed in a technology can be done by looking at what a certain technology makes its users do as well as by asking what the rationale for this directed action is and what its effects are. Observations may start by looking at simple actions, such as pushing a button, switching on a computer or inserting a thermometer into an orifice. Then it may become clear to what end such actions are undertaken, what problems they address and what might count as a good or bad outcome. Such interpretations may then be compared to the intentions that motivate the implementation of a technology, which almost certainly will be informed by very different ideas and ideals.[36]

Folding time

Empirically studying the good requires folding together concepts and practices. The history of ideas is a great resource for finding interesting concepts. Juxtaposing the writings of theorists and historians from the past with my empirical observations in the present – as I do in this book – is a way of bringing together different forms of understanding that are dispersed over time. It is a way of making writings and observations speak to each other without ignoring their historical specificities.

Care practices are articulated and enacted, which also means they are, in a sense, 'theorised' by participants. An ethnographer can contribute to these interpretations. Similarly, social theorists interpret the historical context in which they do research by adding their particular reading of history. Both historical actors as well as social theorists therefore shape the manner in which history is told. Historical narratives are empirical and conceptual as well. Historical texts are layered. They not only narrate the past, but they also simultaneously demonstrate how historians use tools and methods to reconstruct history. It is this dual analytical manoeuvre that is of interest to my folding exercises. My question for historical texts has less to do with whether some time period has been reconstructed 'correctly', but more with how history is reconstructed in an empirical-conceptual manner by linking words and practices. How is history made to speak to the readers? What does its description allow us to see? Is it, say, a history of great men, great women or great battles? Or does it foreground everyday life in the past?[37] In my book the question is, of course, what a historical text can teach us about the values of everyday life and how these may be conceptualised.

Bringing together various forms of understanding the world that have been dispersed over time is an attempt to make them speak to each other without ignoring their historical specificities. Folding is a metaphor that Michel Serres introduced for thinking about time.[38] While I use the metaphor of puff pastry, Serres invokes the handkerchief. The handkerchief may be stretched out and ironed flat to present a linear conceptualisation of time in which one event follows another. Folding the handkerchief, however, brings together points in time that were previously unconnected. In this way historical events are brought together, which allows one to talk about contemporary problems with unexpected interlocutors.

Why folding?

As simple as Serres' metaphor of the handkerchief may seem, applying it to an academic text is complicated. A major difficulty is selecting which points to fold together. There are no foolproof criteria for making this selection; the repertoire of possible stories and connections is endless. A key requirement is that the things that are folded together – texts, events, places and so on – speak to the topic at hand and are capable of *generating insights*. But there are no guidelines or rules for delineating what texts should be included or when 'enough' variety has been unfolded. Due to the cross-temporal and cross-disciplinary nature of folding, a scholar who wishes to employ this method must relinquish any notion of completeness or closure. There will always be different texts, different stories, different periods and different contexts. Various folds can be made. One particular fold can always be contested as not being the most relevant one. There is no certainty here, and no endpoint.

Another risk is that the folding approach may seem disrespectful to 'great thinkers'. Folding seeks to find new forms, tropes or ways of thinking rather than to do justice to someone's oeuvre. Certain elements and ways of thinking are privileged. Historical and theoretical texts can therefore seem to become a mere means to an end. I suggest that this is not a matter of disrespect but rather a means of making use of the support that *friendship* can provide. The Renaissance philosopher Petrarch regarded books as his friends (see Chapter 11), and his writings are always in dialogue with human friends as well as book friends. I find this an attractive metaphor to think with, as I experience this supportive dialogue-through-writing-and-reading myself as well, even if such a dialogue requires physical solitude. Friendship is a trope we will encounter frequently in this book because it is an important theme in philosophies of the good-life-as-practice.[39] Friendship allows us to speak frankly with each other. The aim of friendship is to give support and to collectively make sense of problems at hand in order to solve them or find relief. Obviously, a friendly relationship with historical texts cannot be abusive, and the various historical contexts of such friends need to be considered. The interpretation of historical texts should be as accurate as possible. However, interpretation also has to be evaluated based on its generative ability, namely the potential to create new researchable objects and ideas.

Rather than cautiously avoiding the risks of folding, however, one may also celebrate its possibilities. Folding is a process that is never complete and is always ongoing. Others may add different, interesting and illuminating lines of thought, allowing for more and more varied interpretations or the emergence of new objects of inquiry. Folding may allow multifaceted and evolving objects to be pieced together. Both the justification for and the criterion by which to judge the success of a fold, in this book, is that it should *generate concepts for a pressing problem of our time*. Put more specifically, the problem is how to address the values of everyday life. Rather than its historical correctness – which is, of course, also relevant – the success of a fold is determined by its *success in making historical stories speak to present-day concerns*, such as, for example, allowing care practices speak to other practices in relevant ways. The intended reader of this book is therefore not a specialised historian or philosopher, even if such scholars provide building blocks for meaningful foldings. The intended reader of this book is someone who is attempting to grapple with present-day concerns. Folding together certain ideas that have appeared throughout history is a generative attempt at interpreting the times we live in. Folding invites scholars to reflect on what their concepts or methods might generate and encourages them neither to take 'good methods' for granted nor to get stuck in a style of critique.

Making ideas 'speak' to one another across different times calls for a particular approach. Historical ideas can only be properly understood within the context in which they made sense. This goes for our contemporary ideas as well. I will therefore combine 'archaeological' analyses that dig up historical forms of life – or 'ethnographies of the past' – with empirical studies of contemporary care practices in the Netherlands, or what one might also call ethnographies of the present. Unfolding these historical forms as well as the ways in which historians made them visible helps me to create concepts and tools that are productive for speaking about everyday values in contemporary care practices for people with chronic disease.

My dual analysis of social theory texts, namely of their historical descriptions as well as the conceptual tools and questions that guide these descriptions, is important for two reasons. First, it is a hermeneutic device for unfolding multiple meanings in a text. And second, it allows me to unravel a text's dual layers of meaning, one derived from the author as well as another from the historical subjects. Social theorists writing about certain historical situations, thinkers and ideas interpret the values of everyday life in ways that are helpful for learning how we may address such values today.

I will also discuss texts that tell us how everyday life values have historically *disappeared* from academic discourse. To find concepts for articulating the values of everyday life as well as to understand the disappearance of these concepts, this book will travel between various time periods, events and developments: from the present to pre-modern philosophy, the Renaissance, seventeenth-century civil wars, the emergence of the Enlightenment, and the transition from feudal to modern society.

Folded concepts

Concepts have a history that actively shapes how we see our world. John Law writes that 'concepts and descriptions can be seen as having performative workings, helping to present one version of reality rather than another'.[40] I previously referred to 'performative working' in my discussion on the creativity of methods. In this section, I specifically examine the use of concepts to re-scribe a situation. Writing about a particular practice in a new way means presenting a particular *version* of this practice. Hence, concepts are tools that 'help us speak the world'. By putting observations into words, we create a new object, namely the world as a text.[41] Many stories can be told about the same situation. It is possible to describe the reader of this text as a semiotic being, as zillions of molecules, as a set of metabolic systems or as a sceptical intellectual who is considering whether to accept folding as a hermeneutic method or not. All these descriptions would be truthful but would perform different objects – readers – by re-scribing worlds and words.

However, due to the meanings that are folded within them, concepts also 'make us speak the world'. What can be made visible or not is dependent on what concepts allow us to say.[42] It is a well-known rhetorical strategy in academia to say that the use of particular metaphors by another scholar *reduces* a phenomenon to one of its parts. For example, someone might say that statistical analyses reduce people to numbers. 'Reduction' suggests that a wholeness is narrowed down, as if the numbers are part of people but not the 'whole story'. This then turns into an epistemological discussion in which 'reduction' is reinterpreted as 'qualitatively different ways in which *specifications* are made'.[43] In this reading, statistics are a method that is employed to tell *specific* types of stories about people that sit alongside, and that are distinguishable from, other, qualitatively different stories about people. The logic of 'reduction' or 'specification', 'quantitative' or 'qualitative' differences, brings with it a different worldview. Such nuances are easily lost to a habitual and heedless speaker of words, but they are objects of acute interest to the conscientious (un)folder.

As if

Folded concepts are words, theoretical ones, that fold meanings and practices together. After unravelling a concept's history and its inscribed meanings, one can start to navigate between these meanings even if one is not at liberty to completely change them. Concepts defy attempts at random redefinition by persistently and stubbornly speaking their history and by shaping their practical use. Folding needs to be done carefully and with respect for the material that is being folded.

In both everyday life and scientific studies the relationship between words and things can constitute objects differently, but often metaphor and reality collapse. The 'as if' of representations disappears, and the metaphor 'becomes' the world. Douwe Draaisma argues that psychologists do not study the human psyche 'as if' it works like a computer, rather that they study 'human cognition' by understanding humans as *being* computers.[44] Draaisma's work shows how technological metaphors have influenced research in psychology and that flashy, new technologies often provide metaphors for understanding humans. The technological metaphor of choice for Freud was the steam engine, with the unconscious 'id' collecting steam that needs to be contained by the ego and the superego. But for cognitive psychologists the metaphor is that of the computer that stores, retrieves and processes information, whereas for up-to-date neurologists it is neural networks that are modelled after the internet. The intricate relationship between concepts and practices now becomes clear. Steam engine psyches and neural network brains are concepts, but these conceptualisations depend on developments in the world while also structuring how we approach the world. It is at the borders of practices or concepts, or both, that one can work towards new understandings.

Words as well as things change when they are linked in certain ways. 'Describing' an object performs this object in a particular way, or re-scribes and represents it, thus highlighting certain understandings rather than others. It may be true that 'we are our brain', but this statement is of limited value for theorising about a just society or for understanding the beauty of an artwork. Concepts evoke certain language games or practices of use and therefore project different meanings. The work of an analyst who uses folded concepts, such as Draaisma, is to re-establish the 'as if' in order to see what other 'as ifs' there are. It may well be that this will cause metaphor and reality to collapse again. People cannot act in daily life if they must consider the potential meaning of all things all the time. People treat material-semiotic things as one and the same real thing, thus making them 'real in their consequences'.[45] Concepts and reality merge in established routines. The example of folded *objects* will further demonstrate this.

Folded objects

Amade M'charek has further developed the concept of folding through the introduction of the folded *object*, a 'thing' with a history that is made of different materials that are seemingly more difficult to fold than a handkerchief.[46] M'charek's object is a DNA reference sequence. The particular DNA sequence that she writes about is called 'the Anderson sequence', or 'Anderson' for short, after the author of the first paper on this sequence. Anderson is a list (a sequence) that geneticists use to ascertain where a piece of DNA that they have isolated is located on the genome. In her paper, M'charek analyses not only the historicity of Anderson but also what came to be folded into the sequence. For instance, there is the notion of timeless reference to nature in which Anderson has always been there, even if scientists had not discovered it yet. Anderson came to stand for nature itself, the metaphor collapsed with reality. The Anderson sequence was not designed at a certain time but was always there.

The geneticists, too, were involved in some interesting folding work. M'charek traces Anderson back to its original materials and shows that Anderson was made up of placental cells, cells from a cow, and cells from the HeLa cell line. HeLa refers to Henrietta Lacks, the person from whom extremely aggressive multiplying cancer cells were taken to be cultivated in laboratories all over the world. Henrietta Lacks and her relatives were never even informed that this took place.[47] By showing what is folded into Anderson, M'charek also tells the story of what has been *left out* of the history of genetics, most notably the racial subtext (Lacks was a Black woman), the identity of the donor materials as both human and animal, and Anderson's later incorporation into the Cambridge reference sequence.

However, history left a material trace in the Anderson sequence in the shape of 'an extra C'; a letter that refers to 'nucleotide position 14,766'. M'charek states:

> At one particular locus, the makers of Anderson in 1981 had reported two Cs, a so-called 'CC doublet at positions 3106 and 3107'. The re-sequencing of placental mtDNA in 1999 showed the mistake. There is actually only one C, meaning that the extra C is a technical artefact. Yet the revised sequence of 1999 continues to encompass that error. It still contains two Cs instead of one.[48]

The extra C shows how history was materially folded into the sequence even though that C is not found in the human mitochondrial DNA. Removing it from Anderson would mean renumbering the sequence from position 3107 onwards, which would mess up all earlier research done with Anderson as a reference. And so, the extra C remains. It silently testifies to the fact that Anderson was constructed over time rather than, 'once upon a time', discovered in nature where it was waiting to be found. The double C does not fit but it is there nevertheless as a testimony to its history. Anderson can ultimately never be described as 'found in nature' due to that extra C.

Words and things

I would like to follow up on this 'material trace' in my elaboration of the *folded concept*. How can we consider concepts that are rich in and performative of meaning, either explicitly or forgotten, as concepts into which history is folded in particular ways? Or more specifically, how may words and materials both be used to create new objects in ethnographic and theoretical research? Stefan Hirschauer argues, like John Law, that ethnographic work is constructive and performative. Because, he argues, researchers put things into words that did not exist before, researchers create new material-semiotic objects.[49] Hirschauer lists multiple categories of objects that exist before there were words to describe them: the quiet workings of technologies and other 'things'; tacit knowledge; taken-for-granted matters; mute things like facial expressions; things or people without speech or voice; or things that cannot be named because of local traditions or beliefs. It is exactly the act of 'putting things into words', Hirschauer states, that creates an object-that-can-be-articulated-in-language, an object that was not there before. 'Ceci n'est pas une pipe'; an image of a pipe is not the same as the thing it represents. The representation 'turns a thing into an image', which is made of different 'stuff' than the original object. Hirschauer talks about objects that are not words, or objects that lack words, for which a researcher then has to create words.

Does this mean a striking victory over the linguistic turn and the final revenge of the mute materials? Not quite. Anderson's extra C reminds us how words or symbols may be turned into solid things. Hirschauer ignores or overlooks the point that unspoken taboos are also semiotically structured, just as facial expressions and technologies contain a particular 'social grammar'. We understand them as meaningful situations, not as semiotic problems. In this sense even dolmens (stone age tombs) 'speak', although one has to keep in mind that such talk emerged at a particular time. Things are material-semiotic objects, or objects that M'charek in another paper describes as entanglements of both 'fact' and 'fiction', materiality and meaning.[50] Things speak to us, and act on us, too.[51]

Folding and unfolding concepts means disconnecting them from particular contexts, materialities and narratives, and reconnecting them with others. The interpretative technique of *pointing* shows how concepts may be *re*-folded in order to generate new meanings. Pointing indexes objects that lack words for their articulation, or otherwise indexes the interpretative directions one may take, or may want to move away from by pointing 'there, in that direction, not the other way'. It is a way of describing potential pathways to conceptualising things that have not quite yet been put into words. By pointing one may slowly start refolding one's object of interest, which in my book is the values of everyday life. I did not 'know' this object from the start; it was not clearly articulated. I traced its shapes in practical examples and received hints of its appearance by adopting some concepts while rejecting others. I started with observing care practices and by asking questions about how these practices sought to achieve something good and what this good might be. I added historical concepts that pertained to everyday life values. This book is therefore an exercise in folding together historically different ways of conceptualising everyday life values in the present. Why are everyday life values so difficult to study today, and how might we go about studying such values in future research?

I use techniques of folding and pointing to *generate* new concepts. The tension between linking words and practices – things that are already there and things that are brought into being – is, I argue, exactly why folded concepts can be generative. On the one hand, different strands of meaning are folded into an object or concept, but these only become visible when a persevering researcher draws them out and refolds (interprets) them in a particular way. On the other hand, such strands are already present in the folded object or concept, and they can speak to a researcher if they do not articulate, argue against or steer away from them. Not any kind of thread can be spun from any concept. Folded concepts offer a lot of creative possibilities, but these are not endless. For example, practices can turn out differently than expected, researchers can be more, or less, experienced in discerning different materials or in asking helpful questions, and words may resist being fit onto certain practices, and so on. Or practices may resist words. For example, emancipatory mental health care providers have abolished the term 'patient' and now refer to 'client' or 'service user' instead. Explorations of folded concepts may result in a beautiful new object, but also in a tarnished, messy one, the latter being a common phenomenon in the early phases of qualitative research. The result could also be a sequence, a list or a piece of music. This depends which 'topoi' (places on the cloth) are folded together. The result depends on the success of creating something from material that simultaneously was and was not already there.

Generative hermeneutics

Concepts fold different times and places into themselves, and therefore the folded concept is a metaphor for both historical and interdisciplinary work. The concepts created by ancient thinkers and their interpreters can be unfolded and refolded to fit contemporary problems and solutions. The folded concept can thus become a generative concept, a concept that provides new understandings and possibilities for acting. In this book, the philosophy-as-practice of the good life is made to speak to the present-day values of everyday life, particularly to those of people with chronic diseases or disabilities. Amid the interdisciplinary work called upon in this book to trace the values of everyday life through different disciplinary realms (history, philosophy, ethnography, social theory, medicine, ethics, aesthetics), folding is being done to translate findings and analytical techniques from different disciplines into others. This is what I call generative hermeneutics; by folding forms and situations together one can generate new possible interpretations of complex and not yet fully articulated problems.

Generative hermeneutics may travel from one historical context to another or from one scientific discipline to another. It is an attempt at evoking an object of research by learning how it may be articulated. What can be made visible by combining these particular sets of methods, concepts and working disciplines with these empirical situations? What can these combinations make visible and why should we care about them? Are the insights into the values of everyday life generated by this book helpful and to whom?

A demonstration of folding and pointing: the concept of dignity

To illustrate the hermeneutics of generative pointing and folding and to make this technique more concrete, I discuss an example from my research on dignity. My exploration of dignity was an important inspiration for wanting to learn about the values of everyday life. In my study of care practices, I folded the concept of dignity together with another folded concept, namely aesthetic values. By retrospectively reconstructing some of my pointings and foldings, I want to show how several strands of thought were embedded in these concepts and how I navigated between them. These strands of thought sometimes helped to make sense of the events I witnessed, but sometimes they were unhelpful. This navigation helped me map out the direction that I wanted to take – and the concept allowed me to do this – in my analysis of dignity. In this way, I gradually refolded the concept of dignity until it started to resemble something I could *only retrospectively* describe as 'the object I was looking for'. I was not certain how, or even *if*, I could get to know this object when I started my research. However, I suspected that I might be able to find some of its constitutive elements. I could point to these even if I did not yet have the words to name them.

Because I want to demonstrate the process of folding, I will not show the 'completed' object (the 'results' of the study). Instead, I will show the ways in which I went about looking for this object. This means organising and editing time, too, so that I can present a clear trajectory wherein one thing happens after another. 'Results' will be presented in the next chapter.

Pointing out dignity: 'the bedsore case'

I first encountered the folded quality of 'dignity' in a residential home in which psychiatric nurses were working with elderly patients who had been living in psychiatric hospitals since their early twenties. In this residential home, patients were attended to by geriatric assistants who had previously been looking after a very different group of patients, namely people with dementia. Their encounters with these new patients led to many misunderstandings that were informed by various concerns, values and conceptualisations of what counts as good and professional work. The conceptualisations of these geriatric assistants were accompanied by deeply held feelings about what is good to do and what one should never do. I was reminded of one particular event – involving many misunderstandings and hurt feelings – in which I first encountered the concept of dignity. This event was one of the first constitutive elements of the object at which I could point. It involved a discussion about the care (or lack thereof) given to an old lady who had died the previous week. This discussion evoked – and amplified – the differences in values between the psychiatric nurses and the geriatric assistants.

In an interview, one of the psychiatric nurses explained to me:

> We do deputise for the geriatric nurses on other wards, out of office hours. One day a person was on the brink of dying. And those girls [geriatric assistants] were running around, they were extremely busy. So there was no time to pay attention to the dying person. And the girls said this about dying alone: 'Oh yes, this happens now and again.' You see? I think it's terrible! I talked about this with my colleague, with Nettie, about how this could be possible. A person on the brink of death will not get dirty and get bedsores, that is the kind of care they will receive. They'll wash him all right and turn him around in bed a few times. But with us [psychiatric nurses], we will sit at the bedside of a dying person who might be dirty and have bedsores, but at least we're *there* [laughs], we're *with* him! On the other ward they will wash you and turn you in bed, no problem, but beyond that you must fend for yourself. It's very strange. I could never work like that! Never.

My very emotional informant seemed to forget that bedsores can be extremely painful. The separation of 'care for the body' and 'care for the soul' presented here makes this an excellent empirical argument against mind–body dualism. But I want to underline that there are apparently different ways of thinking about the dignity of dying patients, ways that involve different practical approaches to handling a situation that are diametrically opposed, yet that are each of the utmost importance to those involved. One of my colleagues – who was a neurologist in training at the time – recounted a similar story in which neurology nurses considered it unbearable *not* to wash a patient and turn her in bed, even if this washing and turning would be painful and disturbing to the dying patient, a discomfort that could be avoided by not washing her.[52]

There was a point to these stories, and I suspected it was an important one. But what was it exactly? I could try to explain what happened by referring to the training of nurses and geriatric assistants or to the broader differences between psychiatric and hospital nurses. I could try to 'unmask' one of the concerned parties as having got it wrong. But these did not seem to be very interesting and illuminating options if I wanted to understand what meanings the concept of dignity might hold.

In a later publication (in Dutch) I provided the quote above to illustrate some of the different repertoires of good care that exist in residential homes and how each repertoire foregrounds different values. At the time, however, I was not able perform a thorough analysis of the situation or to formulate how what happened might point to concerns about dignity. I was faced with a difficult situation as well as a lack of words, and an intuition that dignity played an important role here even if I could not yet capture this role in words. This 'bedsore case' is a 'situation to think with' in my quest to find fruitful ways for understanding dignity.

I had the chance to think more about such situations when a colleague in my department received a grant to study dignity and generously invited me to conduct the research.[53] With the bedsore case in mind, I turned to the relevant literature. I had no intention of performing a 'systematic review' to find and evaluate 'all that has been written on the topic before', as my medical colleagues might do. Moreover, this literature is *vast*.[54] The history of 'dignity' and its various meanings began to unfold. What threads were there to discover?

Unfolding dignities in the literature: new things to point towards and steer away from

I have found, (very) roughly, two approaches that are frequently intertwined: on the one hand, dignity is of interest to philosophers of law, and on the other, to doctors and researchers working in health care. In both strands of literature dignity is a *serious* matter, indeed it is often described as a *fundamental* issue. The agony expressed by the nurses in the bedsore case resonates with this sense of seriousness. They felt terrible if they could not wash their patients.

Western philosophers found themselves on solid ground when they took dignity to be the foundational principle for the universal rights of man, that is to say, *all* human beings have dignity simply because they are human.[55] Protecting dignity was taken to mean protecting humans and humanity itself.[56] Their theorising ran out of steam, however, when dignity was treated as a value that expresses *differences* between people. Enter the ghost of Cicero.[57] The unease started with Cicero's assertion that one citizen can be regarded as having more dignity than another because of their social position and the status and responsibility granted to them by society. This understanding of dignity is completely unacceptable to contemporary Western thinkers. Dignity is at the core of what it means to be a human being, and this distinguishes humans from other animals or plants but not from one another.[58] Accepting that there might be differences in dignity between humans implies an abandonment of the principle of equality, which is a cornerstone principle in a just society. It signifies an introduction of meritocratic principles in its stead. Such a distinction would, it was feared, ultimately lead to the acceptance of a difference between first- and second-class citizens, or citizens and slaves. Human rights philosophers would ultimately run into a dead end with the Roman philosophers who had given them so much. They folded Cicero *out* of their conceptualisations of dignity. But Cicero stuck to the concept, much like the extra C in the Anderson sequence.

In many of the situations that I have encountered in my research on dignity – as in the bedsore situation above – there are *different* understandings of dignity at play: some that involve cleanliness of the body, and others that involve more psychological and spiritual matters. Such differences are confirmed in studies by medical researchers who take an empirical approach and who ask people in fraught situations (such as hospices and nursing homes) about their particular understandings of dignity.[59] Such researchers analyse interviews using a grounded theory approach. These studies rarely lead to a comprehensive understanding of dignity. They tend, instead, to provide a long and seemingly randomly ordered list of 'elements' that express dignity. The 'human rights approach' that stresses equality and the 'Cicero approach' that emphasises differentiation are both present in these expressions of dignity, which demonstrates that different meanings are folded into the concept of dignity. These meanings articulate the cultural heritage of the term. Medical researchers who take an empirical approach do not unfold the different conceptual elements of 'dignity' or trace them back to their theoretical origins. They analytically list them.[60] Consequently, there are almost as many classifications of dignity as there are studies of the concept.

A third approach is found in the Catholic use of the notion of dignity, which does not grant dignity to any individual in the same way, but to any individual in their particular 'mode of existence'. For example, the dignity of embryos is considered to be different from that of middle-aged women in that their destinations in life are different. Rosen discusses the Catholic meaning of dignity and how this meaning stands in contrast with the ideas of human rights theorists.[61] The Catholic approach to interpreting dignity is often used to argue against both abortion and euthanasia. An ironic unfolding of history has left dignity in the hands of human-rights watchers and pro-life activists alike![62]

Weaving the cloth for new dignities: refolding

How to fold dignity in a different way? Enter the construction works! I chose to do some preliminary theorising by discerning two sets of values, which I dubbed, on the one hand, *humanitas,* or citizen values and ethical principles, and on the other hand, *dignitas,* or aesthetic values, thus folding Cicero together with *aesthetics* rather than with a politics of justice or a philosophy of law. I derived the names for these two sets of values from earlier research that was done in residential homes and psychiatric hospitals where dignity was used as a concept, such as is apparent in the bedsore case.[63] Psychiatric nurses brought values of citizenship into their care work and tried to support patients' autonomy, freedom and independence. Geriatric assistants, however, cared for *patients,* people 'who could not do certain things any more'. The geriatric assistants pursued aesthetic values, such as 'doing nice things with residents' or taking care of clean bodies and clothes. These goals were informed by their interpretations of dignity. The goals of psychiatric nurses were, in contrast, informed by their interpretation of the notion of privacy as a way to express dignity. This idea of dignity made psychiatric nurses reluctant to interfere with the actions of their patients. These nurses aimed to 'let people be who they are' (*in hun waarde laten*).[64] For geriatric assistants, dignity meant assertively organising patients' lives, looking after their cleanliness and maintaining their self-worth (*voor hun eigenwaarde*). I introduced the concept of aesthetics to analyse how this form of dignity emphasised an orderly – dignified – appearance.

For the technique of pointing and folding, the notion of aesthetics brought me to sociologists such as Pierre Bourdieu who *unmasked* the love of art as an artefact of class.[65] This provided another pointer – 'Not this way!' What better ways of interpreting can be invented or folded into the analysis? The point here is the pointing. The big, folded concept of 'dignity' was going to be more useful if I combined it with another big, folded concept, namely aesthetics. Doing so allowed me to point to an object of research pertaining to the cleanliness of the body, which I later named *dignitas.* My more aesthetic conceptualisation of dignity was not yet well described and needed words, arguments, demonstrations and connections to practices. This pointing was a first step in the design of this object of research as well as the ways in which it could be folded. I wanted to find out how I could fold – and hence interpret – concepts and situations, such as 'the bedsore case', in a different way, namely as involving heartfelt aesthetic values in concrete situations.

So, at that point in time, the task at hand had been pointed at even though it had still not been described with adequate words, let alone thoroughly connected to care practices. The next step was to look for practices that were relevant to learning about *dignitas*. I looked for good empirical cases to further substantiate and nuance what *dignitas* might mean.[66] When do aesthetics matter in care practices? What *are* the aesthetic values found there? Where might I find practices that can provide words, activities (images? sensitivities?) or other kinds of terms for developing the concept of *dignitas*?

Refolding words with practices

I did not simply want to trace the *word* dignity. The existing literature had convinced me that doing this would result in conceptually weak 'folded talk' about principles and values that had already been 'dug up' from interviews by other empirical researchers. I did want to pursue this thing I had called *dignitas*, the yet-to-be-articulated non-identical twin of the term *humanitas* used by human rights scholars. The principle of equality is strongly present in care practices, such as, for example, in the upholding of the principle of patient autonomy. The popularity of general principles continues despite the fact that there is little room for generalisations in care practices. The variability of everyday life is immense. Every new patient who arrives at a clinic and each possible treatment leads to a specific situation that is different from the previous one. *Humanitas* was not the kind of thing I was pointing towards. So how might I conceptualise *dignitas* while trying to avoid being overshadowed by the much better-developed and -conceptualised term *humanitas*? How to put everyday aesthetics into words?

I encountered a situation that involved, without any doubt, *dignitas* as a signifier of aesthetic values, even if my informants were not using these terms. The huge hospital where I worked resembled a small village. My topic was right in front of me when I walked in through the main entrance. There was a small but expensive hairdresser that, in addition to cutting the hair of customers, sold wigs for people who had lost their hair as a result of disease or, as is more common in a hospital, because of chemotherapy. Hair and wigs shape what people look like and how they are aesthetically appraised by others. The hairdresser was a place where everyday aesthetics could be studied and where their importance in relation to frightening diseases as well as care work could be examined. I was certain that, with this new site, I would find out how and why aesthetics *mattered*, and how I might begin to understand aesthetic values. You will find the results of this analysis in Chapters 7 and 9, which are the core case studies of Part II.

To end the journey of pointing and folding

More pointing followed. I could now assemble a list of the aesthetic values of everyday life. These terms were not just about things that can be seen, such as wigs or bald heads, but also about what may be felt, heard, tasted and so on. Aesthetic values, I learned, are commonly used to qualify relationships with people and with things. Whereas at the beginning of my research I had problems identifying aesthetic values, now I saw them everywhere around me. New questions emerged, such as ones about the relationship between the doctors' aesthetics and those of the women they treated, or about the relationship between the saving of lives and the quality of those lives, or about the available repertoires for thinking about the self in terms that were different from those of the 'autonomous individual'. And so on and so forth. A new object – that had been there all along – was born.

This book is the result of my quest. Unfolding and refolding the concepts of dignity and aesthetics was – and is – a generative activity for pointing towards which directions to go. Unfolding the folds of these historical concepts and refolding them allowed me to recreate the object of *dignitas* that had been replaced by *humanitas*. My approach is a way both of *making* and of *finding* this object. 'There it is, it has such and such characteristics, and here are the practices that may help draw connections between words and situations.' I created my object by pointing at what is unarticulated, underarticulated or no longer articulated, and by pointing at what *is* articulated but that is diverting our attention. My pointing and folding is informed by the generative and creative work of theoretically oriented ethnographers who put things into words and words into things. This connecting of words and practices is not just a matter of putting theory into practice or 'applying theory' by examining a practice through a conceptual lens. And the connections are also not just about formulating theories about practices. I generate theory not only by articulating meanings and characteristics or by observing a concept's practical use, but also by articulating empirical situations using new, tentative and generative concepts. The generative object of research, then, is a concept-object, a material-semiotic entity, an intertwinement of words and practices.

Notes

1. I borrow the term 'articulation' from Donna Haraway (1988), who uses it to indicate that every empirical study is an attempt at putting a certain, situated way of knowing into words. Articulations are partial, as they join some things together and separate others.
2. On care for obesity as an 'object multiple', see Vogel, 2016. For objects multiple see Mol, 2002.
3. I use the notion of re-scription to show how descriptions are not neutral 'de-scriptions'. But re-scriptions are not normative prescriptions that tell people what to do. My use of this terms indicates a different normativity, namely one that comes with knowing objects through particular methods, concepts and research traditions. See Harbers, 2005; Pols, 2015. The metaphors I use in the book are 'folding' and 'folded concepts', which I used to explore particular ways of re-scribing.
4. These different examples do not 'add up' to one coherent worldview. Different registers of understanding the world are never complete, or if they are, they are not coherent. See Mol and Hardon, 2020, for a nice example of genres in thinking about coronavirus.
5. One of the lessons my philosophy professors Lolle Nauta and John North taught me is to not be *too* respectful of the, admittedly sophisticated, Grand Philosophers whose writings we struggled to wrap our heads around. Instead they encouraged us to ask critical questions ('If Descartes writes that God has all the virtues, does he also mean to say that God is blue?'). I see links here with Foucault's (1984) notion of *parrhesia*, which involves frankly speaking the truth: a particular mode of examination often employed by philosophers of the good life, such as Socrates. See Chapter 8.
6. Thévenot, 2001. Elsewhere, I have used the notion of empirical ethics to describe this, even if the notion of 'ethics' here does not clearly denote what is commonly understood as 'ethical values'. It is exactly this broadening up of what may be studied as good that is part of my project to reinvent ethics as the study of the values of everyday life – whatever these values may look like. Empirical ethics implies studying the good in practice without limiting oneself to certain values that can be predefined as 'moral' (see below, and Pols, 2004; Pols, 2015; Willems & Pols, 2010). A nice example is Thévenot's study on 'a good road' (2002).
7. Elsewhere, I have made use of the term 'loose concept', but I now feel that this does not adequately represent its meaning. The term 'sensitising concepts' is quite similar (see Blumer, 1954), but I opt for the notion of 'open concept' because I want to draw attention not just to how it sensitises one to different meanings but also to how it *structures* what we can see.
8. See Mol, 2002.
9. See Pols, 2012. This is common in qualitative research, but very strange for quantitative researchers and academic ethicists, who often see rigorous concepts as a prerequisite for conducting good research.
10. There are big books written about what practices *are* (e.g. Bourdieu, 1977; Nicolini, 2012; Knorr Cetina et al., 2000). My preferred use of 'practice' is, however, as a tool for getting out of the office and learning what is out there in the world. Of course, one needs some open concepts for doing this, and these will be provided below. An oft-cited challenge for practice research is what Marilyn Strathern calls 'where to cut the net' (1996; see also Strathern, 1991). One has to decide, considering the aim of the research, which links to follow and where they might lead. But this can never be solved by one theoretical rule or another. It is a matter of finding out and making decisions during the research.
11. Or, if one wants to use the notion of care for other types of practices, it would be aimed at improving certain kinds of situations. An example is scientific practices aiming towards 'good science' (see Pols et al., 2022).
12. To be sure, there are notions of the good in any practice, even if in practices one may see as bad (see Pols, 2012). It may, however, not be interesting or desirable to adopt a perspective on the good. For care practices, however, striving for something good is a crucial characteristic of these practices even if this intention can lead to not so good outcomes. Such efforts to achieve good are rarely explicitly articulated, but they are crucial for understanding care practices, as I will show in Chapter 3.
13. There are practices that can inform abstract reasoning (see Mol, 2000). The abstraction, however, aims to hide contexts from view rather than to foreground them. In this book I will try to unearth these contexts.

14 In theoretical physics there is a recognition of the influence that observation has on the phenomenon that is being observed. However, this is not considered a subjective influence but an artefact of the method of observation. It is this particular understanding of the influence of methods that I am interested in, but in the context of the social sciences.
15 Daston & Galison, 2007.
16 Ruppert et al., 2013; Law et al., 2011; Mol, 2000; Pols, 2012. See also Zuiderent-Jerak, 2015, who argues that interventions should not only be formulated as words but also lead to concrete actions.
17 A common metaphor employed in STS discussions about normativity in research is that of 'intervention', which highlights the normative consequences of methodologies for the field being studied (see for example Zuiderent-Jerak, 2015). This metaphor stresses that research is *active*. The re-scription metaphor foregrounds creativity and hence locates normativity in the very concepts and methods used to 're-scribe' situations.
18 See Rorty, 1979, for a cheerful and erudite discussion on the use of metaphors that 'mirror nature' in the history of philosophy.
19 See Mol, 2002 on multiplicity.
20 See Timmermans & Berg, 2010.
21 I made this point in Pols, 2012. See also Pols et al., forthcoming.
22 Ceci et al., 2017; Mol, 2010; Pols, 2015; 2017a; 2017b; Sharon, 2015; Swierstra, 2013; Thygesen & Moser, 2010; Willems, 2010c; Willems & Pols, 2010.
23 See Mol, 2012, for a demonstration.
24 The speedbump example is from Latour, 1992.
25 Zizzo et al., 2017; Brodwin, 2013; Banks et al., 2013; Banks, 2016; see also Pols, 2008; Pols, 2015; Kohlen, 2009; Hoffmaster, 1992.
26 Law, 1999, p. 3.
27 Pickering, 1992; Law, 1997.
28 Ethnography is a social scientific method that consists of participant observation and interviews. The researcher becomes part of the practices they want to learn about by participating in everyday activities and by observing, recording and reflecting on what takes place around them. I draw upon studies in actor-network theory using the notion of 'enactment'. See Mol, 1998; 2002. Earlier studies use the metaphor of 'production'. See Latour, 1987a; 1987b.
29 Law, 2004.
30 It can be asked *how many* worlds there might be. Like Foucault's discourses, Boltanski and Thévenot paint with rather broad strokes (six worlds), whereas Latour describes 14. Students of 'modes of ordering' (Law, 2004; Moser, 2005; Pols, 2006b; Vogel, 2016) do not restrict orderings to a certain number, but study local modes of ordering 'in practices'. These 'small-scale' varieties are more empirically grounded.
31 Law, 1994; Moser, 2005.
32 Pols, 2004; 2006b.
33 See for 'politics without a program' Pols, forthcoming, a. This attunement to the specificities of practices, in which an intervention might work after adapting it to the specificities of a practice, is diametrically opposed to the lessons of evidence-based medicine. Here, 'proven effective' interventions need to be copied as faithfully as possible. The difference in understanding what a good intervention might be is a nice example of how methods shape objects of research.
34 See Pols, forthcoming, a.
35 See Pols, 2005 and Chapter 12 of this book.
36 An unawareness that similar technologies are frequently used for different purposes, and hence that their effects depend on how they are used in a specific practices, is one of the reasons why the implementation and evaluation of new technologies frequently run into problems. See Pols, 2012.
37 Schama, 1988.
38 See Serres, 1995, and Draaisma, 1992.
39 I call these philosophies of the good-life-as-practice, which is in contrast to normative or prescriptive philosophies of the good life that instruct one on how to live well.
40 Law, 2004.
41 Hirschauer, 2006.

42 Remember the quote from Wittgenstein, 1921: 'Wovon man nicht reden kann, darüber muß man schweigen.' Or, what cannot be put into words, cannot be talked about.
43 For examples of quantitative reduction versus qualitative specification in the practice of self-measurements, see Pols et al., 2019.
44 Draaisma, 2000.
45 'If men define situations as real, they are real in their consequences' is the famous quote from the sociologist William Thomas, 1928, p. 572.
46 M'charek, 2014.
47 Recently, Henrietta Lacks's family has become involved in discussions around (and particularly publications about) the HeLa cell line. It is fascinating to see how Lacks's individual cells came to stand in for many human cells and could even come to include cow tissue.
48 M'charek, 2014, pp. 17–18.
49 Hirschauer, 2006. Kristine Krause is warmly thanked for the reference!
50 M'charek, 2013.
51 So much for Giddens's 'double hermeneutic' (1984), which would distinguish the social sciences from other sciences because they have an object that is self-reflexive. See, for the discussion of the symmetry between humans and things, Latour, 1993.
52 Washing is a fascinating topic to study. See Pols 2006a; 2006b; 2013a.
53 Thank you to Dick Willems who got this grant from the health research funding agency ZonMw in 2010 (Willems, 2010a).
54 Some scholars have suggested that we give up the concept of dignity because it has too many definitions. See Pinker, 2008; McCrudden, 2008; Tadd et al., 2002; Woolhead et al., 2004. Matiti & Trorey (2008) state that 'dignity' is used in care practices to represent values that are of great importance. I agree with this later position. See Pols et al., 2018.
55 Barilan, 2012; Byers, 2016; Kateb, 2014; McCrudden, 2008; Waldron, 2012.
56 Leget, 2013 calls this intrinsic dignity.
57 See M'charek & van Oorschot, 2019 about ghosts.
58 But see the discussion about animal rights in Singer, 1995; Abrahamsson et al., 2015.
59 Chochinov et al., 2002; Masson, 2002; Matiti & Trorey, 2008; Nordenfelt, 2004; Van Gennip et al., 2013.
60 More precisely, they fold them into models that seek to address 'all aspects' of dignity. However, I can now, after years of study, confidently say that such models will never succeed in capturing all these aspects, especially because of the multiple ways in which the concept has been theorised.
61 Rosen, 2012.
62 Gabriela Arguedas & Lynn, 2017.
63 This case is developed in the next chapter.
64 In Dutch, dignity is *waardigheid*.
65 The reference is to Bourdieu, 1984: see Chapter 1.
66 This is empirical philosophy in its shortest version: conducting theoretical research through empirical studies, and vice versa. For Dutch readers, see Mol, 2000 on empirical philosophy. For English-language readers, see Mol, 2002; 2015.

Part I
Shaping the good life – and the end of its theorisation

My empirical Chapters 3 and 5 examine how ethical principles play a role in contemporary care practices, and how such principles differ from the values of everyday life. Ethical principles were introduced in care practices with the aim of countering malpractices from the past and improving the governance of care practices by regulating them. These principles eclipsed local moral, religious and aesthetic considerations in care practice and everyday life. By way of introducing principles, morality was enforced from the outside rather than from within.

My examination of care practices shows, however, that the negotiation of everyday values is crucial to understanding such practices. General principles need to be translated into everyday values before they can play a useful role in specific situations. Ethical principles enter care practices that contain myriad everyday-life values. Some of these values might be classified as ethical, but others might be economic, scientific, aesthetic and so on. Caregivers need to negotiate principles with these different values. General ethical principles can therefore not be thought of as a substitute for everyday values. Even more so, any attempt to govern or rationalise care work runs the risk of threatening the capacity of caregivers to take the specificities of certain situations and values into account. Rather than *posing questions* about what matters here and 'what to do', ethical principles tend to *provide answers*. The universal and abstract character of such principles provides general norms that are used to guide care activities, but the risk is that caregivers are hindered in their requirement to take the specificities of situations into account.

In this part of the book I discuss, first, how dignity is used as a principle in long-term psychiatric care, and second, how autonomy is used as a directive in care policies and practices pertaining to people with learning disabilities. Both these principles have, broadly speaking, eclipsed the role of everyday values in the sense that the latter are rarely still discussed. I contrast these two principles with everyday values and problems, which may shift from day to day and demand persistent negotiation and evaluation. These everyday values and problems are informed by – yet also surpass – the etiquette and morality of professional practices or what is considered good by Dutch professional associations.

Everyday negotiations that draw on different sources do not create a coherent set of norms. Instead, such negotiations demand a reconciliation between different sets of norms and values, and this creates a constant tension between them. Everyday negotiations can be a matter of weighing qualitatively different registers, such as, say, opting for an aggressive chemotherapy to reduce the size of a tumour or pursuing a good life in the short run. Preventing the risk of falling may be at odds with the happiness that people with dementia might gain from being able to move around the wards of their nursing homes.

The academic shift towards principled ethics and the disappearance of the values of everyday life from discourses about care practices, everyday life and society has a long history that I trace back, in my historical chapters, to the transition from pre-modern philosophy to modernity. In doing so, I identify several important tropes that played a role during these transitional stages. Modernist thinkers, contrary to pre-modern philosophers, were concerned with building coherent, systematic theories and philosophies about the nature of the world in the form of a logical, mathematically informed order that is deduced from a set of uncontested assumptions. Everything, from astronomy to ethics and from music to state government, would find a place in this system. Modernity 'on the ground' involved a shift from religion and other forms of moral authority towards techniques for regulating people by channelling their 'natural inclinations' or by guiding their decisions via abstract ethical principles. The conceptualisation of the 'rational' (read: calculating) and 'self-interested' individual was born.

For social theorists this implied a shift away from conceptualising individual morality as the basis for individuals to regulate themselves and to create a good society. The civil wars of the seventeenth and eighteenth centuries formed the context in which the failure to create a stable society was blamed on an over-reliance on morality, which was now seen as a recipe for conflict rather than for peace. Stability was seen as crucial for emancipating citizens, who were modelled after the rising class of bourgeois merchants. Emergent modernist social theories aimed to identify the means through which to create social stability and predictability. One way in which theorists attempted to do this was by homogenising values that could create possible sources of conflict. Substituting the rich vocabulary on virtues with a general notion of self-interest was one way of achieving this.

Social theorists developed understandings about and different techniques for governing nations. Evolutionary theory, the budding field of quantitative economics and the social sciences each provided models for trying to understand how and why people behave as they do. Using these explanatory models, governments could 'socially engineer' the natural behaviour of their citizens and thus create more peaceful societies. Ethics was also reinvented. Ethics was taken out of the realm of motivations, passions and conventions, and instead grounded either in universal rules and principles (deontological ethics) or in objective calculations of effects (utilitarianism). The move towards grounding ethics in universal and true principles is an historical event in time and is therefore informed by particular historical practices such as the secularisation of society. This form of modernist ethics is still the dominant form of academic ethics today. But there remained a role for Aristotelian virtue ethics, empirically oriented care ethics, and practical forms of ethics such as moral debates. The division of labour between ethics and the positivist sciences – which concern themselves, respectively, with values and facts – resulted, however, in persistent dichotomies such as nature versus culture, fact versus value, 'is' versus 'ought' and subject versus object. The following chapters show that this division of labour is unhelpful for examining situations in which everyday values and problem definitions need to be negotiated. Problems and values in everyday situations cannot be defined beforehand. In everyday practice, specificities rather than universalities matter. Care studies and empirical ethics, which are the traditions that this book draws upon, provide alternative ways for thinking about the type of normativity that is relevant here and how one might study this empirically.

Attending to the aesthetic values of everyday life allows us to see the different ways in which people organise themselves through aesthetic *motivations* rather than through governance. This requires a relinquishing of the modernist hope for achieving unity, generality and coherence in our understanding of the relation between society and individual activity. However, this does not mean a complete fragmentation of our conceptualisation of society in which the only available explanation is that different individuals strive to uphold different values. My focus on aesthetic values presents a fresh (or refreshed) approach to understanding the ways in which people organise themselves or how they are organised by others. My approach insists on attempting to grasp the complexity of the social as something that is made up of different coherences. This is an important alternative to conceptualising the social as the channelling of the activities of individuals engaged in the pursuit of particular and unrelated interests. The idea of multiple coherences also presents an alternative to the idea of regulating individuals by appealing to one set of universal or common goods. I argue that the philosophical tradition of the good-life-as-practice, which examined the specificities of everyday life and its problems and values, needs to be revived from its pre-modern slumber and refurbished for present-day use. The upcoming empirical chapters show why this is a vital necessity for understanding care practices, and, eventually, also for understanding social dynamics.

3
Dignity in long-term psychiatry: principles and everyday values for caregivers

In this chapter I analyse how 'modernist' ethical principles enter care practices and the work they do therein. I will first discuss the difference between principles and aesthetic values as well as their interrelations. I then move on to examine care practices and show how different types of values play a role in such practices by discussing how the concept of dignity is used differently in various care settings. Dignity refers to a state of worth for all people, but it is also a concept that is interpreted and given shape through various care practices.

The chapter ends with an analysis of the position of 'the caregiver' as a particular, even exemplary, character for understanding the morality and aesthetics of everyday life. Caregivers strive to achieve or create something good. Their work is impossible to understand without considering this orientation and its intricacies. The caregiver is an interesting moral figure that became obscured by the emergence of modernist ideas about new public management and accountability as well as neoliberal policies. These ideas and policies foreground efficiency and rationality rather than everyday morality and aesthetics. The neoliberal conceptualisation of individuals as isolated, calculating and self-interested actors provides no helpful concepts for understanding care practices. The next chapter will provide the historical background of these neoliberal concepts, and show how ethical principles replaced the values of everyday life.

A second character that emerges in this chapter is that of the patient who is dependent on caregivers to get through their days. I will analyse such patients, and the values and principles that impact upon their situation, in more depth in Chapter 5. This fifth chapter explores how caregivers and policymakers understand the principle of autonomy as a tool to 'make patients speak' for themselves. Autonomy, as a guiding principle in care for people with learning disabilities, leads to unexpected types of practices, and competes with everyday values in the shaping of what counts as good care.

How values work

How do ethical principles such as dignity or autonomy function in care practices? Principles have a universal or general character that applies to many cases and situations, which is why principles are often used to provide rationales for laws and regulations in the governance of care practices. Principles are made concrete through norms or rules that are motivated by these principles. This means that such norms and rules tend to be formulated in general terms.

A well-rehearsed example of general principles in medicine is that of the four principles of medical ethics: these prescribe that doctors should do no harm, should protect patients' autonomy, should do good and should act towards justice.[1] Everyone should be granted autonomy, and nobody should experience avoidable harm. An important norm is that patients have the right to refuse treatment. Principles are abstract, and therefore cover a broad variety of situations and cases that need to be treated on equal terms. They do not always apply to all practices; many studies in ethics are on exceptional cases and special situations or seek to figure out whether one principle should be prioritised over another. Medical ethics committees are a good example of institutions in which such principled ethics are used. The protection of patients is operationalised through a set of guiding principles, such as proportionality and not doing unnecessary harm.

The values of everyday life are under-theorised.[2] They are usually discussed in human-interest stories and social media or by the wellness industry and in private conversations rather than in the medical sciences or ethics journals.[3] Aesthetic values tell us something about the things that people find good, beautiful or appropriate in their lives and in their interactions with others as well as with objects. Indeed, everyday language is full of aesthetic qualifications: a wonderful goal, a good death, a pleasant appearance, a friendly nurse or a beautiful machine.[4] Everyday-life values are context specific. They may differ between people and situations, they may change over time and they may differ in accordance with cultural preferences, conventions and fashions. We may, for example, like or dislike certain kinds of music. The values of everyday life motivate people's actions, are embedded within technologies and inform the concepts and methods people use to understand particular situations. Scientific methods have aesthetics too. The representation of statistical results in a beautiful graph is a good example of how a certain design reflects the robustness of results.[5]

Much like general principles, everyday-life values may have particular effects. But because they have historically, and increasingly, been considered 'matters of taste', they are difficult to use in (liberal and social democratic) governance. Matters of taste in liberal discourse pertain to the expression of individual freedom. In a liberal society, it is the responsibility of the state to protect individual passions and interests. What people like and how they want to live their version of the good life is not a concern for the state; these are private matters. Conflicts arise when aesthetic values are applied as legal principles. There are many common examples of such conflicts in discussions about cultural differences, such as wearing headscarves and the ritual slaughter of animals. It makes a big difference whether such issues are seen as a matter of fashion or taste – a particular choice of clothing or a religious ritual of cleanliness – or whether they are seen as a matter of morality and law, akin to the wearing of religious symbols in public or the maltreatment of animals. Religious symbols and animal abuse may be regulated or banned in public life by establishing laws. Aesthetic practices such as fashion and cleanliness cannot be dealt with in this way because that would imply a harmful restriction of the freedom of individual citizens. Aesthetic values, as expressed in privately motivated acts with no effect on others except for the potential eliciting of disapproval, cannot be regulated by the state. However, governments nevertheless strongly influence the good life, for example by promoting a healthy population or through the upholding of *laïcité* (the separation of state and religion). For governments to interfere in such questions is a delicate matter.

In care practices, understandings of the good life inform everyday activities, but such activities are also informed by ethical principles. A clear example of this is the importance of choice and autonomy for patients.[6] In the first part of this chapter, I compare the principles and values of everyday life – under the heading of 'dignity' – to illustrate how difficult it is to classify them in any strict form or manner. For principles to function well in practice, they need to have the flexibility of everyday-life values. However, I frequently witnessed how the aesthetic and moral values of everyday life were imposed with iron discipline. How do these aesthetic and moral values organise the subject position of patients, and how do they allow patients to do or value certain things rather than others? I will show that, in practice, principles and everyday-life values cannot be characterised without first learning about how they function. Our ability to classify various values as either principles, principles-in-practice or everyday-life values ultimately depends on the way they function in practice.

The case of dignity

The history of the concept of dignity illustrates how general principles differ from the values of everyday life as well as how principles and values are imbricated in practice. In my discussion of dignity as a folded concept, I showed how dignity is articulated as a principle in the context of human rights, where it is used to represent the intrinsic value of any individual human being. However, dignity is also articulated in the context of everyday life. In such a context, dignity often appears in expressions of what people deem to be a good life or not, and this is frequently articulated in terms of aesthetic values. Examples of this are found in our notions of beauty or appropriateness, such as getting washed or dressed. Such terms appeared, for example, in the bedsore case discussed in the previous chapter in which the importance of washing patients was debated.

Dignitas

After several years of research I had to conclude the obvious: dignity does not have one uniform meaning. Fortunately, that was not the only thing I could say about this term. First, in the bulk of the literature on dignity there is a discussion about 'the two faces of dignity', which suggests that dignity has multiple meanings and that these meanings are analysed differently.[7] Second, I learned that, when dignity is discussed in the context of care practices, there is something important at stake.[8] Dignity is a value that matters to caregivers and policymakers alike. It is an important notion in palliative care,[9] but it also appears frequently in critiques of the delivery of elderly care. An example in the Dutch context is that of the 'pyjama days', which refers to a period when elderly people in nursing homes remained undressed due to a lack of staff. This caused public outrage at the time.[10]

Another notorious example in the Netherlands involves the mother of the state secretary for health in 2016. Her husband – the father of the secretary of state – complained that 'urine was running down her ankles' when he visited her in the nursing home, which he took as a sign of undignified care.[11] This episode had great consequences because it launched a series of policies under the rubric of 'dignity and pride'. The aim of this programme was to restore the dignity of patients as well as the pride of caregivers. In care practices dignity has a clear aesthetic connotation, because the concept refers to what people envision a good (dignified) life to be. It is not a right that can be enforced through legal procedures. Merely claiming a right to be washed and dressed properly would not have had the same effect as articulating one's outrage in a public debate.[12]

In situations where dignity is at stake, discussions often revolve around what the Dutch call *ontluistering* (tarnishing), which means that life has lost its shine, beauty and worth. The term is used to describe things that people find embarrassing or humiliating, such as shame or a loss of face.[13] It refers to 'ugly' situations in which the good life, and hence a person's dignity, is at stake. It appeals to values that people find crucially important in a good life or to values that many cannot bear to see disrupted.[14] This everyday, aesthetic understanding of dignity is something I call *dignitas*.[15]

Humanitas

In modern philosophy and the philosophy of law, dignity is studied as a principle, such as the foundation for human rights or as a form of *humanitas*. In this context, dignity means that people have fundamental rights because they have 'an intrinsic kernel of dignity'.[16] This kernel should be respected and protected, which is why all individuals have equal rights. Their dignity should be upheld, everywhere and always, which indicates the power of such universal principles. The bracketing of the relevance of context is a reason why critical scholars have accused human rights of reflecting 'Western values'.

As a fundamental principle, dignity refers to what every individual (and for some, this includes non-human animals) has in common with others. Differences or exceptions do not hinder the force of a principle. And when there are irrelevant differences, these can be dealt with using certain techniques, such as Rawls's 'veil of ignorance', so that they can be ignored and proper judgement can proceed.[17] The veil is needed to bracket, for instance, differences in the positionality of people in order to judge the situation by its merits rather than, say, people's status. One's social position, religion, ancestry or income should not matter when justice is at stake. Dignity motivates human rights, such as the right to food, shelter and freedom from torture.

Relationships between *dignitas* and *humanitas*

The values of everyday life and the principles of *dignitas* and *humanitas* are in tension because of their respective foregrounding of the differences and distinctions between people versus their normatively postulated equality. But the tension also concerns the different affordances of each type of value. One important difference is that principles allow for the formulation of rules and regulations that make principles effective and that give them direction. The values of everyday life are more difficult to concretise through rules and regulations. Even though there are constant negotiations about how to classify things of importance, it is difficult for governments to regulate the various forms of good or aesthetic lives that citizens seek. Should they be healthy? Well dressed? Vegetarian? Free to express themselves in any way? An imperative to wear red jackets reminds us of dictatorships rather than of liberal societies. In liberal societies, the private sphere is where tastes (appreciations, values, motivations) are allowed to circulate freely, and this is something governments need to *protect* rather than regulate.

However, social organisation and the association of people who share particular aesthetic concerns and ideas of a good life operate differently, namely through the motivations of individuals, whatever these motivations might be and however far away people might live from each other. People may be motivated to organise themselves or to reject particular forms of the good life. Eventually these 'informal values' may impact on governance, as was the case with the 'flower power' hippy understandings of goodness. The hippies proclaimed that their values were very different from what was widely considered beautiful and proper at the time. Their long hair and colourful clothes were symbols of a more subversive understanding of how people should live together. Free sexual relationships and horizontal organisations were the trademarks of hippy culture. The hippies' colourful way of addressing issues of power and social convention by challenging conventional dress codes still resonates today. Their impact on democratisation processes in public institutions is still a strong part of the Dutch cultural heritage.

What made these aesthetic values subversive was that they were not, or at least not *only*, asserted through good arguments or decided on through democratic choice. Some things may just seem more interesting, nicer or prettier than other things – so let's do it this way, without further ado. The relationships between motivated values and principles of governance are complex. The tensions between these different forms of dignity are most visible when inequality is addressed in the domain of law because there it tends to become obscure whether individual freedom is unduly limited or injustice is done. There is a lot at stake. If there are different forms of *dignitas*, might this also legitimise the notion that some people have more rights than others? Could there be a difference between first- and second-class citizens or even between citizens and slaves? More and less dignified citizens? Here the human rights activists hit their target. Even if social differences will never disappear, human rights activists need a normative vocabulary to argue for equality and the dignified treatment of all individuals.

This is a form of theoretical, prescriptive equality, not one that 'is' but one that 'should be'. The question of how to deal with *actual* differences is, however, an important one for our times. The differences between citizens of a nation state and stateless refugees puts this discussion back on the European agenda, which, of course, has strong resonances with the Second World War. M'charek and Casartelli write about how dead and living refugees are turned into 'informal' citizens when people help them, thus making them part of their community and perceiving them as humans whether they are illegal or not.[18] Dányi shows how people supporting the 'sans-papiers' who are on hunger strike resist formal regulations that distinguish between those who are and those who are not entitled to food, housing and work in the country they find themselves in.[19]

Yet things become even more complicated when everyday-life values and principles change position. How can we know if a certain good is an important or a trivial aesthetic value or instead a principle that should apply to everyone? The relationship between rights and aesthetic values puts questions about rationality and the role of governance back on the political agenda. Kwame Anthony Appiah asks himself how it is possible that certain social practices, such as duelling, Chinese foot binding and slavery, could have persisted.[20] He shows that arguments against these practices were already well articulated at the time of their occurrence. Rational arguments, Appiah claims, did not lead to the abolishment of these practices. These practices only changed, he argues, when they were no longer seen as honourable and instead as despicable, ugly and 'not done'. As undignified. Not rational thinking but aesthetic disapproval of these practices was ultimately what led to their demise. Aesthetic motivations have more power than social theorists have acknowledged.[21]

Dignity in care

The principle of *humanitas* is informed by both a vocabulary for and a practice of enforcing rights, whereas the aesthetical values of *dignitas* are found in vocabularies for the good life. Each set of vocabularies points to different ways of bringing certain people together and separating others, of organising social life. How may we understand these two different ways of valuing in care practices? My first example is from long-term psychiatry. People who used to live in psychiatric institutions for most of their lives were, as they got older, eventually moved to residential homes for the elderly. The idea at the time was that psychiatric patients could benefit from state provisions for older people, and thus live in society in a more integrated way. However, there was a second group of people: those who were not able to leave the psychiatric institutions and who never made it to these residential homes.

The settings

Long-term mental health care and elderly care

First, a quick introduction to my work on long-term mental health care. I conducted ethnographic fieldwork on innovative mental health care practices in the Netherlands.[22] My fieldwork involved two different kinds of site: four long-stay wards in two psychiatric hospitals, and five residential homes for elderly people.

The long-stay wards in these psychiatric hospitals housed people who could not be accommodated under contemporaneous deinstitutionalisation policies. They could not be turned into 'citizens' capable of living outside of a psychiatric hospital. They could not manage on their own, resisted moving out of the hospital or were simply too vulnerable and unable to survive without the protection offered by the hospital ward. My fieldwork sought to address the question of how the ideal of psychiatric rehabilitation could be translated into practical improvements for people who had to continue living in these institutions, which was something that teams working in these hospitals were striving to achieve. At the root of the ideal of psychiatric rehabilitation was a critique of institutional life, but the big question was whether nurses could develop care practices in wards that were acceptable to those who were dependent on these care practices. Among the many issues discussed were questions about the possibility of having private space, to what extent patients should be allowed to independently decide things pertaining to their lives, and to what extent it was possible to limit institutional power.

My second field site was the residential homes that housed people who had grown old in psychiatric hospitals. The idea was that these residential homes could provide better services and facilities for older people as well as offer them a way to live closer to their families and other social networks. Along with these new patients, new professionals entered the residential homes, namely psychiatric nurses. They had to work in these residential homes alongside geriatric assistants who had experience with and training in caring for elderly people with dementia. I conducted extensive ethnographic research in both the psychiatric hospitals and the residential homes by observing care practices, hanging out with residents and interviewing caregivers about this new idea of 'good care', which involved things such as 'good washing'.[23] I analyse how ethical principles as well as values of the good life work in concrete practices by pointing towards the notion of dignity and the various guises it takes on in these practices.

Dirt and dignity

My concerns about dignity emerged while I was examining the different judgements that are made about cleanliness and the tolerance for dirt in psychiatric institutions. In one of the long-stay wards for younger adults in psychiatric care, notions of hygiene and cleanliness seemed to have been forgotten. According to the common standards of those who live outside such institutions, the ward was extremely dirty. One reason for this was that patients did not seem to mind. They contributed to the pollution of their living environment by spreading ash and cigarette butts and by spilling coffee. They actively resisted showering and changing their clothes. Because of this disinterest and resistance, staff did not prioritise cleanliness, either. This was in sharp contrast to the residential homes where immaculate corridors and shiny floors seemed to be the top priority. Clean residents and spick-and-span buildings were maintained with a strict routine. In both cases caregivers referred to notions of dignity to justify their practices.

Dirt is beautiful?

Apparently, dignity can be found in both very dirty and very clean living environments. Let us first look at the dirty ward. The psychiatric nurses working in these not-so-clean wards referred to principles of citizenship to justify their practices and concerns. Psychiatric patients needed to become citizens, the nurses argued, with the same rights and possibilities as other citizens. This meant, foremost, that nurses should not approach patients as a *group* in order to create space for more individual approaches.

> Rehabilitation coach: We discussed this in the team. 'Yes, we are always there to make sure he takes his shower. But do we have to be there? If he has his towels and his things, he can manage without us.' And thus, people [nurses] began to think about it.

In this individual approach, matters of hygiene became private concerns. Nurses no longer hounded patients to take a shower. People were free to make their own choices about when to shower, what kind of soap to use and what colour of towel to pick. Their citizenship started by living according to their own rather than to other people's preferences.

> Psychiatric nurse: People can be who they are on this ward, with all their handicaps and all their odd behaviours. That's our vision of rehabilitation. In principle, people are allowed to behave crazily as long as you can manage it on the ward. People are allowed to stay in bed for a whole day if they experience strange things. They are not obliged to get up and go to therapy. Let people just be people to start with. They have so little left for themselves.

Another psychiatric nurse:

> These patients are here for a long time, and you might say they are very hospitalised. They lose their sense of dignity. And I think they don't really care what they look like; they just hang around the hospital. This is what you hear some of them say: 'What do we have except for our coffee and cigarettes? Why would I take care of myself? I am locked up in a madhouse.' And with some people it has to do with their disorder. Like Mrs Andersen, she says, 'I must be dirty or terrible things will happen to me. If I take a shower and wash, my skin will fall off.' That's very extreme. Some people have

bizarre notions of their bodies. And her hair is not supposed to be washed, either: it has to remain greasy, otherwise she thinks it will all fall out.

Patients had to become private persons, namely people who are entitled to make their own choices and be left in peace if this is what they want. Dignity was paraphrased as, 'you can be who you are'. To just be human for a while, or, to be more precise, to be a private individual, meant living according to one's own tastes and characteristics. If one's preference was to be not quite so clean, this is a position in life that had to be respected. Dirt appears here not as a common good, but as an accidental aesthetic consequence of 'letting people be who they are'. Each individual is entitled to live according to their own values, particularly when 'at home'. Ironically, the community that patients are supposed to become part of as citizens lives *outside* the doors of the institution. Fellow patients on the ward were not seen as citizens but rather as 'inmates' or 'fellow convicts' with whom one shares nothing but bad luck. Hence patients were not seen as having to negotiate norms among themselves.[24]

In another, not quite so dirty long-stay ward with permanent residents, on the other side of the country, psychiatric nurses placed more emphasis on the aesthetics of private life. They actively supported the development and cultivation of people's tastes:

> Psychologist: You can ask yourself: why didn't we do this before? It's so obvious. You deal with people, they may be a little bit ill, but they're people with tastes and desires. However ill you might be, you can still appreciate the difference between, say, nuts and crisps. There are always differences in taste. Everyone can understand that.

Hence, everyday aesthetic values were seen as necessary for grounding the general idea of what a citizen is or what the good life can be for a human being.[25] This resonates with the notion of the individual as a consumer with tamed private passions or tastes (which I will discuss in the next chapter).

Cleanliness first!

In residential homes, where cleanliness was a central value, cleanliness was not employed to create *individuals* but rather *relationships* with others. The dignity of a clean and well-kept appearance derived its meaning from within the community of the residential home. Here, cleanliness was a clear aesthetic value.

> Geriatric assistant: You see, we just don't have the time. I would really like to talk to my people in the morning, have a nice shower, take an hour to do it, great! We would like to do more, spoil them a bit, do something special. But you just don't have the time. It's like this: out of bed in the morning, washing, making sure they look a bit nice [netjes], so that they at least feel good about that. I find that really important, it's their sense of dignity [eigenwaarde].

Dignity or self-worth was directly linked to the social life of the residential home. As a resident, you have to look good in relation to others so that you are not expelled from the community of the residential home. Clothes should be clean, unwrinkled and without stains. A combed head of hair may compensate for some of the other issues one may have, such as chronic psychosis or dementia. Personal appearance and cleanliness were not a given; they were an *achievement* in a place where such things are constantly threatened. It was the geriatric assistants' responsibility to take care of such matters.[26] Maintaining the everyday aesthetics of their patients was their core business. This turned each of their residents into a human among humans.

In the residential homes, attention to cleanliness and hygiene was important to residents because it created the possibility of sharing pleasant moments together. This also shows the importance of social life in the residential home.[27] Much to the horror of the psychiatric nurses, who were keen on treating their patients as independent people, the geriatric assistants took over a lot of tasks from the residents. The assistants deemed patients incapable of doing much by themselves.

> Geriatric assistant: Personally, I think that the homeliness of the residential home is very nice for most of the residents. And I see this as the main difference, at least from what I gather, between us and the nurses who came from the psychiatric hospital. This is typical for geriatric assistants, we just do it all, and we make it nice and cosy. We take the time to go downstairs and get a packet of cigarettes, we make sure the Christmas tree is in order. And the psychiatric nurses are different. Colleagues who have been there say: 'Jeez, if you saw those rooms, they [the psychiatric nurses] don't do a single bit about them.' They think that the residents should take care of that themselves. But these people are here

because they are unable to do certain things. So we arrange a lot. I think their time wouldn't be as pleasant if we didn't.

The geriatric assistants were astonished at the austere conditions of the living spaces in the residential home in which the new arrivals from the psychiatric hospital were placed. They saw this as a failure of the residential home's staff; *they* should try to make life as pleasant and interesting as possible for the residents. The interpretations of dignity by psychiatric nurses and the geriatric assistants – what it means and what role it plays for patients, but also how dignity informs who patients are and how they should be treated – were diametrically opposed.

Citizenship or cleanliness?

There appears to be a clear difference between the principles of citizenship and individuality that are cherished by psychiatric nurses, and the aesthetic values of cleanliness and friendly relationships that are upheld by geriatric assistants. The practices of psychiatric nurses are motivated by a general principle, whereas the practices of geriatric assistants are informed by values concerning the aesthetics and sensuality of everyday life (see Table 3.1). Caregivers in psychiatric wards were very cautious about interfering with patient lives in their efforts to respect the dignity of patients as individuals and as citizens who have a right not to be disturbed. In contrast, caregivers in residential homes were very assertive in helping the people who were dependent on their care, and they worked hard to preserve the dignity of residents as members of the social and aesthetic order of the residential home.

Table 3.1. Forms of dignity

Dignitas: cleanliness	*Humanitas*: citizenship
Everyday-life values, aesthetic values	Principles
Differences	Equality
Values, motivations, passions, appreciations	Rights, laws, norms, rules, obligations
Local, situated, contextual	Universal, abstract
Permissive, motivating	Prescriptive, directive

However, the distinction turned out to be less stark than this table suggests.[28] Citizenship values turned out to be guidelines that reached their limits when patients became *too* dirty. Different conventions and values disrupted the principle of citizenship. When this disruption occurred, the freedom of choice and personal discretion of the new citizen was abruptly withdrawn; patients were put under the shower whether they liked it or not.

Such interference from caregivers turned out to be difficult to justify. Nurses did not have a vocabulary to argue otherwise within a discourse of citizenship that emphasises individual choice and freedom. The faint objection was made that 'dirty patients hinder others'. But fellow patients were not at all bothered by dirt. In the local, popular discourse on citizenship, patients did not figure as citizens vis-à-vis each other. A patient's relationship with their 'family' was a better argument for justifying a shower, even though family members did not visit the ward frequently. Generally it was the nurses themselves who were the ones feeling troubled, because they empathised with a filthy patient or because they were concerned about the smell. Nurses had the feeling that not washing a patient 'goes too far'. Principles, then, turned out to be adjustable, and nurses could switch to another register for justifying the treatment of patients if these principles were no longer applicable or if different values came to the fore.

> *Fieldnote:* Nurse William said he could no longer stand the way Bill looks, all dirty and with scabs on his face (he has a skin problem). They tried 'personal responsibility' and gentle insistence; they even forbade Bill from entering the common room in this dirty state. They had tried long enough with no result. This morning, William ordered Bill out of bed, dragged him under the shower and scrubbed off all the scabs. 'Harder!' Bill shouted. He was in the shower for almost two hours. William put clean sheets on the bed and beneath it discovered approximately thirty empty cartons of apple juice. Now Bill is in the common room; his head is red as a fire engine. Nurse Martha says there is an ointment that will alleviate this.

The urge to interfere was deeply felt as well as approved of by other nurses, even if intervention was hard to justify in terms of citizenship. The intolerability of Bill's appearance, both visual and olfactory, became part of the equation. But these objections were difficult to justify in terms of individual preference.

> Psychiatric nurse: I think these things are unplannable. On one day, you can say, 'Hey, Ben, let's go for your shower!' And then I think, 'That is nice, I can talk to him in an informal way.' And the other day,

I think, 'Ben, today I am not going to ask you this.' There is no standard that works in all cases. Some other time, I would probably say, 'Ben, you can do it on your own,' or he says, 'I won't do it.' I think it is very hard to determine rules for doing such things.

In terms of the value of cleanliness in residential homes, in contrast, there was much less margin for discussion. Cleanliness was obligatory, for everyone, every day. It was not something that could be negotiated.

> Geriatric assistant: A person who can take care of him- or herself and have a wash and get dressed, you give them a good cleaning in the shower once a week for a check-up, for hygienic reasons. And in doing so I want to wash them from head to toe, even if this person could do it herself. Of course, you let them assist you, but I want to inspect the skin to verify that nothing is wrong, because otherwise, if something is wrong, nobody sees it. That is our [the geriatric assistants'] responsibility, because very often, people do not tell us these things. They are ashamed, they have doubts, and when you take care of them, you are confronted with the problems.

What could be handled flexibly were *ways* of washing. A person used to taking a shower once a week did not have to take one every day. Washing at the sink was permitted and a bathtub was available. The value of cleanliness itself, however, was not up for discussion. The aesthetic value of cleanliness, one might say, was used as a principle for regulating life in the ward even if this particular principle would never be considered as such in handbooks on medical ethics. Cleanliness was not a *motivation* for the elderly residents, even if it was for the care professionals. Cleanliness was put into practice through the prescription that individuals and their surroundings must always be clean. The value of sharing a comfortable life with others, however, is much more permissive, motivating and variable. This value retains its aesthetic character and openness to contextual realisation. Yet cleanliness as a means to an end turned out to be a strict prescription. It became a condition for *humanitas* – for being human.

So it matters considerably whether cleanliness is taken as a principle that applies to everyone, or whether it is taken as an everyday value that can be adapted, privately pursued, negotiated or shared with like-minded others. This is, however, not always an *intrinsic* characteristic of a particular type of value. Even tough values of cleanliness or beauty can be classified as aesthetic values, they may nonetheless also function as principles. Rules of etiquette can, for example, be very strict. Principles and values of everyday life obtain meaning in the context in which they are found. They may function either in aesthetic or in more principled ways. Dignity does orient care work towards particular understandings of the good, but this good can take on different shapes. Dignity could be interpreted as receiving respect in the eyes of the self or others, but also as being human, or rather, as being an individual. Dignity refers to very different states of worth. This concept also allows us to see how the bedsore case from Chapter 2 brings together two different states of worth. The dignity case shows that principles turned into everyday life values when put into practice.

Tales about dignity

In a study on dignity at the end of life, we learned that dignity was a value that was invoked by caregivers to underscore that something was a matter of ultimate importance to them.[29] The exact meanings of dignity may vary – it may be unclear what norms dignity can inform or what actions it would motivate, and whether its character is aesthetic or principled – but for the persons concerned, dignity always refers to what is of great value to them.

We asked physicians and nurses to join two focus groups to study how dignity emerges as a concern in end-of-life care practices. One focus group consisted of five medical doctors and the other of six specialised nurses. The group of doctors (four women, one man) was made up of a neurologist, an oncologist, a pulmonologist, a general practitioner and a geriatrician. The group of nurses (five women, one man) consisted of three pulmonology/gastroenterology nurses, a hospice nurse, a neurology nurse and another neurology nurse from the hospital's palliative care team. We asked participants in advance to reflect on situations concerning end-of-life care in which they had participated and in which dignity had been at stake. We then asked them for detailed observations of clinical situations concerning the end of life, and to adopt an ethnographic gaze on their own practices. This allowed them to describe the material context, their activities, feelings and thoughts as well as those of the other participants. This was not a 'proper' ethnography in the sense that an observer maps positions and events. In this study, the perspectives of the dying persons and their families are not always extensively reported on because our team did not speak to these groups. This method did, however, provide us with rich case studies that indicated where and when medical professionals felt dignity was at stake and how they acted on this.

The professionals took end-of-life situations very seriously, even if it was sometimes hard to find the words to talk about such situations. The conversations were intimate, respectful and intense, with the medical professionals presenting cases that were close to their heart. Everyday clinical language is not very useful for describing a good end of life. Similar to what I observed in other studies, a dignified end of life was often described in aesthetic terms, namely as a 'beautiful death', as a 'proper' way to go, as fitting the lifestyle of the dying person, or as 'horrific' or 'sad'. At the same time, the intensity of these conversations highlighted the significance of various values and how these related to dignity for dying people.

The medical professionals in these focus groups contributed to my analysis through their active engagement with each other's stories, by asking questions, highlighting points they considered relevant to dignity, and occasionally providing comfort to a colleague reliving an intense situation. They did not act in a moralising manner by judging each other. Cases about dignity were cases that mattered to them both personally and professionally. It was clear in both focus groups that conversations about dignity evoked concerns that were deeply felt by the participants.

Dignity in end-of-life care

The case below, recounted to me by a general practitioner, exemplifies how dignity is an important matter to medical professionals. It concerns a man in his sixties who was terminally ill with lung cancer. In his case, different elements that would have allowed for a dignified end of life could not be aligned in a way that was satisfactory to all participants.

> GP: He [the dying person] wanted to die at home, and he wanted to be cared for by his partner and her daughters. And his partner also wanted to do that for him. The problem was that he had many debts, and his partner was illegal. She did not even exist, so to speak. It was winter, and his situation was getting worse. He received pain medication and home care because he was in bed most of the time. At that point their gas and electricity were cut off because of unpaid bills. So, the electric high-low bed did not function any more, and because of that the home-care nurses were not allowed to visit him any more. You know, labour laws and all.
>
> Notwithstanding the electricity we borrowed from the upstairs neighbours to operate the bed, home care workers were not allowed

to visit any more. The house was lit with candles and heated with a gas stove. My assistant occasionally helped out with cleaning the bed. And this man refused to be taken elsewhere because he knew, 'if that happens my partner has to leave the country'. This would eventually happen anyway, but we did not know how to manage this. We tried to convince the municipality to turn the electricity back on, but they could or would not do anything on such a short term. And so, this man spent the last weeks of his life in a very marginal situation: in a cold house, candles that seemed nice but were not, with insufficient care, and insufficient support for his partner, who was very sad and desperate about her husband dying and her own future being so insecure. We went there a lot to do whatever we could. But it all felt very wrong. The only good thing was that they were together, but this was a very undignified setting to die in.

It is clear from this description that all participants were very concerned about the (dignity of the) situation. There were important values at stake. The situation illustrates the role of socio-economic status both for the dying person (his debts) and his partner (having no legal status that would allow her to remain in the country, even in the face of her partner dying), but also the role of the material context, namely the cold and unlit house, and the abandonment by official institutions (home care, the housing company). There was, however, support from the GP practice and the upstairs neighbours.

Did dignity fail to emerge, as the GP suggests? Our position as outsiders and analysts applying a material-semiotic approach allowed us to see something else emerge as well. Notwithstanding the difficulty of the situation, the GP and his staff did not abandon the patient and his partner. They administered whatever care they could provide, which ranged from calling the municipality to visiting frequently and arranging clean bed linen. There was pain, but also the killing of pain. The value that was expressed as being the most important by the patient was upheld: he died in the presence of his partner, even though the circumstances were terrible.

From an outsider's point of view, it is also apparent that the people involved in this situation were remarkably concerned with dignity. This engagement made participants pursue dignity, even if it was clear that it could not be fully realised. This shows something crucial about dignity. The caregivers' engagement was not so much in realising the values at stake; they could not achieve this. But an action may be good even if the good is not achieved. Rather, it is the *engagement* with these values that revealed the importance of dignity, even though the values associated with the concept of dignity could not be realised in full. Dignity is at stake when the good is of such importance to someone that it is persistently pursued even if this good cannot (fully) be attained. The caregivers demonstrated, by not giving up on the patient and his partner, that their own dignity was dependent on the dignity of those they cared for. To give up on the dignity of the patient would also have meant a loss of dignity to themselves. Their merit as medical professionals depended on their engagement with the patient and his family. If they had given up on caring for the patient, they would have given up on their own dignity.

This example also shows that in concrete situations it is frequently quite clear how to define dignity. Similar to the psychiatric nurses and geriatric assistants, it was very clear for caregivers *themselves* what they meant when they said that dignity was at stake. I therefore suggest that it is not the exact meaning of the concept of dignity that makes it important for care. This more contextual meaning of dignity is interesting and important. It brings different values and different ways of organising care to the fore. Yet the reason why dignity moves people to act is that it signifies what people find of utmost importance. It points to concerns that make them act.

Dignity as engagement

Dignity did not simply emerge as a universal kernel of worth, a universal value residing in every individual. Dignity obtains its meaning when a person perceives some threat to their dignity. This places people in a moral and aesthetic relationship with others. A state of worth, or a threat to this worth, gives the situation its importance.[30] People's ability to value and to direct their activities accordingly is the key to understanding someone's motivation to act. I suggest it is not *what*, but *that* we value, which motivates our efforts towards improvement in cases where dignity is at stake. It is a concrete and motivated engagement, it does not follow from protocols, guidelines, rules or norms. Caregivers aim to achieve a state of worth for their patients and themselves. This motivation relates to the workings of everyday life values.

Note, once again, that this does not mean that good motivations always lead to good outcomes. Motivations are embedded and put to the test in social and material practices. There need to be conversations and exchanges between medical professionals in order to ascertain their notions of the good and the values that are at stake. For example, every so often there is a criminal case in which a caregiver has terminated the lives of patients under their care because they considered these lives undignified. The embeddedness of individual motivations in social conventions requires checking if all concerned would agree that the right conventions are being lived up to. As we know from Smith's moral theory (see next chapter) and pragmatist understandings of ethics, it matters with whom one talks.[31] Aesthetic or moral aberrations highlight the importance of aesthetic and moral communities and the role they play in care situations. These communities make clear that differences in valuations are possible. Concrete practices, situations and collectives are ultimately the touchstone for determining whether care has been good. *Humanitas* takes shape in the concrete negotiations that are found in practices of *dignitas*.

The position of the caregivers: morality regained

The moral subjects discussed in this chapter were not some exemplary practitioners of the good life. They were caregivers striving for the good in less-than-perfect situations. What caregivers do cannot be adequately explained as motivated by self-interest or the following of rules or as a striving for the maximum gain for most people. Of course, care work is a profession that is also a source of income. But care work cannot be comprehensively described as merely a source of income or as a set of pre-given rules or logics.[32] It is an everyday, case-based moral, aesthetic and professional activity that caregivers try to accomplish to the best of their ability. Care work involves a constant movement between specific situations and the values that are relevant to these situations. These values have to be weighed against each other to grasp their concrete significance in the here and now. In this chapter, I have made clear that caregivers strive for something good through their practices, namely to achieve a stable situation for their patients, to provide them with freedom of choice, with a clean appearance or possibilities to function in their communities. These efforts are aimed to improve the patients' situation. There are many routine aspects to care work, but there are also many situations in which the values of good patient care are overtly at stake. In situations where the notion of dignity was evoked, it was clear that a state of worth was at stake both for medical professionals and for patients. The dignity of the patients coincided with the dignity of the caregivers looking after them.

The caregivers in this chapter cannot be easily understood as liberal subjects making their own choices, pursuing their personal tastes or working to make care as efficient as possible. Rather, they work in a collective of other caregivers, with patients and families, in which norms and values are collectively experienced and negotiated. Clashes occur when there are different understandings of what the right way to act might be. Individualised everyday morality can lead to original additions or adaptations, but also to idiosyncratic understandings of situations that are harmful to patients. Shared socialities, however, often give rise to complex negotiations involving various values in difficult situations: putting Bill in the shower or not, providing good reasons for (not) doing this, deciding *how* to do put Bill in the shower, and so on. These decisions and activities require skills for negotiating everyday-life values, professional evaluations and understandings of what is good or 'appropriate' given the circumstances. These considerations may sometimes seem to have intuitive solutions, but they are preferably evaluated together with colleagues or other people who might want to dispute their legitimacy, or who may simply improve a situation by suggesting a helpful ointment to ease the pain after one has been cleaned. Care work is hence a collective process that seeks to negotiate measures that will provide a good life to patients as well as medical professionals. Care for patients is thus an exemplary situation for thinking through the negotiations between aesthetic and moral values as well as the other values of everyday life.

Care work cannot be properly understood if one fails to acknowledge that it strives to do good. We have discussed examples of psychiatric nurses who shared their motivations for developing practices of citizenship for their patients, even if these patients were unable to live independently. These nurses were actively looking for ways to shape the citizenship of their patients through care practices by allowing them to be – or turning them into – private individuals with personal preferences and characteristic particularities. The motivation to creatively shape their care work informed their practical approach. Similarly, geriatric assistants displayed their conviction that cleanliness was an important thing to work towards because it was deemed good for their patients. They were genuinely shocked by what they saw as the neglect of helpless people. Likewise, the doctors and nurses from the focus groups conveyed values that deeply mattered to them. Their own dignity as a caregiver depended on the dignity of their patients. These accounts show that everyday (aesthetic) values are crucial to care practices.

So, caregivers emerge as subjects striving for forms of the good who are operating within a framework of everyday aesthetic, moral and other values. These values emerge within contingent situations where they are collectively negotiated and put to the test. This collective aspect means that different conventions, values and ideas about what is appropriate emerge and are dealt with simultaneously. One could say that collectivity is needed to safeguard good decision making in care practices, which always contain multiple and partial perspectives on what is best to do. Caregivers, I claim, are exemplary professional, aesthetic and moral actors, but not in the sense that they already know what is good or how to live the good life. Caregivers are exemplary in the sense that they are actively examining and responding to contingent situations in what seems the best way to deal with them from their perspective. They do this by living with their patients and their professional colleagues, by spending their days with them and by actively engaging with their everyday concerns.

These professional practices are directly related to how caregivers frame and enact a situation. Are these patients individuals with their own preferences? Or are they foremost patients who are dependent on your care for having a good life? Exactly *what* kind of good life might fit a certain reality? Does a person need a wash, a good conversation or an ointment? The creative ways in which caregivers move with and understand their patients as well as their values and the tools they have to hand to navigate their practices all hang together. Form and content are interlinked.

Conclusion

My analysis of dignity in this chapter focused on the principles and everyday-life values that are present in particular care practices, and ended with a discussion on the creative and moral work of care professionals. This chapter shows that the principles and values of everyday life can take each other's place, depending on the way that they are deployed, namely either as universals and imperatives or as everyday-life values and motivations. It is also clear that an abstract principle that exists in a theoretical space needs to be made concrete in everyday life. In practice a principle becomes a norm, a rule or an everyday-life value that is negotiated in a specific case, context or social situation, and hence is made to relate to the specificities of that situation. In practice there is no abstract equality or dignity; there are only concrete forms of these principles. Dignity emerges both as a principle and as an everyday value.

The concept is used by caregivers to express what is crucially important to them, which is why it motivates them to engage in care work.

What is striking about dignity is its power to motivate and engage people. It drives people to take action and strive for situations of worth, both for patients and for themselves. The difference between principles and values is that the latter are part of the social and material setting in which care work is done. The multivocality of the chorus of partial participants, in addition to the specificity and contingency of situations, implies that outcomes always have a certain unpredictability. That there is space for unpredictable outcomes signifies that specificities are indeed taken into account, because these specificities are contingent on a particular patient, a concrete situation, a certain mood and so on. These can never be completely anticipated. Rigid moral systems or rules cannot replace the practical need to work with specificities; practical aesthetic morality must be creatively shaped on a daily basis in response to newly emerging situations. This open-endedness makes it uncertain which values will prevail in concrete cases. This does not mean that 'anything goes' and that there are no moral footholds. Rather, there is a multitude of values, each more or less strongly felt or advocated for, and each belonging to a different set of coherences (medical, aesthetic, moral, professional and so on).

The role of caregivers can best be understood as one in which they strive for something good for their patients. Neither self-interest nor rules, tastes nor calculations helps to understand professional care practices as they creatively and morally evolve. The professional skill of negotiating different values is an everyday moral, aesthetic and professional activity that involves other professionals as well as patients and families. Indeed, the suggestion that the professional is an individual acting alone is misleading. Multivocality and reference to social conventions are necessary conditions for discussing and evaluating activities as well as for obtaining different points of view. The caregiver is hence an interesting figure for examining creative practices in which the aesthetic and moral values of everyday life are prominent. Caregivers have a professional task 'to do good', even if there are different registers for determining what good might mean.

The open-endedness of these practical and creative negotiations is a crucial element of attempts to improve particular situations. Pre-given codes of conduct can be instruments and tools to support such endeavours, but they can never be the final answer to all new situations. Patients may just become too dirty. They might not behave as individual choosers of value, but as people acting in, say, aesthetically clumsy ways, as people who fail to aesthetically craft a good life in relation to others. Patients may not act according to caregivers' ideals of who they are, what they want and what effect they should have on others. Values are not fixed and, to a certain extent, must be reinvented in particular situations, and always with uncertain outcomes.

It is for this reason that principles have ambivalent effects on care practices. As motivations for general norms they provide direction and guidance, but they can never replace the day-to-day negotiations between values and social conventions. In care practices, general principles become specific and concrete, and they must be weighed against 'less big' values. Hence care practices cannot be improved 'from the outside' only. They must be lived, translated and tinkered with from within.

Notes

1. Beauchamp & Childress, 2001.
2. The exception is Aristotelian virtue ethics, which is extensively theorised.
3. There is a particularist ethics, but this is an abstract form of reasoning about values that seeks to give prevalence to particulars rather than to general norms for grounding values and judgements. See Dancy, 2017. A nice exception to this approach is the moral debates that are organised in care practices. Moral debates discuss everyday problems that emerge at a certain point in time.
4. The machine is a reference to Adam Smith: see Chapter 4.
5. Aesthetic values may be part of other modes of ordering, such as science or statistics mentioned in the example, in which values pertaining to knowledge are central. Aesthetic values themselves can also be central, for instance, in the practice of artistic expression.
6. Hoffmaster, 2017; Wolpe, 1998.
7. Spiegelberg, 1970; Nordenfelt, 2003a; 2003b; 2004; Edgar, 2004; Pullman, 2002; Gallagher, 2004; Jacobson, 2009; Malpas & Lickiss, 2007; Leget, 2013; Van Gennip et al., 2013; Oosterveld-Vlug et al., 2014.
8. Pols et al., 2018.
9. Lutz, 2011.
10. NOS Nieuws, 2014.
11. Landeweer, 2014.
12. Different activities demand different styles of accounting for these activities. See Pols, 2006a on this.
13. Margalit, 1998; Lawton, 1998.
14. Meyer, 2009; Meyer & Verrips 2008; Hennion, 2007; Pols et al., 2019; De Laet, Driessen & Vogel, 2021; D'Hoop, 2021a; 2023.
15. Pols, 2013a; 2013b. For aesthetics in medicine and the beauty of the body, see Dekkers, 1999; Düwell, 1999. Maio, 1999 analyses texts about doctors' etiquette and proper conduct.
16. Rosen, 2012.
17. Rawls, 1971.
18. M'charek & Casartelli, 2019.
19. Dányi, 2020a, and Law & Mol, 2020. To analyse the citizenship status of long-term psychiatric patients, I coined the term 'relational citizenship'. This concept posits a notion of citizenship that relies on metaphors of being outside society (living in institutions) or inside (subscribing to societies norms). One becomes a citizen through one's relationships with others and through one's embeddedness in socio-material practices. This is also a good way to shift the conceptualisation of citizenship from an abstract ideal towards observable and concrete relationships. See Pols, 2006b; 2016.

20 Appiah, 2010.
21 It is my understanding that aesthetic depreciation is also the reason why people in Western countries increasingly quit smoking. Education and scary pictures on cigarette packets did not help curb smoking. Turning smoking into an abject and anti-social practice was far more effective. Aesthetic claims are risky arguments in governance because they involve existing aesthetic appreciations. 'Uncool' suggestions will miss their target. This makes the strategy of winning votes by pleasing the electorate a daunting one, as we see currently see in the Netherlands in the scramble for the populist vote. Populist voters are not a homogeneous group but one that quickly changes its styles and adherences.
22 Depla et al., 2003; Pols et al., 1998; Pols et al., 2001.
23 Pols, 2006a; 2006b.
24 The term is from Goffman, 1990.
25 See Pols, 2013a, on washing and dignity.
26 Pols, 2006b.
27 This interest in cleanliness and an agreeable social life stems from the emergence of the residential homes as luxury housing and places of care for well-to-do elderly single people (Bijsterveld, 1995). Cleanliness also has its roots in turn-of-the-century notions of hygiene and mental hygiene, which stretched from physical cleanliness to social cleanliness and attempts at educating families with low income and dubious morals (see Boschma, 1997). After the arrival of the psychiatric nurses and residents from psychiatric hospitals, geriatric assistants were instructed to help people wash themselves independently (see Pols, 2006a).
28 See also Alenichev, 2020.
29 See Pols et al., 2018.
30 A state of worth could also be imagined for some*thing*. For instance, works of art with historical meaning may also raise concerns about values that overflow a situation. Examples are the blowing up of artworks (e.g. by the Taliban) or its opposite, their preservation (such as the Stalinist heritage found in Treptower Park, Berlin).
31 See Liszka, 2013.
32 This is a reference to James, 2010, who argues that moral activities are always situated in unique situations where different goods are at stake. This means that moral judgement is always a way of 'improvising', as no situation is ever the same. This is an argument against a general ethical framework.

4
The end of morality: Adam Smith and the taming of the passions

My research on psychiatric care practices illustrates how general principles entered care practices, and how these were translated into concrete everyday-life values. These values had to be related to emerging situations on the ward, which required caregivers to carefully negotiate which values to prioritise in which situation. This negotiation of everyday values lies at the core of the work of caregivers. However, the abstract and imperative character of norms and principles frequently made it difficult to take the specificity of a situation into account. It is difficult to accept dirt and strange behaviour as forms of dignity in places like residential homes where a lot of work is put into maintaining a certain social order. And citizenship was difficult to uphold if patients did not develop 'proper tastes'. The neoliberal emphasis on efficiency and rationality as well as the principled approach to ethics, however, made it difficult to conceptualise professional care practices as a negotiation of everyday values as well as moral, medical or other values. Managerial mindsets and regulations based on abstract principles only prioritise certain values and seek to 'implement' them. Everyday values thus disappeared from academic, professional and popular understandings of care practices.

The neglect of everyday values is not limited to care practices but is part of a set of broader developments. This chapter explores eighteenth-century social theory to trace some of the precedents for the demise of the values of everyday life as a relevant topic in academia. Learning about the disappearance of everyday-life values from academic discourse is instructive for understanding how such values were and may continue to be conceptualised. How was thinking about the values of everyday life marginalised and problematised in social theory? How were everyday-life values conceptualised? How may such conceptualisations help us to think about the values of everyday life in the present?

I will contrast discourses on the moral and aesthetic values of everyday life with ideas about social life as well as society and its governance. To do this, I will analyse texts discussing civil wars in seventeenth-century Europe as well as the shift towards new forms of governance that could accommodate the concerns of the emerging middle class of wealthy traders. New models of governance were needed to safeguard peace and to provide alternatives for absolutist monarchies and the privileges of the nobility. I will show how ideas about everyday life and its values came to be disconnected from social theory and were replaced by values relating to the good of society. Morality was increasingly seen as the wrong approach to creating orderly societies.

To examine the conceptualisation of everyday-life values, I will freely use philosophers' and historians' interpretations of eighteenth-century thought, and in particular interpretations of the work of Adam Smith.[1] Smith is a key philosopher in this chapter because of his engagement with moral theories and ideas about the emergence of modern society and the post-feudal economy. Analysing Smith's work makes it possible to learn about the relationship between the values of everyday life as well as contemporaneous questions about society, its governance and the role of individual morality for the greater good of society.

My aim is not to do justice to eighteenth-century thinkers or the ways in which their work should be interpreted. Historians and philosophers at home in this era will find that many things are glossed over or interpreted in ways they might want to contest. Interpretation of the philosophical works of this time is still hotly debated and forms a specialised domain in itself. My main goal is not to add my perspective to debates about what history or historical thinking was 'really like' or what the intentions were of these theorists. My aim, the reader will remember, is to 'dig up' concepts, forms and tropes that are useful for thinking about the values of everyday life. This chapter will seek to do this by unearthing previous critiques of everyday-life values and their suitability as a tool for governing individuals – or as a means for making them govern themselves – and how these critiques provided the backdrop to new ideas for organising the nation state.

More specifically, in this part of the book, I want to learn through which mechanisms the values pertaining to everyday life *disappeared* from academic and political discourse as well as social theory, and why these values were increasingly seen as useless and problematic. Moral values were central topics in seventeenth- and eighteenth-century discussions, and there are long lists of virtues and vices that we have long since forgotten. Individual morality has become (almost) irrelevant to social theory. The reasons for this disappearance, I claim, can be traced back to ideas that circulated in this period in history, namely the dawn of modernity, liberalism and the Enlightenment. Social scientific explanations of human behaviour that rejected individual morality as a social force of interest became the dominant way of understanding society.

My approach is to look for perspectives on human morality and psychology in seventeenth- and eighteenth-century social theory. What is the place of moral and aesthetic values in the history of ideas of this particular time, and specifically in the countries that are best documented, namely England and France? My concerns are present-day ones, which are obviously different from the concerns that preoccupied these eighteenth-century thinkers and their interpreters. I want to bring historical concerns to the fore within their own context to examine how the 'behaviour', 'passions' and 'drives' of individuals became central to understanding society. Simultaneously, however, these passions were perceived as threatening social order. Governance of the nation was an important theme in this era, in which feudalism was slowly transforming into new forms of governance amid the turbulence and bloodshed of civil war and the emergence of a new class of bourgeois traders. These transformations gave rise to very specific concerns that are very different from those of later social theorists and economists. My historical analysis does show, however, that there is a long-standing social-theoretical disinterest in individual moral and aesthetic feelings as well as a reluctance to study not only the practice of everyday life but particularly *care* for everyday life.

The Adam Smith problem

The seventeenth and eighteenth centuries are the source of liberal ideas that are still dominant in our day and age, on both the left and the right of the political spectrum, even if they have been adapted and evolved into different forms.[2] This time period witnessed the emergence of capitalist society and the emancipation of workers and merchants.[3] I am interested in the relation between the emergence of liberalist thinking and the depreciation of the values of everyday life. I will use the work of Adam Smith (1723–1790) and its reception to examine the relationship between the triumphant emergence of the economic and psychological individual in social-scientific understandings of society, and the simultaneous downgrading of the conceptualisation of individuals as moral beings. The work of Adam Smith and the debates about its interpretation announce the end of social theorising about everyday-life values.

Adam Smith is widely known as the founder of economic theory, and even as the godfather of capitalism. However, he is also, but a little less widely, known as a moral philosopher. Interpreters of his major works wrestle with the relationship between morality and economic theory. I will examine several interpretations of Smith's work in which scholars try to reconcile morality and social theory by accommodating individual moral or virtuous behaviour with economic productivity and a good, smoothly running society. Scholars of Smith's work generally, and quite rightly, argue against claims that Smith is simply an arch-capitalist or a pre-eminent proponent of the virtues of self-interest. They take his moral theory, which is described in one of his two major works, seriously. In his moral theory, self-interest did not appear as a positive passion but rather as its opposite.[4] The problem of reconciling morality with a flourishing economy that is driven by self-interested individuals became known as the 'Adam Smith problem'. This problem is, in Mandeville's words, 'the creation of social virtue from private vice',[5] or in other words, the creation of a good nation through individuals who behave badly.

But other interpretations are possible. I will show that there are roughly three possibilities: a) individual morality *does* have social effects, which leaves open the question what these effects might look like and how they may be influenced; b) morality has no influence on social effects, and hence can be regarded as an individual matter while theorists concern themselves with social developments; or c) morality is important in and of itself, even if it does not have any social effects. The Adam Smith problem signals a shift from locating goodness in individual, private or moral conduct to locating goodness in society more broadly. The concern here is more with how *society* can be good and less how *individuals* can or should be good. As an instrument for governance, the regulation of individual conduct – which in Smith's time was done mainly through religious practices – seemed too weak and dangerous an instrument to prevent warfare and bloodshed. Also, the very personal style of governance by rulers during the ancien régime (see Chapter 6) did not leave much hope for peace, as kings and nobility made their subjects fight wars over the most outlandish matters of honour. This style of governance provided little space for peaceful trade and the emancipation of new citizens. However, in the emergent social theories of the day, there were also other assumptions about what individuals are, what they do and why they act the way they do. I am interested in how individuals and their everyday values were conceptualised in the social theories of this time.

Governance and civil war

Reading the work of Adam Smith takes us back to eighteenth-century Scotland and the so-called Scottish Enlightenment thinkers of whom Smith was a representative.[6] I read Smith's work as a moral philosophy concerning social theory, psychology, economic theory and politics. I place Smith's thinking in the broader social and intellectual context of his time. The eighteenth century is a rich source of budding social theories, and there are many flavours and debates from which to taste and learn. It was also a time of great societal shifts. Civil wars had marred the seventeenth century. Economic activity had become increasingly important in Europe, and together with the growth in trade, it gave rise to a middle class of men who wanted to have a say in the governance of the nation. Absolute monarchy and the feudal state were questioned; new models for politics were invented. Labour and income became more important topics in thinking about society, at the expense of topics such as nobility and rank. Simultaneously, the influence of religious institutions decreased, leaving Europe in turmoil and in search of new ways to organise society and bring an end to civil wars.

I do not pretend that it is possible to cover this long and complex history in a couple of pages, and obviously there were many differences between different countries and cities. Nonetheless, I want to highlight some of the major tropes, terms and themes that emerged in this period to ascertain how these new terms played a role in the fate of everyday-life aesthetics. I will, for instance, use Albert Hirschman's insightful analysis of seventeenth- and eighteenth-century interpretations of passions, and how such passions were turned into their rational counterpart, namely interests.[7] In a nutshell, interests were passions that were tamed by (economic) Reason. Hirschman's concern with the fate of the passions resonates strongly with my questions about the values of everyday life. He enters this history by asking:

> How did commercial banking and similar money-making pursuits become honourable at some point in the modern age after having stood condemned or despised as greed, love of lucre, and avarice for centuries past?[8]

Part of Hirschman's answer is that the passions, such as the desire to acquire wealth, could be seen as good when they were reformulated as calm and calculated interests. At the same time, however, the multitude of passions was gradually reduced to a single passion, namely the pursuit of wealth. Social theorists' perceptions of the work of Adam Smith are a good illustration of how this reduction might have taken place and how it came to play a central role in social theory. Hirschman describes developments in social theory that are relevant for understanding our current time period, in which politics and economics have become intertwined in complex ways and capitalism has lost the benign appearance it had to eighteenth-century thinkers.[9] Taming the values of everyday life by turning them into private 'matters of taste' was a general tendency in the new social sciences.

The British intellectual and political climate of the eighteenth century was somewhat milder than in France, where civil wars started long before and included the bloodshed of the French Revolution. Nevertheless, the urgency of coming up with new forms of governance for the nation and the desire to end civil war both inform much of eighteenth-century thought. Shapin and Schaffer have argued that social developments are tightly connected to the historical emergence of scientific and philosophical practices.[10] Philosophers and natural scientists of the time drew connections between the question about what one can know about the world and the problem of how best to organise society. They did this by proposing ways to optimally deal with disagreements. Scientific practice was drenched in concerns about the restoration and maintenance of peace, even if suggestions for a solution differed greatly. For instance, mathematical reasoning was seen as a means to arrive at one irrefutable truth. Such an argument was forwarded by Thomas Hobbes, and the pursuit of a single truth also undergirded his argument for having one sovereign ruler of the nation who would be capable of ending all disputes. Alternatively, one could also organise exclusive spaces in which select groups of people could calmly and politely disagree. This mode of organising new experimental sciences was proposed by figures such as Robert Boyle.[11]

In light of these texts as well as the fading interest in everyday-life values, I argue that the passions – and with the passions also moral theory and concerns about the values of everyday life – were gradually removed from social theory. There were four reasons for this: 1) Discussions about the moral concerns of individuals were gradually replaced by a psychological language that described human drives. This demonstrates a shift in concerns about what individuals *intend* to do towards concerns about how they 'naturally' (or causally) behave; 2) Moral justifications were joined together in one passion that contained and summarised all other passions, namely self-interest.[12] Similarly, self-interest was understood as a passion that could be tamed by reason[13]; 3) The idea of a *rational* or *calculating* individual led to new ways of thinking about society as an economy. According to Smith, society is a 'beautiful machine' that either operates independently from the intentions of individuals or that is propelled by the actions of further unspecified human self-interest (the 'Smith problem'); 4) The passions were removed from social theory because they were increasingly seen as dangerous. Where ancient Greek thinking conceptualised human motivation as a drive towards the pleasure of truth (see Chapter 8), seventeenth- and eighteenth-century thinkers feared unruly forms of motivation, such as the wild passions. Civil wars increased this fear of differences in opinion and desire. Stability and predictability became denominators of the common good that needed to be achieved to establish a prosperous nation based on peaceful trade.[14] To this end, the passions needed to be channelled or tamed.

Adam Smith: morality versus economy?

The 'Adam Smith problem' is created by the inconsistencies – and later attempts to argue that there are no inconsistencies – between Smith's two major books. The first book is *The Theory of Moral Sentiments*, in which Smith presents 'a systematic explanation (or theory) of the origin and nature of the moral sentiments of mankind'.[15] Here he develops a moral theory about individual conduct. The second book is *The Wealth of Nations*, which is Smith's more famous text on economy and society at large. In this book, morality seems to have been sidelined as irrelevant. Instead, society operates best as a beautiful machine, independent of individual intentions, or alternatively, operates optimally when individuals strive for their own interests.[16] This claim either disconnects individual striving from a flourishing economy, or connects it to the pursuit of self-interest. Either interpretation obscures the role of morality. Individuals create a good society without intending to do so regardless of whether they act out of virtue or vice. This is reminiscent of Mandeville's question on how the vice of self-interest could become a virtue for society.

Most scholars argue that there is continuity between Smith's works, namely that the prudent man in *The Theory of Moral Sentiments* is the same figure as the economic man in *The Wealth of Nations*.[17] By focusing on Smith's biography, Jesse Norman makes it very clear that Smith himself did not think that his two books were contradictory. He discovered that Smith first wrote *The Theory of Moral Sentiments* in a couple of years, before completing *The Wealth of Nations*. After that he spent some time refining the former book and then finally rewrote the latter book. Norman shows that Smith, once done with his masterpieces, made sure to destroy his unfinished works and loose papers so that after his death only his best works would remain to remember him by. Smith took great care to finish his two most important works thoroughly, and thus to safeguard his legacy. We do not know how he himself conceived of the connection between his two major works, but we can presume that he did not see them as contradictory considering the meticulous arrangement of his intellectual heritage.[18]

I will not take sides in the debate on the Adam Smith problem. I am interested in understanding how this debate paved the way for the historical interpretation of Smith's work as promoting self-interest rather than the morality of everyday-life values. This foregrounding of self-interest eventually made the values of everyday life irrelevant to social theory. Once self-interest was conceptualised as a passion that unconsciously drives individuals to work towards economic growth, self-interest could also be posited as the driver of the economy in (social-scientific) theories that relied on Smith's work.[19]

Smith's work on morality: sympathy and the impartial spectator

Smith's moral theory exemplifies how human psychology became central to social theory at the time. To discuss the difficult relationship between *The Theory of Moral Sentiments* and *The Wealth of Nations*, I engage in a close reading of Macfie's analysis of these two books from 1969. I focus on Macfie because he proposes an integrated and consistent reading of Smith's two books, which contrasts with the claim that these books are irreconcilable. I will follow Macfie's attempt to read Smith as both a moral philosopher and social theorist to explore how Smith did – or did not – succeed in connecting moral philosophy and social theory, and hence how he perceived the relationship between everyday-life values and the stability of society. Doing so will show both how everyday life values disappeared from social theory and how everyday-life values were conceptualised as relating to conventions rather than to universal principles.

The good for Smith is 'virtue'. Virtue stands for propriety or appropriateness. Macfie shows that the idea of virtue as propriety is an *aesthetic* ideal about the beauty and appropriateness of social processes such as the economy. For Smith, this beauty was, literally, the beauty of a 'well-contrived machine'[20] that has 'a thousand agreeable effects'.[21] This machine could also be jarring, however, and would then 'displease' and be 'necessarily offensive'.[22] The smooth operation of the machine is achieved by lubricants that make the 'wheels of society' turn. Hence, beauty, alignment and flow are the aesthetic touchstones for determining whether society is virtuous and appropriate. Beauty and smoothness pertain to the whole of the social machine, not to individual acts. However, in Macfie's reading, individual activities are virtuous if they support this social beauty. A virtuous act must contribute to the way in which individuals live together, namely the common good (which here equals the wealth of the nation). The common good, what it was and how to achieve it were the main concerns of the era.

Macfie stresses that Smith's theory differs explicitly from the utilitarianist ideals that were popular in Smith's time. It is not merely the 'pleasant consequences', but the 'sense of propriety' or 'agreeability to truth and reality'[23] that Smith regards as essential.[24] There is a moral and aesthetic joy in seeing a machine that runs smoothly. 'Likewise, anything that contributes to the happiness of society recommends itself directly to our approbation and goodwill.'[25] This is what a virtuous person perceives and wants to contribute to, namely establishing a happy (and therefore wealthy) society.[26]

Smith uses mechanical metaphors to describe the good of society, but he uses more anthropomorphic metaphors to describe individual morality and behaviour. The main source of morals in *The Theory of Moral Sentiments*, Macfie writes, is the passion[27] of sympathy (today we would be more likely to use the term 'empathy'). Sympathy (in Macfie's interpretation) allows one to imagine oneself in another person's situation. Experiencing a situation as others experience it allows us to evaluate it in turn. We do this not by taking note of what the other feels, but by sensing ourselves in that situation. Smith contended that it is quite possible that an outsider could feel a situation more intensely than the person in the actual situation.

But 'being in the shoes of the other' is not enough for morality to emerge. The passion of sympathy needs what Macfie calls 'a tool to operate on it' or a way to decide what to do. This is necessary because unmediated feelings of sympathy would otherwise be without direction. They would not tell a person what to do even if they feel empathy for another person. To provide this direction, writes Macfie, intellect is needed in addition to feeling. Smith hence adds rational support for the passion of sympathy. He does this by invoking the judgement of the 'well-informed impartial spectator'. The impartial spectator, who is internalised as the 'man within the breast', is an outside spectator who evaluates the propriety of a situation.

Macfie argues that the impartial spectator, as a means for providing moral direction, should be a general or disinterested person. He is, however, Macfie argues, not an abstract or universal person but one who is socialised in the same society as that where his actions are called upon. Everyday values, contrary to later modernist principles, relate here to convention rather than abstract theory.[28] The socialised person has internalised the social norms of his day to form a kind of superego *avant la lettre*.[29] This superego reflects the conventions and morality of his time. The superego is impartial in its approach to a certain situation but not in the tools that are used to judge that situation. The prudent man is therefore situated in the conventions of his time. In this way Smith interprets 'propriety' as being 'appropriate to our natures' (he describes sympathy as a natural passion) as well as being a form of reason that is obtained by being socialised and socially educated in a certain time and place. Both nature and convention direct the sympathy of the impartial spectator.

A situation and its appropriateness are informed by contemporary social institutions and values. This makes the impartial spectator a *situated* spectator. The impartial spectator can judge a situation precisely *because* they are informed by the social context in which they speculate. For Macfie, this relieves Smith from the obligation of formulating clear moral standards that might direct sympathy. The standards are already out there, so to speak: they are part of society and can be established empirically. The moral individual who is assessing appropriateness is utterly social. Macfie and other interpreters hence stress that Smith's morality is an *inductive morality*. By observing and reflecting on many cases, a society develops norms and institutions that can safeguard and further improve the good along the way.[30] Smith writes about a gradual progression towards becoming a moral subject rather than about an engagement with a finished moral system. If the feelings of the spectators emerge from the shared social context and living conditions, people will automatically develop a 'fellow feeling', which makes them capable of sympathising and evaluating.[31] They can place themselves in the situation of others because they share both natural (innate) passions and social education. They observe others and hence learn, through social experience, what is appropriate.

Morality, then, is informed by habits, customs and conventions of what is good and beautiful. Moral sense reflects the social. It is not just intuitive but dependent on concrete social situations. A recurrent trope used to argue this position is that of Robinson Crusoe; according to Smith, when one lives in the way that Robinson did, one has no moral concerns.

Robinson only has his own interests, and has no possibility (and, one might add, no need) for comparing himself to certain standards. Morality, then, is not, or not only, the *result* of social relationships; it is first and foremost *formative* of social relationships.

Adam Smith's moral theory as a theory of the good life

How does Adam Smith's moral theory relate to theories and practices concerning the good life? Macfie, as Jesse Norman also notes, situates Smith's moral theory in the social conventions of his time. The impartial spectator can only get a sense of direction in relation to the common norms and understandings of the society that the person who is evoking him lives. Smith's moral theory, Norman claims, is not a substantive or prescriptive theory of moral values:

> It [Smith's moral theory] is naturalistic and descriptive, not prescriptive . . . It does not offer a specific criterion or rule of moral action. Like the utilitarian rule that one should act so as to maximise the greatest good for the greatest number. Nor is it intended as a detached, Olympian account of universal moral principles to which any rational being is supposed to subscribe, in the style of Kant.[32]

Rather, Smith's moral theory is based on the conventions of a moral community. To place oneself, through the figure of the impartial spectator, in the shoes of others is, writes Norman, to 'locate oneself in a world of reciprocity, of mutual recognitions, and obligation'. There is no standard or independent viewpoint that can be achieved, and 'Norms emerge, tacitly or explicitly, as the outcome of human action, not of human design.'[33] Hence, Norman interprets Smith's moral theory as a descriptive, psychological theory about what men *are* and how they naturally behave rather than about what they *should* do.[34]

I am not so sure that Smith (or Macfie) would agree with this interpretation. It is too 'scientific' and explanatory, and it misses a normative component that indicates what people should do. Alternatively, one could interpret Smith's moral theory as a theory about the good life. It is not based on prescriptive doctrines but on actual practices. This interpretation would locate Smith's moral theory in the realm of practical philosophies of the good life. The impartial spectator can then be seen as a 'technology of the self', a technique that can be used for exercising morality. The impartial spectator is, in this case, a normative tool for making practical decisions. This normative tool is, however, not useful as a prescription before the concrete situation has been explored. The impartial spectator is informed by and situated in actual practices that respond to actual problems.[35] When reconceptualised as a tool, Smith's theory resonates with the practices of the philosophers of the good life as well as that of the ancient Greek and pre-modern humanists which I will discuss later. Such a move repositions Smith as a *pre-modern* moral theorist rather than a modern one.[36]

This repositioning of Smith makes a link to theories and practices of the good life possible. Indeed, this connection can help to shift these theories towards reflections on morality, truth and aesthetics in the lives of ordinary people rather than exemplary men. The moral subject develops an *ethos* through the use of the impartial spectator, which is a figure that is coloured by the conventions of its day. There are no external standards for judgement, and the user of the technology of the impartial spectator operates within the norms, values and aesthetics that are ready to hand. An empirical ethics *avant la lettre*!

From the individual to the social

But how did Smith connect living *through* a witnessed situation with the workings of the social machine? How could social theorists connect everyday life with an understanding of the functioning of society? Here the notion of the invisible hand turned out to be useful. According to Smith, the invisible hand is a divine force that brings together individual actions and aggregates them to achieve a social effect that surpasses the intentions of individuals. It is a metaphor that speaks to the imagination, but it is only occasionally used in Smith's *Wealth of Nations*, as several scholars have noted. It is mentioned only twice.

There is an ambivalence in Macfie's use of terms such as 'social beauty' and the 'good' in individual situations as a method for determining appropriateness. There remains a gap between the individual good and the social good or outcome, even if morality is informed by shared conventions. It is exactly this gap that the invisible hand bridges. The invisible hand aggregates all individual activities and turns them into social effects. The total of this social order is more than the sum of its parts, as individuals may contribute to the social good without knowing or intending to. Individuals are *deceived* about how they have helped to achieve this social effect, writes Smith. Nature – or God working through Nature – creates this deception. So why would individuals need to act in a moral way even if their actions are informed by the morality of their historical context? They do not *have* to act morally to support the beautiful machine. But if contributing to the beautiful machine is not a condition for achieving it, why would individuals take the trouble to lead a virtuous life *at all*? Or should we think of a moral life that is organised *apart* from the social machine, for its own sake or for morality's sake?

This is the explanation that Macfie provides. References to the deception created by the invisible hand, he argues, are explicit but inconsistent in Smith's work. And because they are inconsistent they should be ignored. Macfie claims that it makes more sense to conceptualise the good behaviour of an individual as *the same* as a good social effect. Macfie cites Smith's example of vanity. It is a vice but it can be developed into pride. Pride represents 'true glory' or merit. It is justified when based on what one has achieved. In this way, pride is better than mere vanity. Yet its ultimate shape as a virtue emerges when pride turns into magnanimity (generosity). Then vanity has turned into a virtue in itself. It is a passion to want to be loved by others, but it becomes a moral virtue when one is actually deserving of this love.

There are several nice examples in Smith's work of how vice can be transformed into virtue. For example, that men tend to admire their superiors rather than their equals or inferiors can be good – next to the desire for justice and peace – if it becomes a motive for organising a society that consists of peaceful traders. Restlessness of the human mind may lead to the building of philosophical systems. A wild imagination is tamed by the ability of seeing connections. A desire for variation may lead to a striving for various goods. Vanity can make one behave appropriately in the market. This is what Hirschman calls the 'channelling' of the passions, as I will discuss below.

In a similar way, self-love can be turned into prudence. Through sympathy and judgement of propriety by the impartial spectator, self-love can become a good. 'Bettering one's situation' is also a good for Smith as it works towards the preservation of the species. A ruthless increase of individual wealth, however, is wrong. Dispassionate pursuit of one's interests, on the other hand, leads to a good for society. This suggests that everyday values are still important, but that they must be tweaked and muted if they are to become a virtue rather than a vice.

Self-love, then, can be a moral exercise (by working with the sympathy of the impartial spectator) as well as a natural drive. Morality is needed to establish what *proper* self-love is. Macfie argues that later thinkers conceived of self-love as too subjective an emotion. They assumed that whatever a person was *feeling* was akin to self-interest. But Macfie argues that one should regard this from a more rational standpoint (and this is also Hirschman's argument: see below). When the passions are rationalised, they can be moderated into something good, thus leading to morally right behaviour. I will write more about this below when discussing Hirschman's interpretation.

Is there more to say about the beauty or good of society? I would suggest that this good can easily be reformulated as simply becoming wealthier, particularly when speaking of money as a 'moveable property'.[37] Wealth might be a way to synchronise the values of individuals with those of the social machine. Individuals as well as the social machine both strive for the same value, which is an increase of money or wealth. And it would also be a way to channel the passions into one direction, namely economic profit.

This is, however, clearly not what Smith argues, as his theory is not a utilitarian one (unlike many other theories of his time) but instead based on the 'approbation' of situations. The aspirations of individuals can be different, such as the preservation and expansion of mankind or the establishment of social order and security. The state should guarantee 'peace of mind' so that individuals do not have to fear violence or theft. Predictability and regular development of the social system, according to Smith, coincide with the tranquillity that individuals desire. Tranquillity also appears to be a greater good that makes nations flourish after the turmoil of civil wars.[38] The ultimate goal, then, is not wealth, but instead a stable society with an 'appropriate' (beautiful) social order. It seems that violence and social unrest were the ailments that dispassionate economic activity would have to cure. Not strife but the industrious work of individuals towards the goals they all want to pursue would keep them busy and happy; individuals do what is in their own interest in accordance with their natural inclinations.

The end of morality

Improving one's situation for Smith, then, is seen as good unless the impartial spectator is disturbed. And this happens, if we follow Macfie, when striving for improvement is not done in the right degree or mode, or, one could say, in the correct manner through which the passions are enacted: calm, deliberate, rational. It is in this sense that Macfie finds a continuity between the prudent and economic man. The passions are tamed and channelled. The motives or drives of individuals can become social and they may be well aware of this. They do not know exactly *how* the social machine is influenced by their actions, but they do know that their actions are good. Calmness and modesty establish a link between individual passions or behaviours and their social effects.[39]

But the trope of the invisible hand remained, and this was picked up by interpreters of Smith's writings. The invisible hand appears to dismiss the need for good intentions and judgement because it shifts attention from judgements to behaviours. The trope represents *the effects* of individual activities rather than their moral substance, scruples or particular qualifications. Vanity seems to lead to the same results as pride or magnanimity. The invisible hand is morally blind to ruthless and greedy people seeking self-enrichment as well as to dispassionate and modest traders. The hand deceives both. Here, there is a relationship between individual acts and social results. Yet it is not through morality that men's natural behaviours are coordinated, but rather through the mystical intervention of the unknown workings of the invisible hand.

In this way, both the 'Adam Smith problem' and the invisible hand trope create ample opportunity for dismissing individual morality as irrelevant to the common good. Macfie tries to reconcile these positions by insisting on the sociality of morality (its givenness through social institutions). To this end Macfie deems conventionalised passions to be congruent with good social effects. Proper judgement (calmness, rationality, generosity) would lead to the best economic outcomes guided by an invisible hand that does *not* deceive.[40]

This is a positive interpretation that Smith would have liked in regard to his life and his two masterpieces. However, Smith's theory also allows for different readings, and it was indeed used to justify free competition and markets based on (any form of moral or amoral) self-interest. Smith's theory allowed for an interpretation of his work in which individual moral behaviour is detached from social effects, or alternatively, to simplistically conceptualise human behaviour as propelled only by a desire for profit. A cool calculation of what would provide the best outcome for an individual would lead to the greatest benefit for society. The invisible hand could be demystified, or rationalised if you want. Smith created the conditions for understanding a new entity in social theory, the economy, as an outcome of individual inclinations towards self-interest.

In this different interpretation of Smith's books, it becomes difficult to use his techniques and repertoires for understanding moral behaviour, or to position these techniques and repertoires in relation to his theory on everyday or normative ethics. Smith's theory about the sympathy of the impartial spectator could therefore become merely a matter of 'etiquette', a guideline for behaving in an appropriate manner that is relevant for its own sake. Morality makes life better even if it has no effect on the social machine. To make life nicer and better would become an aesthetic matter rather than a moral obligation or necessity, which means that niceties are not essential for social development or only ambiguously so. Calmness is necessary for peaceful trade, but former vices such as self-interest do not disrupt the smooth operation of the social machine.

And so Smith's puzzle remains. One possible solution is to avoid interpretations of the invisible hand as a deceptive force, such that individual morality can be thought of as bringing about social beauty and hence giving morality a driving force. This would promote virtues leading to the greater good, such as calmness and calculation. The problem then is to turn vices such as greed into virtues such as magnanimity. Alternatively, individual intentions are of no import and social beauty is achieved regardless of individual aspirations. Another option is that morality is important in itself even if disconnected from social effects. Ethics and aesthetics would then exist in their own sphere of rationality. If Smith can be understood (at least partially) as a pre-modern thinker, he would not have aspired to a modernist logic of all-encompassing coherence in his philosophical work. His main works may then indeed be about different topics, written in different registers, using mechanical metaphors for society and anthropological metaphors for individuals.

Macfie concludes, sadly, that, whatever had been Smith's intention, the separation of moral behaviours and social effects has become the dominant interpretation of Smith's work. The self-interest of individuals has been used as a means for understanding and justifying free competition on the market. But as a taken-for-granted premise it is no longer relevant to economic theory. The market was conceptualised in social theory as a new public–private sphere that functions without morality and through individuals' natural inclination to look after themselves.[41] Self-care appears here not as a virtue but as the desire for private gain, disconnecting the individual aspirations of common men from their true social, ethical and aesthetic duties and pleasures. In this manner, the market signifies the end of morality, or at best its privatisation. It is left up to individuals to decide how they want to relate to morality. Smith's work, in other words, helped set the stage for framing morality as a matter of individual taste.

Tamed passions: the calculating work of the interests

This overview of Smith's reception makes clear how the space for discussing morality in social theory was reduced. Hirschman has developed a detailed argument on how interests can be understood as rational or 'tamed' versions of the passions. He comments on the shift in the Renaissance as well as the seventeenth and eighteenth centuries from a normative theory on how one should behave towards the description of 'man as he really is'. This is a shift in the relationship between psychology, economy and political theory, as well as a switch from moral philosophy to social science, and a move from ethics and religion towards psychology, economy and sociology. These developments signify a shift in thinking about people's behaviour and how to manipulate it rather than attempting to understand and regulate people through morality. Instead of being propelled by moral rules, techniques or outcomes, people are affected by their *nature*, by things that are outside their volition.[42] Their activities are effects of natural inclinations. These are all different repertoires for influencing individuals.

Hirschman links this shift to a general breakdown of trust in moral theory and religious instruction as ways for taming destructive passions. Moralising became useless because it was no longer an efficient technique for organising people. People did not seem to act in virtuous ways, and when they did appeal to morality (or religion), this led to bloodshed and civil war rather than peaceful conduct. Appeals to morality were no longer useful for governing individual behaviour and hence the nation. Meanwhile, the governance of the nation remained an urgent concern.

Hirschman shows that, particularly in the seventeenth century, the passions of men were seen as destructive. Seventeenth-century thought was preoccupied with the question of how to turn the passions towards something good. Hirschman's main claim is that interests, in the shape of 'reasonable self-love', were mobilised to turn passions into more rational endeavours. Interests are the rationalised siblings of the passions. Rather than striving for the immediate gratification of desires, interests make people contemplate their (greater) benefit in the long run. For larger groups of people this is often seen as wealth, property and financial profit. Fame, still crucial in Hobbes's political philosophy, became less and less important. However, *any* aspiration or passion could be interpreted from the perspective of interests. It does not matter if one strives for order, efficiency or discretion. Through clever exchange and calculation each individual could achieve what he (yes, *he*, and especially a he with a certain amount of wealth) wanted. Rationality came to mean *that which is best from the perspective of individual gain*.

Hirschman argues that 'interests' increasingly became the paradigm with which human conduct could be explained. At the end of the seventeenth century, passions were regarded as destructive and reason was seen as ineffective in counteracting them. The notion of interests, however, promised a fruitful pairing of both drive and reason. In the eighteenth century, the passions were rehabilitated as a creative force. An overly stable social order was seen as boring, uninspired and too predictable. Such a social order lacked humour, curiosity, creativity, gratitude, generosity, hospitality and friendship. However, predictability and its promise of stability were exactly what had earlier made interests an attractive basis for social order. To achieve a predictable social order one needs what Smith had asserted, namely avarice, or the love of personal gain. According to him, this passion will always be there, from the cradle to the grave. Everyone has it.

Hence, greed was a way to influence people based on their interests and natural drives. Greed accommodated their passions, rationality and calculations. Simultaneously, it seemed a feasible aim to incentivise people to work towards their own self-interests. This would bypass the need for morality or ethical standards as guidelines for goodness. Allowing people to do what they would naturally and spontaneously do would be conducive to social order. This belief gave rise to the first forms of social engineering, Hirschman writes. He shows that individual passions could be channelled along the lines of the mechanics involved in taming a passionate river. Once it became possible to tame the passions, one could also try to engineer their direction and flow.

Taming the passions, Hirschman argues, could be done in three ways. The first was to *repress* the passions through the power of the state. This was not a popular strategy in times in which the problems of government left little hope for assuming the benevolence of the repressive sovereign. Because sovereigns were also plagued by passions, they were an unreliable containment for the rivers of passion. Moreover, their own passions would also have to be tamed, but by whom? The second strategy, according to Hirschman, was to *harness* the passions by turning them into something better. We saw examples of this given by Smith above. Vico, for instance, also provided suggestions for turning ferocity towards the good of national defence, greed into commerce, and ambition into politics. In this way power, wealth and wisdom could be promoted through the natural inclinations of individuals. Passions could be turned into something good. This involved the fine craft of *channelling*.

The third way of taming the passions was through the use of 'countervailing passions'. This could be done, for example, by using innocent passions to weaken or tame more vicious ones. It was in this vein that Mandeville argued that luxury is bad, but that it may be better than sloth (slowness, apathy), which would result from a ban on striving for luxury. Hume argued that a love of pleasure could be counterbalanced by a love of gain, which he thought was better and certainly less likely to lead to unrest. Designing counterbalances is the task of reason and engineering, namely to manipulate which passions to pursue, so that they could lead, by force of nature, to the general wealth and happiness of the nation. Hobbes wrote that the aggressive pursuit of riches, glory and dominion was tamed by the desire for peace, the fear of death, and the hope and longing for a good life. It is for these reasons that people accepted constraints on their liberties and that they organised themselves as a nation state. They wanted to escape the violent state of nature, which Hobbes famously depicted as a 'war of all against all' in which there are no victors. The countervailing passions were mechanisms to contain violence. The passions may be many and diverse, but the idea was that a balance between them would eventually lead to a stable web of interdependent relations between interested groups.

Commerce was increasingly seen as having good effects on politics, society and even morality. Commerce demanded and created predictability as well as continuity rather than the 'diverse' passions (Hobbes), which are capricious, go in and out of fashion and differ among individuals. Monetary gain made a meaningful reduction of different interests possible; money is desired by everyone and makes social life predictable. The desire for wealth is never satisfied. Money is always good to have, and it is never disappointing to have more of it.

Hirschman shows that this desire for profit was, at first, seen as a calm and dispassionate passion. In the sixteenth century the merchant was not much of a hero. The merchant was depicted as a mean, grubby and uninspiring individual.[43] But during the emancipation of the middle class he became seen as harmless and his status increased. Montesquieu called commerce *doux*, which means soft. He wrote that commerce gave rise to an industrious spirit, modesty and regularity. He contrasted this to the whims and passions of the aristocrats, which were preoccupied with heroism and grandiosity. Aristocrats went to war to gain money and prestige rather than engaging in peaceful trade. *Le doux commerce*, on the other hand, blossoms in a society of polite interactions, gentleness and calm passions. The idea of good manners and utility triumphed – and this in the age of slavery! It was not until much later that the violence of (colonial) commerce was criticised as benefitting only a few at the cost of harming countless others. The works of Karl Marx and Friedrich Engels are a marked example of this critique.

So the passions were studied anew and were classified in new ways in the eighteenth century. There were the *good* passions, which were *natural affections* such as benevolence and generosity. These passions served the private as well as the public good. The less good passions were *self-passions* that served only the private but not the public good. *Unnatural affections*, such as envy and inhumanity, did not lead to any good. Economic activity was seen as belonging to the category of the self-passions, but, if done in moderation, could be promoted to the class of natural affections. However, the passions could also be demoted to the level of unnatural affections when pursued in excess. Hirschman shows how Hutcheson distinguished between wild or unruly drives and calm desires that are enacted with calculation and rationality. The calm passions were to replace the violent drives of men.

Politics and possessions

Many thinkers made a difference between the possession of *unmoveable* goods or land and *moveable goods* such as money. The visibility of unmoveable goods could lead to envy and jealousy, it was thought, and could hence result in social unrest. Moveable wealth, however, was seen as much less troublesome.[44] Others – including the sovereign – could not see what was in one's pockets. Moveable goods gave less rise to debate and jealousy, and, I would add, they also allowed for a translation of values, namely from well-described particular passions and preferences to the value of money that could give access to any type of goods. Displaying one's wealth was seen as a vice of the monarchy and nobility.

These reflections on commerce and economy were deeply intertwined with the search for a proper politics for organising societies in non-violent ways. Sir James Steuart worried about the different interests of the sovereign and the rich citizens. The power of the sovereign had been reduced because of the growth of the middle class and the increase in commerce. The sovereign, he argued, could not rule in arbitrary ways because this would have huge economic consequences. Both Montesquieu and Steuart saw the growing economy as means to reduce the power of the sovereign. Commercial interests could channel tyranny to the benefit of citizens.

John Millar, another thinker of the Scottish Enlightenment, also discussed how the middle class could limit the power of the sovereign. Millar predicted that there would be more individual liberty and equality in trading nations than in feudal nations, as well as more collective actions through urbanisation and the concentration of commerce. The wealthy trader, merchant or banker became the countervailing power to the power of the sovereign. The traders enacted this power, contrary to the farmers who lived scattered across the countryside and who were difficult to mobilise. According to Quesnay and Mirabeau, one cannot simply rule over merchants because a sovereign does not know what moveable goods they possess. The ruler must govern cautiously, as rich merchants can easily take their moveable goods elsewhere if taxes are too high, which would not be in his interest.

These thinkers were all concerned with disruptions to government and with coming up with mechanisms for creating an orderly nation. There were even ideas to 'interest' the sovereign, for instance by making him the co-owner of all wealth in the state (this idea is an of Linguet's). Somewhat less radically, Hobbes deemed the private interest of the sovereign as concordant with the interests of his subjects. A sovereign can have a good reputation, strength, wealth and security as long as his subjects are happy.[45] Weak and poor subjects would do nothing for his glory. Ruler and subjects have interests that can be aligned.

There were of course also dissenting voices. Classic republicans thought that commerce would lead to decadent luxury and corruption.[46] Smith also feared that luxury would make men 'effeminate' (a major offence for a man in republicanist thought) and 'dastardly' (which translates as 'wicked' or 'cruel'). An overemphasis on trade and profit could lead to a rejection of education, or to its neglect, because education does not lead to personal enrichment.[47] Rousseau also warned about corruption and decadence. In contrast to the myriad passions that earlier thinkers such as Hobbes discussed, Hirschman argues that Rousseau reduced the passions to either *amour de soi* (self-love), which contained real needs and goods, or *amour propre* (proper love), which is gained through the admiration of others.[48] This is an enormous reduction. Smith's contribution, according to Hirschman, is to leave only one passion remaining, namely seeking economic advantage to gain the admiration of others. The 'great mob of mankind' (this is the term that Smith uses) emerged as a trope and was used to signify a group of people that is primarily interested in material wellbeing. Hirschman concludes that, as a consequence of the reduction of the passions to the pursuit of personal gain, countervailing passions were no longer needed. The passions have turned into interests and are channelled as such.

The 'average man' emerged as a category, and social theorists juxtaposed their behaviours and passions with those of the aristocracy. The nobility does not have to 'care about the necessary things': they are not fearful, hungry or needy and so they have more time to pursue honour.[49] For them, conflicts between passions and theories about their intricacies fostered the creation of literature, conversation and play, but, at their worst, they could also lead to war. Ordinary people, on the contrary, needed to put a meal on the table to survive, and they wanted to improve their material circumstances in order to safeguard their existence. In the reception of Smith's work these passions were collapsed into one general notion of common welfare. When the Napoleonic wars smothered the last hopes of *le doux commerce* in blood, the passions had already been reduced to the mere interest in material gain.

The evils of capitalism

The idea that the pursuit of commerce is a *doux* activity may sound strange to the modern ear, writes Hirschman, and the recent economic and planetary crises can only confirm this. But already in the eighteenth century criticisms emerged. These critiques often focused on the values that would be lost when a society concentrated only on predictability and commerce. Ferguson deplores the loss of sociality in the trading nations where, he observes, there are no tribes but only solitary beings that are detached from others.[50] These beings see others as means to a profit and, Ferguson claims, this hinders the formation of affective bonds. People are joined in civil society but also disconnected because they are only interested in their own profits. Rich people were anxious about losing their property, particularly when the wheel of fortune turned the wrong way.

There were also concerns that the peace and efficiency that were so desired by traders would be enforced by a rigid regime of law and order. Tocqueville warned that money may come to rule the nation. In that case, public affairs would become less important than private fortunes, which would directly threaten to disrupt the stability of the nation. He expressed doubts about the supposed harmony between private and public interests, and argued that traders are only interested in profit rather than in good governance. Tocqueville also warned that law and order may become an end rather than a means. If the government's task is to maintain order, 'the nation is already a slave', meaning that the public good will become subordinated to profit.[51] A desire for order, he feared, could lead to a blind acceptance of dictatorship. Later, Marx addressed the extreme enrichment of the bourgeoisie that was taking place at the expense of workers who were alienated from the products of their labour and who lived in poverty.

In these sombre reflections, the interests have suppressed the passions and killed civic spirit, thus directly challenging the governance of the nation. A sociality based on interests is a sociality in which the passions are ignored – or left to individuals – except the one passion that seeks material gain, which encourages people to spend their income on whatever they see fit. Such a sociality leaves no space for public goods such as creativity, morality, care and affective relations. Even though troubles with capitalism were already visible at the time, these were long seen as mere teething problems. Only in the nineteenth and twentieth century, writes Hirschman, did the misery of capitalism truly manifest itself as the extreme accumulation of riches, worldwide poverty, unemployment through economic depression, and an erosion of the arts and the sciences as well as the environment.

Hirschman concludes that profit and its acquisition are no longer *doux*. Acquiring wealth has become wild and destructive. He ends his book by wondering how to keep societies from falling apart and how to better organise them. Such a reorganisation would, I think, make space for everyday values and morality, which at this point had effectively been written out of social theory. They had no use for the governance of nation states.

To conclude: the fate of everyday-life values in early capitalist thinking

We can see shifts in ideas about the state and civil society that emerged during the seventeenth and eighteenth centuries in the aftermath of the feudal societies. These shifts profoundly shaped the conceptualisation and fate of the values of everyday life in modernity.

First, there was a shift in focus away from individuals towards the economy, the nation and the good of society. Social science was born, and its concern was predominantly the study of different forms of social and economic life. Society functioned through various mechanisms and could be studied as an object in itself. By conceptualising economic order as a machine, the workings, effects and maintenance of this machine could be studied independently from the values and intentions of individuals. By conceptualising the working of this machine as deceptive to the individuals, which is a possible reading of Adam Smith's work, aesthetic and moral evaluations could be moved out of the daily lives of individuals and into the beautiful machine of society. Moral evaluations were informed by efficiency, and according to Smith, also by the beauty of the organisation of society rather than by individual conduct. This fits well with contemporaneous utilitarian understandings of morality in which the maximising of pleasures or profits is the main criterion of goodness. This paved the way for the much later shift from morality to science in which conducting epidemiological *effect* studies demonstrates 'maximum gain for most'. This shifted the interpretation of the effects of individual activities from moral theory towards science. Effects (and hence also the good or the bad) were things that naturally emerged and that were unrelated to individual aspirations. Effects were acts of nature that fit into a framework of thought that shifted the emphasis from morality to science, from values to facts, and from acts of will to natural drives.

Second, in the shift from good individuals to good nations, individual thoughts and activities remained important, but the connections between them were loosened and became ambiguous. It became possible to think of the social machine as bringing about effects that were not straightforwardly informed by individual aspirations. Morality and the aesthetics of the good life as well as concerns about daily life and individual conduct were seen as less and less relevant to the creation of a good society. A good society developed either autonomously from individual intentions and morality or through the channelling of individual passions into one particular passion, namely self-interest.[52]

Morality was increasingly seen as an ineffective instrument for guaranteeing that individuals would behave well. The multitude of religious disputes and civil wars exemplified this failure. Instead, there was a third shift, namely from the perspective that saw individuals as moral actors towards an understanding of individuals as having natural drives that make them act in certain (selfish) ways. Rather than waiting for the effects of moral insights to take hold, it became clear that 'social engineering' could be a solution. This belief was based on particular understandings of human behaviour and how this could be manipulated. This shift was informed by the idea that inherent passions characterise human behaviour, and that these could be channelled to achieve a desired social order. Social theorists of the time rejected the idea that individuals could be governed through moral imperatives that could guide their conduct. Social theorists developed a psychological theory that justified their attempts to 'engineer' social life.

Using Adam Smith's work, one could alternatively argue that morality was still important as a separate sphere of conduct, even if morality was no longer relevant to the entire nation. However, even if one wants to save morality in this manner, it is no longer a term of much influence. Morality became a private activity within the sphere of individual endeavours and motivations. One could argue that ethics became aestheticised in the sense that ethics were similarly turned into a matter of individual taste. One could engage with ethics but also choose not to, because this was largely inconsequential for the greater good.[53] In this way, the values of everyday life were trivialised.

Yet the separation of the social machine and the actions of the individuals remained ambiguous. In some texts, a relationship *was* drawn between individual moral behaviour and the greater good of society, such as, for instance, when the virtues of calmness and predictability were seen as conducive to a wealthy society. Alternatively, some authors also drew a connection between self-interest and economic flourishing, which was thought to provide a harmonious and coherent link between the individual and the social. In this ambiguity the invisible hand could be deceptive at some times, while being propelled by its various parts at other times. The relationship between the individual and the collective was one of the new intellectual puzzles of the time.

The passions were hence not considered as an aspect of moral behaviour but became something that people naturally pursue – simply a part of their universal psychology. It is nature rather than morality that leads to the greater good, which is therefore no longer an individual responsibility. This form of economic psychology reduced the multitude of various passions into one single passion, namely that of self-interest. This is a passion tamed by reason, and reason was defined as self-interest (rather than, say, through the insights of the impartial spectator or the Kantian universal laws of morality that were developed later). With the help of mathematical models in emerging economic theory, constructing a manageable economy with manageable individuals became feasible. These models were abstractions from culture and habits.

Fourth, there is a contradiction in how everyday values are perceived. On the one hand, the values of everyday life were trivialised as mere matters of taste rather than common goods, and on the other, they were thought of as crucial under the guise of the driving force for individual activities that contributed to the wealth of nations. The dangerous passions were tempered, but not in a moral way. The variety of passions was further tamed by making them private. Motivation was turned into taste. This was possible by hierarchically categorising the passions as the search for profit. Money could finance any kind of passion, which meant that earning money could safeguard any passion or taste. Money was hence a powerful translator of differences into shared profit, and thus created a common interest for individuals as well as the nation.

The notion of a peaceful nation driven by *le doux commerce* emerged in social theory. The task of government became to ensure conditions that would allow for peaceful trade. The personal goals of individuals were deemed private, and people were free to enjoy themselves as long as they could afford it. The common good was, however, served through the idea that individuals *will* pursue their goals when these are translated into monetary value. The rational calculations could start. Reason came to equal self-interest. There would no longer be bloodshed but instead trade between parties that each strove for their own benefit.

Fifth, it was also clear that the desire to establish peaceful trade related to the desire to end civil war and bloodshed. The virtues of a trading nation, namely stability and predictability, were a strong motivator for creating such a nation. An effective instrument was again to channel the now reduced passion of self-interest, which made other motivations subordinate. It is easy to argue that this signified the end of individual morality and the aesthetics of everyday life, which were no longer needed for understanding or changing individual behaviour. This is also reflected in contemporaneous critiques. There were, as Adam Smith himself also indicated, concerns about the lack of support for public goods, such as education, art and creativity, but also about the disdain for good governance, because peace could be established and stability enforced even by dictators. For the trading man who is only interested in making a profit, this might be just as well. An interest in one's work and the pleasures of wisdom and play might disappear. But the just distribution of property was threatened if monetary gain was the only goal of the state. The translation of the good life into the rational calculation of interest, in other words, greatly diminished the palette of pleasures, values and motivations.

Sixth, what is interesting, particularly for the quest of this book, is that subjectivity was transformed from the cultivated and motivating feelings of the ancient Greeks, through the unruly passions of monarchs and the nobility, into the calculated reason of merchants. Although passions may determine the *nature* of the goods people want to pursue, reason guides these niceties towards what people actually decide to do. It is not wisdom, insight or moral behaviour that provide pleasure to the self but the dispassionate calculation of maximum gain. Passions became *problems* rather than inspirations for a morally good life. Interests as calculated self-interests could be civil and polite, but they never arose out of altruism or a need to do good for others. This social conceptualisation of pleasure went underground and disappeared from social theory, to be replaced by universal laws of duty and obligation.

Smith on the ward

How do centuries of European thinking play a role in contemporary psychiatric wards and residential homes in the Netherlands? This chapter has shown how the values of everyday life came to be disregarded and trivialised in social theory, even if they continued to be an important yet hidden cornerstone for imagining post-feudal societies. Individual morality came to be disregarded and social and ethical theory lost its interest in techniques of the self, such as the consultation of the impartial spectator. Morality was increasingly seen as having a dubious influence on broader social developments. Ideas and discussions about larger social communities and their regulation (rather than situations encountered by individuals) led to principles and general rules that favoured predictability and order.

In the practices involving dignity that were discussed in Chapter 3, it became clear that applying general principles leads to frictions in care practice. The central challenge in everyday care practices is the various ways of dealing with specificities, namely what is needed in this specific situation, for this particular patient and for those around her, right now. This issue is particularly salient in care practices involving chronic patients. Care work cannot be geared towards curing their disease, but it has to facilitate a mode of everyday life that is as good as possible. It is this concern with everyday moral, aesthetic and other values that is the core business of care practices. Rationalisations in the name of efficiency and utility may be part of these practices, but when they become too dominant or even formative, they disrupt everyday negotiations and silence the values of everyday life. Such negotiations may not lead to grand insights into the governance of care, but their development and cultivation does lead to engagements with and motivations for providing good care 'on the ground'.

Because these negotiations take place in the context of conventions and traditions – and this aspect is also prominent in the moral theory of Adam Smith – shared practices that emerge 'from within' are better guarantees for providing good care than avalanches of broad regulations. In the next chapter, I show how the principle of autonomy plays a role in care for people with learning disabilities, and how 'workarounds' involving everyday-life values are needed to get things done. After that chapter on contemporary care practices, I will revisit in Chapter 6 the historical emergence of general principles in social theory. Whereas the present chapter analysed the conceptualisation and demise of everyday life values, Chapter 6 will analyse how universalist thinking was presented as a social democratic alternative to forms of governance that are based on class or on violence. This type of universalist thinking, however, made its own distinctions that, in turn, created new forms of exclusion.

Notes

1. Smith, 1937; 2010.
2. Theorists such as Michel Foucault use the label 'humanism' rather than liberalism to refer to the central position of man in theories about the world in which humans are on the highest rung on the ladder of evolution due to their cognitive abilities. I use liberalism as well as humanism, as terms to denote more specific strands of thinking about the good life. Today, humanism also refers to the 'secular religion' that forms an interesting hybrid between pre-modern theories of the good life and Enlightenment values.
3. Interestingly, peasants and farmers remained a separate group that was not as central to post-feudalist forms of government. A possible explanation is that they were too scattered to be well organised.
4. Self-interest could be understood as good if it serves the purpose of self-preservation, or the preservation of society: see below.
5. Quoted in Heilbroner, 1982, p. 428.
6. See Winch, 1968. Other representatives are Hume, the Mills, Hutcheson and Rae.
7. See Hirschman, 1997.
8. Hirschman, 1997, p. 9.
9. There are also authors who find arguments in eighteenth-century thought to *promote* capitalism, such as McCloskey, 2010. Her account of history embeds a clear justification of the present, and this makes it difficult to read. Here I do not aim to argue for or against capitalism. Instead, I want to learn about present-day concerns about governance and the distribution of capital. However, it is clear that the problems the world faces today – an increasing accumulation of wealth at the expense of multitudes of poor people as well as the exhaustion of the world's natural resources – demand alternatives to capitalist models. This is also true for the care practices that neoliberal policies run the risk of destroying, as I have argued in Chapter 3.
10. Shapin & Schaffer, 1985.
11. Shapin & Schaffer, 1985.
12. See Hirschman, 1997; Winch, 1968; Heilbroner, 1982.
13. Hirschman, 1997; Norman, 2018.
14. Hirschman, 1997; Shapin & Schaffer, 1985.
15. Heilbroner, 1982, p. 428.
16. Both readings are possible, but the latter is the most common.
17. Heilbroner, 1982. Macfie (1967) is the proponent of such an integrated reading. Viner (1927) argues for the impossibility of reconciling both works.
18. Note that coherence and consistency in philosophical systems was yet to emerge in modernity. Smith scholars repeatedly remark on Smith's messy and wordy writing style.
19. These theorists had a rationalist idea of how individuals 'rationally' behaved by choosing what is in their own best interest (e.g. game theory, prisoner's dilemma, etc.). This signifies to me that individual behaviour was indeed not thought of as very relevant to economic thought. Only recently has 'behavioural economics' emerged, which has created space for thinking about the moral concerns of individuals. One of the founders of this field, Daniel Kahneman, won the Nobel prize for this work (see Kahneman & Tversky, 1979). Norman (2018) shows how models of economic science were based on simplified understandings of individual drives, such as self-interest, and thus often neglected various complexities, such as culture, norms, families, social groups, traditions, pasts and futures, and morality. Norman dubbed this one-dimensional conceptualisation of the individual the *homo economicus*. He characterises this conceptualisation as a combination of utilitarianism, mathematical models, and a desire not only for generalisations on individual (not social) 'behaviour' rather than 'conduct', but also for modelling of the emerging discipline of economics. Much like the models of disciplines such as physics, economic models sought to transcend 'context' and history. See Norman, 2018, pp. 83–4. Hence the discipline economics considered itself as empirical and value-free rather than normative.
20. Macfie, 1967, p. 46.
21. Note that mechanistic thinking was common in Smith's time and context. His theory is an attempt to connect various social institutions that together inform society as a system.
22. Macfie, 1967, p. 46.

23 Macfie considers agreeability to nature as the link between Smith's work and Stoic philosophy. Smith's appreciation for the beauty of the machine is therefore a Platonic heritage. Interestingly, here the link Smith made between beauty, happiness and goodness is also made to explain why people might wish to contribute to the beautiful workings of the social machine, which is comparable to the care for the self in ancient Greek philosophy (see Chapter 8).
24 Macfie, 1967, p. 45.
25 Smith, quoted in Macfie, 1967, p. 48.
26 The rupture with utilitarianism is crucial for Macfie's argument, which seeks to reconcile Smith's two major books. Hence a deontological ethics (rather than a utilitarian one) remains available to situate Smith's moral theory.
27 Instinct, drive, emotion, affect, disposition.
28 This is important for understanding the values of everyday life as concrete and social values.
29 See also Heilbroner, 1982, p. 429, on this point.
30 It was a common belief during this period that societies and histories are always evolving in a good direction. Famous examples are Hegel and Marx.
31 Note that this is exactly Hume's argument against social contract theorists. The disposition to commit to a contract presupposes an expectation of trustworthiness of the other partner. This does not point towards the war of all against all that contract theorists assume will take place, and which they see as the reason for needing such a contract in the first place. This is an argument for understanding Smith's morality as pre-modern rather than modern, as he does not presuppose a 'nature state' that is tamed by calculating individuals.
32 Norman, 2018, p. 268.
33 Norman, 2018, p. 269.
34 This would be empirical ethics *avant la lettre*!
35 This resonates with the scarce but interesting literature on pragmatic ethics. According to such pragmatists, any practical problem is simultaneously a normative problem, because a problem always demands a way for *improving* the situation. Habitual ways of framing situations rarely suffice to solve such problems. To creatively redefine a problem in such a way so that a solution becomes possible is central to pragmatist ethics (Liszka, 2013; 2014; 2021). Through the figure of the impartial spectator such a rearticulation can be made. Smith has four sources for the sentiments we feel when judging the propriety of an action. These are the *motives* of the agent, the *gratitude* of those at whom the agent's actions are directed, the *agreeability* to the general rules of both parties, and the *promotion of happiness* or *beauty of the social machine*. Hence Smith does not formulate rules for us to follow but provides us with a technique ('imagine to be the impartial spectator') to test and improve one's judgement.
36 See Hanley, 2009. These tools could be seen as pragmatic principles. I do not think that the figure of the impartial spectator actually needs such principles, but they may help to sharpen one's thinking (rather than be 'applied' to a situation).
37 The distinction between moveable and unmoveable property was an important discussion at the time, as we shall see below.
38 This is also Griswold's interpretation (1998).
39 See also Folbre, 2009 on this point.
40 Hanley, 2009.
41 Nauta, 1984.
42 Norman, 2018 connects this directly to a notion of an economic individual that is the product of economic scientists' use of mathematical models that can only accommodate a few variables, leading to the *homo economicus* with only one important characteristic: a striving for self-interest.
43 Think also of the anti-Semitic characterisations of Jews throughout history that represent them as greedy and involved in moneylending practices.
44 Hirschman, 1997, p. 80.
45 This is also why Hobbes does not approve of democracy or aristocracy. This would not bring a concordance of public and private interests.
46 Hirschman, 1997, p. 106. See the classic work of Pocock, 2003, and the feminist interpretation of republicanism by Pitkin, 1967.
47 This was also one of Smith's concerns.
48 Hirschman, 1997, p. 109.

49 Hobbes, 1968.
50 In Hirschman, 1997, pp. 119–20.
51 Quoted in Hirschman, 1997, pp. 123–4.
52 In the words of the ancient Greeks: the *ethos* of the exemplary representatives of the good life was replaced by a containment of the *bios* of common men. I will describe this in Chapter 8.
53 Note that this problem is still apparent in current societies where the individual conduct of politicians sits uneasily with public office. Corruption, sexual misconduct and self-enrichment by politicians do not necessarily mean the end of one's career but may even contribute to one's success by emphasising that politicians are 'just like us', namely that we would do the same if we were in the same position. It is clear that these two are in tension.

5
Giving voice or making voice? The principle of autonomy and everyday patient values in care for people with learning disabilities

The current prominence of ethical principles is due to the disappearance of morality from social theory and the development of principled ethics from the Enlightenment on. In more recent history, ethical principles in health care relate to recognition of the atrocities of the Second World War and the extreme abuses of test persons in medical research, such as in the Tuskegee syphilis trials.[1] But the emergence of principles in medicine is also informed by a more general tendency that came to be known as 'medical paternalism'. Paternalistic doctors 'know best', and their patients are not involved in learning and deciding about their treatment.[2] During the process of democratisation in the 1970s in the Netherlands, members of the post-Second World War generation were very critical of hierarchies. Attempts were made to give citizens – and also patients – more room for participating in society and in governance.[3] In this context, the idea emerged that if patients could speak up and make their voices heard they would not accept treatments that were bad for them. This call for including patient voices is one reason for the impact of the principle of patients' autonomy in particular.[4] The current norm is that no treatment should be provided without patient consent, even though there are some well-regulated exceptions.[5] When this principle is applied, it is thought, care work and medical research are in agreement with the concerns and values of patients, or at least not in conflict with them.

In my discussions on dignity and Adam Smith's writings, however, it became clear that principles need to be made concrete in order to function as a value that can be part of everyday-life practices. This chapter explores what role the principle of autonomy plays in care practices, and particularly in attempts at 'giving patients a voice'. The principle of autonomy is supposed to guarantee that people can make decisions concerning their own lives. But how does such a principle take shape in practice? In my subsequent analysis, the role of everyday values will again become apparent. As a directive for care work, autonomy turns out to be of limited use to 'give voice' to patients. Other values are necessary for orienting care work towards something good. I will explore what these values are and how they accommodate the specificities of persons and situations.

Autonomy and learning disabilities

In this chapter, I explore the fate of the principle of autonomy in care for people with learning disabilities.[6] I will show how the principle of autonomy was meant to give *patients* a voice and provide them with a means of self-governance in their care. My ethnographic work, however, shows that autonomy works better in particular situations over others, and that it supports certain voices and activities better than others. The principle of autonomy provided policymakers with an important value for ending the practice of housing people with learning disabilities in institutions and for housing people in ordinary neighbourhoods. Everybody has a right to autonomy in decisions concerning their own lives and this should be no different for particular groups. Patients, no matter how dependent they are on care workers, are moral characters who are entitled to autonomy.

I will analyse how, once patients arrived in their new homes, the principle of autonomy could not be adapted to, and even came to obstruct, this new form of deinstitutionalised care. The principle of autonomy was not useful for determining which characteristics of the good life for patients could be used to orient care practices. Autonomy could only be used to stipulate *procedures* for evaluating if certain decisions were good or not. A good decision is one that is made by a client or one to which they consent. In such a formal description the *substance* of what might be good is not taken into account – it is private. The principle of autonomy does not offer any definitive answer to the question of which decision is a good decision, other than that this decision is made by a person themselves. It is at people's own discretion to determine their personal tastes. Such things are private matters and do not concern formal institutions.[7]

However, it was exactly the *nature* of these decisions that led to conflicts with caregivers, who did not always agree with their clients' decisions.[8] In addition to the problems that surround autonomy-in-practice, my analysis shows that caregivers are unable to provide adequate care without a substantial idea about what might constitute a good life for their clients, or rather, for each client in particular. Their understandings of the good life hence went 'underground' – that is, these continued to inform their activities but became a tacit part of their interpretation of good care. Ideals that continued to be verbally articulated only concerned autonomy.

This view of the good life, I will argue, presents a way of 'making a voice' for patients rather than 'giving' them a voice. *Making* a voice positions patients not as individuals who must not be hindered by others in making their decisions but as people who strive for a good life that can only be lived with the support of other people and within certain material circumstances. Everyday life, one could say, is not about making discrete decisions but about becoming part of a network of relations that allow one to achieve a good life. This good is the outcome of multiple negotiations. Such negotiations never lead to ideal situations or an eradication of bad things, but the situation may be 'good enough' or the best feasible option. This multivocal 'voice in the making' tells us what is good rather than what a single individual desires, although desires certainly play an important role as well. A good life, and even desires, are a *shared achievement*.

Autonomy and institutions

Autonomy was a key principle in the care policies of institutions for people with mild and moderate learning disabilities.[9] Autonomy takes on different meanings in long-term care situations as well as in their regulation, but in the context described in this chapter it refers to the possibility 'to direct one's own life and live according to one's own choices'.[10] The principle of autonomy in care for people with learning disabilities is informed by their long-term institutionalisation. As in the case of long-term psychiatry patients (see Chapter 3), the principle holds that people with intellectual disabilities are supposed to become proper citizens, which means that people can make their own rules and decisions on how to live. The institution can no longer dictate what their day should look like. Because they are living in ordinary neighbourhoods, they are now part of the society that had excluded them for so long.[11]

At the turn of the twenty-first century, policymakers in the Netherlands formulated a 'citizenship paradigm' as a guideline for care work involving people with learning disabilities.[12] The citizenship paradigm provided a model of care in which people live in ordinary neighbourhoods and in an inclusive community.[13] Policy documents, such as the one created by the Organisation for Care for the Intellectually Handicapped in the Netherlands, incorporate the citizenship paradigm's notion of autonomy (*eigen regie*: to direct oneself) as well as the promotion of quality of life.[14]

Critics have accused policymakers of using the ideals of autonomy and citizenship as a way to lower health care costs. Their approach reduces institutional care services and forces people to take care of themselves rather than promoting good care practices and wellbeing.[15] Some argue that the citizenship paradigm is bankrupt for this reason.[16] Independence, critics argue, has come to mean 'do whatever you want, but do not ask for support'. The citizenship paradigm ignores that support is crucial for people with learning disabilities for helping them function as meaningful members of society. Autonomy, then, comes to stand for neglect. If people are not provided with support, they will become marginalised and be unable to meet society's demands. Examples of marginalisation include the lack of job opportunities, low pay rates, digital illiteracy and a higher risk of poverty and imprisonment.[17] This has led Moonen to proclaim that the 'right to support' is the principled basis for a new vision of care work. This right is also stipulated in the Convention on the Rights of Persons with Disabilities.[18]

Whose problem is it?

In 2011, I was part of a study that looked at caregivers' concerns about alcohol and drug use among people with intellectual disabilities. We conducted an ethnographic study of two ambulant care organisations in the Netherlands for people with learning disabilities that were active in two big cities and one smaller town. Brigitte Althoff conducted fieldwork for this study, while working on her master's thesis in anthropology, together with Els Bransen, my colleague from the Netherlands Institute for Mental Health and Addiction.[19] They followed caregivers during home visits and spoke to clients informally.[20]

Alcohol and drug use were of concern to caregivers who witnessed how addictions took hold and social lives were ruined. Were alcohol and drug use the consequence of free choice and newly acquired social privilege, or were people's lives being ruined by excessive quantities of bad substances? And, if the latter was the case, what could be done about this issue?

Autonomy in everyday life

Autonomy was a very clear orienting principle that all caregivers swiftly mentioned when asked what they found important in their care practice. According to the principle of autonomy and the discourse that surrounds it, caregivers are supposed to act only when clients ask for advice or consent to receiving help.

> Brigitte: Does your organisation have a particular philosophy of care?
>
> Sonja: Yes, [it is aimed at helping you] to direct your own life. That's the idea, that you can decide most things for yourself. [laughs] It's funny, but the way I work, and what I find very important, is that the clients can decide things for themselves. We [caregivers] don't stand above them [direct them], but next to them [work with them]. And as long as it's safe [*verantwoord*, responsible] we'll do what the client wants, so to speak. It's a very good philosophy, because everyone has the right to live their own life, and even with a learning disability, they can decide what to do. I find that very important.

The quote shows a clear adherence to the ideal of citizenship in care work. The ideal has to be put into practice, but only within the limits of safety and responsibility, which are issues that apply to everyone. Clients should live the life that they want to lead, and caregivers are there to support this endeavour. Allowing people to make their own choices could, however, be hard work.

> Diane: He [client] overestimates what he can handle. It's gone wrong so often, like whenever he gets a job. He wants to work five days a week, and it's fine for three weeks but then it all goes haywire and he loses the job. But if he worked *two* days a week he could manage. I'd like to explain this to him, by asking him questions. But he's really keen to work, and, in the end, he does what he wants. That is his choice, so, yes . . . It doesn't work well. [laughs] But I have to say that this last job is going surprisingly well, and that's really nice to see. So, it's a dilemma. On the one hand, you want to protect him against the failures that will occur, and on the other hand, he's so happy, and you want to give him a chance to go ahead and try.

Caregivers have learnt to take a step back and give their clients the benefit of the doubt rather than to try and prevent any foreseeable harms. They grant clients the opportunity to chase their dreams and try things out. This does not mean that they let their clients do whatever they want or let them take sole responsibility of their activities. They keep an eye on what is happening and discuss the results with their clients. Experiments are possible and opportunities are generously granted but clients are not left alone. This means finding a fine balance in which habits and common expectations are weighed up against the good of getting a chance to try again.

From our observations of day-to-day care, it was apparent that caregivers not only upheld the ideal of autonomy while helping their clients to direct their own life, but in a particular form, this ideal was also *accomplished*. This form of autonomy consisted of the possibility of ending unwanted relationships. Clients rented their own apartments, and this gave them, literally, the power to close the door to their well-meaning caregivers. The possibility of being cut out was a concern that kept coming up for caregivers in their daily practice.

> *Field note*: Jolanda says that they all have their own apartments. 'You can't control what happens in there. You can have nice chats about things, but if someone goes to the supermarket and fills up his fridge with beer, you can't stop that from happening.' Jolanda then gives an example: 'It's always a give and take with Michael [client]. At any moment he could say, "I don't want any more assistance. Here are your marching orders."'

The move to community housing provided people with their own private spaces. They had the power to legitimately shut people out. Ending relationships could have serious consequences (such as losing a job), but such issues were not part of the abstract ideas that inform the citizenship paradigm. Everyone is entitled to orchestrate their own misery. Autonomy is used here as a procedural criterion: a decision is good when it is made by the client themselves. This is regardless of the reasons given for decisions that are made, or their consequences. That type of content is irrelevant to others; it is a matter of individual discretion. At least in theory.[21]

Concerns and effects

One of the everyday-life values that caregivers tried to achieve was that of maintaining a relationship with their clients. They had no authority over what their clients could or could not do, but they tried to stay in touch with them in order to be able to provide any support at all.

> Joanna: You see, you must know how to address Bert [client]. Because if you are too strict . . . I do set limits, but very carefully, and not that often. That's how you must interact with Bert, otherwise you'll lose him. He closes the door on you, and then he won't let you in again. If that happens, you certainly won't be able to help him.

There must be a relationship in order to be able to support people. One of the main challenges with 'difficult clients' is gaining access to them. Care work (or working with clients) becomes difficult when there are different opinions about what constitutes a problem. This frequently occurred in cases of using alcohol or 'soft drugs', which are legally available in the Netherlands.[22] Caregivers wanted to intervene when they saw clients doing things that they thought were not good for their own wellbeing. At that point, something interesting happened to their understanding of autonomy. Caregivers shifted their interpretation of autonomy as the right to govern oneself towards autonomy as the *competence to make decisions*. Making decisions is something which one can be good or bad at, better or worse. If autonomy is interpreted as competency in making decisions, and this is often how autonomy is interpreted in health care, a client can also fail.[23] Caregivers were frequently concerned that their clients were not particularly good at making decisions. Very often they saw clients making wrong decisions in the sense that they deemed these decisions unhelpful for achieving a good life.

> Thera: You see, José [client] went to a dietitian for her diabetes, and the dietitian didn't understand how this works for people with learning disabilities. She said for instance, 'Do you drink tea?' 'Yes, I do,' said José. 'Do you put sugar in your tea?' 'No.' And then you should stop, move on to the next topic. But the dietitian said, 'Well, if you do add sugar, I'd advise you to start using sweeteners.' And José thinks, 'Sweeteners are better.' And so, she bought sweeteners, whereas it is better to drink tea without sweeteners. Or the dietitian said, 'You're allowed to eat a cake every now and then.' But what

does 'every now and then' mean? José never ate cakes, only on birthdays and such. But now she thinks: 'Ah, I can eat cake! Every now and then I can eat cake.' And now she buys cake. She eats worse now than before she went to the dietitian. [laughs]

We witnessed several instances in which tacit or explicit advice led exactly to the kind of behaviour it was supposed to discourage. The most dramatic example involved Roger, who drank alcohol while taking his medications even though his doctor had emphatically forbidden this. A sticker on the package warned, 'Do not use with alcohol'. That same evening Roger had to be admitted to a hospital by ambulance, as he had drunk alcohol anyway. It was not clear if the doctor had failed to consider Roger's alcohol problem when prescribing the medicine or why Roger had not heeded the warnings. Situations in which clients and caregivers held different understandings of what the problem was and what needed to be done about it frequently proved challenging. One could say that the dilemma is about who can best speak for the client: the self-destructive clients themselves, or their caregivers who anticipate the consequences.

> Thera: See, if you knew that she could make a proper decision or that she could use her freedom to make a wise decision, then you can make an agreement. Then I'd say to her, 'Your diabetes can give you problems with your health, your sight can get worse, you'll have low blood pressure, wounds, foot amputation, whatever.' And if she said, 'OK, I'll make that bargain because this is how I want to live.' Well, then fine. But you can't talk with her like that because she doesn't understand [the long-term consequences]. That makes it so hard.

In these examples, there is a difference between good and bad autonomy, and between good decisions (wise, properly made, in accordance with how one wants to live) and bad decisions (not taking effects into account, not being able to weigh one's options). In both cases individuals govern themselves, but in vastly different ways. What is at stake is not only 'who governs' or who has a voice, but also what this voice is saying.[24]

The flipside of autonomy

When caregivers thought that their clients acted in destructive ways, however, they had little ground for justifying their efforts to intervene.

Formally, within a legal discourse on autonomy, interventions are only allowed when clients meet the legal criterion of being a 'danger to self or others'. In such cases, autonomy was deemed to have failed and caregivers could take actions that were backed up by the law. Such situations involve what I call the 'flip-over' character of autonomy. One is an autonomous individual until it is shown that this is no longer the case. When individual autonomy fails, the perspective flips and rigorous action may be taken without obtaining consent while nonetheless remaining within the strict limits of the law. Discrete situations can be understood as a binary opposition between the success and the failure of autonomy, and one may flip from one position to the other. Once it has been formally determined that a person is behaving in a dangerous manner, self-governance ends and the state takes over. The free individual has firm boundaries.

The flip-over logic of autonomy made it difficult for caregivers to see how they might (attempt to) influence their clients without coercing them. From the perspective of caregivers, it seemed either that they could not influence their clients (because they were making autonomous decisions) or that they had to take complete control over them. However, any ordinary activity in day-to-day care can be seen as influencing a person.[25] When looking at situations in care, people can be seen to influence each another all the time. In encouraging someone to take a shower, supporting the preparation of a meal and attempting to solve a problem, caregivers influence their clients. This influencing happens within the specificity of their relationship and in their striving for a good life. Yet this form of caring does not exist in legal conceptions of autonomy, which mainly concern autonomy 'after the flip', that is, as employed to regulate *problematic* situations.

This 'everyday' form of influence is never coercive. Caregivers rejected the use of force for various reasons. First, coercion jeopardises the relationship with their clients who could close the door on them. The second reason is a pragmatic one, namely that coercion *does not work*. Clients will continue doing what they want to do, but out of sight of caregivers.

> Jane: Well, people drink or smoke, you have to be realistic. Prohibiting things is of course useless. If you prohibit things, clients become invisible. They'll keep doing it behind your back. Our strategy is to make it [the abuse] no longer a taboo and to guide it [the use] towards acceptable proportions. That's the strategy.

There is little sense in using force in care, because it is illegal and does not lead to desired outcomes. Here, the caregiver's problem becomes clear. Caregivers do not want to wait until their clients run into problems that are so severe that caregivers are legally allowed to force compliance. They want to provide support long before this happens. But care guidelines that are based on self-governance provide caregivers with little direction. Caregivers felt they had to 'wait for things to escalate'. They tried to act to the best of their abilities yet remained uncertain about the legitimacy of their actions. But caregivers also found it difficult to respect 'bad decisions'.

Good care in everyday life: creating relations

The discourse of autonomy left little space for caregivers to reflect on the ways they could and did influence their clients. It did not formulate substantial ideals that could inform what care work for people with learning disabilities should strive for, but instead provided procedures for deciding if clients should be left alone. However, caregivers *did* have ideas about what a good life for their clients might look like, which became clear when they talked about the dilemmas they faced in respecting 'bad decisions'. What would a good life look like? This is different for different persons, but the gist is that people need to be embedded in social and material relationships that are meaningful to them and through which they can realise a good life. Rather than leaving individuals to govern themselves or end relationships,[26] this suggests an understanding of the good life as something that is lived in and through relationships with others (family, friends, employers, caregivers), and with things and material infrastructures (income, housing, a place to go to meet others).[27] These relationships are all needed to realise this good life.

Note that, for the researchers, a good life was a *result* rather than a guiding principle. Empirically, one may describe a good life as the result of interactions and affordances. To caregivers, the fragility of their clients' relationships with others made it difficult to create and maintain such interactions and affordances. These relationships were different and specific to each client, and they could also shift. Caregivers worked to creatively craft a good life in relation to others. Even if they had no explicit discourse to justify this endeavour,[28] they *enacted* it in their everyday activities. They kept an eye on things when relationships were threatened. This could happen, for instance, when somebody lost their job, had problems with family members or started drinking to excess.[29]

The core of such relational care is not just about *individual abilities* or individual *governance*, but about *a life achieved together with others*.

When one attempts to rethink autonomy in terms of relationships, it becomes something like 'to be in circumstances that allow one to achieve a good life'. To accomplish this, people need alliances with others rather than just the power to 'say no'. It assumes the givenness of dependencies and of mutual influences. Here, influence is not a negative term but a condition for achieving anything at all. A life that is as good as possible is dependent on what others contribute to this. Life is not static and never finished but always in the process of taking shape.

I already showed that the first step for caregivers is to establish and maintain the relationships between *themselves* and their clients. These professional relationships formed an important basis on which to build and support relationships with others, which required a specific approach for specific persons.

> Wilma: With Jasper you mustn't emphasise the downside too much. Then he gets stuck, keeps repeating things. But if you take a more positive approach he'll move on. I once commented on him skipping dinner. That he should have a certain number of meals a day. The next day again he didn't have dinner. He turns into a bit of a small child then: 'Yes, yes, yes, sorry, sorry, sorry!' He really wants me to be proud of him, and he doesn't want to be told off. That's how I see it. He's scared of rejection. And he has learnt that I'm really happy when he tells me things, that I can support him better like that, because then I know what's going on. And he knows I won't get angry. So then he reports something really hesitantly, such as, 'See, Wilma, something went a tiny little bit wrong . . .' Then I try to respond like, 'Well, now isn't that too bad, how did it happen? Tomorrow is another day, so let's take it from there.'

Caregivers told us that it is a matter of learning which approach works best for whom. Each person has their own characteristic traits and, at times, very distinctive habits. Caregivers need to tune into the specificities of the situation, and they need to find out what works for whom, based on – and through developing – the relationship that they have with a client. This does not mean that caregivers simply do what clients want.[30]

> Case study: Steven is generally very agitated but refuses to take his medication. He smokes cannabis to slow himself down. His caregiver says he understands this, and that it also improves his relationship with Steven. When he had a job he liked, Steven smoked two joints a day and found a good balance. His employer kept an eye on him

and they worked well together. But he lost that job due to a reorganisation, and got a new one he didn't like. He found it too heavy for his back, he thought the pay was too low and that he was being taken advantage of. And so he quit. His cannabis use increased dramatically. Due to his drug use, swearing bouts and refusal to take his medication, it is difficult to make him interesting to employers. His caregiver says that finding a suitable job is crucial for Steven. Steven also acknowledges the importance of a good job, but he is suspicious of being underpaid and discriminated against.

This caregiver expresses what the effects are of doing certain things. This is not always a concern the client shares. Steven did not see his smoking habits as a problem. He also did not consider the effects of being in a daze all day. All this notwithstanding the fact that he would like to have a good job.

Whose voice articulates a good life for him? Do we have to choose? Caregivers attempt to provide support to their clients so that they can achieve a life that is good for them, either because clients *say* it is good or because caregivers see the positive effects of, say, having a job rather than smoking pot all day. There were of course differences between what either party deemed to be good. These differences formed the grounds for negotiations, pleas, compromises and discussions rather than 'either-client-or-caregiver' decisions. The activities, their meanings and the effects of what clients do are part of the negotiations involved in understanding and shaping a good life. Besides what people decide or like, what also plays a role is how their activities affect their relationships. This may be difficult to assess from a first-person perspective, and there may be unintended outcomes. Consequences and voices of others both come into view and are taken into account. In such an everyday relational perspective, a good life is always a shared achievement.

All participants were part of the negotiations involved in creating a good life and in establishing its goodness. Steven might think that smoking all day is no problem, but those caring for him thought differently. This did not mean they could – or would want to – force their views onto Steven. But they could try to help create conditions for a better life, and they could try to make Steven see a different point of view or nudge him towards a life they thought was better. The good life here is a collective achievement, similar to the 'voice that is made' for and with patients. It is not a perfect life, nor is the good that is achieved always the good that was intended. The good is the result of practical negotiations in everyday life, which may turn out for better or for worse. Autonomy – the ability to say no, end relationships and be left alone – can still be part of these practices. But achieving what is of value to someone in everyday life is something that can only be done in collaboration with others.

Playing the game of the good life: the distribution of agency

The challenge is not to *end* relationships but to build and maintain social and material relationships that contribute to achieving a good life. One caregiver used the metaphor of the game.

> Lisa: You have to play with people. Not aim straight for your target. Try another way as well. You see, I really like Martin, who he is as a person. I don't approve of everything he does, but you must feel for him a bit. I can tell him off: 'Damn it, Martin, you can't do this, you can't go out all night and not tell your partner! She waits up all night for you and is scared shitless!' I can say that to him, but that's also because I'm quite relaxed with him, I tolerate his beers and his shenanigans. And I provide a lot of coaching in their relationship as well.

The metaphors of game and play suggest that the moves of one player depend on the moves of another. There simply is no game if one does not acknowledge this interdependency. The challenge is to keep the game going and to prevent players from dropping out. Rules and positions are not set in stone but are improvised along the way. This involves constant experimentation, evaluation, adaptation, tinkering and improvisation in an attempt to achieve a 'good game'.[31] It is a process of give and take that involves the situation as it unfolds in the moment, as well as the various processes that this situation contains. If one of the players drops out, the caregivers will attempt to re-engage the client – or themselves – in the game or try to find different strategies that might work better.

For example, Steven was kept off drugs through the support of his employer and the routines he established through his job. As caregivers learnt from working with Steven, having a job reduced his use of alcohol and drugs. Directly addressing what they, not Steven, saw as his drug problem had little effect. If Steven's living conditions could not be improved, there was little chance that his drug habits would change. And vice versa, if his life was better, Steven's need for drugs would be less strong.

> Thera: I often think we're more preoccupied with setting conditions for a life without alcohol abuse rather than going straight for the target and saying, 'You can only have two beers.' That doesn't work at all. You work on the things around the problem. You try to get their lives back on track so that people will decrease their drinking in the same go.

The outcome would be a life in which Steven would work, smoke less and be less susceptible to trouble. This is what the caregivers saw as the best option, and they thought that Steven would not disagree once this was achieved – not because he would smoke less pot (he did not care about that) but because he would have a good job. The good life here was good both to Steven and to his caregivers, and this was achieved together with a good employer.

Another example is that of Roger, a troublesome binge-drinker on whom caregivers almost gave up and who pushed other people away by swearing at them.

> Janna: It was two minutes before blast off, so to speak, or maybe it was already blast off. Nobody saw any alternative options. It was really a question of how can we, the team, still coach him? We really didn't see how we could, especially because of the nuisance he caused in the place he lived. The issue was that this was really his last chance. We saw that his housing situation wasn't ideal. He shared a flat, lived with other clients. So we got him a small home away from the other clients, where he's a bit further away from everyone. It worked well.

The first intervention in this 'near-lost cause' was not to target Roger's alcohol use but to adjust his housing situation. This meant nobody else was around to be abused by him when he was drunk. The next step was to help him find a job. Caregivers did not give up on Roger and helped him build a better life by adjusting and improving his material and social circumstances. They helped to build an infrastructure around him, thus laying the foundations for sustaining a way of life that they all found liveable and meaningful.

Agency can hence be seen as distributed across the socio-material network, which caregivers put to good use. One can achieve things with others and within supportive contexts. This means that others do their share and have a role in shaping the outcome. The governance of the self hence becomes a shared governance. How one can 'make a voice' is largely dependent on how one can create this voice with the help of supportive and active others. Without caregivers, people like Steven and Roger might have lots to say but would never be heard.

Here is one last example of how a good life may be achieved amidst different preferences and relations.

> Case study: Rinus has Down's syndrome. This organisation has been coaching him in various housing circumstances since he was 17. Four years ago, Herman, an old friend and colleague from the social employment organisation, moved in with him following a suggestion from Rinus's caregiver, Stefan. He saw that the two men got along well. Herman is autistic. They both work. Rinus had a drinking problem in the past, which was ignored in his previous accommodation. He started to live more healthily after a heart attack. Two years ago, when he moved into his present house, there were excesses. Rinus drank too much, and then would fight with the staff. When Brigitte talked to him, he said he drank one glass every other day. Alcohol is not an issue any more under Stefan's supervision. It helps that Herman positively detests alcohol due to bad experiences in the past. Stefan encourages the two men to work things out between them. And they do. Rinus and Herman cook together. Herman takes care of Rinus's medication, helps him in following the instructions issued by the thrombosis services, and goes with him to the dietitian. Stefan helps with practical matters such as finances and the mail. And he supervises the consultations with the dietitian. Stefan is happy with the way things have turned out.

The three men have established a balanced situation in which each person's tasks are clear. The situation supports relationships that are beneficial to establishing a life that is meaningful to the persons involved. Intricate relational and infrastructural networks can support and influence this good life. With his new housemate and friend, Rinus is not drinking so much. He does not reduce his drinking because of his health but because of his friendship with Herman. Another consequence is that Rinus no longer gets into fights, which is good for the social environment as well. The two men cook and eat together and manage medications among themselves. The caregiver has not withdrawn but takes responsibility for some of the tasks (finances and mail); he also facilitates the relationship between both men to keep things going as they are. The caregiver gets something in return as well, namely job satisfaction. All three men managed to create a shared good life, on however small a scale.

From giving voice towards achieving a good life

The principle of autonomy works in different ways, but it does not always strengthen the position of patients or amplify their voice. The procedural way in which autonomy has been interpreted, as well as its 'flip-over' character, make it difficult to 'apply' autonomy in the achievement of good care. Autonomy affords the capacity to end relationships but not to establish them.

Caregivers worried whether autonomy could be understood as a competence in making decisions that are supportive to a person. They observed many situations in which they wanted to correct their clients' behaviour. But the autonomy discourse made intervening difficult to justify, even if many day-to-day situations in care settings are not about making autonomous decisions. These situations were also not about coercing clients to do something but rather about influencing their lives. When and where interventions might be legitimate was unclear in the autonomy discourse, because this allows for only two positions. Either one is autonomous or one is not.

The possibility for clients to end relationships, in combination with the lack of more substantial ideals for orienting care, led to difficulties for caregivers who were doing their best to develop and maintain relationships. Such relationships might be between themselves and their clients, but could also involve socio-material relationships with other relevant persons or with the material infrastructures that clients moved through. The nature of these relationships could make a vast difference for the acceptability of clients' behaviours and their effects on others. Adjustments to the environment could make problematic clients function well.

Agency was hence nicely distributed across the network. Clients did not act alone and could not govern themselves alone. Issues such as drug use and bad housing arrangements acted on them. This raised the question of who can 'speak the truth' about the subject. Who can do that best and how is it best done? Not only what people *did*, what they *decided* or *intended*, or how they *understood* their situation was important for improving the patient's position, but also the *effects* of their activities on others. The goal therefore became to establish a set of relationships between clients and their socio-material environments that were as good as possible.

Building relationships and networks does not, however, give any indication of which values to pursue. Values could be flexibly related to individual situations even if individuals were unable to make themselves heard. Conventions played an important part in this process, but also the ideas of caregivers, the presence of clients and supporting others, the availability of jobs, friends, proper housing and so on. Rather than being premised on self-governance and independence, care was based on the idea that one can only achieve things within relationships. These relationships could be good or bad, which was, again, something that members of the network evaluated and worked on. Rather than the metaphor of 'giving voice', these attempts to create a good life dynamically shaped the position of patients and made their life good or less good. Voices were *made* in particular arrangements.[32]

Notes

1. In the Tuskegee trials, male subjects with syphilis were studied to observe the natural course of the disease even though a cure was available at the time. The fact that the test persons were African American increased the level of public horror when the 'experiment' came to light. Petryna et al., 2006; Petryna, 2007; 2009. Jacobs, 2022, argues that this historical background is often cited as the reason for establishing ethical committees, but that an alternative reading is that these committees gave doctors the possibility to govern and control their own practices
2. Some have described this as a doctor–patient relationship that suits some patients better than others. See Emanuel & Emanuel, 1992.
3. Bartlett & O'Connor, 2007; Carey, 2009; Ootes et al., 2010; Pols, 2016; Tonkens & Weijers 1999; Tonkens, 1999.
4. Wolpe, 1998.
5. The Dutch law regulating such exceptions is the 'Wet op de Geneeskundige Behandelingsovereenkomst' (WGBO).
6. There is much debate about the label of intellectual disabilities, which are now called 'learning disabilities' in the United States. Some people who have been given this label have rejected it because they do not agree that it reflects their concerns. At the high point of discussions about the correct terminology, the notion of 'people with possibilities' was suggested, but this provided no possibilities for claiming a right to professional care. See Dronkert, 2018.
7. The reader can hear a clear resonance with the faith in the passions described in the previous chapter.
8. The term 'client' is a way to address people in a more emancipatory way. There is much debate about such labels. Here, I follow the term currently used in the field.
9. The ideal of citizenship central to the deinstitutionalisation policies caused patient autonomy and self-determination to become core values (Pols, 2006b). As citizens, everyone, including people with disabilities, should be allowed to live according to their own rules, norms, values and choices (Meininger, 2001).
10. Pols, 2003; 2006b.
11. See, for the spatial metaphors in this context, Pols, 2016, and on social space, Muusse et al., 2020.
12. Van Gennep, 2000; Frederiks et al., 2009, p. 7; Renders & Meininger 2011, Lord & Hutchison, 2003.
13. Wilde, 2015.
14. VGN, 2007. *Eigen regie* (autonomy) and quality of life are listed next to one another as core values. Quality of life is described in the report as involving support for health care, personal development, participation in society and so on. How potential frictions between core values should be resolved is not described in the document. On VGN's website, interestingly, the core

value of autonomy is not mentioned (accessed 21 May 2019). The key values listed are: trust, involvement, professionality, care services that meet the demands of clients (and parents) that seek to achieve an as worthy existence as possible, and a good quality of life. Quality of life is a second way of operationalising 'patient values'. A recent policy document that envisions the situation as it will develop until 2030 presents a quite different approach. Core values are now: living a meaningful live together with others, and getting support to do so.

15 Gennep, 1997; Frederiks et al., 2009.
16 Moonen, 2015.
17 Moonen, 2015; Woittiez et al., 2014.
18 United Nations, 2006. See also Hendricks 2007; Flynn & Arstein-Kerslake, 2014.
19 Althoff, 2014.
20 In February–June 2014, the two fieldworkers followed 11 community caregivers on 26 home visits to adult clients with learning disabilities. They also followed 11 caregivers of clients who had alcohol or drug problems, or problems that posed a dilemma to caregivers, namely of wanting to address issues their clients did not perceive as such. Informal conversations were conducted with other clients and caregivers. The fieldworkers also interviewed the leader of the team and one caregiver they had not followed. In both organisations, fieldworkers attended team meetings and conducted focus groups with their caregiver informants. The groups discussed concerns with alcohol problems, perspectives on care related to autonomy and to caregivers' own ideals as well as some of the dilemmas they encountered. The fieldworkers interviewed eight clients, four in each location. We constructed 21 case studies of clients with alcohol or drug problems. The material – case study descriptions – was analysed in a master's thesis (Althoff, 2014) and resulted in the creation of a practical guideline for caregivers (Bransen, Althoff & Pols, 2015).
21 See also Van der Weele et al., 2021.
22 See also Clarke & Wilson, 1999.
23 Discussions about this issue are formalised in Dutch legal terms as *wilsonbekwaamheid*, which can be translated as something close to 'incompetence of will'.
24 This debate has taken place in disability studies as well. When patient organisations spoke up, what they said was often not to the liking of the disability activists. The latter issued a manifesto that outlined which words are appropriate to make demands. See Pols & Hoogsteyns, 2015.
25 See Pols, 2003, for the absence of 'care as usual' in juridical understandings of care. See RVS, 2019, for a perspective on autonomy and influence in ordinary rather than problematic situations.
26 This is a particular way of interpreting 'negative freedom' or the right to be left alone. See Berlin, 1958.
27 See for this argument also Gómez, 2015; Danholt & Langstrup, 2012; Langstrup, 2013.
28 See Muusse et al., 2020, for the situation in Trieste, where caregivers did have an explicit discourse at their disposal.
29 See note 19 in Chapter 3 about 'relational citizenship' in the context of health care for people with long-term psychiatric problems; it is not by grace of *where* one is that one becomes a citizen (e.g. by not living in an institution any more). It is through a network of material and social relationship that one becomes part of a society. This network includes formal and informal contacts, and hence also speaks to notions of 'motivated sociality' as elaborated in the next chapter.
30 See Driessen's (2018b) notion of 'will-work', as an everyday practice that tries to influence what another person wants in order to achieve a shared wish to do something together. She coined this concept in her work on dementia care. The will to do something can emerge as something relational as well. See also Hume, 1978.
31 On tinkering, see Chapter 1 of Mol et al., 2010.
32 More on 'voice' follows in Chapter 10.

6
The particularity of universalism: life in the salons, or citizens against aesthetics

The previous chapters showed how aesthetic and moral values of everyday life were pushed into the background in eighteenth-century thought, and how universal principles and rule-based forms of ethics emerged. The abstract nature of ethical principles, as I discussed in my chapters on dignity and autonomy, is made concrete once these principles are put into practice. Any application of abstract principles or norms leads to concrete practices and effects. The outcome of this process may be hard to predict because general principles first need to be translated into practical activities. Consequently, upholding dignity can mean allowing patients to be unclean, and respecting autonomy can lead to better or worse outcomes for patients.

In this chapter I engage in a historical reading of the effects of using universal claims of rationality. I will show how these claims were made historically in relation to particular practices and concerns. Practices with universalist pretensions often push different forms of life to the margins, condemning them as merely promoting *aesthetic particularities*. At the same time, universalist claims downplay their own situatedness as well as the particularity of their aesthetic form. Claims of universality are often very specific and have exclusive rather than inclusive effects. I will demonstrate that it is important for social theorists to take aesthetic social practices into account. People organise themselves not only because of the rule of government but also because they cherish a certain way of living together. These aesthetic genres of activities are *motivated* forms of social organisation.[1]

Early social theorists wanted to channel individual morality and aesthetics or make these concepts irrelevant for understanding societies. In the chapter on dignity, I pointed out that one can understand very little about care practices if one glosses over the motivation of caregivers to do good for patients. A social theory that merely privatises passions, tastes and motivations, or turns them into a singular desire for self-enrichment, fails to acknowledge the unruly ways in which people – within their material milieus – organise themselves. Even if the motivations of citizens are not transparent to those who govern, the creation of motivated socialities is a powerful way for people to organise themselves. Aesthetic values, then, refer to certain types of social coherence or modes of ordering facts and values. People participate in certain practices because they like them or because they find beauty, happiness and inspiration in them. Acknowledging the role of motivated socialities brings the passions back into social theory. This also implies that social and political theorists must grapple with multiple forms of coherence rather than positing one universal type of rationality.

At the heart of modernity

This chapter reflects once again on the emergence of civil society, but this time it folds together events that took place in the eighteenth century with social theories that emerged after the Second World War. In both these periods the legitimacy and the governance of nation states was at stake. In the eighteenth century, as described in Chapter 4, there was a move from feudal societies and the rule of nobility towards more democratic republics in which rich citizens and traders wanted to be part of government. In post-Second World War theory, the guiding question was how the Holocaust could be prevented from ever happening again.

These concerns and their historical context are helpful for explaining how the aesthetic values of everyday life disappeared from academic thought, as well as for understanding why so much hope was invested in universalist theory.[2] Everyday aesthetic values are inherently empirically situated and embedded in concrete practices. They are connected to the senses, to what one can see, hear, taste, smell and so on. They are concrete. Principles, however, are formulated as universals: they are univocal and clearly defined, and can seemingly be easily applied in different situations to provide shared understandings. This makes them powerful tools for formulating normative programmes. Principles are used to distinguish things that are true and important from concrete trivialities, such as taste or appearance. However, when looking closely at universalism-in-practice, it becomes clear that this, too, is a style that is characteristic of particular, historically situated aesthetic genres.

Moreover, as I will show, these practices are, despite their claims of universality, intolerant of different forms of social life.

The questions of this chapter are: what is the relevance of the aesthetic values of everyday life in social or political theory and in governance? How does a universal notion of rationality become situated in concrete aesthetic practices? And finally, what different forms of sociality become visible when departing from the idea that there is one single rationality?

The emergence of the citizen

I will analyse how Jürgen Habermas has conceptualised the emergence of 'the public sphere' in France as well as the role of a new political figure, namely the eighteenth-century *citizen*.[3] The citizen, Habermas claims, sought to establish a free space to argue for the common good in universal terms. I will then present a feminist critique of Habermas's work by the philosopher Joan Landes. Landes argues that Habermas's conceptualisation of a single public sphere, however inclusively its claims might be formulated, marginalised other public spheres, which contained other styles and ways of organising than the public sphere that Habermas's new citizens had proposed. She is particularly interested in the salons, which were a form of semi-public life where well-to-do women ruled. The salons were criticised by both the old regime and by the new citizens. Landes shows that both lines of critique appealed to different types of masculinity that were mocked within salon practices. The rhetoric used by the citizens is revealing of how everyday aesthetic values became suspect. Transparency and clarity were seen as related to justice and truth and were played out against masquerades and literary games. The latter were equated with falseness and treachery, hence pitting aesthetics against truth and justice. Simultaneously, the vocabulary of republicanism, which appealed to the conception of muscular masculinity, saw itself as in threat of being corrupted by the seductive games and sly manipulations of the *salonnières*. These discourses provided a potent mixture of terms for condemning the unruly semi-public sphere of salon life.

The changing structure of the public sphere

Jürgen Habermas is a sociologist and philosopher from the Frankfurter Schule (Frankfurt School) in Germany, and his work should be read as belonging to this tradition. The Frankfurter Schule was founded at the beginning of the twentieth century by Theodor Adorno and Herbert Marcuse, and is famous for what later came to be known as critical theory. The most famous work of the Frankfurter Schule is the *Dialektik der Aufklärung* (*Dialectic of Enlightenment*), which was written by Max Horkheimer and Theodor Adorno while fleeing the Nazi regime. The first edition appeared in New York in 1944. Their work should be seen in the context of Nazism in Germany, and their theory was drenched in post-war concerns about democracy and reason 'after Auschwitz'.

Habermas's work should be understood in this critical tradition, and the stakes are therefore high. Democracy had to be redesigned in ways that would make it impossible for the atrocities of Nazi Germany ever to occur again. This normative imperative explains the interwovenness of Habermas's empirical work with the ambition to theorise about the normative conditions of democracy. He wanted to ascertain how the emergence of a new public sphere might inform present-day understandings of democracy. This goal resulted in an ambivalence in his writings, namely whether the public sphere was an empirical phenomenon or whether it could be theoretically interpreted or enriched as an ideal type of public sphere – that is, the public sphere as it should be. The public sphere is a concept to reflect on the conditions that are necessary for democracy. Habermas wanted to analyse the conditions under which democracy can function by focusing on procedures that facilitate unity and agreement between citizens – the *herrschaftsfreie Kommunikation* or *Dialog* (anti-authoritarian, non-hierarchical deliberation).

Habermas's first book, which is of central importance to this chapter, is *Strukturwandel der Öffentlichkeit* (*The Structural Change of the Public Sphere*).[4] This book was empirically historically oriented, much more so than his later normative book, the *Theorie des kommunikativen Handelns* (*Theory of Communicative Action*). In *Strukturwandel der Öffentlichkeit*, Habermas analyses the emergence of a new public sphere in eighteenth-century Paris. He describes this new public sphere as forming a rupture with the federal public sphere of the ancien régime. The creation of such a public sphere – by rich, predominantly male citizens who were traders and wanted to break the power of royalty and nobility – was necessary to take part in the governance of the nation. Habermas formulates the public sphere as a category between the state, the working life of civil society, and the private sphere of the family. He describes this public sphere – and this is crucial for understanding his book – as an assemblage of private persons who meet in public in order to develop a public opinion that represents the common good. The common good is formulated as the process of rational debate between equals.

From representation to deliberation

Habermas contrasts this emerging public sphere of new citizens with the representative sphere of the ancien régime. The notion of representativeness signifies the visual representations of the power of the feudal monarchy. In the ancien régime, it is the person and body of the king that is represented and that embodies and signifies his power. The nobility and members of the household of the king also represent this power by being present and visible in public. Power was directly *shown* to the public. The private sphere of the court and the relationships between those living there were a public affair. Courtly life was presented to the people through theatre, music, parades or other public manifestations. These public spectacles were concentrated in the courts and demonstrated royal splendour. Life in the courts was theatrically presented to the people.

In these times, Habermas argues, there was little possibility for people who were not nobility to have a say in how the country was run. The king was authoritarian and the people had to obey his imperatives of conduct. Public affairs were all about taste, style, appropriate behaviour and virtue. One had to dress and behave like royalty to participate. By adopting narratives about a general, civilised human being, the *honnête homme* – the gentleman or non-noble person – could attempt to gain entry to the courts. To do so, it also was important to develop knowledge, civilised manners and good taste – that is to say, *Bildung*. *Bildung* (education and cultivation) thus allowed for a limited form of social mobility. Non-aristocrats could become a member of the courts if they demonstrated excellence or good taste and, one might add, if they had good connections.

Habermas argues that, with the flourishing of commerce, the representative public sphere and its expressive forms became less important. Courtly life could become the target of mockery by rich emancipated citizens who considered the courts' imaginary worlds ridiculous and absurd.[5] The rise and flourishing of commerce benefited from direct channels of communication, such as the press, which were becoming more independent and gradually became an important factor in the creation of the new public sphere. The importance of the press was rooted in a growing exchange of letters for trade. The writing of letters increased as well as the writing of novels, which provided new forms of exchange between people. Civil society developed while commerce was privatised. Private persons were informed about national news through newspapers. They started to assemble in public to debate the pressing concerns of their times. And so, writes Habermas, the public sphere of the free citizens was born.

From private to public

It is important that Habermas describes the modern public sphere as emerging from the private sphere. For the argument of my book, it is also helpful that Habermas shows how the values of everyday life were framed as private rather than public concerns. This development started in the public sphere of literature, Habermas claims, where people deliberated and put forward public opinions about *art*. Habermas describes the literary sphere as a public sphere that has not yet reached its full potential because it does not address political matters.[6] But the emergence of the literary sphere was a first step towards the development of a type of 'civil identity' or, one could also say, towards the creation of the modern individual who could think for himself (yes, *him*). Such a subject is a necessary condition for conceptualising the public sphere. In these literary gatherings, Habermas claims, *arguments* were important, not just authority. This is a first step in the emancipation of the public away from the representative power of the king. Books were read not because some noble person recommended them but because readers liked these novels. The literary novel was an important vehicle for developing an understanding of a common humanity. Novels could be written in the form of a correspondence through letters that revealed individual 'movements of the soul'. Novels were an intimate kind of literature about individual contemplations and feelings that could be shared with fellow humans. Literature supported the ability to imagine an abstract or individual identity, which eventually paved the way for further reflections on freedom and equality as important characteristics of a general humanity.[7]

According to Habermas, the autonomy of the private individual was one of the pillars of the new society and its forms of citizenship. Citizens became emancipated and discovered and cultivated their individuality in private (see the privatisation of the passions described in Chapter 4). The Enlightenment trope of the emancipated[8] individual made it possible to form a public sphere in which each citizen could have their say. In Habermas's writings, the person with possessions (*bourgeois, homme*) served as the model for the private person who was the cornerstone of the public sphere. As such, Habermas writes, they could be the instruments for creating a rational public opinion. This 'public opinion' was created through deliberations between free and autonomous private persons.

With this achievement of a rational public opinion, it is clear that Habermas is writing as a hopeful social democrat rather than as an empirical researcher. Later critics have pointed out that the exclusion of different (poor) classes and women from the public sphere as well as the

Enlightened conceptualisation of personhood both cast doubt on the idea that this was truly an open sphere for public deliberation. Meanwhile, as critics have also argued, the notion of the human being became linked to the character of the *citizen*, which connected ideals of freedom, equality and humanism predominantly to a certain class of rich bourgeois citizens. The political emancipation of citizens during the Enlightenment and after was framed as *human* emancipation, but the definition of the human was a very particular one. Habermas has always countered this critique by pointing out that the *principles* of the deliberating public sphere allowed for the inclusion of everyone.[9] It was, Habermas claimed, only a matter of time before women and 'unwashed' citizens could also claim their right to participate in the public sphere, because they were included in the terms used to describe this sphere. So even though the public sphere was exclusionary in practice, the principles on which it was founded were not. It is not an exclusion *in principle* but a contingent historical imperfection, or so Habermas argued.

From the literary public sphere emerged a 'proper' public sphere, according to Habermas, after political concerns had become a topic of debate. This could lead to more informed opinions. The printed press was crucial here because public opinions could be published, which meant that the category of the public was expanded to include anyone who was able to read. Habermas analyses the French Revolution as a consequence of an emerging public opinion that citizens sought to institutionalise. Traders wanted to turn the deliberating public into an organisational foundation of the state through the institution of parliament. General interests, as formulated and argued for in public, would be able to exert control over the state and set its goals. Books of law were written and further elaborated upon through public debates that firmly inscribed the principle of equality and freedom to participate in it. Rational covenants and contracts between consenting partners were instated to replace the power and authority of the nobility. Private differences could be channelled through rational debate. Rather than being propelled by self-interest, Habermasian citizens strove for the common good by applying rational means. One could see this as the return of *public* morality through the search for the common good. Interests were not simply informed by a calculation of individual gain but by ideas of what was good for the nation as a whole. 'Rationality' in Habermas's theory is not an interest or calculation but a search for truth and justice.

Public opinion

It is important to understand how Habermas constructs the notion of public opinion. As the product of free argument and discussion, it is the key to the formation of new social relationships. Habermas distinguishes between different kinds of opinions, which he situates on a scale of varying degrees of publicness. There is 'public opinion' (*öffentliche Meinung*) and there are 'mere opinions' (*nicht-öffentliche Meinungen*). These 'mere opinions' are prejudices or beliefs that are often held unreflexively or tacitly. They are not purified and rationalised through open discussion. Habermas also calls these beliefs 'sub-literary opinions', and they are often related to morality or sexuality. People who hold these opinions may not even be aware of their existence or their implications as they are not publicly shared and scrutinised.

A sub-set of these mere opinions are 'experiences' of which people are aware. These are not yet rational because they have not been debated in public. Another sub-set is that of the 'post-literary opinions' that are overt and shared as well as taken for granted. These opinions are about matters of taste, fashion, norms, traditions and human relationships. One could say, in the terms of this book, that these are about everyday understandings of the good life. These opinions emerge from the intimate sphere of private life. They may be discussed among people, but this is not done in the presence of a general public audience. Private discussions are not brought to a conclusion. They are held without obligation and take place merely because of certain habits and beliefs.

These half-baked opinions are sharpened through public debate, which transforms them into a rational public opinion. For this to happen, an open communicative procedure for the exchange of information is necessary. This idea would lead Habermas to write the *Theorie des kommunikativen Handelns* (*Theory of Communicative Action*), in which the conditions for *herrschaftsfreie Diskussion* (power-free debate) are formulated. The procedures of public debate can be seen as the Habermasian variant of Smith's invisible hand; private striving is transformed into rational goals for all. Here, however, the hand of public debate is not invisible or misleading. Rather, it is transparent: a system of argumentation that can be witnessed and criticised by everyone. The power of rational arguments is that they will result in the same conclusions for everyone and that they are accountable to all.

Earlier ideals concerning the expression of public opinions about political matters were criticised, for instance, by Alexis de Tocqueville and

John Stuart Mill. They worried about the role of 'the masses' in the public arena. They feared there would be too many contradictory interests, which would cause a *majority* to dictate decisions in public debates rather than decisions being made through rational agreement. In his book, Habermas agrees that this is what ultimately happened, but he calls this the *demise* of the public sphere. He ends his book with a description of the continuing breakdown of the public sphere, wherein consumption takes precedence over reading and the private sphere is increasingly dominated by the state. Advertising replaces rational argument and causes sentimentality and consumerism to take the place of rationality. Similarly disruptive, he states, are party politics, which institutionalise the interests of specific groups of people. Although surveys are conducted, these only reveal the 'mere opinions' of the public, which are not processed and developed through public debate. Habermas's sombre conclusion in the *Strukturwandel der Öffentlichkeit* is that present-day citizens have become private consumers rather than public debaters. Rationality was not been achieved, and its ideal served critical theory but did not lead to ideal societies. This is a situation in need of repair, and for which Habermas provided the theoretical blueprint in his later work.

The public sphere of the salons

It is clear that Habermas's normative goals interfered with his empirical descriptions. The philosopher Joan Landes took up the challenge of criticising Habermas's theoretical ideals in her book *Women and the Public Sphere in the Age of the French Revolution*. She brought new empirical descriptions to light and thus proposed a re-scription of this period in history as well as a different perspective on how this new form of society was created.[10] She formulated a counter-story to the success and attractiveness of the public sphere of citizens. Similar to Habermas, Landes analyses the transition from ancien régime to civil society, but she explicitly contrasts her feminist analysis of this transition with the analysis presented by Habermas in the *Strukturwandel der Öffentlichkeit*. Her most important critique is that Habermas does not acknowledge that the public sphere of citizens is created through the explicit exclusion of women. This exclusion, she claims, is not a mere historical imperfection waiting to be corrected, but an artefact of the very terms used to conceptualise the public sphere. The exclusion of women was a condition for its emergence, a *sine qua non* rather than a promise that would be fulfilled later. Landes also notes that is important to take note of the gendered language of republicanism. Republicanism referred to the ancient Greek *polis* where virtuous and masculine men were supported by republican mothers whose task it was to give birth to and take care of the next generation.

Landes proposes that the salons were an alternative public sphere, and in doing so changes the terms of the debate. She shows how the conceptualisation of the public sphere – as a rational and accessible debate between citizens – is a highly stylised idea of *just one* of the 'publics' at that time, and one that was far less coherent than Habermas would like to maintain. Landes analyses public spheres (plural) by examining their 'cultural and political forms of representation' as well as the ways in which they 'organise experience'. She explicitly includes codes of behaviour and etiquette as well as styles and conventions of speaking and dressing that serve to distinguish one social group from another. Put in the words of this book, Landes analyses the aesthetic values embedded in social or public life. She argues that the citizen style is just one particular style among others, and one that is particularly intolerant of 'other' styles. Landes also shows that the salons contained aesthetic social practices that were affected by the shift from ancien régime to civil society.

Ancien régime

In her analysis, Landes also discusses modes of cultural representation during the ancien régime in France, and in particular life at the courts of Louis XIV. The body of the king represented the hierarchical organisation as well as the unity of the nation. The king was the representation of a regime that was organised in a personal and patriarchal way. The most important means of cultural and political representation is, Landes argues, the *icon* rather than symbols and texts. Like Habermas, she points to the directness of iconic representation – the king *is* the state and his vassals *are* his power. Either they must be present in person or images of them will make them present. The king is represented on coins, in paintings and through insignias that mark people's rank and relationship to the king. At the court, spectacles such as coronations, plays and parties were organised to highlight the grandeur and power of the king. Landes argues that the court functioned as a theatre. The personal life of the king and the private affairs of his vassals had consequences for the entire nation. If you wanted to gain influence in government, the court was the place to be. You had to become part of the royal icon.

Landes also analyses the gendered subtexts of the representative power of the courts. Female influence could become possible because men and women were equally powerless. Maintaining good relationships with noble ladies and remaining in their favour was important in court intrigues. They cultivated conventions of good taste and influenced the making or breaking of the careers of aspiring participants. Republicanist thought, Landes shows, criticised this unmanly subjection to women's whims as the 'effeminisation' of men.

The salons

The salons emerged in the seventeenth century and were dominated by noble women. In the seventeenth century, only members of the aristocracy could join these salons. This changed in the eighteenth century, when lineage became less important. To join salons one had to display erudition, artistic capacity and an ability to fit in with the salon *style*. This was a breach with the ways of the ancien régime. Non-aristocratic newcomers were welcomed and were taught new manners and habits. They learned to obey codes of behaviour and to use particular ways of speaking.

The salons were strongly influenced by the tastes and preferences of female members of the aristocracy and bourgeoisie. They formed a 'polite society' with its own styles and codes of conduct. Currying favour with the *salonnières* was crucial, while romantic engagements could also be helpful as they enabled one to enter salons through personal relationships with insiders. Important in the salons was to see and be seen, to be able to engage in quick and witty conversation or word games, and to display a certain flair or be knowledgeable about literature. In the salons, novels by and correspondence with popular authors were read aloud and discussed.

In the salons art was of crucial value. Here, 'literature passed into life, and life into literature', according to Landes, and imagination was therefore of great importance.[11] Dressing-up parties and masquerades were among the pleasures offered by the salons. One could dress up as a favourite character from a novel or partake in plays. Appearance and illusion were, as in the courts, nurtured and cherished. A commitment to the *particular* – to jokes, plays and references that were only recognisable to those in the know – was one of the pleasures of life in the salons. Imitating and playing with particulars was highly regarded, which was in strong contrast to the strict laws of symmetry and the eternal values of truth of classicism that were popular at the time. The Rococo style suited salon life with its abundance of curls, curves and details.

Salons under fire

Salons were criticised at the time in two ways. First, there were the new citizens who articulated their critique using a liberalist, revolutionary vocabulary. They loathed the opacity of the salons' particularist style and posited transparency and universality as an alternative. They also promoted the universal principles of equality, freedom and fraternity. In the emerging press, they criticised the salons for being 'effeminate' and rejected the ambiguous language that was used there. These citizens saw the salons as an extension of courtly culture and were suspicious and antipathetic to them for this reason.

The second style of critique was articulated using the vocabulary of republicanism. Republicanism is informed by virtues and notions of masculinity that were borrowed from ancient Greece. According to republicanist thinking, the salons represented luxury, which was tantamount to corruption. Men who attended salons were seen as weak and effeminate, and therefore a potential threat to the nation. Virtuous public men conformed to the style of the salon out of politeness and an eagerness to please the ladies rather than to stand proud and defend the nation. The ideal republican male was a brave warrior. The ideas about romantic love that circulated in salons were thought to weaken the institution of marriage, which republicanists considered a virtuous institution that ensured procreation and heredity. Heredity was of great concern because money was the entry ticket to the new class of citizens. In contrast, *précieuses* (*salonnières*) considered marriage a matter of convenience or a strategic game. This was unacceptable to republicanists. They saw marriage as a pillar of the nation, where virtuous mothers would give birth to and raise the new warriors and statesmen of tomorrow. A strong nation starts with a strong family.

The playfulness and artificiality of the language used by the *précieuses* clashed with the classic understanding of language as a natural means to straightforwardly speak the truth, which was held both by republicanists and citizens. The analysis hence juxtaposes two styles of aesthetics. Word games, irony and jokes about important masculine words were not appreciated by the serious and virtuous representatives of the nation. Their concerns were informed by the virtues of classical art, where naturalness, transparency and universal principles were valued over artificiality and pleasure, and where particularities were rejected in favour of universals. Clearly, to create a virile state, women had to stay at home and become mothers. Landes shows how the female public sphere of the salons was seen as a threat to the state both by republicanists and citizens. They deliberated in a style of discourse that paired citizenship with masculinity. Female influence had to be placed in a supportive role to the state, that is, in the private sphere.

New forms of representation, different public spheres

Landes shows that, with the advent of civil society, new patterns of political and cultural representation also emerged. These new forms of representation were not organised around images but around texts. Texts did not merely make things present, they also conveyed important values and therefore functioned as a particular kind of rational public debate. Print media and the emergence of newspapers transformed oral culture into a literary culture. Anonymous pamphlets and newspapers started to circulate, and people could read these in newly founded libraries and reading rooms. Printed books could also be borrowed in these places, which allowed the public sphere to grow even more. Printed material was also read aloud to the illiterate, which made printed words an effective means of communicating with these audiences as well.

Textual representations were more abstract and less personal than the iconic representations of the ancien régime. Texts often touched on topics that were more abstract. Written texts discussed abstract laws and the rights of the citizen rather than merely making the body of the king present. The universalist style of these writings is relevant to Habermas's arguments about the rise of public opinion, which was influenced by the many conversations, texts and deliberations about the common good. This universalist style, as noted above, was also part of the critique of the salons because citizens associated this style with the ancien régime.

This analysis resonates with Habermas's arguments, but Landes shows how yet another literary tradition also emerged at the time. Although there were many newspapers, pamphlets and books, there were many poor writers who could not make a living from their literary or journalistic work. If they could not find a patron among the aristocracy or in the salons, they became impoverished and started to form a kind of underground public sphere that existed alongside the spheres of the salons and of the writing and deliberating citizens. Such impoverished writers met in cafés, and wrote anti-aristocratic, sexist and pornographic pamphlets that mocked the ladies of the salons.

The style of writing of the private reading cultures in bourgeois houses was about private concerns, such as pedagogy and self-disclosure.

Landes points out how rather than addressing general humanity, hyper-individualising reading conventions emerged. Rousseau is an example of an author in this genre of writing. His texts are characterised by the relationship between two individuals in which one candidly reveals things about themselves to another. This is an earnest as well as a sentimental and moralistic exercise. Self-disclosure, the process through which a transparent and authentic self is constructed, was the predominant style of these new texts. This type of literature was also critical of the salons. The fashionable, inauthentic and playful culture of the salons was considered an offence to people who thought of themselves as serious and authentic.

By highlighting the existence of these various groups of public figures and their different vocabularies, Landes fragments the coherence of the public sphere and its forms of representation. She shows that there were pluriform cultures of reading and writing as well as different and oppositional public spheres. The universalist public sphere presented by Habermas is but one of this multitude of spheres. Landes also asserts that class interests particularised universalism and rationality. Her argument, which is crucial for my book, is that *the universalist-style public sphere of citizens can only exist by ignoring or opposing other public spheres* and other styles of representation. Universalist language dismisses particularities, including the 'particular' public spheres of the salons and of impoverished writers. By declaring one style of deliberation to be universal and rational, other styles were condemned to being mere particularities that could not be justified by recourse to rationality and reason.

As a consequence, Landes argues, reason came to oppose femininity. Femininity came to signify play, pleasure, erotics, artificiality, style, appearance and particularity. Reason, she argues, has its own aesthetics: transparency, authenticity, seriousness, masculinity and universality. Reason is about principles such as truth and justice, which were defined in opposition to private tastes. The rhetoric employed by citizens was about *unmasking*, about bare truth rather than disguised pleasure and fancy dress. Communication had to be direct and truthful and geared towards uncovering truth. This approach was a clear critique of the ancien régime and the female privileges that it upheld. The 'personal-public' sphere of the salons – involving casual conversations and handwritten notes – had to preserve itself against the anonymous and uniform public opinions that were expressed through the printed press. The opposition was one between different aesthetic styles rather than Habermas's juxtaposition of reason and aesthetics.

The aesthetics of politics

Both the salons and the public sphere of citizens can be understood as *motivated* forms of sociality. This form of sociality was not organised by the government or another authority, but instead argued against these authorities or presented an alternative that was based on people's motivations and inspirations. The ancien régime that was resisted by these publics was a very particular structure of absolute governance. Its regime of truth and power was aesthetically enacted through life at the courts as well as through occasional wars and massacres, which happened for reasons that were hard to explain to outsiders of the royal court. The king and the courts *were* the state. There was no space for individual citizens who were, strictly speaking, not citizens but part of the body of the king. They did not have an identity or authority of their own. It is for this reason that Habermas needed to show that citizens are private persons. Framing citizens as *emancipated* individuals who can speak for themselves is a way of granting them a degree of agency as well as a rightful claim to political influence. Truth and reason have clear authority here.

The salons, as another motivated form of social life with their own aesthetics and beauty, took particularity as their preferred style. They conceived of salon life as a work of art, and artistic pleasure was the primary motivation of *salonnières* and visitors of the salons to participate. The moral effects of salon life may have been accidental rather than intentional, but the salons did provide opportunities for social mobility. People could become part of salon life by playing along with the games of the *salonnières* and by adopting their aesthetic styles. Aspiring participants had to cultivate their appearance and way of speaking in order to be of interest to the *salonnières* and to gain access to the salons.

Speaking as a way to relate to truth was not a big issue in the salons, but it was acknowledged that intimate knowledge could lead to power over others. Salon life involved games of inside knowledge as well as puzzles and intrigues. Salon life was akin to a play that participants could act in and through which they could display their creativity and wit. Indeed, the salons represented a good life that was to a large extent aestheticized. Their purpose was to please participants, but participation could also lead to upward mobility and wealth. Yet the moral relationships of salon life extended mostly to insiders. Nonetheless, it is important to note that it was the aesthetics of salon life that brought the visitors of the salons together and that led to the creation of a social group with some influence. The salons, one could say, performed politics through aesthetic means.

Aspiring citizens, however, resorted to the use of serious classicising language and identified with the aesthetics of straight lines, universal principles and naked truth. It is not surprising that Habermas considered citizens' deliberations as a form of striving for rationality, and eventually, if the right procedures had been followed, truth and justice. Habermas wanted to create better terms and conditions for democracy by grounding them in a singular rationality. In this way debates could be brought to a conclusion and disagreements could be solved. However, Landes argues, their universalist regime of truth excluded those who did not want to subject themselves to its rules. The public sphere of citizens provided a closed system with clear rules and outcomes. There was no space for alternative forms of rationality, such as those geared towards pleasure. The salons were seen as artificial, false and untrue. The aesthetic rationale of the salons was unacceptable to the new citizens. It was rejected by the new citizens because there could only be one single rationality, one which led to agreement rather than play.[12] This also implied that there could only be one form of aesthetics that was seen as acceptable to politics. Yet this was not recognised as an aesthetic form because the targets were justice and truth.

Habermas argued that the exclusion of some groups from the public sphere may have been an empirical truth, but also that this exclusion was not a normatively necessary one. Everyone who felt excluded, he reasoned, could appeal to the principles of freedom and equality to gain access. His conclusion is that there was nothing wrong with the principles of the public sphere. However, Landes shows that this is only true if one *accepts the terms* of the new citizens. Accepting the principles of the public sphere of citizens was not possible according to the terms of the *salonnières*. If they wanted to participate in the public sphere, they would have needed to give up their games and pleasures and become earnest pursuers of the common good rather than playful pursuers of particular tastes. They would have to dress differently and ignore matters of gender. The various styles of public life and what these could reveal were incompatible; one could not exist within the other.

Principles and the values of everyday life: theory versus practice?

Landes argues that the abstract vocabulary of citizenship, which centred on freedom, equality and fraternity, was supplemented by a gendered vocabulary of virile and virtuous masculinity as well as a specific conceptualisation of women as mothers of the new citizens. Warfare and heroics were also an explicit part of this vocabulary. Under the guise of neutral and transparent speech, a specific class (bourgeoisie) and type of people (male owners, traders) were granted the ability to speak 'for everyone' (the common good) in a language that was highly specific and that privileged one particular style of thought over another.

What failed to emerge in historical practice is the singularity achieved by a power-free discussion.[13] Landes's argument, in contrast, centres on the role of aesthetic values. Habermas struggles with acknowledging the role of aesthetic values because they do not fit well with his ideas about the universal rationality of public discourse. I will unpack this issue a bit more to show the problems that aesthetic values pose to a universalist discourse. Habermas separated *herrschaftsfreie Kommunikation* (power-free discussion) into three different spheres or discourses: truth, justice and expression. Although Habermas mentions that these spheres all come together in concrete speech acts, he nonetheless classifies and analyses various utterings as belonging to different spheres by making a theoretical distinction between three kinds of utterings. The first are *descriptive* utterings, which relate to the objective world. The criterion for their validity is truth, namely that what is said should be the case. Descriptive utterings are used in a theoretical *Diskurs* (a verbal discourse). The second kind are *normative* utterings, which relate to the social world and its norms. Here, the validity criterion is *rightness* (justice). Normative utterings are used in a 'practical *Diskurs*'. The third kind are *expressive* utterings, which Habermas relates to a subjective inner world. Their validity criterion is authenticity. Because of the connection between authenticity and subjective interiority, expressive utterings cannot become relevant to rational discussion. One cannot check the truthfulness of people's interiority though the procedures of public deliberation. According to Habermas, 'expressive' utterings are hence part of a *Kritik* (critique) rather than a *Diskurs*. A critique is not a dialogue but rather an *expression* even if the authenticity of the speaker may be criticised.

In his *Theorie des kommunikativen Handelns*, Habermas visibly struggles with expressive utterings, which he uses to describe the characteristics of art. Habermas interprets art in a particular modernist way, namely as being the most individual expression of the most individual emotion. Art remains in the realm of values and mere opinions that are, according to Habermas, not as general as norms. Norms can be intersubjectively formulated and recognised. Values, on the contrary, are private things that relate to the inner state of a person who might express this inner state through art. Such values are difficult to verify or argue for because the human subject who holds these values is the only one with access to their own inner world.[14] Authenticity or truthfulness, which according to Habermas are the validating criteria for expressive speech-acts, can only be judged by seeing if the subject *acts* according to their expressions. Hence Habermas claims that psychotherapists and art critics need to unmask inauthentic utterings – that is, statements that are not truthful and that serve different purposes, which are perhaps only known to the inauthentic speaker.[15] Expressive utterings are individual rather than social, subjective rather than intersubjective. They are made by isolated individuals rather than by socially and culturally embedded persons. Aesthetic values, then, are private, even idiosyncratic, rather than social values for Habermas. This is in line with modernist understandings of aesthetics. In Habermas's work, aesthetics take on a particular meaning, especially when compared to Adam Smith's writings on the passions and the embeddedness of aesthetic values in conventions.

Landes's analysis, on the contrary, shows that people aesthetically shape the practices of daily life. Her 'turn to practice' transforms universalism into a particular style that is characteristic of a certain group of people and their way of speaking. Hence, she makes universalism one particular style amid several others. Universalism, then, becomes a particular style characteristic, as is seen in, for example, classical art. Here we find a profound clash between these two philosophers. It is very important for Habermas to deny that the public sphere involves the interests of particular groups. It was crucial for him to speak about universal 'humans' and about universal truth in the singular form. This was a way to create a potentially rational unity for the nation through which one could hold debates and collectively conclude what would be good to do. Committing atrocities would never become acceptable through rational deliberations. But Landes's examples show that this unity is a theoretical unity rather than an empirical one; the purported universal language remains both exclusive and particular in practice rather than inclusive to all.

Individual differences are, again, both essential and trivial to thinking about the public sphere of the new citizens. Their differences are essential because they inform the psychological make-up of the emancipated, enlightened and rich subjects who are inclined to achieve the shared goal of finding the common good through rational deliberation. Individual differences are trivial in the sense that their concrete content or substance is of no interest. These are private matters, and they can only become of common interest through the procedure of rational deliberation. Individual passions and beliefs are private, whereas the public good is general and shared. The common good is cleansed of chit-chat about literature even if private reading practices had been formative to establishing what counts as the common good. Aesthetic and moral differences are safely contained within the private sphere.

However, the historical case of the salons – and this counts for the practices of citizens as well – shows that aesthetic styles could unite different groups of people, and that such styles granted salon participants a degree of influence over the lives they busily sought to craft. Rather than being mere trivialities, aesthetic values formed the core of what made the salons a type of public sphere, and this was also the reason why salons were criticised. Aesthetic values hence provided an important means for social analysis and political organisation even if these analyses and organisations were styled differently than the parliaments promoted by the citizens.[16]

To conclude: aesthetic and universalist particularities

What is made clear in the discussion between Habermas and Landes – and, by extension, between citizens and *salonnières* – is the precarious but nonetheless important role that is played by aesthetic values in social theory. For citizens, aesthetic and moral values should remain safely contained within the private sphere. Aesthetic values are personal matters of style that are difficult to judge, whereas questions about governance and the procedures to achieve justice and truth are more important. These procedures should be devoid of aesthetic particularities in order to be transparent. And in this context, transparency is not seen as an aesthetic qualification but as a characteristic of truth. Salon gatherings, however, are an example of a social practice that is explicitly oriented towards a particular form of aesthetics. Here aesthetic values are social values that organise the social practice found in the salons. And this aesthetic has a different – if ironic – understanding of truth and morality.

In this chapter, the empirical grounding of abstract normative concepts has achieved three things. First, it revealed that citizens' practices are also characterised by a particular type of aesthetics. These were concrete, historically situated practices despite being inspired by notions of universality and equality. Such empirical historical practices come with a particular aesthetic style. Second, empirical analysis showed that separating aesthetics, ethics and truth and assigning them each to a particular realm is not possible when studying concrete practices. Landes notes that the aesthetic characteristics of citizens' practices are intrinsically linked to citizens' understandings of truth and justice. The same goes for the practices found in the salons, which were not merely aesthetic practices but also practices that interfered with particular notions of truth and justice, however ironic. Third, citizens' universal claims rested on the assumption that a singular truth as well as a singular model of justice could be achieved if people with different opinions 'refined' those opinions through rational debate. Aesthetics, in this view, remained more or less particular to a particular person. The shift to practices, however, allowed for the articulation of different aesthetic social coherences that each had their own particular style for approaching truth and maintaining appropriate relationships with others.

The struggle between the two forms of social practice – salons and citizens' public gatherings – was interpreted by Landes as involving important matters of aesthetics, and can therefore be understood as confrontations between different everyday-life values. This distinction pitted seriousness against play, authenticity against artificiality, transparency against masquerade, and masculinity against femininity. Thinking about social organisation as an aesthetic style was, for universalists, a dangerous move because it acknowledged the difficulty of verifying statements and opened up the possibility of disturbing the principle of equality. The possibility of rational agreement is threatened when participants do not articulate differences 'in the same terms'. Aesthetic values did not promise solidarity of all with all but instead foregrounded differences and incompatibilities.

The idea of a singular and universal reason was empirically challenged by demonstrating the existence of different styles of reasoning that each had their own internal coherence and aesthetic form. This once more emphasises the importance of aesthetics for understanding social life and the analytical power of this category. For the purposes of this book, it can now be argued that the modernist containment of aesthetic values within the private sphere blinded social theorists to acknowledging alternatively motivated social assemblages as well as the situatedness of historical practices that made claims to a single rationality. The public performances of the citizens, as well as those of the *salonnières*, could be analysed as motivated forms of sociality that were brought about by the appeal and pursuit of things that are of value to their respective participants. Aesthetic values are social values. They are not universally strived for but they are nonetheless of great importance both to the creation of certain forms of sociality and to their change.

Coda: individual citizens in the community

The notion of citizenship has been a powerful emancipatory concept from modernity until our present day and age, and it has become central to contemporary care practices as well. Citizenship is connected with notions of autonomy and equality, which are cornerstones of present-day thinking about what constitutes a good and inclusive society. The 'individual' and the 'human being' have become the central characters of modernity, but with a particular understanding of what it means to be an individual. A key point is the characteristic that all individuals or human beings share, namely their equality and capacity to reason as well as their reasonable ways of distinguishing between their passions and particularities and the common good. This heritage of terms is reflected in present-day care practices, which makes it difficult to discuss differences in ways of living and reasoning.

A difference with the era of Adam Smith is that the understanding of the individual has shifted from being a 'natural' thing that could be explained by psychology or evolutionary biology towards being a cognitive and social being that is able to identify a common good. In this chapter, citizenship was defined by an explicitly prescriptive normative theory. The imperative was to treat people as citizens and to strive for citizenship so that they could be governed by rationality rather than by passions or other notions of beauty that may be unappealing to some, and difficult to justify or verify. Living as a citizen implies leading a life as a private and free individual who achieves their potential as a cognitive being that is eager to reason about the common good.

Examining care practices shows that there is also variation in conceptualising citizenship as a prescriptive ideal. Present-day citizens have variable characteristics, which can range from the skills they acquire to the personal tastes or preferences they develop, as well as the relationships they form.[17] In care practices, however, ideals of citizenship and humanity, and the hierarchies that come with these categories, are transformed by caregivers who focus on the morality of everyday practices that are 'good enough' for a specific situation. These practices are better on some days rather than others, and never completely succeed in eliminating bad, difficult or imperfect things. In the 'messiness' of everyday practices, hard dichotomies and hierarchies between terms – such as reason and passion, fact and normativity, nature and culture – dissolve. Studying the negotiations of aesthetic values that are made in everyday life shows that situations are constantly re-scribed in order to be dealt with, and that different understandings of what counts as a problem or a solution are continuously evaluated and adjusted.

There is a need for collectivity among patient-citizens and their caregivers, but this is not a community that purifies arguments through debates about a common good. Instead, this community works together to weigh different values and conventions against each other to solve day-to-day problems and to bring them to a temporary conclusion. Conversations about everyday ethics and attempts to shape a good life do not result in general rules but in provisional problem descriptions and solutions that may later be put to the test. Experience in doing this sensitises participants to what might be important in difficult situations.

A variety of genres

Similar to the public spheres of the nineteenth century, in care, different practices are characterised by particular aesthetic styles. I already described a tolerance for dirt in psychiatry, an imperative for cleanliness in elderly care as well as virtuous non-intervention in care for people with learning disabilities. This variation is why it is important to distinguish between different styles of care and the different forms of the good they entail. This is particularly the case when the question is not how to cure people from disease or disability, but how to support disabled or ill subjects to live their everyday lives in good ways. What is the place for different aesthetic styles in care, ones that can be smelly, intoxicated or not so clever?[18] What effects might flow from these different styles, and how can we evaluate them?

More broadly, an attention to the aesthetic styles found in the organisation of social life calls for further exploration of the terms as well as the material and social relationships that people use to create social forms. Aesthetic values unite people, even if they do not unite all people at the same time or through the same means. Understanding motivated socialities is important for imagining possible forms of living together and for finding new ways of shaping such assemblages. The question of how people want to live together with others is a fair and productive question to pose to 'new citizens'. It involves exploring how they may want to be social beings as well as members and co-shapers of particular aesthetic communities. This is a fundamentally different endeavour compared to the demand that they adapt to the given norms of a society in which they are only tolerated to 'participate as citizens' without being able to establish its conditions.[19] If social conditions cannot accommodate newcomers, chances are small that their new social life will become a success.

Rehabilitating everyday life aesthetic values and using them to understand social life gives rise to a new question for social theory, namely *how we might live with different coherences* ('rationalities', 'aesthetic genres', 'modes of ordering') even if these may seem unwise, unappealing or dirty.[20] Or, as Isabelle Stengers puts it, how can we live with an *ecology of practices* rather than with an assumed universal whole or unity?[21] What are the implications if we no longer organise society with one truth or a single understanding of goodness in mind, but instead live in a world that includes different forms of understanding? This is particularly important when 'bad things' cannot be resolved and instead must be lived with. This can be done for better or for worse, and particularly if the better or worse can be determined along different parameters.

These are complex questions that I must leave here for now. Chapters 10, 11 and 12 will continue to discuss how we may develop research practices that can accommodate the things that people value, particularly when they cannot easily 'make their voices heard'. This, as we have already learned, is a quite limited way of determining what might be of value to anyone, but particularly for those who have difficulty in thinking about or expressing themselves. But before that discussion, the next cluster of chapters will expand my analysis of everyday aesthetic values as social in their origin and effect, as well as what this implies for conceptualising 'a good life'.

Notes

1 I use the notion of *motivated* social organisation in the sense that such a form of organisation is driven by inspired individuals. It is unspecified where the action should be located, namely in the individual who is motivated or inspired, or from the cause that inspires or motivates it. More on this in the next chapter. See also Latour & Girard Stark, 1999.
2 Note that the Nazi regime also had its particular aesthetic preferences.
3 Habermas, 1962.
4 Habermas, 1962.
5 Note that irony and mockery are aesthetic disqualifications of the nobility rather than rational arguments against them. A good case for the importance of honour as a form of aesthetic (rather than rational) justification for some practices to exist and others to be rejected is made by Kwame Anthony Appiah, 2008.
6 See also the work of Hannah Arendt, 1958, in which the household figures as a sphere of necessity and reproduction, and where the promise of being human is fulfilled through becoming a political being. This hierarchy makes it difficult to study care practices. See, for a tasty critique, Mol, 2021.
7 This generality could denote reason, but also sentimentality, as Rousseau's work shows (1979). Enlightenment and Romanticism go hand in hand, but one should be aware of the existence of a private space for the sentiments in contrast to the public space for reason during these periods.
8 *Mundigkeit* is the term Kant used to describe this (1996).

9. Habermas made exceptions for 'irrational' people, such as children and disturbed individuals, in order to uphold his particular ideal of rationality. See below.
10. Landes, 1988. This mode of argumentation fits with the one used in this book, bringing events and situations to theory to analyse where they would make it necessary to amend theory.
11. Landes, 1988, p. 25.
12. In a similar way, a logic of universal rationality was to protect nations from the horrors of Nazism.
13. See Habermas, 1981, for more on his *Theorie des kommunikativen Handelns*.
14. Habermas, 1981, p. 422.
15. Habermas, 1981, p. 445.
16. Note that there are also aesthetically oriented forms of sociality with a less ironic relationship to truth, as I will describe in the next chapter. This truth is, again, always partial and situated (see, on situated knowledge, Haraway, 1988).
17. It is tempting to engage in empirical *psychology* as well: see Pols et al., 2019. For an analysis of the social and political implications of notions of citizenships, see Chapters 3 and 5, and Pols, 2006.
18. Habermas explicitly states that madness should be excluded from discussions about citizenship, which according to him is a failure of the capacity to express things authentically.
19. Pols, 2016. And see Part III of this book for how such ideas might work out in research practices that are established 'on the terms' of the research subjects.
20. Populism poses a comparable question.
21. See Stengers, quoted in Ceci & Purkis, 2021, p.15. Ceci and Purkis use this framework to interpret dementia care at home as a 'practice among practices', where people have to negotiate different forms of formal and informal care with situated problems.

Part II
Reconceptualising the good life

The cluster of chapters in Part I analysed the demise of everyday-life values in social theory alongside their stubborn reappearance in practice. This second cluster of three chapters further develops my conceptualisation of the good life by attending to the social nature of aesthetic values in everyday life. This endeavour once again puts the relationship between sociality and individuality on the agenda. Each conceptualisation of sociality implies a particular understanding of its constituent parts, and vice versa, each conceptualisation of individuality has implications for how individuals might live together and form a sociality.

The chapters develop the theme of how aesthetic values, which have been conceived as individual and private values from modernity until today, can be understood as social values. In Chapter 6 I showed with the case of the salons and the citizens how aesthetic values organised and motivated concrete social practices. The central empirical focus in Part II is a case study of women who have lost their hair due to chemotherapy (Chapters 7 and 9). This case highlights the importance of aesthetic values in everyday life because hair loss can be seen as an aesthetic problem. Hair loss is a problem that unfolds as a social problem in both its origin and effect. My analysis shows that aesthetic problems in everyday life are not just individual matters of taste. The image of a bald woman resonates with extremely negative imaginaries from the past (witch hunts, punishment, dehumanisation) and with conventions about what a woman should look like in the Netherlands and elsewhere.

The women in my study notice how their changed appearance affects their social life. Their hairless heads somehow present a more confronting truth about cancer than narratives can achieve. Having no hair is more detrimental to the women's social relationships than having a disease that is invisible to outsiders. My analysis highlights the creative efforts that these women undertake to repair or maintain their social lives by recreating their individuality and femininity. Individuality appears here as a *state of worth*, a valued state that must be achieved and accomplished every day anew. It does not refer to the fixed or given entity that is often called an individual.

Analysing individuality – as a valued state that must be achieved and recreated again and again, rather than as a given entity – casts a different light on studies that take the individual, or individual bodies, as a starting point. How do separate individual entities relate to each other? How different is one individual from others, and in what ways is this the case? If an individual is neither unique nor identical to another, say, by sharing the same physiology or the same drive towards self-interest, autonomy or the common good, then how may we think about their relationships? My analysis of the values of everyday life shows that aesthetic motivations create or represent social coherences, such as was the case among the *salonnières* and citizens striving for emancipation and political influence. Individuals, however, may partake in different aesthetic genres or forms of sociality. These motivated socialities link different individuals together by simultaneously connecting them to some people while separating them from others.

So how might one think about the good life, and in what sense can one say it is good? With these questions in mind, I read the final lectures by Michel Foucault, in which he explored conceptualisations of the good life by examining forms of living the true life in ancient Greece. There are multiple resonances between these lectures and the methodological approach taken in my book. Foucault approaches the good life as a practice of everyday life (*bios*), which took on different social forms in ancient Greece and in later humanist practices of the good life. The good life in these different practices was lived by way of examining it and teaching others about it. Crucially, the good life in ancient Greece implied an interconnectedness and inseparability between the good (the ethical relationships with others and oneself as a moral subject: *ethos*), the true (to examine the good life, and to speak truth about it: *parrhesia*) and the aesthetic (a state of worth that one can strive for and put to the test as well as techniques for creatively giving shape to everyday life and practising its truth in 'care for the self': *melei moi* or *epimeleia*). This interconnectedness between truth, goodness and aesthetics resonates with the idea that describing a practice is also a way of re-scribing it, that is, connecting what is taken to be true or problematic about a certain situation with what can be done about this situation and how. In Chapter 6 I already signalled the impossibility of separating beauty from truth and justice when empirically studying practices.

Foucault's work explicitly addresses the aesthetic dimension of practices, albeit briefly, as his interest is primarily in the good life as a *true* life. Understanding this aesthetic dimension helps to move away from a *prescriptive* normativity, which states how everyone *should* live a good life, towards an enquiring approach that asks what the good life is in particular situations and whether this is something that can be researched by analysing how people discuss, cultivate, maintain and test what they believe the good life to be. In this manner, striving for the good can become part of social scientific studies again, without an a priori *judgement* of the goodness or the *effect* of such efforts. Three mutually related sets of questions may therefore be addressed when studying the good life as a practice: what kind of truth is lived (or enacted) in such practices? How is everyday life oriented towards forms of the good both in relation to the self and others? In what way is everyday life aesthetically shaped, and what notions of appropriateness inform this process?[1]

The variety of social forms of practising the good life found in ancient Greece were informed by the different values that were held by different 'schools', such as the Cynics, the Stoics and so on. The philosophers of these schools practised and examined the *exemplary* good life and taught and questioned others about their lives. It is, however, the subject-position of these *others* that I find interesting as a model for thinking about 'ordinary lives'. How do less-than-perfect citizens muddle through their daily life? Such citizens are striving for something good but they cannot eradicate the bad. They are often weak, hindered by difficult circumstances, pursuing goals that are not so wise or failing in their attempts to do good.

In the last chapter of Part II, I return to the case of women who have lost their hair in order to ask how aesthetic socialities may also *change* social conventions. What is the political relevance of everyday life aesthetics? In the previous chapter on life in the salons, it was clear that aesthetic motivations were powerful incentives for supporting or creating new social forms. But it is not only motivations that are necessary. New social forms often depend on the very same conventions that they want to move away from. This chapter analyses how women in my study work within existing conventions and adapt or shape these to their advantage. There are also examples of women *subverting* conventions. Subverting aesthetic conventions, and hence creating new forms of sociality, is, however, very difficult and is informed by several material and social contingencies. There are many women who lose their hair because of chemotherapy, but sheer numbers are not enough to change social practices. Part II ends with an exploration of what an aesthetic-social and conventional self 'looks like'.

Notes

1 I borrow Adam Smith's term to foreground the conventional nature of the 'beauty' of the good life (see Chapter 4).

7
Aesthetic values as social values: women losing their hair due to chemotherapy

In this chapter, I explore how women who have lost their hair due to chemotherapy perceive and deal with baldness as well as how others respond to this.[1] In doing so, I unravel the multiple social relationships between the aesthetics of feminine appearance and baldness. These women are not merely negotiating individual preferences or a shared dislike for baldness. Nor is there a clear or more or less coherent aesthetic 'culture' that bald women can refer to, even though it is obvious that female baldness is commonly seen as bad. I will show that the ways in which these women (and those around them) perceive and appreciate baldness are informed by historically contingent imaginaries, conventions and perceptions of beauty as well as the meaning and appropriateness of certain ways of being visible. It is in the interplay between individuals and their social environments that aesthetic values gain their importance.

Life, death or aesthetics?!

At the start of my study, I focused on exploring the relationship between aesthetic values and dignity (see Chapter 3). Situations in which dignity was evoked often involved concerns about losing face, being humiliated, losing independence and so on: in other words, concerns about what the good life might be and what kind of aesthetics it has or lacks. I was anxious about bothering people who are being treated for cancer with questions about how their looks had changed. They were probably worried about more pressing concerns, such as their illness and the availability of various treatments. The threat of death looms large in one's mind after a cancer diagnosis, even if cancer has become treatable in many cases, thus turning it into a chronic condition rather than a fatal disease.

My worries about the relative insignificance of one's looks, however, proved to be unjustified. Appearances directly influence the position of a person within their social environment and can pose a serious threat to that position. Even if we are not familiar with all the people that we might meet in a day, we nonetheless see people all the time and we – tacitly or openly – deal with their evaluations, judgements and norms. Strange or scary appearances may threaten the predictability of social life.

My pre-fieldwork concerns *did* show that my thinking was already influenced by medical language and its priorities. 'Saving a life' is a central value in an academic hospital, such as the one where I work, and the hardships that result from treatment are things that need to be endured towards this good end.[2] The dominance of this 'life-saving' discourse is strengthened by the lack of a vocabulary for talking about the aesthetics of everyday life. This deficiency of words makes it difficult to express what you or I perceive when looking at the consequences of a treatment, such as a bald head. This problem has parallels with the difficulty of talking about visual art forms. How to describe a painting that stirs emotions, an image that shocks, an ugliness that repels? There are, however, specialist vocabularies and conventions for speaking about these matters in the art world. There are very few words for expressing aesthetic appreciations in everyday life. What does a bald female head evoke?

The problem of putting visual things into words caused my research also to become a quest for words. My informants made great efforts to express their experiences, and by comparing and drawing connections between these stories, we together unfolded an everyday semiotics of female baldness. This is not a general theory or philosophy but a localised reconstruction. The role of the Dutch language was crucial because it contains phrasings (metaphors) that provide vivid, image-based expressions that are difficult to translate, such as 'losing face', which is an example that is known in other languages as well. These phrases are not to be taken literally (no physical face is 'lost'), but they quite vividly illustrate what is at stake. But I also noticed that these perceptions emerged as a messy set of contingent associations, fears and images that were derived from historical events with which observers were familiar. This tacit semiotics of baldness was dependent on Dutch cultural imaginaries (if that was the country where the research subjects grew up). But cultural imaginaries can also be American, because people in the Netherlands can and do widely access American cultural resources.

Perceptions of baldness were therefore informed by particular events that had taken place in the past, and these events varied in meaning and relevance for my informants. It was impossible simply to link certain perceptions to an assumed homogeneous culture of a country or social group. My analysis shows that cultural perceptions are instead capriciously related to particular events that may have been witnessed, learned about or lived through. Perceptions of baldness are informed by fragmented and diverse global, cultural and historical influences.[3]

I identified and analysed the cultural, social and historical frames and events that informed visual and social perceptions of bald women by focusing on a mundane but pivotal technology that many women use as a tool – the mirror. By analysing women's narratives about what they saw in the mirror, and by analysing how others responded to their lack of hair, we managed to articulate what my informants and others saw. Through these conversations we learned about the everyday aesthetics that are at play in presenting oneself and the hazards of hiding or revealing baldness, as well as the effort and courage needed for camouflaging baldness rather than making it disappear altogether.

An underlying issue that this chapter addresses is the relationship between *seeing*, *knowing* and *evaluating* something, as these are actions that are embedded in the act of perceiving or describing women without hair. This resonates with my notion of re-scription, and more specifically with Foucault's ideas about the clinical gaze and with discussions about what 'putting things into words' might mean.[4] Foucault's clinical gaze is structured by the logic of the clinic. This clinical logic was a breach with the classificatory logic of diseases that doctors used previously. 'The clinic' provided a practical space and way for thinking through as well as ordering relationships, and this became the new material and epistemological setting that informed how clinicians came to regard patients and diseases.

Foucault's concern is with *knowing* the self or the other, and how this turns a person into a particular kind of subject. My goal is to shift the focus from the activity of knowing towards the practical relationship between knowing and *appreciating* (implicit) or *valuing* (explicit) things. This includes 'knowing' or having a certain idea about facts (what something is, such as what one sees when looking at a bald woman) but also, importantly, the act of valuing and evaluating.

Fieldwork

I recorded and transcribed 13 interviews with women who volunteered to talk with me after participating in a series of workshops called 'Look good, feel better'. These workshops were organised by a not-for-profit organisation and run by volunteer beauticians or cosmeticians with support from various cosmetics companies that provided the beauty products used during the workshops. Participants were invited to learn 'hands on' how to use make-up to look better after treatment had affected their face and skin. Workshops involved 12 steps in which participants learned to carefully clean their vulnerable skin, apply foundation, hide spots, draw in eyebrows and make up their face. A specialised barber gave advice on wigs and headscarves that could be tried out on the spot. Advice was also given on dealing with common side effects of chemotherapy, such as loose nails, blistered feet and very dry skin, and on taking care of the skin of recently exposed scalps.

I observed three of these workshops in two different hospitals. The workshops provided a sheltered place for reconsidering and re-enacting appearances and social relationships. At the beginning of each meeting, women were invited to take off their wigs and hats if they felt comfortable doing so. This created a space in which baldness no longer needed to be concealed. Some participants found seeing other people's bald heads very confronting, particularly when they had not lost their own hair yet. The 13 interviews often developed into intense conversations. Stories about hair loss and the importance of 'looking good' were inextricably entangled with stories about cancer, treatment and the disruption of everyday life and social relationships.

Facing the facts?

In the history of ideas, the connection between beauty and goodness, and between ugliness and badness, is often emphasised. The stories provided by bald women, however, often featured a strong relationship between what is seen and what is *true* before considering how it ought be judged. There is a Dutch saying, *Ik heb het met mijn eigen ogen gezien* ('I have seen it with my own eyes'), which is a way of indicating that one has first-hand evidence and that an event therefore cannot be doubted. What you saw was really there because you actually witnessed it.

Psychologists have asserted that witnesses are generally unreliable because they are poor reporters on what actually takes place. In everyday psychology, everyday phenomenology and the perception of daily life, however, the link between visibility and truth remains strong. This was also the case for women who had lost their hair. They often used phrases such as 'being confronted' to describe both the way they looked and the reality of having cancer.

> Leana: [about her visit to the hairdresser to have her hair cut off]. She [the hairdresser] put on my wig and I went home. She said, 'You should take a shower and act as if you are washing your hair, then you can get used to it, to how it feels.' And I did. And I am a tough girl, and I can sympathise with anyone, cry for everyone. Just say the word, and I am there for others when they need me. But not for myself . . . No. I don't know . . . In the shower, I think the whole neighbourhood heard me because [hesitates] I cried so hard. And then I covered the mirror with a towel. I did not recognise myself. And I am good at confronting myself with things, but in that moment I couldn't do it. I just couldn't.

Losing her hair was a double disaster for Leana. It was a signifier of having cancer and of losing herself. Jane describes, similarly, how seeing her bare head in the mirror was a 'reminder' of 'how things are'.

> Jane: It still gives me a fright when I unexpectedly see my reflection in the mirror. It's like, 'Huh. Oh, yes.' You have such a different image of yourself. And then you look in the mirror and you think, 'Oh, yes.' Not like, 'Oh, how terrible!', but just that you had forgotten how you look now.

Losing one's hair is such a dramatic change that one needs to be constantly *reminded* of one's new look in order to come to terms with oneself as no longer having hair.[5] Seeing an image of oneself that is so different from what one might expect is hard to get used to. The same is also true for one's loved ones. Even if Anita is relaxed about her now bare head, her kids are not.

> Anita: My kids never saw my bald head; they didn't want to. I asked them, of course, and my daughter saw it when my hair started growing back. But the boys absolutely didn't want to see it. Sometimes they wanted to feel with their hand under the cap. They would say, 'I

can feel something already!', but they didn't want to see it . . . I think, if I hadn't had children, I would have dealt with it differently. With less consideration perhaps, a bit more relaxedly, yes.

The reason for not wanting to be 'confronted' with a bare head, to be reminded of disease, may have to do with the fact that people can occasionally accept having to think about disease and mortality but that they cannot do this all the time. This observation was also made in a study on palliative oncology care involving patients who could not be cured and who would eventually die.[6] The people I interviewed wanted to plan ahead for their demise, but they did not want to do this *all* the time. They wanted to live the life they still had left to live, which included discussing everyday things such as the colour of the curtains or the grades of their children in school. People can accept that they are mortal, but they cannot preoccupy themselves with their mortality all the time. Contemplating life's ending is but one part of living it.

So, if seeing symptoms or signs of disease makes the disease present, a bald head signifies this presence *constantly*. Apparently, what one does not see, and hence is not confronted with, can easily recede to the background. Words are much better suited for negotiating the presence of disease. Showing oneself, or being seen, often feels too direct, especially compared to using words that can much better be weighed and controlled, and that can hide the harsh reality of an inescapable truth.

> Jane: It is very strange. I have been very open about it. If people asked me, 'How are you?' I said, 'Do you have a minute? Yes, I have cancer.' So, everybody knew immediately. That may have been confronting but at least everybody was up to date. But last weekend, a friend came over. I hadn't seen her for a long time. And then I thought, 'I need to wear a wig.' [She was used to wearing a cap or being bare headed in her home.] It is different if you *tell* people. It's less shocking.

A truth communicated in words is not the same as 'disclosing' a disease through visual means, such as confronting a friend with one's baldness. 'Being perceived' in a negative way makes the subject passive, whereas being able to craft a story about oneself allows one to be actively in charge. The moment of 'confrontation' can also be extended over a longer period. One may change or soften a topic of conversation, but a bald head – as both a signifier and presence – is constantly there.

Not showing may, then, be a solution. It was not that these women did not want to accept their disease; it was rather they did not want to *see* it. These were different realities. Some women covered their mirrors. Getting told by a dear one that they have cancer is not the same as 'seeing a dear one without hair'.

Protecting others and managing responses

There are differences between people and the ways they perceive baldness. These differences are hard to control or influence.

> Laura: I didn't apply make-up like I used to, I didn't feel the need. And my idea was, 'If you don't like it, please, [gestures] look the other way.' Until I met my neighbour last week. He said that he had seen me the day before. He said, 'I got the fright of my life yesterday. Because I hadn't recognised you.' And then I thought, 'Wait a minute. I don't want to give people a fright.' And then I started to be more careful and to apply some make-up again.

It is probable that the neighbour's shock was due to their recognising a person that had been unrecognisable before. However, even though Laura and Anita were not very concerned about their bare head, they told me others were. This concern made both women adapt their repertoires for dealing with their bare head by employing strategies of concealment. The differences in people's ideas about female baldness made it difficult to anticipate responses. And the unpredictability of the looks and reactions of others could feel threatening.

> Sally: You can't hide any more, you know. They *see* you. They see that you are ill, and that I find extremely painful. Normally [when you have hair] you can, well, you can keep up appearances and act strong [*je groot houden*]. And now they see it. Now the world sees you. And I notice I find that very difficult, too.

Sally expresses how she feels that her bald head 'betrays' her by exposing and revealing the truth of her disease. It renders her passive and stigmatised. She can no longer play with her appearance and health state. Disease has become truth. Bald heads cannot be ignored; *the world sees you*. She stands out among the crowd. Many people may be ill, but if nobody knows this about you specifically, it can feel less harsh and true.

The women I interviewed used metaphors such as feeling naked, cold, exposed or unprotected to express this imagined, punishing gaze of others.

The way one looks is not only perceived and evaluated by the self but also performed, 'confronted' and relentlessly seen and evaluated by others. Reactions to one's appearance are difficult to control when sporting a bald head. It is for this reason that many women choose to *shape* the responses of others by restyling the appearance of their head. This is an aesthetic and motivated act of subject formation that seeks to create ways of living with baldness.

Looking bad, good or beautiful

Assessments of truth involve appreciations of what both my informants and their real and imagined audiences had witnessed. Bald women are not positively responded to at all. What types of appreciations can be distinguished in conversations with them? Bald women, when looking at themselves in a mirror, roughly classify themselves in one of three categories: they look bad, good or beautiful. Looking good means displaying various degrees of ordinariness, and involves seeing the self as usual or recognisable and as not standing out from the crowd. Good looks are a broad category that signifies that one is safely within a particular social order. One is 'OK', beyond the judgement of others.

Looking good is demarcated by its exceptions. Looking bad is the negative exception, which entails associations with disease, a loss of individuality and sociality, punishment, and ultimately death. Looking beautiful is the positive exception, which applies to celebrities or pop stars and can be achieved on an occasional night out. Some women with a feel for what pleases the eye were able to fold beauty into their everyday lives. But my informants taught me that looking beautiful could also be a risky or undesirable strategy involving an even greater loss of ordinary life. I will map the normalities of looking good by carefully analysing the exceptions first.[7]

Looking bad

Looking bad is an exceptional state, but the stories that women told indicate that this can be more easily dealt with if there is concordance between how one is diagnosed, how one is feeling and how one looks. Feeling bad could match with looking bad.[8] Three registers of badness, namely doing, feeling and looking, are aligned.

> Lena: You see, if I don't feel well, it doesn't matter one bit. I put on a scarf and go shopping. And I just don't care. I don't have to look good if I feel awful! It is just the way it is. And you don't care what others might say or think ... When I was that ill, I didn't apply any make-up. I didn't want to. I thought to myself, 'get lost'. Not even a little bit of lipstick. Nothing. I had this idea, 'to hell everyone!' I feel bad, and the whole world may as well know this.

In this quote, the body that looks bad corresponds with the body that is in trouble. Appearances, doings and feelings are all aligned. This bad state implies a clear cut with one's social ties. Lena says, 'I don't care what others say or think,' and tells others to 'get lost' or '[go to] hell'. She places herself outside the social order that she no longer cares about when she feels bad. She is indifferent to the gaze of those representing this order ('the whole world may know this') because she is excluded from this order by badness. The subjectively lived state of baldness fits with this exclusive space.

However, many women reported they had not been feeling (seriously) ill when they were diagnosed with cancer. Sometimes they were diagnosed after a routine preventive breast cancer examination. They did not have any symptoms, or at least not symptoms they associated with a serious disease. The disease had been a latent presence, but from one day to the next these women had the very surreal experience of suddenly becoming patients, which disrupted their daily life immediately and drastically.[9] There were *discrepancies* between doing, feeling and looking.

> Ella: You see, I am ill, but I don't *feel* ill. With cancer that is really the case. At least, well, some people get ill from the chemo. But I don't. And so, notwithstanding my *being* very ill, as a matter of fact, I don't *feel* ill and I don't particularly want to *look* very ill, if you see what I mean.

Here, looks no longer mirror the true/bad state of the body as they did in the 'all bad' situation. One's appearance is disconnected from one's illness. It was at this point of (dis)connection that the 'Look good, feel better' workshops became relevant. Appearances could *influence* feelings, and they could also influence social positions. The idea behind the workshops was that women with cancer *feel* better if they *look* better.

> Petra: Yes, it's true what they say, 'Look good, feel better'. I think that it makes you feel better. Because there are days that I just walk around the house, I don't get dressed, and I don't feel like doing anything. But then you feel less good. Or the other way around, you

> don't feel well, but after you've had a shower, you've taken care of yourself and you've gotten a sense that you look good again, then you feel better, surely. You must recognise this, when you've had flu, and you have been feeling bad, then it's great if you can take a nice shower and wash your hair, apply some cream. These things make you feel better right away, don't they?

Looking bad here relates to being dirty, not being dressed properly, and to a body that is not being cared for and hence 'feels bad'.[10] Women talked about this way of looking bad as having a body that was not 'in proper shape'. They might say, 'I look (like) nothing' (*Ik zie er niet uit*); what you see is incomparable to anything recognisable. 'Feeling better' is a sensuous state that is only partially informed by the visual. One cannot see one's appearance constantly, but one may feel that one looks good all the same (the cleanliness and softness of the skin, the nice clothes, feeling well).

Looking good, here, does not reflect some truth about the body but rather a way of manipulating this truth. As one woman said, 'You have to put some work into it' (*Je moet er werk van maken*, which is a Dutch expression). A bad (looking, feeling, acting) body is an uncultivated or unshaped body that is not fit to be shown to others. It is a body alone in a house dressed in pyjamas; it is not a social body. The social implications of one's looks are, again, very clear. Looks are an important determinant of one's place in the social world, even if the work that is necessary to maintain one's looks is routine for most people.

The way one looks can hardly be called a trivial matter or a matter of individual taste. If looking bad means stepping or falling out of the everyday order of things, looking good can also be a way of getting back in. A social life is at stake, which can be rejoined by wearing wigs or scarves and by applying make-up. Yet doing this can also come at a price.

> Josie: Yes, they said, 'Gosh, you look so good!' [after she came home from the workshop]. But that is not always nice to hear. Because you are ill. So on the one hand, the organiser of the workshop set things up so that not everybody could see that she was ill. She wanted to have her ordinary life back, and I can understand that. But on the other hand, you do want some special attention when you are ill. You don't want to be treated as a healthy person because you are ill.

Not looking ill could, for better or for worse, also mean 'not being treated as ill'. The downside to 'passing as normal' is that there is an obligation for patients to remain positive, or even to 'fight and conquer' cancer. This 'demand to think positively' does not distinguish between ways of looking good or looking bad but turns looking good into a tool to conquer the bad. The women in my study were very aware of these distinctions.

Nothingness, illness and death

What was it that these women, and others, saw when they looked at a bald female head? What do bad looks signify in this context? A strong imaginary[11] of looking bad was to have 'chemo head'. A chemo head is a head that 'looks like nothing' because it no longer has any defining characteristics. It cannot be compared to or recognised as anything familiar. This theme emerged particularly when eyebrows disappeared. A face without hair or eyebrows is an 'empty' face that looks like a 'bare bottom' (*blote billen gezicht*), according to a particularly unforgiving Dutch expression. It has no structure, shape or distinction.

> Patricia [about the workshop]: Oh, speaking of those eyebrows, that woman didn't have eyebrows. And when the beautician drew them on, that made such a big difference. Just the eyebrows. It is really important that people learn how to do this. If I had lost my eyebrows, I would have been very happy to know these techniques. It instantly makes a face lively. And without the eyebrows, there's just nothing. You have no facial expression. I didn't know this before, but then I saw it. That woman looked so much better by the end of the morning, only because she had eyebrows again. That makes all the difference. A face is misty [vague/indistinct; in Dutch, *mistig*] without eyebrows.

Patricia describes faces as 'not being a face' (*het is geen gezicht*) or having 'no expression'. A vague or indistinct face is one that is devoid of meaning and expression. This can be contrasted with the Dutch turn of phrase *sprekende ogen*, which literally means 'eyes that speak' or 'express'; these are eyes that are apparently *addressing* others. They are not 'mute' like a face without structure that communicates nothing. Patricia also speaks of 'making a face lively'. The connection between looking bad and 'looking like nothing', or like illness or death, is a recurrent theme in these women's stories.

> Vanessa: You don't look really alive. You look more like . . . [thinks] like you really have a serious disease [laughs]. And that is exactly what is the case of course!

Vanessa sees herself and her fellow patients as *halfway to the grave*. Being ill and having a bald head was also frequently interpreted as no longer having any individuality, as if illness implied a loss of self, giving way to a more general form of existence. This 'general existence' was often 'the cancer patient'. The cancer patient that emerged from the stories told by these women is not an individual but a category.

> Alice: Yes, when people see me, they think 'cancer'. [As a person without hair] you really are part of the sick people in society, that sort of feeling. People think: see, now you are really ill, now we can see it. Something like that.

When marked as belonging to a certain category of people who look bad, a person loses her sense of self as the individual she once was. The self is 'unmade'. One literally loses the self. Laura articulates this transition poignantly.

> Laura: You've lost your own head. I had a head like those in the images we had seen of people who had received chemo. I wasn't completely bald at that time, but the effect was the same. The hair was so short that I could see the shape of my skull.

'Losing your own head' and comparing it to the heads of people undergoing chemotherapy is a striking way for expressing the transition from individual to category. In a Dutch movie featuring a beautiful woman with cancer, one of the most arresting scenes is when her hair is being cut off, thus dramatically showing that she is being 'dehumanised'.[12] The images in the movie are very strong, but it is quite different from the way many of my other informants described this situation. In these instances, cutting one's hair was more of an anticipatory act that allowed one to take control over a situation rather than waiting for one's hair to fall out by itself.

Being oneself as a state of worth

'Selfhood', or feeling and being oneself, emerges as a state of value here. 'Self' is not a signifier to merely index a particular person or being, but something good, a state of worth. I want to suggest that this state of worth does not only involve a notion of authenticity, as if the face only expresses something that is rooted in an individual and their habits of seeing themselves. Individuality, instead, refers to aesthetic positions that are socially valued. The women can no longer see their old self, and hence look for recognisable images that they can compare to what they see in the mirror. In this way they try to make sense of what they see. In Laura's case, what she saw was 'a chemo head'.

Losing one's head is, once again, an indication of exceptionality (ordinary people have individual heads; they are not categories). When confronted with their bare heads in this manner, women positioned themselves somewhere between being alive (as a recognisable individual), being halfway gone (a category) and being dead (the ultimate nothingness). These increasingly categorical looks fit into a life that was literally outside common daily practices such as going to work or school. Treatment and survival filled the days of these women. One of the things they could do to counter this marginal state, however, was to modify their appearance. Indeed, enough was at stake for them to take wearing wigs and painting eyebrows more seriously.

Facing death and punishment

In addition to belonging to certain general categories or being a part of nothing, there was another register of badness. Being a social outcast was strongly evoked by one of the most dreadful images that women saw when they looked at their bald selves in the mirror, namely the concentration camp.[13] Being bald meant being excluded and set apart, with nothing to hope for.

> Sally: Erm . . . when I heard that they diagnosed me with breast cancer, my first thought was, 'I will lose my hair. I will lose my hair.' I found that *extremely* devastating. [Sally starts talking about the strategies she explored to prevent her hair from falling out.]
>
> Jeannette: Why did you find losing your hair so terrible?
>
> Sally: Hair was the most terrible . . . I immediately made associations . . . with Jews, the burning of witches [she cries]. To be set apart from others. That is, I still feel that. Oh, now I immediately start crying. Yes, hair, that is the most sensitive part, so to speak. I always found that really terrible.

For Sally, the prospect of losing her hair had a more immediate impact on her than the diagnosis itself. The concentration camp is a terrible image, and this was certainly not evoked for everyone. Concentration camps and the burning of witches are both related to historical events that have become part of collective imaginaries. Images of these events have a varying impact on people, depending on their familiarity with these events and the emotional impact of these imaginaries. These impacts are hard to control or ignore. They involve images that have become stereotypes or archetypical social fears that may or may not be shared by particular individuals. They carry connotations of being set apart, being stigmatised as the one person who does not fit into a crowd of people who are all 'OK', and there is very little that one can do about this. Life is disrupted until further notice, and hair loss is the most visible marker of one's exit from social life. Baldness becomes the instrument that effectively enforces this expulsion. Bald women are on their own, an easy target in a world full of animosity. These imaginaries also connote a sense of punishment, particularly for women who have been marked as deviant or bad.

Such feelings of animosity and punishment are also informed by Dutch imaginaries about the treatment of female 'collaborators', women who engaged in relationships with German soldiers who were occupying the Netherlands during the Second World War. After the war, these women were rounded up and their heads were shaved in public, and sometimes also covered in paint.[14] In short, they were publicly humiliated. This particular imaginary was not brought up by my informants, but it may have influenced their sense of social humiliation and punishment.

The imaginary of the concentration camp is a complex one. Bald women associated different physical conditions with this social and technological setting. A thin body that is mutilated by operations was seen as a sign of not being human anymore because it could not be recognised as partaking in any form of aesthetic sociality.

> Catherine: In the evenings it was worse. You would take off your wig and see yourself completely naked. And because you don't have breasts any more [due to mastectomy], the image that you see . . . And I said, 'Now I look like people in a concentration camp.' Extremely thin, scars on my belly from the operation [that had removed most of her intestines] and the [now removed] colostomy bag, no breasts, a bald head. That whole combination. That was, well . . . it was confronting.

The problem here is not just the body itself, a body that others (in this case doctors) have stripped of various body parts that are important for shaping one's sense of (feminine, human) identity. Again, it is *seeing* this bare and mutilated body that is the problem. For the women I interviewed, the easiest way of dealing with this problem was to not look in the mirror. Strategies for avoiding seeing one's image in a mirror involved covering it with a towel, not switching the light on in the bathroom or using smaller mirrors that could still be used for applying cream or make-up without providing a view of the whole body. The body was covered with clothes, the head with wigs or hats. The result may not have been perfect but it worked to keep associations with concentration camps at bay. This again shows the 'magical' performativity of seeing or not seeing things. Making things invisible can indeed perform a different truth.

Looking beautiful

Most women considered looking beautiful an exceptional state, something that is positive and achieved on a night out, or by exceptional and famous people such as Sinead O'Connor, a celebrity who was periodically bald and who was able to combine her baldness with being sexy and famous. Another, older Dutch celebrity was Sugar Lee Hooper, a singer and entertainer who expressed cheerful extravagance through her shaved head, colourful dress and sturdy posture. Being beautiful, however, did not have to resemble the beauty of a movie star. Beauty could also be displayed through creativity and style.

For the more creative types, interestingly, looking beautiful did not involve disguising one's baldness completely. The bare head was taken as a starting point and dressed up as such. The technologies these women used for being beautiful were scarves that creatively shaped and ornamented their bare head rather than wigs that concealed their baldness. The scarves also engendered a sense of 'self' to those who found wigs uncomfortable to wear.

> Annemiek: It [wearing a wig] doesn't feel nice. I feel as if I am wearing a bathing cap. You can feel the edges, much like when you are wearing a cap. But I never wear things on my head, so I don't find it comfortable. And you must be more careful, look out for rain for instance. I have a raincoat and a hat, and if I want to take off the hat, I need to make sure to hold my hair [the wig], and then take off the hat. And it may move if you reach above your head, for instance,

when you store luggage above your seat in the train. Or when it's windy or there are branches, sometimes you fear that you will lose the wig.

Entirely hiding one's baldness is difficult. Some women found wearing comfortable headwear an acceptable alternative, at least when they were at home. Wearing headwear is a risky strategy when going out because it does not hide and can even emphasise baldness.

> Jeannette: OK, but why not wear scarves or hats?

> Ellen: Oh, no, never! That is *so* cancer. I find that so bad, and I notice it right away in the street. Fortunately, there are not that many women who do this, thank god. Most women wear wigs when they go out. It marks a cancer head so distinctly, a scarf with nothing underneath. Yes, if it was more acceptable, I would walk around with a bare head, but *never ever* with such a thing [scarf]. No, it's such a stigma, it writes 'CANCER' on your head with big capital letters. With a wig, you look somewhat normal, but with scarves? No. You can see that it's bare.

Yet to others who aspired to look beautiful, baldness could have its own beauty as well. I discussed this with my informants. Some of them were more beautiful without hair than most people are with hair. Being around many bald women during my research made me used to seeing this aesthetic. I had no problem with seeing bare heads. I visited most women at home and they looked fine and comfortable in their home with minimal covering. But how could the norm to conceal be so strong that it also implicated the hiding of beauty?

> Lisa: My partner says, 'See, look at her on the TV, she wears a scarf, too. You are more beautiful wearing a scarf than that wig.'

> Jeannette: Why does he think this?

> Lisa: Well, I lost a couple of kilos and the lines on my face are stronger. I look fit. So he says, 'You were beautiful, but now you are also beautiful. Just show it.' Whenever I put on that wig to go out he says, 'You are so much prettier with a scarf!' He says the wig makes me look older.

Jeannette: So he says the wig does not make you look the way you used to, like you hoped?

Lisa: Exactly!

For Lisa, her new looks were not a new self but just a temporary look. She wanted to resemble her old self as much as possible. She *never* left the house without her wig. Her partner was capable of admiring her new appearance and appreciating its new beauty. This shows that there is a tension between the desire to look 'as before' and the wish to 'be beautiful' and to receive affirmation of the 'new self' one has now become, whether this is temporary or not. Lisa's partner got used to and appreciated what he saw and how this may also look good. Lisa could only accept the image of her old self. This is what most women expressed, they wanted to look *good* rather than *beautiful*.

A Dutch novel – *Girl with the Nine Wigs* – may help clarify the dilemma between looking good and looking beautiful.[15] The young woman portrayed in this novel, a student of political science, takes her temporary baldness (due to chemotherapy) as an opportunity to experiment with new looks, and particularly with wigs. She buys different wigs at flea markets and party-supply stores. She goes out into the city as a short-haired redhead one day, and with an afro or with witch's hair the next.

Playful experiments with one's body were, however, not something most women acknowledged as something they enjoyed. They were trying to regain a lost sense of self rather than inventing and experimenting with new identities. These women were striving for the normality of looking good without standing out or attracting people's attention. They just wanted to fit in and be 'OK' rather than 'stunning'.

Looking good

Now the meaning of 'merely' looking good is taking shape. As mentioned before, this is a way of looking that can involve a wide variety of appearances and that is demarcated by its negative and positive exceptions. The women in the study were longing for the 'normality' of looking good. There were three ways in which they could look good: first, when they resembled their former selves, and second, when they did not stand out socially (and when they were not reduced to nothingness). The third way turned out to be the most difficult one, namely to be who they had become, a worthy person with cancer.

The first way, to look like one's old self, is a lot to hope for when one fears a loss of self.

> Ellen: You just want to be who you are. You change so much already because of that chemo stuff. And then it's nice if you can put on a thing [wig] that allows you to look a bit like what you used to look like. There probably will be people who try something new. But I did not have that urge.

The self from before the illness was perceived as the real self, whereas the self without hair had a tough time in passing as acceptable outside the home.

> Annette: You just want to be yourself as much as possible. Because you've lost yourself. And I read a book in which women had two wigs, one blonde, because that would attract more attention from men. But then I think, 'That is not what I need right now.' I like to try things out. But you try new things when you feel good. And that is not how I feel right now. I am not in the mood for doing nice new things. That doesn't work during this period. You want to be yourself.

Being ill rarely engenders a sense of creativity that might lead one to experiment with beauty. These women were looking for conventionality and continuity rather than new looks, however beautiful these looks might be. When the familiarity of one's own face is threatened, the leap towards the opposite exception – a beautiful face that attracts looks because it *takes advantage of* rather than conceals the baldness of the head – was too far for most to be a viable alternative.

The second way of looking good involved passing as normal and not being gazed at. This did not always mean that one was not noticed by others. The technology of preference for effectively avoiding if not the gazes then at least the comments of others was the wig. Some modern wigs are of such high quality that only experts can identify them. The message conveyed by the wig to those who can identify them as such is, however, to not comment on them. The wig is a technology of visual concealment and an effective tool for avoiding uninvited comments.

The last way to enact the self as looking good was 'to be who you have become', a woman with cancer. It 'takes courage' my informants said (and demonstrated) to act against 'bad' norms and to show one's bare head to the world. None of my informants took the risk of doing this, because it could cause embarrassment or shame.

Joanna: That [being bald] was really tough, also when I looked at myself in the mirror. I suddenly looked very much like my brother [laughs]. You know, I thought it didn't look like a face [*Ik vond het geen gezicht.* Something that 'doesn't look like a face' is something that looks like nothing; one cannot really look at it.]. You really feel a bit ashamed that you thought, 'Ooh!' How can I explain this. It is cold as well, you see, I always found it cold, a bald head [*kale kop*], no face, it doesn't look good. I thought I had a bit of a sick head.

This jumble of metaphors exemplifies the search for meaningful comparisons to describe what Joanna saw in the mirror. Again, it is a mix of physical sensations (coldness), exceptional looks (no face) and social feelings (shame): a literal 'loss of face'. Baldness led to badness and isolation because having a 'bare' head visibly marks one as 'out of order'. To prevent this, women armed themselves with wigs and mirrors. This indeed is a cruel fate for people who are already having a tough time while dealing with cancer.

The bald female self that looks good emerged as a fragile entity. It had to be shaped and adapted in order to become more ordinary and socially acceptable. It is very clear that the bald self has a hard time 'being what it has become' because it breaches the norms of how a woman is *supposed* to look. There are very few conventional socialities or aesthetic genres in which one may be 'ordinary' as a bald woman. This makes it more difficult to accept baldness as a part of the self, however temporarily this state might be. When selfhood is a valued state, it is difficult to link it to powerful imaginaries such as badness.

Conclusion: connecting the bad, the good and the beautiful

The women were not alone while staring into the mirror. In the privacy of their bathrooms, their own gaze was tinted by the multiple gazes of others. But it was not a homogeneous frame through which baldness was perceived. Imaginaries could differ as well as the emotions attached to them. There were different ways of perceiving and valuing. The conjunction of knowing and valuing the self here indicated that selfhood and being oneself did not refer to fixed states or predetermined individual entities. They referred to a state of worth. 'Being oneself' means that one is in a valued state and recognisable as an individual with a degree of continuity. But this also implies that one is part of some form of sociality.

Perceiving a new reflection in the mirror entailed comparing that image with other images to make sense of what is seen, thus connecting truth and evaluation through social conventions.

Even if the women themselves were relatively unaffected by the loss of their hair, it was hard to ignore that others did take notice. A bad-looking body, in its most mild form of badness, is an uncultivated, unshaped and non-individual body that stays within the privacy of the home. It is not something for others to look at. So these women could no longer just live their life as it unfolded; they had to find or create ways of *living well* with baldness. This meant actively shaping the self and *manipulating* one's body and appearance in order to connect with a meaningful form of sociality and individuality. Cultivation and manipulation of one's appearance with scissors, mirrors, wigs and scarves became a necessity. These creative activities provided ways of relegating 'badness' to playing a limited role in one's life. The drawbacks of not shaping one's looks, and hence granting illness only a limited role, were severe: it could mean a loss of individuality by becoming 'nothing', or it could mean becoming a category ('cancer patient', 'chemo head') or standing out in a crowd and running the risk of losing dignity in social encounters.

There were clear relationships to truth (the truth of illness, or of certain stereotypes), goodness (not wanting to scare others, remain socially functioning, taking responsibility for the effect of one's appearance on others) and beauty. The last category was ambiguous. It included notions of beauty as an exceptional state, but this was only occasionally a concern for some women. Their relationship to beauty was less to beauty as an exception and more to beauty as a mundane experience (looking good), which is a form of beauty that involves normality and convention as well as 'being oneself'. The exception and the norm define one another, but it is important to note that, unlike a work of art, these women did not want to make a statement to an audience.

Aesthetic values emerged here as values that are informed by social events and social practices. Being able to appreciate one's appearance is influenced by contingent forms of social life and historical events. These are more erratic and contingent phenomena than the logic of Foucault's clinical gaze, which involves a more disciplined, coherent and professional stare. There is no unified discourse on what bald women are and how to approach them, but there are different imaginaries that are differently valued by those who are looking and being looked at. The uncertainty and messiness of these ways of looking, moreover, makes it difficult to state simply that 'interpretations are culturally informed'. This is the case, of course, but the imaginaries that are evoked are different. There is always *someone* looking at something or somebody. What is being seen may lead to semiotic problems such as simultaneously recognising and not recognising someone. Something that is witnessed is always interpreted in relation to other things, such as cultural imaginaries, and to other instances of perceiving the self or others. Examples are 'before and after', (tacit) expectations and positions of the observer, or a similarity to one's brother.

The importance of one's appearance in this context is informed by social death rather than biological death. Social death may take place before the body dies. It involves being excluded from any acceptable aesthetic, which was most powerfully expressed by the imaginary of the concentration camp but also by references to nothingness, the loss of individuality and 'not looking alive'. Social death involves a body that is stripped of its relationship to any acceptable sociality. The body 'looked like nothing' or had 'no face'. It was not recognisable as an individual. These are harrowing experiences.

There was no formal recognition of the impact of baldness, but this problem may have been influenced by the particular hospitals where these women were being treated. Baldness was not considered to be much of an issue by doctors. The workshop was a volunteer event that relied on advertising by health care staff. Wigs were paid for by the health insurance. In contrast to other countries, remedies such as the 'ice cap' are not actively promoted in the Netherlands. Hair loss was mainly seen as a (hopefully) passing inconvenience that had to be endured for the greater good of being cured.

So these women were in a specific social position, which thus far had not led to a motivation to organise themselves. There seemed to be no positive motivation for getting together and thinking of ways to live well with baldness. Any potential efforts to organise were also impeded because women themselves were affected by certain social imaginaries. Some women felt liberated when taking off their wig at the workshops, but others felt extremely hesitant. They judged themselves by the same cruel standards as others did.

Some of the women rebelled against these norms by insisting on dressing beautifully or by going against the norms that forbade them to go out with a bare head. None of my informants tried actively to breach these norms by showing their bare head in public; this is almost impossible to do for an individual. Normalising female baldness might become a possibility through social action or through other ways of creating a new aesthetics of individuality and sociality. Such a hypothetical sociality of female baldness would have to create space for cancer as a potential fact of life, which is at odds with the dominant medical rhetoric and practice of aggressively curing cancer by 'making it go away' as well as with the cultural fear this disease still evokes.

I will address the possibility for social change in Chapter 9. For now, I want to point out that aesthetic values, such as how one looks, are social values. These values are strongly related to conventions that suggest a norm or show an exception. These values make a big difference for being part of certain forms of sociality or for falling outside them. One's appearance is an essential part of being social, but people whose appearance is not frequently challenged by odd looks hardly ever notice this. Aesthetic values are indeed crucial for understanding how social relations may be built as well as for how subject positions may be shaped. To become a subject is to become part of a social order. Even if that social order is messy, or if it consists of different orderings or snippets of powerful images, subject-positions are marked by aesthetic perceptions of the self and by the perceptions of others. Such perceptions reveal certain forms of truth as much as they urge one to respond to that truth, even if only for the sake of others.

Notes

1 Women's baldness due to chemotherapy is understudied, but this is even more true for male baldness. I did not explore chemotherapy-induced male baldness because my informants were participants in a make-up workshop in which no men participated. Hair, and in particular body hair, is, however, an important marker of masculinity. More research is needed here.
2 This is not a static discourse. Concerns are changing due to the increase of chronic disease and the 'chronification' of diseases that used to be lethal. Different forms of cancer are clear examples here. When 'health' is beyond reach, people may arrive at a point where they find the burden of treatment too heavy and instead opt for 'quality of life' without treatment, even if that means hastening death. Another example in which quality comes to trump the extension of life involves people who are 'tired of living'.
3 For a history of the meaning of hairdos, see Welch, 2009.
4 Foucault, 1975.
5 There are important differences here between women. In a society that is more oriented towards heterosexual relationships rather than other relationships, heterosexual imaginaries weigh heavily on ideas of beauty and the importance attached to this term. A colleague of mine who was married to another woman one day showed up to work proudly sporting a bald head. When I asked her about this, she explained that she was not so concerned about social norms about how women should look. This colleague left behind an impressive set of stories about the trajectory of her illness (Cato, 2016).
6 Pols, 2012; 2019b.
7 Another reference to Foucault (1978) is in order. The normal can often best be grasped by looking at its deviations. Here, Foucault builds on Canguilhem, 1989 (originally published in 1943), who used the pathological to learn about the normal.
8 The phrase 'doing disease' rather than '*being* ill' (Mol, 2002) sounds a bit awkward, but it avoids assigning an objective state of 'being' that is informed by medical research and treatment, whereas other categories (feeling and looking ill) are denied such a reality.

9   The modern way of 'doing all the tests' in one day saves patients from having to wait and being left in uncertainty, but the speed at which their fate unfolds is often very hard to keep up with. Most women talk about this time as an emotional whirlwind that they could not make sense of in any way.
10 The symbolic meaning of cleaning is also a literary theme. In my study of washing practices, this theme emerged when one of the psychiatric patients that I was following was recovered from the bed in which he had been lying for weeks without being washed or dressed. His care worker helped him into the shower so that he could shave and put on clean clothes. He was full of surprise when he looked at himself in the mirror and said, 'There hides a human in me.'
11 An imaginary is a mode of interpretation that is culturally available and that can make what is witnessed an example of something.
12 R. Oerlemans (dir.), *Komt een vrouw bij de dokter* [*Stricken*], 2009.
13 The concentration camps of the Second World War, to be specific, where inmates were de-individualised by being prohibited from having distinct hairstyles or clothing and by being forced to wear prison uniforms and having their heads shaved. This was done to make it easier for guards to see inmates as inferior life forms.
14 Diederichs, 2005.
15 Van der Stap, 2006.

8
Imperfect lives: Foucault's archaeological reading of the Cynics

Historically, studies of the 'good-life-as-practice' have drawn a connection between everyday life and its values. The good life was referred to in ancient Greece and Rome as a set of practices and ways of thinking. After the decline of the Greek and Roman civilisations, there were a variety of humanist traditions that renounced these ancient roots in their reflections and practices of the good life. These pre-modern humanist traditions came to an end with the advent of modernity, as the first cluster of chapters showed.[1] Questions about the good life for individuals, together with religious matters, were increasingly privatised because rulers feared that the passions would divide rather than unify the nation. Social theory sought ways to channel the passions.

The privatisation of passions did not mean that the individual became irrelevant to social theory. Instead, the individual gained a new identity under the abstract guise of 'the human', which eventually became the cornerstone of emancipation during modernity. However, the abstract concept of individuality had very little to say about concrete social life and its values. Statistical models and abstract theories strove for identifying generalities rather than learning about specificities. The case of women who have lost their hair provided an illustration of how everyday-life values are not general but social in their origin and effect, which is a theme upon which this chapter further elaborates. This case also showed how thinking about aesthetic values as social values can lead to a lasting understanding of what an individual is, namely someone who is striving to create their individuality as a state of worth.

In this chapter, I will analyse Michel Foucault's work on the true life as presented in his lectures of 1984.[2] My aim is to develop an understanding of how everyday life was turned into an object of study by philosophers of the good-life-as-practice, how they understood its goodness and how this may be adapted to contemporary studies of the values of everyday life. These philosophers provided examples to think with that can be used to develop concepts for understanding the values of everyday life. Whereas philosophers who practised the good life sought to live their lives as examples that others could learn from, I look for ways to think about the goodness of *ordinary* lives. My aim is not to judge everyday lives or provide guidelines on how to live one's life but to learn how such lives are practised and how they are informed by values. This chapter will therefore elaborate on questions of normativity that are central to studying the good life. How may conceptualisations of the good, as found in the lives of philosophers of the good-life-as-practice, help to understand ordinary and imperfect lives as good lives, and how might we understand this conceptualisation of the good if it is neither exemplary nor intentional or prescriptive? Works by ancient Greek philosophers of the good-life-as-practice hence form the starting point for my analysis. After a thorough analysis of how Foucault conceptualised the ancient Greek conceptualisation, I will link this project to the questions of this book. How can the ideas of these philosophers of the good-life-as-practice generate concepts for my inquiry about the values of everyday life?

Foucault's lectures on the good life

I explore conceptualisations of the good and true life by ancient Greek philosophers and how these were, in turn, conceptualised by Michel Foucault. This double hermeneutic, or double archaeology, is a crucial part of the puzzle that is being pieced together in this chapter. I read about Greek concepts using Foucault's work to determine how both may be used to study the values of everyday life as a good life. Understanding Foucault's particular way of analysing ancient Greek lives requires some background knowledge on what he was seeking to achieve. To this end, I will first situate the work that I draw on, namely Foucault's final lectures.

Foucault's lectures were a work in progress, which makes them fascinating to read because the reader can follow his 'thinking in action'. But this also means that there is no 'final coherence' to these lectures; Foucault died before he could turn them into a book. Foucault's erudition is spectacularly obvious, but he does not provide many references to the works of others and the lectures trace his thinking as it evolves. This makes the lectures a generative and generous read; there are many ways a reader may draw lessons from these lectures, and I will gratefully try to do so as well.

Because philosophers of the good life were interested in *practising*, that is, in actually *living* the good life as an exemplary life, Foucault undertakes what we may call a *historical ethnography*. The aim of philosophers of the good life was to *live* the good life, and hence they also wanted to put assumptions about the good life to the test. Foucault's goal is to learn about these philosophers' lives by placing them in the context of their everyday practice and by putting them in relation to how other citizens considered these lives. I read Foucault's lectures as an attempt to articulate conditions, or to create a conceptual space, for studying the various forms of the good life that were lived in ancient Greece. As I will show, the subject-position of the *audience*, or the pupils, of the philosophers of the good life – the imperfect citizens who are being taught by these philosophers – is important for being able to grasp their understanding of everyday life and its values among 'ordinary' (rather than exemplary) people.

Positioning Foucault's lectures

Foucault's lectures of 1984, which are in retrospect dramatically situated just months before his untimely death, were given as a series of seminars at the Collège de France. The published text is a transcription of the many recordings made by the students who were bulging out of the classroom at the time. The lectures presented Foucault's unfinished work on articulating and exploring the contours of how we may study the good life as *concrete forms of life*. Foucault used an 'archaeological method' to 'dig up' concrete examples of everyday life and to learn about everyday practices in ancient Greece.[3] Foucault conceptualised the good life as a practical form of everyday life so that it could become an object of social scientific and historical study. The cases he focuses on are the exemplary lives and teachings of the Cynics as well as the various interpretations of Socrates' call to care for oneself.

Foucault explains why a history of the forms of everyday life (in Greek: *bios*) has not been attempted before, which is of great relevance to my goal of studying specificities. The reason for the historical neglect of the study of everyday life, Foucault argues, is that for centuries scholarly interest was directed towards the *universal* and transcendental character of the self. This is called the *psukhe*, which Foucault translates as 'the soul'. *Psukhe* works in the same way for any human and exemplifies a form of ancient Greek psychology *avant la lettre*. Studies on the *psukhe* developed ideas about the essential nature of the soul and the activity of *knowing* oneself through knowing the soul. *Bios*, however, is variable, concrete and specific. It is difficult to study in terms of universals without overlooking its specificities and concreteness. In *bios*, the crucial theme was not *knowing* the self but *taking care of oneself* (*epimeleia, melei moi*), and by taking care of the self also taking care of others. Taking care of oneself implies having a certain type of knowledge or the ability to speak the truth about everyday life. Foucault persistently strove to articulate this truth as a specific form of truth that exists next to other forms of truth.[4] Foucault remarks that there is no present-day equivalent to speaking the truth about individual lives and how individuals organise themselves as moral subjects (*ethos*). This form of truth has disappeared, he argues, or was transformed from being an individual consideration into an institutional matter through religion, psychiatry, medicine and education. Foucault wanted to understand how the connection between truth and individual life was understood before these were conceptually separated.

The activity of caring for the self is done by *examining the truth*, that is, by using the soul as one's touchstone. This, at least, is how the Cynics and Socrates put it. Rather than identifying the universal characteristics of the *psukhe*, the Cynics and Socrates explored the truth that could be found in the forms of living they saw around them. The Cynics were not concerned with the universal; for them the *elementary* was the crucial term. This meant that they were not interested in abstract knowledge about the world (*physis*) but in the knowledge that is needed to support everyday life in its specificity.[5] By living their life in the way that they did, the Cynics posed questions to themselves and their contemporaries about what a true life really needs (that which is elementary to it) and what it can do without. The Cynics tested assumptions about what life might need by putting these into practice, for example, by seeing if they could live without the luxury of a house.

It is important for Foucault that the good life of the Cynics is shaped by their practice of *parrhesia*, which means 'courageously speaking the truth' about everyday life. *Parrhesia* is a way to turn philosophy into practice. 'Parrhesiasts' spoke the truth about everyday life to citizens in ancient Greece. For the ancient Greek philosophers, *courage* referred to the fact that their frank message was not always welcomed by citizens. For instance, the Cynics rejected fame, good manners and wealth as unimportant to the true life. But these values were very important to Athenian citizens. In contesting these values, the Cynics risked the ire of their fellow citizens. But to the Cynics this was a serious matter because they deemed it central to the good life. Their lives were dedicated to exploring this truth and simultaneously demonstrating it to the citizens.

Famously, Diogenes lived in a barrel to show that one could live without the luxuries that were so cherished by his contemporaries. The Cynics educated and advised citizens on how to examine their lives, and thus lead a true life, even if they did not want to have anything to do with this. It was the life mission of the Cynics to live the good and true life through self-examination and by courageously confronting citizens with the truth.

Situating Foucault's final lectures within his oeuvre

At the end of the lecture series, Foucault suggests that he, or others, could write a history of (exemplary) forms of life and their relation to speaking the truth. These lectures can be seen as a first exploration of some of the cases and terms with which to write this history as well as providing the possible contours of what such an history might look like. These lectures extend Foucault's work on care for the self, which he had started in his 'history of sexuality' and further developed in his (unfinished) work on technologies of the self. In this latter work he was examining the various possibilities that surround the 'freedom' of individual subjects. That is to say, he sought to conceptualise freedom as the potential to turn oneself into a subject rather than as the liberation of some authentic self from the oppression of others.[6]

Foucault, in this way, also sought to address the (feminist) critique that he leaves no space for the agency of subjects, which he often presents as being disciplined or subjected to grand discourses of truth. Foucault's work, his critics argued, turned the modern, Western and thinking subject into a docile victim of subjectification who is at the whim of powers that cannot be resisted. His work left little space for political action. This is a common interpretation of Foucault's work, but in these later lectures his struggle with this deterministic view is clearly visible. I will return to the late-Foucauldian subject who yearns to exploit aesthetic forms of living for creating the socialities it desires in Chapter 9. For now, I concentrate on the emergence of the Foucauldian subject that is acted upon but that also retains certain degrees of freedom. Having a chronic disease such as cancer may well be seen as an example of being acted upon, whereas shaping the self with wigs, make-up and scissors may be seen as practices that display both conventional ways of subjectivication, but also a modest but crucial degree of freedom to shape the self.

Notwithstanding – or might I say because of? – the unfinished nature of thoughts that have not quite settled, the lectures provide an utterly absorbing read on the topic of the good life. The complexity, thoroughness, clarity and depth of Foucault's analyses generate many footholds for conceptualising the good life. The lectures exemplify Foucault's development of the practice of 'generative research'. In these lectures, he persistently and assiduously attempts to articulate what has not yet been put into words. My reading of these lectures cannot possibly do justice to their richness. By unfolding or reconstructing what Foucault makes visible with his method as well as what he obscures, by highlighting some details and downplaying other things, I attempt to create a theoretical space for articulating and understanding everyday life and the values that are relevant within it.

The true, the beautiful and the good

Before discussing Foucault's interpretations of the Cynics in more detail, I start with some words on the relationship between the true, the beautiful and the good in ancient Greece as well as in Foucault's approach. This is crucial for the exploration of aesthetic values in everyday life because the good life in ancient Greece was simultaneously a true and beautiful life. Truth and goodness, whatever concrete forms these might have in practice, were not assigned to separate spheres in the way they would be under modernity (see the discussion of Habermas in Chapter 6). This separation only started to make sense many centuries later when ethics, science, art and religion obtained their own realms of relevance, and after morality and the passions had been privatised. For understanding values in everyday life, it is key to reconnect truth, beauty and goodness in order to empirically specify the relations between them.

In Greek thought, and in the study of everyday-life-as-a-practice, concerns about truth, beauty and goodness are brought into a certain relationship with each other even if multiple alternatives for crafting these relationships remain. The Cynics, with their rejection of wealth and institutions such as marriage, provided extreme examples of how to live. Epictetus, for instance, softened their demands by mixing Stoicism with Cynicism, hence approving of modesty rather than demanding poverty. Socrates was a married man with a modest and conventional private life. But for the early Cynics, violating conventions and enduring the strong reactions this led to was part of the courage it took to speak and live the truth as well as a way of putting truth to the test.

Goodness – in the form we would now recognise as beauty, morality or justice – and truth are connected in ancient Greek thought. They are always found together. *Foucault*'s interest, however, was primarily in the good life as a particular mode of relating to *truth* within an exemplary form of the good life. This relationship to truth emerges by practising *parrhesia*. Foucault's interest in – or perhaps obsession with – the history and workings of truth colours his investigations and leads him to foreground a particular understanding of the good life as something that relates to truth.[7] In contrast to Foucault, my interest is in the implications of thinking about the *values* of everyday life or what makes the good life good.

The good-life-as-practice for ancient Greek philosophers is informed by *examining* the truth about everyday life. The person living a true life relates to its truth by testing it and by attempting to live it. How does this life that is actually lived relate to truth? For the Cynics, truth meant that what one is doing is essential for living and cannot be rejected; true is what is elementary to life. Such a life implies an ethical relationship with others who will be, voluntarily or not, educated about what is true and what is not. The Cynics engaged in dialogues with their fellow citizens to put their conventions to the test. They tried to make appeals to their soul to test assumptions about what might be true or not.

Crucial for the philosophers of the good-life-as-practice is that it is not clear from the start what a true life is or whether its truth exists as a doctrine or theory that can be put to practice. The true life is instead a practice of generating knowledge by actively examining what holds true or not. The truth of life must be investigated and one needs to train and transform oneself to explore this truth.[8] Foucault later described this as a *technology of the self* (see Chapter 9). For instance, the Cynics asked what they actually needed to live a true life and what they could do without. They learned about the true life by putting it to the test. As the Cynics became older, they got rid of more and more of their possessions. The Cynics found out that they could live without these possessions by gradually abstaining from them.

The true life was an *exemplary* life, an example for others to witness and learn from even if the lesson was sometimes hard to swallow. For fellow citizens, the Cynics' lives seemed to be more about indecent behaviour than truth. This was the case because the Cynics took what is natural to be good and true, which meant they did not conceal the bodily functions that others deemed better to keep private. They relieved themselves in public because they did not hide the truth and beauty of nature. Precisely in this way, Foucault argues, the exemplary life gained the characteristics of a work of art. It is a life that is actively practised and constantly refined through persistent testing and finetuning. Life's truth was simultaneously its beauty, no matter how unconventional or repulsive such a life may seem to others.

Foucault's preoccupation with truth is very clearly expressed in his archaeological method. Foucault articulates how the good, the true and the beautiful relate to everyday life (*bios*). The true life is articulated in relation to truth, ethics and aesthetics (as well as, in a more complicated way, to the political life of governing the *polis*, which will be discussed below). Through his archaeological approach, Foucault provides readers with a picture of the *practical* form that the Cynics' lives could take on rather than only focusing on their ideas and doctrines. What did the *parrhesiasts do*? How did they live and what did they want to achieve by doing this? What were the effects of their actions?

Foucault provides us with glimpses of everyday lives that were actually lived or that could have been lived. These are forms of life that can be empirically traced and 'unearthed' from historical texts. This method provided Foucault with a lens to study these texts. For the goals of my book, the true life of the Cynics provides an example of how the good life might be conceptualised. As I will show later, these concepts cannot be directly applied to present-day situations but first require a shift to conceptualising less-than-perfect lives.

The true life of the Cynics

The Cynics examined the truth or put it to the test (and therefore led a true life) by enacting their ideas in practice. For example, to practise the true life the Cynics tried not to become involved in matters of opinion and convention. These were not about truth according to them. Truth was to be found in nature rather than culture. What were deemed real concerns – that is, concerns relevant to living a true life – were the things that were necessitated by or which followed from nature. Through their lifestyle, as people without possessions or any ties to cultural conventions, the Cynics showed there was *a lot* one could do without. Their contemporaries compared the Cynics' lives to the lives of dogs; they were not interested in proper clothing or decent behaviour and admonished others by barking at them.

Foucault's descriptions of the Cynics' approach to truth is insightful for understanding why their exemplary lives provoked scandal. To the Cynics, the true life was: 1) *unconcealed*, 2) *independent*, 3) *straight* and 4) *sovereign*. Their concern for the truth informed how they valued beauty and rightness. By listing these characteristics I can show how truth, beauty and goodness are connected in everyday-life practices.

First, according to the Cynics, the true life does not hide anything. It does not acknowledge shame or dishonesty, which are conventions rather than truths. For the Cynics, true life unfolds along the lines of nature (it is *straight*). Truth is not to be censored or hidden away. Truth is guided and supported by the watchful eyes of friends who dare to speak the truth to each another (*parrhesia*) and who dare to accept this truth. Such an *unconcealed life* does not require one to have a house to hide in to keep secrets from others. This life requires only a minimum of clothing and there is little need for privacy from others. What is natural is good, true and beautiful. If one only follows one's natural needs, then there is nothing bad that one should need to hide. And this was scandalous to the citizens of Athens. In this sense, the Cynics' lives were radically different from the lives of Athenian citizens. Dirtiness and ugliness in the eyes of their contemporaries were of no concern to the Cynics.

The second characteristic of the true life, *independence*, signifies a life without 'mixtures', bonds or dependencies. Such a life is identical to itself, and the soul is freed from material cravings and disorderliness. The self takes care of the self and does not worry about things that are beyond its control. In this sense, such a life was also a life of 'indifference'. Foucault describes the ways in which the early Cynics enacted this form of life by living in poverty. Their independence, however, involved being dirty and offending others in a society where graceful conduct, physical beauty and cleanliness, in addition to personal reputation and honour, were highly valued. The Cynics actively sought out situations in which they would be humiliated to challenge the conventions that govern such situations, to train themselves not to have opinions or to participate in these conventions, and to teach others to do the same. For instance, Foucault describes a situation in which some men have a meal and throw a bone to Diogenes so that he can eat like a dog. Diogenes retrieves the bone to chew on it, and then pisses on the guests like a real dog would. Rather than being humiliated by these men, Diogenes confronts them with their own conventions and demonstrates how to defy such conventions.

This particular account also refers to the third characteristic of the true life, namely *straightness*, which means that one should live according to the *logos* (laws) of nature. This is an animalistic way of living. For an animal, nothing that is natural can be wrong. What is natural is self-evident. Hence the many stories about Cynics publicly relieving themselves. An oft-quoted example is that of Diogenes masturbating in public. As a dog, however, Diogenes considers only the demands put on him by nature. The Cynics only ate as much food as they needed and they had no house or family. Diogenes was at some point even sold as a slave.

The metaphor of the dog also illustrates the attitude of the Cynics towards others; they figuratively barked at citizens by confronting them with their concerns about things that were not of real importance. The Cynics bit and attacked people in their effort to challenge vices, misleading conventions or untruths.

The fourth characteristic of the true life is *sovereignty*, which refers to a clearly directed life that cannot be corrupted. One should belong to oneself and be sovereign over every aspect of one's life. Such sovereignty leads to pleasure and the enjoyment of *owning* oneself. By enjoying oneself through one's sovereignty, the true life also becomes beneficial to others. The Cynics sought to provide spiritual guidance and assistance to others. They taught them to care for themselves by putting their lives to the test. Foucault uses the metaphors of the doctor and the teacher (rather than those of the king or emperor) to describe this type of sovereignty. The philosopher relieves pain and gives both encouragement and guidance on how to conduct one's life. The sovereign life of the Cynics is hence a life that is lived in assistance to others. This assistance is provided through their exemplary lives as well as the narratives about and demonstrations of these lives and through examinations of what people hold to be true.

Diogenes and Alexander the Great

Foucault cites a parable in which Diogenes meets Alexander the Great. The parable demonstrates how the greatness of the Cynic's life is more powerful than the sovereignty of the king. Monarchy, the tale shows, is illusory and precarious as well as constantly under threat. Alexander is dependent on his empire to be king, whereas Diogenes needs nothing. Alexander needs training but Diogenes does not because he merely needs courage to live the true life and reject the things he does not really need, which makes him immune to the opinions of others. Alexander needs to defeat others but Diogenes needs only to overcome his own errors and vices. Alexander can lose everything, Diogenes nothing. The Cynics test themselves for humanity. They interfere with the lives of others, but they do not interfere with just anything. Only those things that are of interest to *humanity* are of interest to the Cynic. This includes the life of the Cynic himself. He is like the 'general who inspects the troops' in that the general looks after his troops in the interest of all people. As such, the Cynics are distinct from the people they want to educate. They are moral examples with which to teach others, which means there is a clear hierarchy.[9]

These characteristics of truth are also aesthetic and moral characteristics. It is bad to cling to what one does not need. Living a true life means living a beautiful life and proposing notions of beauty that mock aesthetic conventions as well as dedicating oneself to truth. *Parrhesia* means 'to say everything' (*pan rema*). It has a pejorative connotation when referring to 'just saying whatever', that is, speaking for the sake of speaking without reference to reason or truth. The positive connotation of *parrhesia* is 'to hide nothing' and to say things without reserve, rhetorical flourishes or mannerisms. This demands courage and frankness because it involves running the risk of offending others. It may evoke anger in others and may even put the life of the speaker in danger. This is why such spiritual guidance works best within a friendly relationship even if *parrhesia* may also challenge this friendship. *Parrhesia* demands courage to speak as well as accept the truth. This is different from rhetoric because in rhetorical speech there is no relationship between the person who is speaking and the truth. One can say things beautifully and skilfully without meaning one word of what is being said. *Parrhesia*, however, is not a technique in the rhetorical sense. It links persons to the truth and rightness of *what* they are saying and *where* they are saying it. It is a virtue to practise *parrhesia* because it is a modality of speaking the truth.

Parrhesia and other modes of speaking the truth

Foucault understood *parrhesia* as a particular mode among other modes of speaking the truth. This is important to acknowledge because it allowed him to delineate between the true and good life as practices that aim for truth and other, different practices of speaking the truth. Foucault articulates four modalities of speaking the truth in ancient Greek thought that link a subject to a form of truth and to ways of verifying that truth. First, there is the *prophet*. The prophet does not speak for himself but on behalf of others, namely the gods who speak through him. The prophet mediates between gods and men, and between the present and the future, by predicting what is to come. Speaking the truth serves here as a corrective to blindness by making people see the future that they are heading towards. The truth articulated by the prophet may be enigmatic, but it can be verified when reality eventually unfolds.

The second mode of speaking the truth is that of the *wise*. The wise man speaks on his own behalf but keeps his wisdom mostly to himself. He only speaks the truth in public when he is called upon to do so. If he is not asked to speak the truth, he lives a withdrawn life. The truth he utters is not an advice but pertains to the state of *Being* of the world. It provides general statements about the world (*physis*). In the wise man we may also recognise the scientist who speaks about the world in terms of generalities.

Then there is the *parrhesiast*, the figure in which Foucault is most interested. A *parrhesiast* speaks not about general concerns but about 'the singularity of individuals, situations and conjunctures'. The *parrhesiast* cannot remain silent as the wise man might because he has an obligation to give advice to humankind. To the *parrhesiast* the general knowledge of the wise man is 'useless'; it cannot be used to better one's life.[10] It has no pragmatic value. Only the knowledge that is needed for living one's life well is of interest to the *parrhesiast*. Hence, the *parrhesiast* must speak out even if he puts himself in danger by doing so. Speaking is to validate this truth. The *parrhesiast* helps other people shape themselves as moral subjects and to shape their *ethos*. This is his mission.

Finally, there is the *teacher* or *technician*. This may be a doctor, a musician, shoemaker or carpenter. The knowledge of the teacher is *techne* or knowhow. It is a form of knowledge that is shaped in practice and that can be acquired through apprenticeship. Rather than being a theory, *techne* is mainly something that can be learned through exercise and experience. Teachers can teach this knowledge, and they have to do this to allow this knowledge to survive because it is a form of technical knowledge that is embedded in a tradition. Once the tradition is lost the knowledge will disappear too, as it needs to be transferred from master to apprentice in order to be passed on. This process can be done in a friendly manner, and the teacher may take pride in their skills, but there is no *risk* in passing on *techne*. This is the most important difference with *parrhesia*. For the purposes of this book, learning-through-tradition is clearly of interest for generating knowledge about certain forms of everyday life.[11]

Foucault hence discerns four regimes of truth or veridiction: *prophecy* is in relation to fate because it pertains to what will unfold in reality. It can be enigmatic and hidden. *Wisdom* relates to Being, namely that which is (always) there in the order of things (*physis*). Next there is *parrhesia* or providing knowledge about individual ways of living well (*ethos*). And last there is the expertise of knowhow – *techne*. This is knowledge about how to do things. These four 'modes of veridiction' are each related to a different character (the prophet, the wise man, the *parrhesiast* and the craftsman) and involve different domains (the future, nature, individual life, skills).

However, these characters should not be understood only as specific types of persons. Different modes of veridiction can be connected to each other. For example, *parrhesia* and wisdom can meet in philosophy, and *parrhesia* and prophecy can meet in Christianity. In the Middle Ages, teaching and *physis* were connected, and in present days, prophecy may become connected to revolutionary discourse (in Foucault's time) or terrorism (in the twenty-first century).[12] One could say that knowledge about Being was institutionalised in the sciences, whereas knowledge on how to live a good life was the subject matter of religious institutions or the market. These are clear examples of attempts to separate the spheres of truth and goodness.[13]

Socrates' political *parrhesia* and his search for truth through inquiry

The four modes of veridiction had no clear relationship to the governance of the *polis*. In this way, Foucault could make clear why the philosophers of the good-life-as-practice did what they did – it was their mission to speak the truth. Foucault goes to some length in analysing the relationship between the *polis* and *parrhesia* by exploring the relationship between political *parrhesia* and *parrhesia* in relation to *ethos* or individual life.[14] In discussions about political *parrhesia* and democracy, *ethos* is a crucial term for understanding doubts about the value of democratic governance that emerged in ancient Greece. The problem with democracy was that the 'majority' (a group of people) did not possess a soul and therefore could not be educated. A king or a tyrant, however, *did* have a soul and hence had the potential to be educated and understand truth.

Socrates' life is the most vivid example of the relationship between ethos and political life. Socrates asserted that he would rather die than stop speaking the truth. But he explicitly excluded political *parrhesia*, which is a form of frankly speaking the truth in democratic assemblies. Socrates did not engage in political *parrhesia*, he said, because this would cost him his life. How to understand this paradox of wanting to sacrifice one's life for truth, on the one hand, while renouncing this on the other? Clarification can be provided by distinguishing between the practice or mission of *parrhesia* and the goal of speaking truth in politics (political *parrhesia*).

Through his practice of *parrhesia*, Socrates took care of his contemporary citizens in the manner of a father or older brother. In his *Apology*, Socrates gives two examples in which he spoke the truth in an assembly and ran the risk of being killed. Foucault shows that it was not Socrates' fear of death that kept him from engaging in political *parrhesia*. Rather, it was his *mission* to speak the truth and, in doing so, to express care for the Athenians. Dying in the political arena would prevent him from being able to care for others through useful, beneficial and responsible relationships. Socrates hence chose to speak the truth as a philosopher or *parrhesiast* rather than as a politician.

So, political *parrhesia* is speaking the truth about governance before an audience that may take offence at this truth and thus threaten the speaker. A tyrant or a prominent member of the assembly might punish one for such words. This shows that there is a difference in the normativity of these different types of *parrhesia*. Political *parrhesia* makes statements about what governments should do. Ethical or aesthetic *parrhesia*, however, is a *test* of the truth that takes place in the confrontation (in dialogue) between souls. Both are modes of speaking the truth, both imply danger for the speaker as well as for the listener. Each mode of *parrhesia* pertains to a different domain, namely the governance of the *polis* or of individual life. But the assembly or 'the majority' cannot test the truth even if the individual members can.

This issue of the distinctiveness of *parrhesia* can be analysed in terms of the four modes of veridiction or speaking the truth. Socrates' practice of speaking the truth is based on the prophecy of the oracle at Delphi,[15] but he did not test this prophecy by waiting to see how reality or nature would unfold according to the prophetic mode of veridiction. Instead, Socrates *examined* the truth spoken by the oracle. He allowed it to be tested by his soul – the touchstone for this type of truth – in his investigations. There is no transfer of knowhow, as with *techne*, but there is a confrontation with other people about what they know or think they know about their lives. *Parrhesia*'s mode of verification is the testing of statements about one's life through the soul and through conversation with others.

Foucault analyses Socrates' interpretation of the famous prophecy given to him by the oracle of Delphi. The oracle was asked which Greek man was wiser than Socrates. The oracle said that *no man* is wiser than Socrates. Nobody understood this answer and neither did Socrates himself. Yet he was determined to find out what it meant. He did not wait to see if reality would somehow verify or clarify the statement. Socrates set off to put the oracle's statement to the test in order to learn and care for himself. He went out to question and investigate the oracle's prophecy by engaging in the mode of veridiction that is *parrhesia*.

Socrates started this inquiry, or this particular 'game of truth', by speaking to others about wisdom. He travelled to meet politicians, poets and labourers to ask them about what they know. Socrates determined that politicians thought that they were wise but that they made many mistakes. Labourers knew far more than politicians about issues they had expertise on. But all of them shared the idea that they knew things they did *not* know when they were put to the test. And this was what Socrates learned, namely that he knew that *he did not know* things. He was aware of his own ignorance. The oracle was proven right, as this made him wiser than others.

Having the courage to speak and investigate the truth was more important to Socrates than proving that he did not fear death. His mission to tell the truth could not be obstructed by his dying for reasons that were not related to this mission. This mode of *parrhesia* and veridiction is very different from the detached wise man who speaks only when forced to and who otherwise remains silent. It is also different from the knowledge held by the doctor who knows how to set a broken leg. Yet it is a mode of veridiction that could, theoretically speaking, be applied in the political arena. But because of the *parrhesiasts*' particular mission of *parrhesia*, this could not be done in practice. Socrates' mission and responsibility were to educate the citizens rather than to risk his life in the political arena. He had to take care of others and to make them take care of themselves, of their soul and of truth. Political *parrhesia* was too risky and would jeopardise this mission. Losing his life would make it impossible for Socrates to pursue his mission.

Aesthetic values

The notion of 'having a mission' brings us to the motivation of *parrhesiasts* for practising *parrhesia* and how they understand its value. What drove them to conduct these tests with others and to risk social condemnation and other hardships? Here, I again follow the example of the Cynics. The Cynics tried to live the true life in order to train themselves and to teach others how to take care of themselves (*epimeleia, melei moi*). The Cynics were educators but they did not only seek to educate those around them. They wanted to change humankind. The domain they focused on to interfere with humankind, however, was individuals' moral lives or *ethos*. *Ethos* refers to the ways of life or conduct through which a person constitutes and enacts themselves as a moral subject. But why did they want to do this? Here we reach a point on which Foucault is silent, apart from some snippets of various thoughts that can be found in his lectures. But these snippets are very interesting and I will piece them together here.

Foucault conceptualises the motivation to care for oneself as an aesthetic motivation, which is also an ethical motivation as well as a desire for truth. First, Foucault argued that everyday life (*bios*), under the guise of the good life (*ethos*), has become an object for aesthetic evaluation. *Bios* is shaped into an object with a certain aesthetic form and can thus become a work of art. Adjectives that could previously only be applied to things or words can now be attached to practices of the true life. The true life is a creative practice for shaping this life and it is informed by varied aesthetic forms. True lives have an aesthetic form that builds on the same values that are established when testing the truth (unconcealed, independent, straight and sovereign).

Diogenes was said to live a dog's life – a life without modesty, shame (the unconcealed life) and respect – because he did in public what only dogs dare to do. The Cynics were indifferent to the course of history and happy to satisfy only their direct needs. They barked at enemies and served humankind by exemplifying how to live a good and artful life. The true life was therefore also an aesthetic life even if one did not subscribe to the particular style of this aesthetic. For the Cynics, life was open, without dark secrets, and allowed or even obliged to show itself. Life was clear about its intentions and true to what the Cynics said about this. The true life did not involve cheating or combining goodness with badness. True life was a unity and it was in line with what the philosophers knew to be true. Leading the true life took courage to state the opposite of what everyone thought. It was offensive because it showed that people were wrong. Not only did the subject courageously *speak* the truth, it also courageously *lived* or impersonated this truth, and therefore made it an aesthetic *performance*.

Aesthetic motivations

There is a reference to aesthetic *motivations* or *inspirations* in Foucault's lectures. At the start of lecture 7, Foucault analyses care for the self (*epimeleia, melei moi*).[16] He complains that it is unclear where this term comes from or what its root is. In a description of a discussion with Dumézil, a specialist in Greek language, and on the subject matter of *epimeleia* in ancient Greek philosophy, Foucault suggests that the origin could be *melos*, which means *melody*. After an initial rejection of this suggestion, Dumézil eventually agrees that it is possible. In French, *ça me chante* means 'it appeals to me'. This is not a call to duty but a call to freedom and pleasure. 'I do it because it appeals to me.' It is a duty that appeals. It demands an active-passive subject that both is being called and is motivated to follow this call.

The two scholars – Foucault and Dumézil – identify connections to metaphors of warmth. In Latin, *camera* means being hot as well as 'caring about'. In French *chaloir* also means 'having an interest in something'. *Melos* is also the call (*le chant d'appel*) of a shepherd calling their flock.

The sheep come running because they *like* to meet the shepherd even if it is also their obligation. *Melei moi* – the song summons me, calls out to me, it says something to me (*Ça m'interpelle*). There is a latent aspect of musical appeal in care for the self and therefore also in care for others. It is motivated by pleasure and is hence also an aesthetic appreciation.

If I apply these insights to Socrates' practice, we can learn that Socrates' task was in fact a *mission*. He *had* to follow its call, it was unavoidable, and he had to engage with it. Simultaneously, it gave him great pleasure to pursue this duty. The melody of the call motivated and rewarded the ethos of a true, good and beautiful way of life. The *parrhesiast* found intellectual pleasure in discerning truth from untruth (by putting it to the test) as well as in doing good by turning their own life into an exemplary life that could educate others and improve humankind. The subject of the good and true life is a subject that is motivated to live this life in order to find the truth and do good.

This understanding of the active-passive character of both 'being called' and 'being motivated' to care resonates with the motivations of the caregivers discussed in Chapter 3 to support their patients in living a life that is as good as possible. Doing so is their professional duty and obligation, but it is also a motivation that informs their practices without which these cannot be understood. Pleasure in morality and truth appear here not as private passions that are only of interest to the individuals themselves. Pleasure and the call to craft a moral and truthful life form the motivation to live a good life and to help others create one as well.

Archaeology, *bios* and *ethos*

What does Foucault's analysis of the good life of the Cynics provide for understanding present-day concerns in everyday life? The Cynics lived exemplary lives, but what makes it possible to fold their story in with contemporary concerns is not the *content* of the ways they point us towards the good; I cannot imagine that appeals to start living like a dog would find a sympathetic ear today, and this approach does not seem to be particularly nice or caring. And neither would contemporary society facilitate conditions for living in such a way. I suspect that a contemporary Cynic would be jailed for vagrancy and indecent behaviour. Yet there are other forms of exemplary lives that are possible to imagine in present-day care practices. One might think of communities where people organise their lives differently, for instance because they want to attempt to live in an anarchical society or in a better democracy, or to lead more climate-friendly lives. But we might also think of the lives of caregivers who are trying to achieve something good for their patients. These can also be seen as exemplary lives, as ways of showing that different forms of life are possible.

What may be refolded are Foucault's concepts of *bios* and *ethos*. Foucault unfolds and folds these new objects to make them amenable to historical study, thus providing analytical directions for scholars interested in everyday-life practices.[17] I consider Foucault's analysis of the Cynics as a generative approach to finding concepts that enable one to write a history of the good life. Foucault makes specific and concrete forms of life visible (rather than, say, general knowledge about the soul) by shaping this 'new-old' object with the concepts and methods that he derives from the Greek language. In Foucault's archaeological method – and also through the form of his lectures – the activity of *examining* and *crafting* comes to the fore, which is very different from the more passive approach of discovering or mirroring the truth of nature. Foucault's lectures provide tools for an historical approach to understanding the ways in which people were made, and the ways in which they made themselves, into subjects with a particular relation to the truth. This allows researchers to re-scribe contemporary varieties of the good life.

How do the concepts of *ethos* and *bios* help with the study of everyday life as a good life? The 'ethos' is a form of everyday life (*bios*). *Ethos* demands a subject that is normatively inclined, through an aesthetic and/or moral motivation (it is both a duty as well as a pleasure), to speak the truth and to aesthetically shape the *ethos* – and hence also shape itself as a moral subject. This particular *ethos* exists alongside other possible forms of *ethos* and next to the less coherent and more messy forms of the *bios* of citizens. *Ethos* has, or aims to have, ethical implications for the lives of others. Both *ethos* and *bios* refer to the everyday-life practice and conduct of individuals, and help with thinking about the types of normativity found in everyday life that can either be tacit and varied (*bios*) or more explicit and more structured (*ethos*).

Ethos

How can we understand *ethos* as a specific form of *bios*? First, the different forms of *ethos* found among different schools of thought can also be seen as works of art. This is the case because these forms are intentional. They are not coincidentally emerging forms of life but are purposefully created by a subject or group of subjects. The subject who is cultivating an *ethos* is intentionally doing this even if it is often not clear what it will lead to and how this will affect their audience. This is a matter of constant examination, testing and training. One can compare this to the work of an artist who knows that she strives to create a work of art even though she cannot completely control the process no matter how skilled she might be. She also cannot control the *effects* that this artwork will have on her audience.

Second, the forming of *ethos* is hard work; it has to be aesthetically *crafted*. To live the type of *ethos* that the Cynics proposed means working hard to improve one's performance, and testing this to see how it may be expanded, trained and improved. The practice of crafting life makes it a work of art. It is not something that 'merely happens'. It is a motivated, purposefully pursued and creative process. This also means that it relates to particular practices, namely those that are shaped in efforts to be exemplary so that others can learn from them.

Third, forms of *ethos* can be understood as works of art because they create possibilities for seeing things differently by articulating different layers of meaning and ways of acting differently.[18] In this way, these forms of life challenge singular and conventional ways of accepting what is good and true. They do this by adding different possibilities and by making things that are taken for granted strange again. Without disregarding their seriousness, the exemplary lives that the Cynics and Socrates performed can be seen as theatrical in nature, containing specific messages about morality and truth, and expressing particular ideas about what is beautiful, elementary or appropriate. Indeed, it is clear that in these practices of the good life, everyday values about how to live one's life are foregrounded (what to wear, where to live, how to behave in relation to others, how to relate to the truth, what to find important). These are not prescriptive rules or doctrines but repertoires for challenging and training the self as well as for teaching others by altering their understanding of their own lives. The good life can teach citizens because philosophers present a qualitatively different form of the good life than citizens are used to seeing.

Fourth, *ethos* is not important in and of itself: it is a way for teaching others. The *ethos* implies an ethical relationship to others, namely those for whom the example of the practice of a good life is a means for being educated and taught about what is important in life and what is not. The good life is a serious thing. Living the good life is a tool to 'improve mankind'. Or to put it into my own words, the good life aims to achieve something good for others.

The study of *ethos* as particular forms of the good life is an element of the history that Foucault proposed to write. It shows how questions of ethics, aesthetics and truth are connected to techniques for examining and training the self in everyday-life practices. In ancient Greek examples of the good life, truth, goodness and beauty are inseparable. But this connectedness was also informed by their object, that is, everyday life. One can suggest different ways of connecting these terms, but in the study of practices, truth, goodness and beauty always come together 'as a package'. They involve perceptions of what the world is and what its problems are, how to relate to others in this world, and how to shape one's subject-position and *ethos* by doing certain beautiful and true things rather than others.

Bios

When placing *ethos* within *bios*, and hence within actual practices of everyday life, *bios* becomes incoherent as a 'performance' of everyday life. *Bios* may involve a mosaic of different understandings of the world and possible actions – as well as *ethos* – within it.[19] However, the Cynics folded *ethos* and *bios* into each other: they lived *exemplary* lives through their day-to-day practices. They aimed to synchronise *bios* and *ethos* or bring them in conversation with each other in the act of examining the truth. For them, there was no strong difference between doing good and preaching about the good. They embodied and personified the good life. It existed as an exemplary practice that was relatively coherent in comparison to the lives of their contemporaries.

Note that there is a great difference between this understanding of the good life and Habermas's rationally achieved common good, which is created through public opinions that emerge from individual opinions or morals and their articulation in public debate. *Ethos* does not emerge through the procedure of refining beliefs that are found in everyday life (*bios*). On the contrary, the exemplary, scandalous lives of the Cynics represented the *other* compared to the lives of the citizens that were directed by conventions. *Ethos* is a specific and rather more coherent form of *bios* and the former is antagonistic to the latter. More modest schools of the good life were milder, but they still differed strongly from ordinary lives.

The links between *bios* and different forms of *ethos* were much looser and more varied for 'ordinary' citizens, who pursued different values and lived in accordance with habit and convention while moving from one everyday problem to the next. Acknowledging the imperfections of the subject-position of citizens helps create a theoretical space for thinking about the good life for other ordinary people, such as people with a chronic illness. But to develop this idea further, I first need to show

how Foucault's approach to truth, paired with his utter dislike of what he calls 'humanism' (and I call modernity), can nevertheless provide conceptual handholds for thinking about *values* in everyday life. I therefore need to learn more about why, according to ancient Greek thought, philosophers of the good life as well as citizens were doing what they did and what their psychological state was.

Truth and motivation

Foucault reinscribed *ethos* as a form of *bios* in the history of ideas by using his archaeological method. But he also explored the linkages between political life (*politeia*, the demos or the assembly governing the *polis*) and individual life or conduct (*ethos*, where the Cynics advised their fellow citizens) as well as their relation to the speaking of truth. Foucault's focal object throughout his oeuvre is the way in which discourses of truth inform both governance and subjectification. He studies these simultaneously and asks, 'What modes of subjectification are articulated with forms of the government of men, to resist or inhabit them?'[20] Foucault conceptualises subjectification here as a practice that is created by a certain discourse or as a subject-position that one enacts within a certain discourse.[21] Individuals can conform to such positions or resist them.

Understanding what *moves* individuals who resist or actively accept certain subject-positions was not Foucault's most important line of inquiry. His main preoccupation, as we saw, was with the role of truth both in the shaping of exemplary life forms as practices of *parrhesia* and in his archaeological method of 'digging up' forms of life. Certain individuals may resist or value certain subject-positions in concrete situations, but this is not what Foucault was interested in. Individual subjectivity or evaluations have little space in his thinking. Whether other citizens liked or disliked the Cynics' take on the true life is, for Foucault, secondary to understanding what their subject-position *is*. The citizens' responses were, however, the reason why the Cynics needed courage if they were to practice *parrhesia*. They form the context in which the Cynics' way of life became exemplary and obtained its moral function.

The Cynics represented a school of thought, or rather a practice of the good life, not just an individual thing. The Cynics' way of life was not just a collection of reflections, valuations, passions or motivations of unconnected individuals. But even if Foucault is not much interested in individuals as people who value certain things or who are motivated to do certain things, let alone have a *taste* for one thing or another, his lectures show that such valuations are indeed important for individuals who wish to live in certain ways. Motivations are what make living the true life appealing, and they explain why subjects are compelled and motivated to live such a life. The subject practising *parrhesia* is 'enchanted' or seduced and lured into the good life to the extent that they also actively desire to take part in it. They find pleasure in caring for oneself and for others, enjoyment and happiness in owning oneself, and joy in finding the courage to examine and speak the truth. But how can this appeal to shape a certain *ethos* be used to understand 'ordinary' people or people currently living with chronic disease? They may not have a mission such as that of the Cynics, but they nevertheless attempt to live a life that is as good as possible. They strive for the good, even if the nature of these goods may vary and even if these goods may never be achieved – and the bads will remain part of their lives.

Sick citizens and the normativity of a good life

Both citizens and philosophers of the good life were striving for something good in their everyday lives. The practices and values of the ancient Greeks are very different from the challenges that people with chronic disease face in the present. There can be no simple translation of ancient Greek practices to contemporary practices. Greek society was completely different from our society and we would reject many of its elements.[22] Yet there are some interesting possibilities that arise from Foucault's conceptualisation of *ethos* and *bios* for theorising the subject-positions of 'ordinary people' with less-than-perfect lives and who do not have a grand mission to help others.

First, we may consider the particular social and temporal position of the *parrhesiasts* living the true life. In the last lectures of the series, Foucault stresses that the true life is also the life of the *Other*, that is, the life of a dog, an outsider and an exemplar. It is exactly because the Cynics' lives are so *different* from those of their fellow citizens that the Cynics can confront and educate them. They enacted the true life and they managed to have an effect because of their demonstration of the differences between their lives and those of citizens. Because the Cynics' lives were different, they could be thought of as good as well as true. These were exemplary lives from which the citizens could learn.

It is striking that the subject-position of the people *addressed* by the Cynics is, to a great extent, absent in Foucault's lectures. Who are these people who form the audience of the Cynics? We learn that the citizens are scandalised and that they are ethically reprimanded by the Cynics. The reactions of citizens are important for explaining why it takes courage to practise *parrhesia*. *Parrhesia* becomes salient because it is in opposition to what others think and because it contrasts with what is generally held to be proper and true. Courage is a virtue for the *parrhesiast*, and this is also why speaking the truth is powerful. Between the lines of Foucault's lectures we can read that citizens were the decadent male elite who, when they were not going to war, spent most of their time arguing, eating, bathing, having sex and trying to look good or beautiful. The Cynics, by living an exemplary life, wanted to show or teach these citizens what is good and how to live a true life. This turned the Cynics into something that is closer to the role of teacher or 'doctor' than that of an ordinary citizen.

The citizens – or at least those who are not-so-good, or, rather, those who are straying from the path of true life because they are unclear about what their *ethos* should be – are being taught. They take the subject-position of 'patients' or 'pupils', so to speak, namely people with problems in need of improvement.[23] This is a very different position and one that is situated in the conventions of that time. Athenian citizens often pursued projects that were wrong or trivial in the eyes of the Cynics, such as striving for wealth and luxury. Citizens muddled through or experienced temporary triumphs but were generally misled by their ambitions and conventions. As imperfect practitioners of *bios* they needed to be challenged and corrected. Citizens *may* become subjects living a true life, but only if they accept the truth presented to them by the *parrhesiasts* and perform this truth through their lives, even if they do not do this as consistently and skilfully as their teachers.

Good lives that are not so good

The subject-position of citizen opens up a theoretical possibility for thinking about the good life in the context of chronic disease. It allows for an exploration of the subject-position of citizens, that is to say, imperfect people who 'live with the bad', which can be contrasted with the subject-position of exemplary people who live the good life. The citizens of Athens were not exemplary subjects, but we can understand their character more positively when comparing their position to that of patients. People with chronic disease live with the 'bads' that are the result of their diseases or their treatments. People with lasting handicaps are not in and of themselves exemplary. They encounter moral and aesthetic difficulties and fail to have insights. They must make the best of their life in conditions that are not optimal. They may want to conceal things, keep up a good face, learn about being dependent on others and find ways to live in this manner, and they may struggle to find the space to move about. They are confronted with the ugly bends and twists of their capricious body and may feel like they are unable to govern their own life. The lives of both citizens and patients are an example of having to live with badness in specific socio-material situations. This is a non-exemplary subject-position in the sense that they do not aim to provide ideals that others might strive after.

I can now compare three subject-positions: there are the exemplary and unconventional lives of philosophers of the good life, such as, for example, the Cynics; the less-than-perfect, conventional lives of the citizens of Athens; and the conventional lives of chronic patients who must 'live with something bad', such as the women who have lost their hair. The people in the latter two positions are striving for something good, but the nature of these goods may be contested. The citizens, for example, were reprimanded by the Cynics because they strove for wealth. They present an example of how one may live with the bad rather than an exemplary representation of how to do this in a good way. One can nonetheless learn from these examples, because they strive for a good life, but also because one can learn from mistakes or other things that might go wrong in the attempt to make the best of things. Hence one can learn about the effects, good and bad, of certain ways of living.

The goods that are strived for in all three subject-positions are not just personal pleasures, tastes or preferences for things that one might be able to do without. The Cynics were serious in practising what they preached. They led a life that was far less comfortable than the lives of other male citizens. For bald women, there were important values at stake as well, such as continuing to partake in their social environment and not being cast out or frightening others. All these forms of the good were linked to the conventions and social imaginaries of their time; for living with them, or by attempting to differ from them, and hence promoting a truth that transcends conventions.

The exemplary good lives of the philosophers of the good-life-as-practice were performed as a *mission*. The Cynics, as teachers, wanted to confront their audience and they underscored the value of a straight and open truth rather than, say, a truth that is hidden by wigs or scarves. They were motivated by their duty to care for others and to teach them about the true life. For those leading ordinary lives there was no mission to help others even if there were strong motivations to do so. The women who had lost their hair had no intention of educating others. Instead, they had the more pragmatic aim of protecting others and living together with them in peace. Their reward (pleasure) was to continue to remain a part of their social environment. Philosophers of the good life wanted to be different in order to provide a mirror to citizens; bald women wanted to blend in so that they would not stand out in a crowd.

In all three positions there is some space for manoeuvring despite certain socio-material limitations. People creatively tinkered with the subject-positions that had been laid out for them, and they did this to find ways of living that were of value to them and that allowed them to achieve a state of worth. In doing so, they creatively worked towards particular notions of what is good and true. This was part of the *mission* of the philosophers of the good life. But for bald women, modifying their appearances and managing the responses of others was something that had been forced on them by conventions that compelled them to deal with these responses in the best possible way. These three positions are connected not by the particular *nature* of the aesthetic values that they pursue but by their active-creative attempts at shaping one's life towards something good.

So, the good lives of ordinary people are not exemplary, but others can nevertheless learn from their adventures and failings. The goodness of ordinary lives is informed by conventions and contingent problems that emerge along the way rather than by doctrines or personal taste. There is no 'mission' that shapes these ordinary lives, but people are active and creative in shaping everyday life regardless, pursuing particular notions of what is good. What do these descriptive characteristics imply for analysing such lives as *good* lives?

Everyday life as a good life

To end the chapter, I can now formulate some ideas about the truth, beauty and goodness of ordinary lives of people with chronic disease or lasting impairments. These lives include goods as well as bads, and do not aim to perform a coherent or prescriptive idea of goodness. A clear conclusion is that questions about how ordinary lives may be good are *empirical* questions rather than normative programmes. Whether expert or novice, or not even aspiring to be knowledgeable about the good life, ordinary people are not exemplary. They are examples of individuals who are striving for something good and who are trying to deal with situations that are either good or not so good. What these goods involve is not a matter of judgement or a prescription about how one should conduct one's life in a good manner. These are not doctrines or normative theories about how one should live well. The normativities that are relevant to leading a good life need to be empirically determined by focusing on the efforts and motivations of people who are trying to achieve something good as well as on the effects of their interactions with the conventions of the *here and now*, that is, in a specific time and place. What is good is the pragmatic and contingent – and sometimes more coherent – attempt at living a life that is as good as possible.

Everyday life (*bios*) refers to the practices through which individuals attempt to mobilise and create social forms of living together. Everyday life has no coherent normative orientation unless one is a philosopher of the good life, or a fundamentalist or terrorist.[24] Rather than a coherent framework there is a patchwork of positions and valuations. And there are also the contingencies to which every new day may give rise. There are, moreover, snippets of *ethos* belonging to citizens/patients who are motivated to make the best of life and who craft ways for getting through their day in the best way possible by moving from one problem to the next. These everyday practices contain elements of different forms of *ethos* as well as theories about what is good to do. For example, there can be a desire to be autonomous, to enjoy a party or to take care of one's health. Different normativities and ways of positioning and being positioned are part of everyday-life practices, both clinical and otherwise. For instance, receiving a serious but life-saving treatment is one concern, but trying to remain part of one's social environment is quite another. Clear hierarchies between goods are not always available and intended hierarchies may fail. 'Healthy living', for instance, may be in competition with being a good parent or sister. Priorities are always made and remade in specific situations.

In ordinary lives there are always *efforts* to lead a good life and to find things that people value even if others might contest them. People enact particular appreciations or motivations both in what they say, and non-verbally, in what they do.[25] What forms of the good are deemed important in everyday life may shift because they are dependent on various circumstances. Goods may be defined as moral, medical, aesthetic, economic and so on. As has become clear, goods are not simply matters of taste but are informed by social conventions and imaginaries. These forms of the good can be as difficult to ignore as conventions about baldness. Goods may be expressly articulated, or they may be tacitly presented, and they might be achieved with the use of certain devices and techniques or through the norms and gazes of others. Ideals of autonomy or dignity may or may not inform the repertoires of one's caregivers. Wigs may be available and affordable or not. Having no hair as a woman may be acceptable or not. Conventions are important providers of goods and bads, and these conventions also inform people's efforts, however authentic and personal these may feel.

The demands of people with chronic disease and their specific situation are foregrounded. They must deal with diseases, impairments, treatments or other influences on their lives that they have no control over. 'Forms of the bad' will remain a part of their lives because they will not be cured of their chronic disease. Finding the good of a *cure* or a panacea to all their problems is not their aim, or if it is, this is a futile one. Their task is to live a life that is as good as possible. This means, again, that there are no general norms, standards or criteria for determining what a good life may be. However, it is still possible to exchange tips and tricks for others to try and test. What are the available ways for dealing with hair loss, fatigue, inaccessible labour markets and so on?

People's capacity to value and obtain value, as well as their preferences and motivations, are hence not 'free'; they emerge through interaction with their specific socio-material environment. This suggests that there is a relationship, or perhaps even a unity, between the person appreciating something and the thing being appreciated.[26] Appreciations are hence both passive and active: that is, they act on the self and are acted upon by the self. They can be shared by some people and rejected by others. There is no 'universal appreciation'; it is an aesthetic, situated notion.[27] The interactions between different forms of the good as well as the circumstances under which they appear make the *effects* of what people do something they cannot completely control. They are unpredictable. An ordinary life as a good life is hence filled with cultural and social contingencies as well as tentative attempts at improving one's circumstances in ways that may turn out to be useful or not.

To end: ordinary lives, the good and the true

With the help of Foucault's understanding of everyday life (*bios*) and exemplary life (*ethos*) it became possible to make an 'empirical turn' in the study of ordinary lives that are good and bad as well as non-exemplary. This required a shift in ideas about 'learning about their truth'. Might it be the case that individual lives have something that is of interest to others in comparable positions? How might these lives relate to each other when they are dissimilar to the relationships between exemplary teachers and pupils? This is a question about conducting research and finding ways of studying the good life. How may knowledge about everyday forms of the good life be developed, and how might this knowledge travel if not through generalisations or universal rules? These questions about research will be the subject of the chapters in Part III. But in the next chapter, I will first revisit the women who lost their hair. I want to learn in more detail how they created the self as a state of worth and how they played with various conventions to achieve this. In doing so, I will also discuss the influence of individual practices on the formation of socialities.

Notes

1 In modernity, humanism evolved into the secular religion that still exists today. Secular humanism puts the human subject at the centre while adopting Enlightenment values, such as equality and individual freedom. This is quite different from previous humanist traditions of the good life, as this chapter will discuss.
2 Foucault, 2011.
3 Foucault, 1972.
4 Note that 'truth' is an open concept. Its meaning must be specified in the context in which it is used.
5 One could call this knowledge *techne*, and it resembles this, but Foucault reserves that term for a particular form of knowing, namely craftsmanship. Foucault considers the examination of the truth about everyday life a 'game of truth' or a way of knowing and generating knowledge that can be situated besides other ways of knowing.
6 Martin et al., 1988, 11.
7 Although Foucault is commonly read as the political philosopher that he in fact was, I read his work foremost as containing theories about knowledge and ways of thinking about truth. Epistemology came first in his work while his political reflections emerged later in his work.
8 See Metselaar, 2015, Chapter 5, on Bonaventura, and how practising the good life requires a *transformation* of the self. See also Metselaar, 2011.
9 Foucault, 1984, pp. 275–7.
10 See Petrarch's humanist critique of academic knowledge in Chapter 11 of this book.
11 Pols, 2013b.
12 One could say that suicide bombers take the idea of the exemplary life to its limits, namely by ending life to obtain the good that it stands for.
13 The failure of this separation is still hotly debated, for instance, in discussions about 'fake news' and 'fake facts'. A better understanding of the mediation of methods in science might bring some clarification to these debates.
14 Foucault's lecture series in the year before was dedicated to political *parrhesia*. See Foucault, 1983.
15 His connection to religion through his visit to the oracle apparently prevented Socrates from being accused of impiety.
16 Foucault, 2011, p. 117.
17 This folding and unfolding has its creative, or re-scriptive moments. One could argue that these life forms were already in existence among the ancient Greeks regardless of Foucault's archaeological discoveries. But Foucault's creativity as a researcher is to 'dig up' these life forms by articulating them and by finding the words for creating this particular object of *ethos* as a form of *bios*. Foucault performs a generative reading of classical texts to make the creation of this new object of research possible, which is an approach that strongly resonates with the method of folding used in this book.
18 The term 'layers of meaning' in an artwork is from Rietveld, 2019.
19 Knowledge in everyday life resembles clinical knowledge, which is similarly an assembly of different forms of practical knowledge that is drawn upon to interpret and act on specific

situations. See Pols, 2014. This understanding of clinical knowledge builds on Georges Canguilhem's (1989 [1943]) distinction between 'the laboratory' and 'the clinic', which may be loosely interpreted as involving different spaces or structures for scientific and clinical knowledge.
20 Martin et al., 1988.
21 Foucault's notion of discourse refers to conglomerations of buildings, practices of doing things and ways to speak about them.
22 For instance, ancient Greek society depended on the labour of slaves and women, which allowed free citizens to participate in battle, politics and the good life.
23 I would not think that cure is an option here, as this would mean that the citizens would become good-life philosophers themselves, which is possible but unlikely because 'converting' citizens was not necessarily the aim of the Cynics; they were teachers.
24 The closest one can get to a coherent *ethos* would be 'role models', and these are, in a sense, modern versions of the exemplary lives of the philosophers of the good life. These may, however, not have deliberately chosen to become a model for others, and their practices may not have had a clear guideline or aim to teach others how to live. For example, think of Stephen Hawking, who serves as a role model but who probably would have thought of himself first and foremost as a physicist. Being a role model is an abstraction of his everyday life. It is not a motivated ethos but one that is attributed to him by others.
25 Pols, 2005.
26 See Gomart & Hennion, 1999; Hennion, 2003; Pols, 2005.
27 Pols, 2013b; 2019a.

9
The self as a practice of worth: on imminent aesthetic socialities

In Chapter 7 I discussed how women who had lost their hair because of chemotherapy saw themselves, and were seen by others, through the lens of social aesthetic imaginaries. These evaluations had little to do with individual preferences or authentic expressions but were instead informed by wider cultural events and images. The nature and intensity of these imaginaries differed among people because of their varying familiarity with certain images and imaginaries as well as the emotional meanings that they attached to them. It was also clear from these narratives that when people are confronted with feminine baldness they perceive this as an extremely powerful aesthetic truth. People see bald-headed women not as individual persons but as representatives of categories such as sickness and exclusion. Such imaginaries left little room for differing identities and individual specificities. This categorical truth ultimately pointed towards death and nothingness. In light of this, it is no surprise that these women sought to reshape their appearances.

The concepts employed by Foucault and the ancient Greeks are useful for understanding how this process of creative reshaping also involves the creation of a pragmatic *ethos* for managing the reactions of others. This is not done to set an example for others or to educate them, but it is a particular way of maintaining good relationships with others – that is, of managing their reactions and thus upholding the potential for engaging in social relationships. Creatively reshaping oneself does not entirely negate the bads of cancer and its treatment, but it can soften some of their social implications.

These women may or may not anticipate the social effects of their hairless appearance and must improvise with the various means and conventions that are available to them. In this chapter, I look more closely not only at how bald women are *influenced* by socio-cultural imaginaries but also at how they work with and within certain conventions to create or change norms of living together. This highlights the obduracy of conventions and the difficulty of changing them. My analysis shows how this can be the case. Why are there so few acceptable options for women to be without hair? This chapter extends my argument that aesthetic values are social values and discusses their impact on the organisation of social life.

Technologies of the self, revisited

To analyse the connections between individuals, the values of everyday life and forms of the social, I revisit Foucault's notion of 'technologies of the self'.[1] Foucault's neglect of individual agency – or perhaps his conviction of its futility – has been the subject of (feminist) critiques.[2] Foucault's subjects appear to be implicated in their oppression when they discipline themselves within grand discourses of truth. But a close reading of Foucault's later work – of which the lectures discussed in Chapter 8 are a part – reflects exactly this tension. His concept of technologies of the self, which one should understand as *practices* of the self, resonates with my attempt to think about the activity of individuals towards forming social coherences.

Foucault conceptualises technologies of the self as the ways in which individuals can influence their appearance and sociality – by their own means or with the help of others – by performing a number of operations that involve their body, soul, mind, conduct and ways of being. The aim of their practices is to transform the self in order to 'attain a state of happiness, purity, wisdom, perfection or immortality'.[3] Foucault seemed to suggest that technologies of the self are an alternative to technologies of power and domination, and that these could be instruments of creativity as well. The question then changes from 'how does the subject create itself by re-enacting directives from discourses on truth' to 'how does a subject turn themself into a subject or a state of worth' ('happiness, purity, wisdom, perfection, or immortality') that is valued by the self and others. And to this I add the question, 'how do practices of shaping the self in turn shape the social world of these subjects?'

With these questions in mind, I will explore technologies of the self as *political* practices not in the classical sense of practices found among the *demos* or political arena, but as practices with which individuals either try to escape from or renew structures of governance and social organisation. I will use conceptualisations of the good-life-as-practice to guide me in this endeavour. This means that I analyse concrete and practical efforts as well as motivations or inspirations to achieve a life that is as good as possible and that represents a state of worth. These efforts are undertaken in circumstances that are characterised by certain goods and bads that influence the potential outcomes of striving for something good in unexpected ways.

By analysing what I call *motivated socialities* (socialities that are formed because they are appealing to people who actively co-shape them), I hope to learn how 'emancipatory' movements (led by women, gay people, ethnic groups, patients and so on) might emerge without losing sight of the various conceptual ways that are available for analysing the power relations involved with the initial subjection and subjectivation of these 'others'.[4] Such emancipation would have to be an emancipation without liberation, a freeing of those who were not previously oppressed. There is no assumption of a fixed and given authentic being that is freed from its chains, but instead a shaping of subjectivity that takes place outside larger power structures.[5] As Foucault put it in an interview, 'I think that there are more secrets, more possible freedoms and more inventions in our future than we can imagine in humanism as it is dogmatically represented on every side of the political rainbow: left, right and centre.'[6]

In this chapter, I further develop the concept of technologies of the self not to extend Foucault's analysis for its own sake but rather 'to think with' this concept and to find tools that might help with understanding the lives and subject-positions of people with chronic disease (and possibly other *others* as well). My aim is to learn about social change while taking seriously people's historical and material situatedness as well as their motivation to act in certain ways or to appreciate certain things.

Shaping the self, shaping the social

My empirical analysis of technologies of the self using the case study of women who lost their hair showed that these women use everyday tools to (re-)shape their bodies in an attempt to achieve a particular valued subject position or state of worth. 'Worth' was an open category that needed to be empirically substantiated. 'Worth' resulted from non-verbal 'appreciations' and more explicit ways of valuing something, which were both informed by the conventions and imaginaries that circulated in these women's contexts. What can practices of shaping the self – using tools and technique such as wigs, scarves and make-up as well as walkers and massages – teach us about the dynamics of social practices and about social change? These women's practices illustrate how selfhood is a state of worth that is constantly challenged not only by their disease and its medical treatment, but also by the conventional ways that they as well as others respond to the effects of the disease and its treatment. By engaging in new interactions, these women sought to influence their plight either by trying to restore the valued subject position of their 'old self' and its predictable social relations, or by engaging in innovative practices of worth that strove for new forms of the self as well as new forms of sociality. This can involve the subversion of conventions as well as attempts to recreate or use existing conventions for improving one's situation.

How do these bald women 'shape the self', what tools do they use and to what effect? What notion of self might this result in? Can we understand these activities as potentially socially transformative activities, that is, as activities that can change, for the better, how people live together?

Restorative practices of the self: of wigs and walkers

To recall, I met these women who lost their hair due to chemotherapy while observing three workshops that were organised under the name 'Look good, feel better'. Participants were invited to learn 'hands on' how to use make-up and look better after cancer treatment had affected their face and skin, and were given advice on the use of wigs and headscarves. The primary tool for looking normal was the wig. 'To look normal' is akin to the 'state of happiness' that Foucault referred to, and this was the state of worth they wanted to achieve by wearing a wig. Bald women constructed looking normal as two particular states of worth. On the one hand, they wanted to restore the self to the way it looked before their cancer treatment. They wanted to look like their 'old self'. On the other hand, normality as a state of worth meant 'not standing out in a crowd' and being able to avoid negative responses.[7] Both states referred to a broad and non-specific range of female appearances that did not breach local expectations of what women should look like. The reactions of others compelled these women to modify their appearance even if they themselves as well as their families were not bothered by baldness. The intense reactions of others made these women shape their self in order to avoid such reactions and to maintain their individual worth. The tool of the wig, then, provided the safest option. It *concealed* baldness to the untrained eye.[8]

The way these women produced worth by trying on and wearing wigs shows that their ideas about worth were not particularly *original*. They were attempts to restore rather than to innovate, and were therefore mostly shaped by existing conventions. Such restorative efforts were informed by the cultural imaginaries and stereotypes to which these women – and those around them – compared their bald heads.[9] These imaginaries, as we saw in Chapter 7, were generally gruesome and referred to a loss of self, to unworthiness (being interned in a concentration camp or prosecuted as a witch), a loss of individuality, a reduction to a single identity category ('being a cancer patient') or to 'nothingness'. These images had strong associations with (social) death. More positive imaginaries did not bring much relief. These consisted of the bald heads of female celebrities, such as Sinead O'Connor or Sugar Lee Hooper, or of characters in novels. These images were examples of unconventional femininities. All my informants found these positive examples too extreme to mimic. In contrast to celebrities, these women wanted to 'be themselves' and not attract attention or experiment with eye-catching new looks. At this point in their lives, experiments did not offer something they valued.

Situated and relational perceptions

The historical events and imaginaries used to attribute worth to baldness underscore the historically and culturally contingent nature of the imaginaries that the women responded to, and hence also the way in which these imaginaries added or subtracted worth. However violent these imaginaries may have been locally, they are always situated in particular times and places. 'Being a bald woman' can mean very different things if moving from the Netherlands to Ghana or Israel. The historical contingency of appreciations also explains why it is so difficult to control the effect of one's looks on others. It is hard to predict which historical events or stereotypes will inform others' perceptions, or to know what the appreciations are of these imaginaries in terms of their emotional intensity. This all depends on the exact nature of the relationship between those looking and being looked at as well as their appreciations of historical imaginaries.[10]

So, the self comes to appreciate its looks by comparing these to cultural imaginaries that may have different meanings for different people. Others, witnessing this self, do the same. Whereas Foucault initially stressed the dominance of 'large' and oppressive scientific discourses, technologies of the self appear to present a 'way out' by proposing a much more contingent and fluid fabric of social relations, cultural activities and events. Cultural events do shape the process of subjectification in important ways, but not by establishing a singular and inescapable truth through discourse – although undeniably there are multiple discourses on femininity at work here.

However, rather than being pinned down for what they are or how they should behave, individuals also shape worth – or futility. Subjectification is informed by an appreciation of contingent aesthetic conventions on how to look good as well as historical events with which one may or may not be familiar and that may leave a greater or lesser impression.

The wig and the practice of the self

The practice of wearing a wig by bald women can be understood as a technology of the self because of its particular aims and ways of influencing others. Wearing a wig works because it reattaches women's looks to particular, historically situated conventions and forms of worth (continuity in looks, not being too different from others). However, the creativity of bringing about these conventional looks, I suggest, is found in how women use wigs to influence the responses of others and thus shape their own lives. Looking good rather than ill allowed women to play with or reject their (worthless) identity as a cancer patient or punished woman. They could get a break from being a patient because they were treated as ordinary (worthy) people.

> Edie: You just have to build up the courage. And they said, 'Just do it, put make-up on your face,' and I did. Then everybody stopped saying, 'Poor kid, you must be feeling bad.' No, everybody said, 'Ah, you're well again, I can see that!' So, you are no longer confronted with your cancer. And that is wonderful. In the hospital you are a patient for some time, but outside of the hospital you're not. You just need some courage!

Wearing a wig and applying make-up can be seen as technologies of the self that take on an active social meaning by granting women the possibility of playing with conventions and cultural values, and thus allow them to manipulate the reactions of others. By making their looks conform to more conventional forms of femininity, they could organise their lives in such a way that cancer and its treatment did not 'reign'.[11] Feminine normality (worth) 'overruled' cancerous abnormality (worthlessness). The context allowed for the transformation of a conventional norm of femininity into a social innovation. Wearing a wig was hence not a technology of the self in and of itself but because of its effect on particular social situations.

However, wearing a wig failed to make feminine baldness more acceptable or to subvert norms concerning the acceptability of having cancer.[12] Rather than changing social relations, old relations were rebuilt. It is paradoxical to change one's social world by restoring it to a former state. This action transforms the meaning of emancipation or liberation from freeing an oppressed self into actively playing with conventions to create possibilities for doing things that are deemed valuable.

From authenticity to artificiality: walkers, clothes and showers

The self that emerges from the practices of women suffering from cancer runs counter to claims about the autonomous individual that has an inner kernel[13] of authentic and personal taste. Rather than remaining a bounded entity that cherishes a set of passions or values and that may be 'dressed up' to change into something that is not particularly real, women made attempts to style or construct their self in ways that could locally pass as proper and worthy.[14] Everyday shaping of the self became a prerequisite for 'feeling good' and 'in shape' regardless of whether one was ill or not. Most people dress and wash in the morning to shape themselves as presentable subjects. 'Authenticity' or being oneself does not equal some raw or naked state of being. Instead, it is a cultivated state that is created within the confines of particular conventions.

Authenticity in the sense of an inner identity is not evoked here, but its opposites are, namely artificiality and sociality. Technologies to transform the self can create a self that is even more itself because they manipulate and enhance the body in a way that is desirable to the self: a desire that is informed by wider social values. Self or selfhood is an *achievement* rather than a given state, a creation rather than a fixed entity. This is even more obvious – and difficult – when the self is struck by disease and needs to be 'repaired'. Elise expresses this pointedly when speaking about her walker:

> Elise: When I walked, I bent over a lot. I walk more upright now, but even more so with the walker. The handles are in the highest position, and then I walk straighter. I find that very important. Your posture is also a kind of dignity. Because, when you bend over, that is so . . . So, with the walker I am more myself than without the darned thing.

The walker serves as a tool to 'be oneself' more than one is without it. The posture of the body, when supported by the walker, makes the self feel more like itself, namely as someone who is facing the world strong and upright rather than bent over and with downcast eyes. This enactment of the self does not suggest a move towards an inner truth or a core identity that is hidden within the self, but instead foregrounds attempts to achieve certain types of embodiment that are valued and deemed worthy of calling 'a self'.[15] Selfhood, then, emerges as a state of worth in itself, as something that is strived for in particular situations and that is akin to Foucault's 'state of happiness'.

Innovative practices of the self

The following examples do not show ways of *restoring* the self and its social relations but ways of *innovating* one's self by creating new situations of worth.

Massage in the hospital: looking for the good in the bad

In the next example, Elise describes how others – or other events as well as the self – can also cause feelings of 'non-value' or worthlessness, and thus contribute to the unravelling or negation of the self. Like in the examples on nothingness, Elise describes this process as negating the body or extracting value from it. Worth and selfhood, then, find their opposite in devaluation or worthlessness.[16] The self is transformed in an unwanted way through the looks and (un)appreciation of others, but also through other modalities of perceiving or sensing the self, such as being touched or hurt.

> Elise: When I was being treated, at the start, I received chemo on Monday and Tuesday, so then I'd get a needle in my arm. Wednesday, I had to go to the lab, again a needle in my arm. Thursday off. Friday to the doctor and another injection. So, four out of seven days I had to be in the hospital and have my skin pierced. And that really gives a very ... erm. When you get a massage, well, that's just heaven, it's wonderful. That there are people who are happy to do that for me. It's a way of being touched in a good way. Well, that goes on until you are eighty! ... So at least once a week my feet receive a massage from these people, as do my calves and legs. I can't describe it, it's so good, endlessly ... I enjoy it so much that I think, 'Yes, everybody should be able to experience this.'

Elise describes the contrast between her skin being pierced and her feet being massaged as two different technologies that act upon the self, one creating worth and the other worthlessness. The differences between them may be hard to describe, but they make a lot of sense if one tries to imagine both situations from a sensory perspective.[17] The self in pain is an example of the self being enacted in a negative sense, or even a negation of selfhood as a state of worth.[18] On a pre-verbal yet still profoundly social level (in different contexts piercing the body can be experienced as pleasant for aesthetic reasons), the self becomes a self – or is negated as a self – in an embodied way. Here, being pierced with a needle is not supportive of a practice of the self. The following example shows how relations that support worth are important for creating value in life and for negating death, pain and nothingness:

> Mary: I have been undergoing treatment for a year. Every three weeks I am admitted to the hospital for five days to receive chemo. So I was in the hospital a lot, and in between those three weeks I also often went there because of high fever or for a blood transfusion. So, I was inside the hospital more than I was outside. And there was one nurse who, if I was at a loss and couldn't keep myself in my bed, came to rub my shoulders. [Silence. It is clear she is still deeply moved by her memory of the event.] That was so amazing. I will never forget that.

The sensation evoked by the massage from the nurse supported a practice of the self that contrasted strongly with the state of being in pain and of experiencing a lack of worth during encounters with others. This was crucial and left a powerful impression on Mary; it became a life-changing event. She was determined that others also experience this dash of worth in a temporarily worthless life. She became a 'new person' after her recovery. She did not return to her old job but instead trained to become a beautician, and eventually also became a leader for the 'Look good, feel better' workshops. The nurse who created worth in a situation that was otherwise worth*less* made Mary realise that it was possible to help others imagine that there is a life that is not halfway to the grave and that may be worth living. Elise, who worked in a children's hospital, reported something similar:

> Elise: I worked in a paediatric ward and I gave massages to the children there, from babies to teenagers. People pay little attention to this but it is really important. Because you notice that if you teach parents to give their kids a massage, this can mean a lot. Parents of

children who are in a hospital and often ill, these parents can do little for them because their kids are severely ill. And a massage is something . . . you can hug your kid but giving them a massage is something through which you can experience something really nice in the relationship between parent and child. And this gets very little attention, it is regarded as luxury. Because there is no evidence that it cures the kids. But there is evidence that it makes the kids and the parents happier.

Massage is an example of a technology that adds worth to the relationship between parents and their severely ill children. Because of the motivation of gaining worth (pleasure, beauty, taste, happiness), a new and valuable way for parents to relate to their sick child is invented. Rather than the usual interactions that take place in medical practices (consultations, operations, chemotherapy), the sick person is related to through the creation of pleasure, and is thus endowed with worth. New relations emerge in the hospital by enacting new situations of worth.

The workshop as a technology of the self

The 'Look good, feel better' workshops, I suggest, are activities that support practices of the self and that provide a new state of worth by allowing for new ways of living together. To understand this, it is helpful to look at the use of a different tool than the wig, namely the headscarf. The wig made baldness disappear by effectively concealing it, hence restoring a former self and state of worth. The scarf, however, camouflaged rather than concealed baldness. This was not approved of by all interviewees. To some, even a hint of baldness was rejected in favour of the restoration of 'normal' looks. This rejection is probably informed by the fact that there are no public practices in which baldness is seen as an acceptable way of presenting oneself as a woman. In these workshops things were different. Here, the wigs would come off, often for practical reasons, but also because 'we are among ourselves'. To some, this was a very distressing event because it confronted them with what lay ahead. Others did not follow up on the invitation to take off their wig because they did not want to reveal their baldness. For most of my informants, however, it was liberating to do so and to have a social meeting with strangers without having to hide their baldness. On the contrary, the women in these workshops were encouraged to show not just their strongly desired 'ordinary face' that 'looked good', but also to work on the possibility of shaping their own face as a 'beautiful face'. The overall feelings that my informants reported were surprise, happiness and enjoyment. Appearances, which would have been depressing representations of disease elsewhere, suddenly emerged as a source of pleasure in these workshops.

> Mary [workshop leader]: She [participant in the workshop] wrote in the evaluation, 'It is wonderful that we are allowed to be seen again! [*weer gezien mogen worden*. This is a Dutch expression that in this context combines the literal meaning of 'being looked at' with 'being recognised as valuable'.] Ah, the tears really welled up when I read that! She really came [to the workshop] with resistance written all over her face: 'Pfft, this is another thing we have to undergo, we are here to be pitied and taken care of.' And then she wrote this on the evaluation form... I could see her cheer up during the morning, she became really happy, eager and full of life. 'Oh, this is beautiful, and that is beautiful too!' And her back straightened up, as if she was saying, 'I can be here again. I don't have to apologise.'

This quotation vividly evokes how having a disease is connected to feeling cast out of society. Being bald (unworthy), having cancer (unworthy) and being beautiful (being worthy) resulted in a new social practice mixing three elements that usually do not go together, or at least not in ordinary life. This potent mixture created states of worth by providing new ways of being a 'self with cancer', without hair, and yet beautiful. At the end of the workshop there was a general feeling of celebration during which everyone was astonished at how great everybody looked: skinny, soberly dressed and beautifully ('naturally', the beauticians said) made up faces. The celebration became a social practice in which cancer and feminine baldness were lived in a new way because it was a practice lived with others, if only for a short period of time.

The workshop was creative, or innovative, in providing a new way for living with cancer and baldness in comparison to the ways there were already available, even if the workshop also relied on existing conventions. The workshop 'worked', intentionally or not, without a particular motive or attempt at resistance, and instead made appeals to these women's appreciations and motivations, which were shaped by their recent illness. The workshop created worth by creating new and attractive possibilities to enact selfhood for women with cancer. It provided a means for being together in a way that made bald women with cancer at worst unremarkable and at best beautiful. This created the possibility of working with baldness and 'making something of it'.

> Annette: Well, I bought that wig. I thought, 'This is the best thing to do, it is the haircut that I have, and I look just like I always do.' So it's a fantastic thing, this wig. But the scarves . . . these are really a thing for me. Wonderful! I think they look nice, I think they look different. Whereas that hair, it's not mine anyway. And with scarves, you have all these colours. And as you can tell, I am crazy about tiger print, see [points at the trousers she is wearing]. So I had an old set of leggings in tiger print, and I cut them up so that I could wear tiger print on my head as well. So you become a bit creative, really. And the woman at the workshop, what she suggested was to wrap colourful stockings around your head and to match your make-up to them. Well, isn't that fantastic?!

Annette decisively brushed aside the idea of restoring the old situation and returning to her former self ('that hair is not mine anyway'). She created new looks for herself by starting from the 'material' she had to work with. Cancer and baldness were not issues to move away from as quickly as possible. As important constituents of her new situation, they were matters with which one could find valuable ways of living. Doing so is an uncommon practice rather than a conventional one, and not everybody can enjoy this type of creativity. It seems impossible for most individuals to find such acceptance on their own, because this would be exceptional, similar to the lives of pop stars and brave characters in novels. There is no practice or genre of female appearances that accepts and includes baldness – and cancer – or the wearing of scarves. This requires new social practices.

> Jane: What I really dislike is that I am not accepted like this. If it were up to me, I would prefer to go out into the street with my [bald] head, to the shops, just like that, without a wig, and without further ado. I never did that. I wear scarves, but now I am wearing a cap because it is so cold. Normally I wouldn't wear anything [at home]. And this is the worst thing. You are ill, and this causes you a lot of trouble. And then you look different from what you used to look like. But you cannot be who you have become without being ashamed or thinking about it . . . You just don't have the courage. If I knew there were more people walking around like this, I wouldn't have a problem with it. But I don't even consider going out without a wig. That is what I find so damned deplorable.

In order for practices of showing one's bald head to become technologies of social change, more people need to show their baldness. For instance, as a creative political strategy, bald women with cancer could collectively set a new example, which would be in line with the current cultural phenomenon of seeing more and more women who are bald as the result of chemotherapy. In this way, technologies of the self, such as the workshop, are 'political' technologies because they create new practices and conditions for living together by providing value to those who participate even if they are not 'freeing' themselves of cancer or baldness. By being collectively enacted, these practices have the potential to become a new aesthetic genre, a conventional way of practising worth. Rather than removing barriers of oppression, technologies of the self show the hard work and motivation that is needed to enact new ways of living together, which involves relabelling as good that what had hitherto been seen as bad.[19]

To conclude: changing social life

Are everyday-life values and motivations formative of social forms and social organisation? What kind of selves do these values and motivations lead to, and how do they succeed? Foucault's conceptualisation of 'technology of the self' was paradoxical because it involved, on the one hand, an historically situated self that enacts itself through discourse, and on the other, a socially active, subjectively engaged and innovative self. If the self is determined through discourse, what 'possible freedom' is there to change the self and one's social situation? Bald women who engaged in practices of self-styling demonstrated how to negotiate such paradoxes. They provided inspiration for conducting empirical analyses of technologies of the self.

Bald women shaped a self by *appreciating* and *valuing* the subject-positions they could take rather than *thinking about, knowing* ('taking the self as one's object') *and judging*. In these women's practices, their 'self' emerged as a state of worth, namely as a position that they valued and that emerged through particular manipulations and enactments (wearing wigs, going to workshops, hospitals and so on). These states of worth were not simply individual preferences but also socially valued positions. This is in contrast with the conceptualisation of the self as an individual with an inner core of passions and thoughts, or as an individual with a body that precedes practice. Selfhood becomes an embodied state of actively creating value within and through practices. The outcome is dependent on the 'materials to work with', the skills to craft these materials and the cultural resources that are available for valuing and organising particular practices. The activity of appreciating or valuing certain things led to the shaping of particular positions, thus highlighting the inseparability of practice and selfhood. These emerge together. In short, the self here is a practice of worth.

The notion of worth – and hence selfhood – anchors the social situatedness as well as the fragility of worth and worthlessness. Appreciation of the self as a state or practice of worth was informed by historically and culturally contingent relations, events and imaginaries. The women in this case study were, as cancer patients, in a situation in which their experienced and perceived worth (selfhood) was being challenged. They, or those around them, devalued their bald heads and sick bodies by comparing them to gruesome, historically rooted imaginaries of inmates in concentration camps as well as condemned and humiliated women. Locally, baldness or cancer could not be connected to worth.

Their historical situatedness did not involve a disciplining process that was enacted through powerful discourses of truth, but took place through the *dispositifs* of contingent events and historically and culturally (de)valued as well as often ambiguous imaginaries. However, the relative weakness of these cultural imaginaries (in comparison to the power of discourses), and the different ways in which they were appreciated by different people, made them unstable. This instability provided space for playing with conventions. The women resorted to conventional forms of femininity to escape their identity as a cancer patient by adding beauty and thus improving their life with cancer. This 'possible form of freedom', however, also made their attempt at innovating selfhood – and to a lesser extend restoring it – a fragile endeavour. One could never completely predict the ways in which others might appreciate one's attempt at creating a worthy self. Wigs could be identified by expert eyes, and scarves or make-up could meet the disapproval of one's children.

In my relational analysis, 'agency', namely the ability to instigate change, is best understood as distributed across people, situations and things. Generally, it is hard to tell in interactions who or what 'came first'. One could, for instance, trace the origins of the 'Look good, feel better' workshops, relate their emergence to the growing number of women who have cancer and who have to live with this condition for a long time, and then focus on the various practices that are being developed to ameliorate living with cancer. The temporary 'end results' that can be observed – namely people engaging in valued positions – may start in different ways. These practices may be picked up or not, be incidentally stumbled upon, be actively campaigned for and so on. There are many contingencies here, too. In this particular case there was no 'movement for the liberation of female cancer patients', but nonetheless fruitful connections were made, affordances exploited and materials used. All these affordances were mediated by historical events and conventions. Rather than providing an explanation for or genealogy of social innovation, ethnographic studies, such as the one presented here, can provide an exploration of existing normativities and the possibilities that emerge within the settings that have been studied.

Departing from Foucault's tentative description given in the introduction to this chapter, technologies of the self can now be described as practices through which people – by their own means or with the help of others as well as tools – attempt to enact themselves as a self (a state of worth or a position they value) by performing a certain number of operations within particular social and material circumstances. Technologies of the self are socially lived, materially structured and historically situated practices that allow people to value, and therefore enact, certain subject-positions. The concept of technologies of the self can hence be used to analyse practices – or the lack thereof – for occupying or creating valued positions for particular people. Such subject-positions provide avenues for living together and for further developing opportunities to do so. In the case study discussed in this chapter, alternative positions to that of being worthless as 'bald women' or 'cancer patients' were as follows: being beautiful as well as being seen as such (as happened in the workshop), engendering good feelings while receiving treatment (as happened when giving or getting a massage), passing as normal (by using a wig), and being 'more oneself' by working on the self (the example of the walker). Different practices may be of value to different and changing groups of patients.

Good practices of the self are hence social and political matters in the sense that they may lead to different ways of living together or socially organising people. Technologies of the self 'change the world' by providing new and valued socio-material practices for living as a self together with others, however modest this may be in terms of scale. Here, women attempted to turn 'life with cancer' into something that could happen to a 'self' – that is, to someone who is worthy. Rather than being liberated from cancer, women modified their relations to attain new positions of selfhood. Analysing and comparing these practices can open up ways for reflecting on and discussing or supporting certain desirable ways of living together with 'others'. This might, for instance, allow us to find better ways of interacting with women who have cancer or other diseases.

Contrary to G. H. Mead's claim that 'critical awareness' or conscious intentions are necessary conditions for individuals to have a political effect, the practices of these women were not informed by a critical discourse about freeing themselves from 'oppressive social situations'.[20] Rather, their self-fashioning activities were inspired by the everyday things that they appreciated and valued or disliked. The foundations of these women's social innovations were neither free will or intentional actions nor some liberated insights that could somehow transcend common beliefs. These social innovations emerged from the possibility of experiencing worth and the goal of subverting worthlessness in a given situation. In this way, receiving a massage in a hospital could be seen as creative and subversive because it created worth where previously there was none. Conventions concerning the beautiful female body certainly played a role, but these could also be exploited to create new forms of worth by enacting alternative, valued ways of living together with others.

Ironically, Foucault's own life, and his participation in experimental practices of living as gay men, provides a better example of the political potential of developing cultural practices through technologies of the self than his pre-modern case studies do. Avant-garde gay men such as Foucault created alternative sexual practices based on their particular tastes. In this way they experimented with a new genre of activities, even if these practices would never become mainstream. My way of analysing active attempts to attain worth draws on pre-modern notions and practices of selfhood, but this classical approach may also be adapted to describe contemporary ones. Rather than liberating their oppressed self, women with cancer enacted a 'possible freedom' by moving away from practices that did not allow them to live in the ways they valued, and by moving towards practices in which they might be able to do so. They did not 'escape from' conventions and power structures, and indeed my analysis shows that doing this is very difficult. They used some conventions, creatively reorganised others, and invented new combinations that were of value to them.

End of Part II, on to Part III

Part II on the social nature and effects of aesthetic values on everyday life ends here. I have shown that aesthetic values are social values, and that they play a role in concrete historical, socio-material practices. There was an excursion to ancient Greece to look at how the concepts of *bios* (everyday life as it unfolds) and *ethos* (everyday life as it is intentionally shaped by someone) might help with analysing how everyday life can be thought of as *good*, and particularly for 'ordinary' rather than exemplary people. The normativity of such lives, I argued, can be analysed empirically as a practice that may turn out to be good or not so good because it also always includes 'the bad'. The chapters in this part of the book listed several concepts for thinking about the good life. This chapter discussed how thinking about aesthetic values as social values can lead to forms of social organisation or living together that are based on motivations and appreciations. It showed that motivations are powerful but that conventions may be even stronger. It is never easy to change conventions. All chapters showed, again, how an understanding of what individuals are varies with how we understand the social.

Using these tools, concepts and technologies, Part III will elaborate on how to *study* the everyday lives of people with chronic disease, handicaps or other problems that remain, and on how researchers can learn about what their informants value. Part III discusses methodologies for conducting such research, and analyses how individuals and their 'social aggregates' are linked through certain research methodologies. Doing so will further specify how form creates content in important ways. Part III will end with an analysis of new forms of 'hanging out', which are unstructured methods for participant research that attempt to enact their object of research – in my case, the values of everyday life for people who are not able to participate in more standard and verbally oriented approaches to doing research.

Notes

1. See e.g. Foucault, 1972; 1986; 2000.
2. Rather than submitting to structures of power-knowledge, feminists choose to find or create concepts and understandings that might help them change these power formations. See, for instance, Saba Mahmood's work on Muslim women who are active in religious practices. Mahmood (2001; 2011) shows how these women change their selves (positions, bodies, experiences) to live a pious life. They hence manage to gain influence in Muslim religious practices. They cannot escape this dominant discourse but modify it from within. They do not move from a position of oppression to one of freedom, but change the nature of their entanglements with power and thus change the social fabric of the society they live in. Mahmood's analysis provides a clear account of how social relationships can change through one's engagement with what one values. See also Heyes, 2007, Markula, 2003; 2004; Taylor & Vintges, 2012; Vintges 2001; 2012.
3. These are various ways of formulating worth. See Martin et al., 1988, p. 18.
4. Scott, 1991.
5. In later feminist discussions, this was also an argument against 'standpoint feminism', which assumed a privileged position for those who see the world from the margins. See for instance: Hartsock, 1983; Harding, 2004.

6   Martin et al., 1988, p. 15. Note Foucault's critical stance towards Enlightenment 'humanism' – or what I call modernity or liberalism – which foregrounds a general, reflexive individual who is striving for individual freedom.
7   In contrast to Goffman, 1956, this practice is not about 'making an impression' but about *not* wanting to make an impression. Goffman maintains that there is an authentic self that is backstage behind the different presentations of the self that are made onstage. This position is rejected here.
8   Women who had experience with wearing wigs were experts in being able to spot wigs on others. There was a tacit understanding that one should not address this unless the other person broached this topic of their own accord.
9   Images that may or may not have existing referents, such as in fairy tales.
10 I quickly came to realise this point when the impact of the Second World War – which has been, and in many ways still is, the most important moral landmark of Europe in the twentieth century – came up in conversations with people from Africa and South America. To my astonishment, they did not recognise this war as a moral landmark, in contrast to the self-evident role these events have played for Europeans and contemporary ethical thinkers. To people from Africa and South America, the Second World War was merely a remote fact in their history books; they had their own moral atrocities to live with and think about.
11 See Moser, 2006, and M'charek, 2010, on the interference of different normativities.
12 Goffman, 1963, would consider this a normalising situation in which women lived up to norms that were 'out there'. I re-scribe this situation by showing that they responded to concrete fears and concerns about themselves and others, and that they creatively manipulated these feelings. But there remains a question, namely whether this is the best possible strategy.
13 The term is from Rosen, 2012.
14 Goffman, 1956, uses theatrical metaphors to describe a true self that is presented or staged to create certain impressions that are inauthentic and that hide the inner or backstage self. See also Landes, 1988.
15 Theorists such as Elias (1978) show that the construction and demarcation of the individual self has become more important over the centuries. In other words, what an individual is exactly has become more and more encircled by a private sphere that hides the individual from the public eye (or nose). This process of individualisation does not relate to a pre-given authentic self. Instead, it is something that is cultivated and eventually incorporated so that the self physically reacts to transgressions, for instance by showing shame through blushing.
16 See Scarry, 1985.
17 This way of arguing is to ask the reader to imagine a sensation!
18 Scarry (1985) describes being in pain as an unmaking of the world. She contrasts this with creativity, which represents its making. For a critique that also shows an understanding of pain as an actor, particularly in the practice of giving birth, see Skeide, 2021.
19 Christine Frost-Hartwig describes an intriguing practice of dealing with baldness and paediatric cancer on Bermuda. By way of fundraising (on St Baldrick's Day) participants have their hair shaved off in public, in solidarity with children with cancer. She shows how this brings a sense of belonging and moral awareness. Thanks to Bjarke Oxlund who sent me Frost-Hartwig's unpublished University of Copenhagen thesis (Frost-Hartwig, 2022). It is intriguing that such a significant experience is lived through for the sake of children, showing a 'motherly' heroism in caring for them.
20 Mead, 2009.

Part III
Researching the good life

In contrast to the ethical conceptualisations presented in Part I, this Part addresses the question of how to *study* the good life of people living with chronic disease or lasting handicaps. The debate here is with scientific approaches rather than with demarcations between ethics and religion. What kinds of research practices are needed to learn about the values that are important in everyday life? Answering this question will again highlight the different relationships between individuals and forms of social life as well as how they shape one another.

There is a problem with 'just asking' people about what they value in everyday life, as I discussed in Chapter 5 on the role of autonomy for people with learning disabilities. Such a question does not lead to unambiguous answers. People do not speak simply 'by themselves' but in situations that allow for some things to be said rather than others.[1] A voice is *made* rather than given – to articulate one truth or another, or to relate to some form of the good or to another – depending on the relationships that allow this voice to emerge. Individuals are always *somewhere*, surrounded by other actors and actants (active things).

For individuals it may be difficult to anticipate or even register the effects of their activities in a particular social setting. Their activities may be motivated by a certain value but may lead to the achievement of quite another. This can happen, in the example of care for people with intellectual disabilities, through the promotion of autonomy. Autonomy can lead to the breaching of relationships rather than their creation. There are many examples of people doing things that are bad for them without themselves acknowledging this as such. An example was drinking too much alcohol, which caregivers found problematic, but not the drinking persons themselves. The values that are important in everyday life may hence be difficult to grasp for individuals. As these are social rather than individual values, there is no 'privileged access' to an inner state for learning about the values of everyday life.

The way in which one attempts to learn about people's values has a major influence on how these values are understood. Some people with chronic disease illustrate this point particularly clearly, for example, when they do not speak in ways that are understandable to a researcher because they have a speech impairment, mental or cognitive disability, or are simply afraid to speak their mind or unable to understand a questionnaire. It is difficult to include these subjects in research. However, a lot can be learned from observing how they go about and appreciate things in their everyday life. This is the only way to learn about the values of inarticulate subjects. Doing this can teach us a lot about more eloquent subjects as well; what truth *may* be said or demonstrated about the good life depends on the methods employed while asking questions. 'Hearing the patient's voice' is one particular – not very specific – method that shapes particular outcomes.

The first chapter rearticulates the 'creativity of methods'. It discusses how patients suffering from ALS use a plastic feeding tube that is inserted through the wall of their stomach. This chapter shows how ethnographic methods can make visible the everyday-life values related to the tube as well as their shifts. I compare the value of a feeding tube to quantitative studies on 'quality of life' by analysing various assumptions about what quality is and how it might be studied. My analysis explains why such studies are unable to grasp how patients value their feeding tube. Everyday-life values are an object of research that is hard to articulate with standardised methods because such methods cannot easily take the specificities of everyday life into account. Their generalised results are difficult to interpret for individual cases. For example, what does it mean for someone to know that, say, 65 per cent of patients find that their quality of life has improved after a certain treatment? People want to know specifically how a treatment or technology works, and they want to relate that knowledge to their own situation. This is a task that clinicians engage in all the time. I will show that whatever it is that quality-of-life research measures, it is not the values of everyday life.

The historical chapter discusses how the Renaissance humanist Petrarch, as seen through the eyes of philosopher Nancy Struever and through a reading of his letters, created a philosophical practice for addressing the concerns of everyday life. His enquiries into the good life employed accessible methods and practices that are well suited for addressing the specificities of everyday life, such as writing letters and engaging in conversations. The chapter also discusses how practices of enquiry co-determine the object that one seeks to study, and what research practices can be imagined to gain access to everyday-life concerns. To address and learn about the values of everyday life, researchers need to adapt their methodological strategies.

The final chapter of the book applies the lessons from the previous chapters, and asks how ethnography can be further refined to examine the everyday-life values of people with chronic diseases and persisting handicaps who cannot easily participate in research through standard methods. The chapter argues that this requires creating conditions for informants to *demonstrate* what they value in everyday-life practices by generating such values *through the research practice itself*. This means that research practices need to be adapted to become valuable to informants. To create space for doing this, the researcher must accept other goals than directly pursuing her research questions and has to cede control over how informants might answer such questions. The task is to develop ways of living together that are generative for producing knowledge about the everyday-life values of research subjects that are acceptable – if not agreeable – to both researcher and informants alike. When one wants to learn about the values of everyday life, opening up research practices – rather than strictly controlling their circumstances – is a virtue rather than a problem.

Notes

1 A good example is the involvement of patients in the making of guidelines; Van de Bovenkamp & Trappenburg (2009) describe how patients' contributions are seen as 'anecdotes' rather than as 'evidence', which needs to be of a statistical nature.

10
'Quality of life' and everyday values: living with ALS and a feeding tube

In this chapter, I explore what happens to values that are relevant to patients' everyday lives by juxtaposing the practice of doing research on the 'quality of life' with the practice of doing ethnographic research.[1] Quality of life is the banner under which the first attempts were made to bring 'patient values' into oncological research.[2] Medical parameters indicated that tumours were shrinking, but patients felt that cancer treatments were threatening their good life. Hence, quality-of-life research attempted to include such 'subjective experiences' and to give patients a voice in the evaluation of their treatment. If 'patient autonomy' is the ethical way of allowing patients to have a say in their treatment, then 'quality of life' is the way to learn about the role of patient values in medical research. This chapter will show, however, that 'quality of life' is a very different research object compared to 'the values of everyday life'.

Our ethnographic study brought many different values to light. Its longitudinal design allowed me to consider how, in individual cases and situations, particular values are foregrounded and how these changed. Ethnographic attention to everyday practical concerns and the ways in which people live with medical interventions articulated these changes. This chapter shows that examining 'quality of life' through quantitative research involves a very particular way of articulating what is of importance to patients, and that this approach did not work well in the case that we studied.[3] Quantitative studies could not say anything about the values that patients have in relation to the feeding tube. Ethnographic approaches, however, can show the values that are at stake. The results of an ethnographic approach can hence inform clinical practices, but in a different way than statistical studies are able to.

The case study

My case revolves around the question of whether a feeding tube helps to improve the life of severely ill patients. The patients considering a feeding tube in my study were people suffering from ALS (amyotrophic lateral sclerosis). They might be considering using a feeding tube, or have been living with a feeding tube for some time already. ALS is a severe and progressive motor neurone disease. Because of the degeneration of the nerve tissue that directs one's voluntary muscles, patients are increasingly unable to move and their muscles start to waste away. The course of the disease is generally devastating. Fifty per cent of patients die from ALS within three years of their diagnosis; most patients are dead after five years. The disease gained a lot of public interest during the so-called 'ice bucket challenge' in July–August 2014. The idea that underpinned the challenge was that one can imagine how it feels when muscles stop functioning by pouring ice-cold water over one's head. A famous ALS patient, albeit an atypical one due to how long he lived with the disease, is the scientist Stephen Hawking.

What is a feeding tube?

Applying a feeding tube (gastrostomy) involves piercing the wall of the stomach and inserting a plastic tube. Liquid food can be fed into the tube either manually with a syringe or with a motor-propelled drip. There are several methods for applying feeding tubes.[4] In the hospital where we did our study (as well as elsewhere), percutaneous endoscopic gastrostomy (PEG) is the most common procedure. PEG insertion requires the patient to 'swallow' a scope that illuminates the stomach from within. The wall of the stomach is then pierced from the inside, thereby minimising any potential damage to blood vessels. PEG can only be performed if patients have sufficient lung capacity and are not dependent on breathing devices. PEG placement is done by a specialist, namely a gastroenterologist, who in our study was associated with the ALS team and knew the patients that were involved from earlier consultations on ways of dealing with dysphagia (swallowing problems that arise due to weakness of the tongue and mastication muscles). When a patient does not meet the requirements for PEG but is able to lie on their back, the radiologist inserts the tube instead. This is called radiologically inserted gastrostomy (RIG). RIG insertion requires the stomach to be inflated with air after which the stomach wall is pierced from the outside. The diameter of a RIG tube is smaller than with PEG, affixed less stably, and the wound needs to be stitched, which increases the risk of infection. The radiologist who performs RIGs generally does not know the patient, and this was one of reasons why PEG was the preferred method in the hospital where we conducted our study. The rationale for this was that, as talking becomes difficult for patients and their body loses much of its strength, a familiar doctor can enhance communication and the feeling of safety and trust.

Research into quality of life and the feeding tube

There are various reasons for patients to consider the placement of a feeding tube. These include excessive weight loss as the result of dysphagia (difficulty swallowing), difficulty with coughing that may result in (an acute fear of) choking, risk of getting pneumonia from food that is stuck in the lungs, and excessive time spent on eating. The literature concerning the effects of tube feeding on the lives of patients with ALS is inconclusive. The main questions in this literature are: 1) Whether tube feeding extends life; 2) If tube feeding improves nutritional status; and 3) What the effects are of tube feeding on quality of life.

There is no solid statistical evidence for answers to any of these questions.[5] One reason for this is that it is very difficult to set up a clinical trial to answer such questions because it would require randomisation. The decision to have a feeding tube inserted would then be beyond patients' control. As we learned from our ethnographic study, this is something patients do not want to consider. The decision to have a tube inserted or not is far too important to them. Other quantitative studies have proved inconclusive in determining the effects of the feeding tube on quality of life.

It is clear that the research practice of studying quality of life is ill suited for answering the important questions that need to be answered. The object of study – the impact of the feeding tube on the quality of life for this particular group of patients – could not be made visible. That there *are* effects is obvious both from the literature and from observations in hospitals where people with ALS are being supported. In the literature on feeding tubes, good quality of life is mostly related to the social practice of eating, whereas tube feeding is related to physiological effects, such as obtaining enough calories, prolonging survival and improving nutritional status.[6] Some authors warn that hampering the ability to eat through the mouth should be a last resort because of the multiple meanings that are attached to eating.[7] Other authors, however, recognise that spending an entire day trying to swallow food can present its own kind of problem,[8] and see tube placement as a minor surgical procedure or a minimally invasive procedure[9] that will enhance quality of life.[10]

Because of this 'lack of evidence', some authors argue that the decision to insert a feeding tube should only be made if an improvement in quality of life is to be expected, rather than a 'prolongation of the dying process'.[11] This may be hard to determine, and patients, their loved ones and clinicians may all have a different stance on this.[12] Others authors argue, however, that dysphagia itself can be seen as a deficit in quality of life, and therefore that the physiological benefit of a person's nutritional status should be a necessary condition for placing a feeding tube.[13]

The discussion in the literature is still ongoing. This means that in clinical practice decisions are made based on individual situations without guidance from the scientific literature. However, the reluctance of patients to have a feeding tube inserted suggests that scientific evidence might be a relatively poor decision aid. What would it mean if the feeding tube is an improvement for 'most patients'? Notwithstanding the difficulty of applying statistical evidence to individual situations, it is striking that quality-of-life research has been unable to ascertain the role of the feeding tube in improving quality of life, even though clinicians evidently recognise that there are clear concerns. Now let us see what ethnographic research can tell us about why this might be the case.

The ethnographic study

For this study, my research assistant, Sarah Limburg, and I interviewed patients whom we had contacted through four means: the ALS Tertiary Care Centre of an academic hospital in the urbanised Amsterdam region of the Netherlands; the 'ALS Stichting Nederland' (a national funding agency for research into ALS); social media; and personal connections. The theoretical design of the study was set up with the goal of enrolling patients in different stages of interacting with the feeding tube, thus varying from anticipation of use to experienced use. We interviewed 11 ALS patients either anticipating (3) or living with a feeding tube (8) or both before and after placement. In total we took notes on and recorded as well as transcribed 15 interviews for this study.[14]

We also interviewed four professionals involved with tube feeding in the hospital at different points in time: a gastroenterologist, a neurologist who diagnosed ALS patients, a nurse specialised in coaching patients with feeding tubes, and a rehabilitation doctor who was the main carer for ALS patients. The rehabilitation doctor helped us by approaching patients and giving them our informational flyer. If patients wanted to participate, they could tell the doctor or nurse, who would then give us their contact details. We discussed our results with the rehabilitation doctor to crosscheck our findings and interpretations.

In addition to conducting interviews, we observed three consultations involving patients and their partners who had come in to discuss tube feeding with the gastroenterologist, and two consultations with the specialised nurse. This is how we managed to learn about what the specialist told patients with regard to the tube placement process and about living with the feeding tube. Patients had already discussed the consequences of tube feeding with the rehabilitation doctor when they came to the specialist. Due to the 'lack of clear evidence', the specialist's approach had to be tailored to the specific situation of each patient. Patients ultimately had to decide for themselves whether to have the tube inserted. When possible, we observed patients using the feeding tube or asked them detailed questions about using it, thus turning patients into ethnographers of their own situation.

Understanding quality of life

A first finding from our study of the literature was that there is a lack of clarity on the meaning of the term 'quality of life'. This term has been widely discussed, and the debate reached a high point during the 1980s. Despite widespread use of the term, it remains unclear what exactly is being measured in assessments of quality of life. Various definitions and operationalisations abound. The World Health Organization Quality of Life (WHOQOL) Group describes quality of life as 'individuals' perception of their position in life in the context of the culture and value systems in which they live and in relation to their goals, expectations, standards and concerns'.[15] This description reveals an interesting problem; measuring quality of life is a *subjective evaluation* ('individuals' perception') as well as a condition that is *evaluated from an external point of view* ('culture and value systems'). There may be discrepancies between these two positions.

Some researchers assess quality of life by asking people for an overall rating of their happiness, that is, the grade that they would give to evaluate their life.[16] Other measurements, such as EuroQol, which was developed by the EuroQol Group, do not involve individual assessments but establish how well patients are *functioning* ('I have no problems in walking about').[17] Sometimes 'mental health' is measured as an indicator of quality, such as done by the Beck Depression Inventory, which is a scale to measure symptoms of depression that is used to operationalise quality of life. There are many different questionnaires for different diseases, and some are used in clinical research while others evaluate patients' clinical situation.

In addition to these questionnaires, there are measurements of QALYs (Quality Adjusted Life Years) and DALYs (where the D stands for 'disability'). To calculate these measurements, the expected extension or shortening of life is multiplied with a score that signifies the quality of life. This number is commonly divided with the cost of a certain treatment. QALY is used in national policies as well as international studies that asses the 'global burden of disease'.[18] Such studies inform the funding and accessibility of treatments and shape healthcare policies both nationally and globally. This means that treatments can be evaluated by comparing QALYs, thus making it possible to decide between treatments that result in the highest quality of life compared to their costs.

The measurement of quality of life has played an important role in formulating health policies and in determining what treatments are offered in clinical settings. This has made some authors very sceptical about its measurement. Quality-of-life measurements, they argue, have become strategic assessments that are demanded by public and private sector initiatives, thus turning them into a means for selling treatments rather than undertaking serious assessments.[19] Some authors also argue that questionnaires claiming to measure the quality of life are included in clinical trials even though these say little about the term 'quality' or patients' experiences of quality.[20]

The lack of clarity on what exactly quality-of-life questionnaires evaluate also makes certain observable facts, such as the 'disability paradox', difficult to interpret. The 'disability paradox' refers to the phenomenon that people with severe handicaps or diseases often report a good, stable or even improved quality of life, whereas others would expect that such people are very concerned about their disability and therefore report having a lower quality of life in comparison to being in a state of health or optimal functioning.[21]

Notwithstanding the widespread use of the term 'quality of life' and its impact on the availability of treatments, the obvious conclusion is that this term is rather messy, and that it is informed more by the content of various questionnaires and free associations with the term than by clear definitions.

Normative and descriptive qualifications

There are several lessons that can be drawn from our study of the values that patients associate with the feeding tube. A first lesson about quality of life from our ethnographic study is that it is helpful to distinguish between the (anticipated) *actual* life changes that result from using a feeding tube and the way patients *value* these changes. Quality can be either a normative or a descriptive category. The normative meaning of quality is that it stands for something that is a good, such as a talent, virtue, preferred activity or capacity.

Colloquially this meaning of quality is found in expressions such as 'I opt for quality of life rather than treatment'. Quality is, here, good in itself; it expresses value. This is similar to the way that quality of life is interpreted in quantitative studies that measure or approximate average 'overall' or 'health-related' goodness. QALYs show that this ultimate goodness, or optimal functioning, is reduced by disease and/or treatment in relation to costs.

The second meaning of quality is descriptive, which is similar to terms such as 'qualitative research' that describe rather than positively valuate a *type* of research (as having such-and-such qualities). In this descriptive sense, quality refers to a characteristic or property that has yet to be evaluated. When quality is a characteristic rather than a value, the question whether a certain treatment results in a higher or lower quality of life is meaningless; it would translate to being a question about whether life with or without a treatment has more or fewer qualities or characteristics. It is, however, important to acknowledge that a treatment may lead to different facts of life for different people, as we learned from the accounts given by patients and their families. The distinction between quality as a term that expresses either values or facts enables analytical sensitivity for learning about how and where certain characteristics and their valuations cohere, how they differ, and when it is useful to distinguish between them.

When we asked patients about their quality of life, they did not *contrast* and *weigh* goods against bads, as Albrecht and DeVlieger have suggested.[22] In our study, people answered questions about their quality of life by interpreting quality in a normative way: that is to say, they recounted the good things that they are still able to experience. These good things represented their judgement of their quality of life as they thought of it; the good things were not compared to the bad things.

> Mrs Ralphs: I just celebrated my birthday. And they [her three kids] put on a heart-warming party for their mum. And I am still lucid. Many days have a silver lining.

Mrs Ralphs can no longer get out of bed but she still considers her life valuable because it contains events and characteristics that she values positively (the love from her children, the clarity of mind, the silver-lined days). She lists the positive things in life rather than dwelling on what she has lost. Disease is not part of the calculation for her. Sometimes there are symptoms, such as nausea and fatigue, that hinder her ability to appreciate the good things. Such invasive symptoms correspond to the negative quality judgements that Albrecht and DeVlieger described. However, contrary to this, we learned that rather than being weighed against each other, negative events only become relevant when they *overrule* the possibility for enjoying positive things.

Interestingly, patients do not appear to compare their being ill to their lives preceding illness. Their illness and its drawbacks had become a 'fact of life': that is to say, these set the stage on which life may be experienced as good or not. There may be 'bads', such as constant pain, fatigue and an inability to communicate. But these are all given things that need to be endured or dealt with in a particular situation. Patients do not enjoy this, but they also do not see this situation as necessarily indicating a lack of quality of life. People 'count their blessings' rather than calculate their overall gains and balances.

When we apply this analysis to other cases, it is unwise to take *functioning* as an indicator of quality of life, as often happens in questionnaires. Of course, one does not wish for a treatment to reduce people's functioning. This is, however, better understood as an effect on *health* rather than as the experience of good things in life as the latter is not correlated with functioning in a straightforward way. One can indeed be disabled and lead a fulfilling life, as disability scholars have pointed out.[23] If quality of life is understood in relation to what people value positively, a change in physical functioning does not in itself influence life quality in an unequivocal way.

Quality of life after locked-in syndrome

Some of the coincidences that happen in the process of doing research are rather nice. Sarah conducted most of the interviews, and she has a father who is a neurologist. At the time that we were conducting our research,

> he was treating a patient with 'locked-in syndrome'. This means a patient's body is paralysed and that they are only capable of vertical eye movement. The treatment team concluded that this patient had a very low quality of life and paid him a visit to say they were going to switch off his ventilator. Much to the surprise of the treatment team, the patient was not at all willing to let this happen. He deemed his quality of life high enough to continue living. This quality consisted mainly of the relationships he had with his wife, children and grandchildren. The team learned to never again be so quick to judge another person's quality of life. We published this case in a Dutch journal for doctors.[24]

Functioning, in itself, does not say much about the *kinds* of functioning that are important to certain individuals. The concern for them may not be that they have difficulty walking, but rather whether they can walk their children to school and get their groceries. Struhkamp and colleagues discussed how the term 'independence' was used in rehabilitation questionnaires for people with spinal cord injury, and how this term was formulated in abstract terms that were broadly related to functioning.[25] They found that an abstract definition of functioning is very different from the concrete and practical role that this term plays at home, where people are concerned with performing specific tasks rather than with accomplishing general functions. Large numbers, abstract indicators and averages make the particularity of individual circumstances (and values!) invisible.

The ethnographic findings underscore the ambiguity of statistical operationalisations and their application in research on the quality of life, which is often measured with quantified techniques, averaged across large groups, and taken to refer to bodily functions or an average rating of happiness. The way that quality-of-life scores are used to signify quality changes the meaning of this word and signals a shift away from its common-sense understanding. People who are asked to rate their physical functioning may interpret this term as having a descriptive rather than a normative quality. Such ratings take into account neither subjective understandings of functioning nor the practicalities of everyday life. The meaning of quality of life becomes even more complex when it is understood as a characteristic of everyday life and the various values and facts that play a role in this, as my analysis of temporality will now discuss.

Temporality

Temporality has haunted the endeavour to measure quality of life from its early days. This issue is most notably discussed in terms of 'response shift'.[26] Response shift is a change in preferences in regards to 'changing internal standards, values and the conceptualisation of quality of life'.[27] The phenomenon that requires explanation is the change in how people answer questions that are presented to them in questionnaires on the quality of life. Eton writes, 'Response shift is . . . a theory that helps us understand how certain psychosocial processes can affect how people answer questions on health-status measures.'[28] This phenomenon has also been described as 'cognitive resonance reduction' by psychologists looking for patterns in human behaviour; the same phenomenon is judged differently at different times. Response shift therefore involves changes in the way people rate quality of life in similar contexts at different points in time. The question is whether these changes refer to actual changes in the level of quality experienced in real life or to measurement errors.

The importance of temporality was brought out by our ethnographic approach when we considered the particular group of patients that we were studying. Interpretations of the kind of intervention that the feeding tube signified for patients and their families shifted over time. The process of anticipating or living with a feeding tube differed between patients and between situations. Next, I briefly describe how the feeding tube takes on a different meaning and materiality, at various points in time, for patients anticipating a feeding tube as well as for patients who have obtained such a tube.

Anticipation in times of diagnosis: the tube as a symbol of deterioration

It was clear to clinicians that patients did not like the feeding tube at all, were reluctant to accept it as a possibility in their lives, and postponed its placement as long as they possibly could.[29] The gastroenterologist preferred inserting tubes at the early onset of the disease, when patients were still relatively fit. At this stage, patients could benefit from the nutrition provided by tube feeding and would not have to spend entire days trying to swallow their food. She was unsure whether patients fully understood what having and living with a feeding tube actually entailed. She observed that many who opted for late placement died within three months of the start of their treatment.[30]

Upon receiving their diagnosis, ALS patients are forced to face a radically new perspective on life and grapple with the news of their impending death. Seeber and colleagues show that such a diagnosis is a shock from which most patients have to recover before they can reorganise their lives.[31] They start at the very end: that is, they anticipate how they will die and discuss how they wish to be cared for at the end of life with their general practitioner.[32]

When they did not yet suffer from dysphagia and weight loss, the patients in our study saw the feeding tube as something they may or may not need until later. But 'later' was deemed to be a state of decline that they preferred not to think about or imagine. At this point, the feeding tube was a frightening symbol of deterioration or even the end of a life that is worth living. That living with a feeding tube was so repulsive to some patients was expressed with the phrase, 'If I have reached *that* stage [to need a feeding tube], I'd rather be dead.' The imagined *quality* of life with a feeding tube was a kind of life they did not want, and they therefore did not even want to consider such a life. It was bad enough to have to consider an early death.

Here we are not even talking about the effects of a having a feeding tube inserted, but instead about its anticipation in the context of a radically changed life perspective.[33] The feeding tube was expected to bring such misery that patients did not even want to think about having one inserted, and they could not imagine that the feeding tube might improve their quality of life.

The tube as a solution

Although some patients indicated that they did not feel they had been given enough time and space to form their own opinion on the feeding tube ('I had no choice'), other patients did recount the considerations they had made.[34] Typically, such patients narrated how they had been 'getting through the day' by various means for a long period of time without questioning if something should or could be done to change the situation. They took things as they came. Then there was a turning point.

Partner: Eating was very difficult and it took a lot of time.

Jenita: I spent the entire day eating.

Partner: And obsessively, eh, because it is also a fight against losing weight. It was really stressful. And now, with the feeding tube, she gains a lot of time and energy that no longer goes into eating and worrying about food. She eats soup, custard, whipped cream, all the things she really likes [via the mouth, as a treat]. And it's no longer the main thing or a necessity.

Obsessive eating has an abstract temporality. There was no discrete point in time that could be pinpointed as the point where this struggle with eating became 'too much'. Limits are shifting all the time anyway, slowly, as bodies change. It is hard to establish when 'enough was enough', and the feeding tube can be considered a solution to this rather than a threat. The rehabilitation doctor acted as a gatekeeper and kept an eye on the *relative* speed of weight loss. But time was fluid until a limit had been determined. The feeding tube became a different thing with different functions and uses.

> Sarah: Can you tell me what happened to make you require a feeding tube?
>
> Mr Jansen: I have problems swallowing and I choke. And eating takes a very long time . . . One month, two months ago, eating dinner took the whole evening. I can't swallow food. So that's why, really . . . And it takes me more than an hour to eat. It takes so much energy. And you leave lots of food on your plate because you give up trying. So, then I lost weight, I was underfed. And I lost more and more weight. So, at a certain moment . . . We have a very good doctor and she wanted to do it [the placement] before she retired. So, we had to think about it a lot before we accepted the feeding tube.
>
> Sarah: What did you have to think about?
>
> Mr Jansen: Well, of course, the fact that you have such a thing in your stomach wall!
>
> Mrs Jansen: Yes, you considered the downside, eh? But then, this explanation [by the doctor], that was really nice. She told us everything about it. And then we knew it just had to be done. We [the family] decided immediately. But Hans [Jansen] said, 'I don't want it.' So we took a leaflet home, deliberated and reflected. That was on Wednesday. And then, the other day, [to husband] you choked terribly, [to Sarah] he chokes every day, but this time we thought, 'This is the end.' And the boys [their sons] were there and

we said to Hans, 'What do you want? Do you want to choke?' And then he said, 'You've convinced me.' And he sent an email straight away on Friday. [to Hans] And you even looked forward to it!

The meaning and identity of the feeding tube changed for Mr Jansen once he realised that the tube would not just be awkward or disfiguring but also provide things that were of value to him. The feeding tube promised no more choking, no more fear of suffocating, no more struggling to eat food – which no longer tasted very good anyway – and no more losing weight. As his wife reported, the prospect of no longer having to deal with such issues was something Mr Jansen actually started to look forward to. The meaning of the feeding tube transformed from a symbol of deterioration into a means to an end; it became a tool to alleviate complaints and concerns.

Mr Jansen's account is an example of how the characteristics of life with a feeding tube and the value of these characteristics intertwine and inform each other. In everyday life, the feeding tube became a different object. It now also provided valuable opportunities rather than just solutions to problems that Mr Jansen did not yet experience or could not yet imagine. These possibilities outweighed his primary, and to him self-evident, reluctance to 'have such a thing in your stomach'. A plastic tube in his stomach was not something he would ever consider for trivial reasons alone. The extremely scary event of nearly choking to death, however, was the tipping point that allowed him to conclude that there might be good reasons to have a feeding tube inserted. This shift involved not only a psychological process or change in perception – a response shift – but also a physical process or change in qualities, that is to say, of no longer being able to eat or of choking on food. When considering this change in feelings related to the feeding tube, the tube is reimagined as a rational response to a changed situation rather than an inexplicable change in values. Rather than a shift in 'response' per se, it signified a shift in the *situation* that he responded to anew.

The tube as facilitator of happy events

The understandings of the feeding tube could transform once more. The tube could become an alleviant of complaints. When people evaluated the feeding tube positively, they praised the tube either as an alleviant of complaints and concerns or as a facilitator of happy events. The latter description was brought up once patients discovered that the time they formerly spent on eating could now be spent on more meaningful things.

Gastroenterologist: The tube does not provide quality of life in the sense that it cures a patient, because they cannot be cured. The quality it provides is that people say that they can get rid of things they did not enjoy, such as the social aspects of eating, 'it takes me hours to eat, my food gets cold'. I had one patient, he was an artist, a painter, who could only draw dots as a result of his ALS. He'd go to the zoo, and he would draw dots with his pencil, make drawings just out of dots. And he said to me, 'Thanks to the tube I have gained so many hours in my day. I used to only have a couple of hours in the day when I was not too exhausted to draw my dots. Previously, I used those hours for eating, and now I don't have to do that any more!'

Paradoxically – and in contrast to the juxtaposition suggested in the literature between the pleasure of eating and the necessity of tube feeding – the tube permitted new ways of eating and enjoying food. Eating and tube feeding are not mutually exclusive, which is a common and unfortunate misunderstanding. Once the pressure to consume enough calories was lifted, eating – or rather tasting – could be organised in new and enjoyable ways, albeit in different forms. Eating had to be reshaped to involve foods that are neither too runny nor too solid and that still tasted good. Food did not have to be 'healthy' or 'fresh', which puzzled some patients and their caregivers. Tastiness, swallowability and pleasure were what mattered. One patient ate one or two cookies a day just for the satisfaction and pleasure of chewing.

For Jenita, food had completely lost any attraction because of the difficulties she had in swallowing. After the feeding tube had been inserted, calories were no longer a worry and Jenita could start eating in ways she liked. The materiality of various foods narrowed the possibilities (not everything can be swallowed easily, and not every kind of food can be made swallowable), but within these limitations she could eat the things she enjoyed in a relaxed manner. Eating could again become a pleasurable activity rather than a necessity to survive.

These examples show that the feeding tube might provide positive things in life that are not in themselves related to the tube but that are facilitated by it. If the feeding tube is not a positive characteristic in itself, it is important that patients consider what they will do with the time that they gain once they have obtained such a tube. The time that is gained, however, could be miserable rather than fun.

The tube as a transformer of misery

The tube could also transform a certain form of misery or unhappiness into another. This could happen, for instance, to people who were unable to administer food through their own tube due to a lack of muscle power and who had no informal carers to do this for them. Particularly when they needed regular feeding (such as every two hours), the feeding tube could be a major source of misery. For example, Mr Gonders had to constantly administer liquid food because his stomach could not handle too much fluid at one time.

> Sarah: Is there anything else you'd like to mention about the tube?
>
> Mrs Gonders: Well, if I may speak on his behalf, the worst was that he couldn't move. When he had to go to the loo, for instance. First, he had to disconnect the power cord of the motor for the feeding drip. Then the oxygen . . . he could take the oxygen with him. And then he had to bring the whole rig with him. He couldn't just get up to get something or go to the door when somebody rang the bell, or to go to the toilet. He couldn't do any of this, which is why he was completely in the doldrums. Not going to the computer or moving to the table because it was so much fuss!

Mr Gonders was hampered by his drip machine and the device providing oxygen. Even if he was physically capable of walking, he could not do so easily because of all the machines attached to him. He could not do the ordinary things that he had always done routinely. Other informants recounted that they spent a lot of time waiting for nurses to replace their bags of liquid food. Being unable to do things, or being unable to do things that one might enjoy, could make the life of ALS patients with a feeding tube more miserable. Instead of struggling to ingest enough food and calories, they were now tethered to machines, sitting and watching as time passed by and their life wasted away. It was time of bad quality, everyday time changed into empty time. This kind of life contained no promise of pleasurable events, and everyday time became devoid of order, activity and meaning.

Different feeding tubes

From the ethnographic study it became clear that the feeding tube is a *complex* and *unstable* intervention, the effects of which depend on where and when it is put to work. The circumstances were of crucial importance for determining what the feeding tube could do for someone.[35] Measuring the effect of the feeding tube on quality of life depended on *when* the measurement was done. A common research design is to measure quality of life before the feeding tube is placed and again at some point after its placement. But does the moment 'before' represent the anticipation phase in which people were still rejecting the feeding tube because it symbolised a life that is not worth living? Or are patients in this moment already experiencing so much discomfort while eating that the tube can become a solution to their problems? As for the second moment of measurement after the feeding tube's placement, do the measured outcomes signify a solution to the immediate and immensely scary problem of choking? Or does this measurement take place during the phase in which it is becoming clear to the patient that the tube can facilitate good or exacerbate bad things? Using aggregated scores to calculate an 'average effect' will inevitably include situations that are incomparable. Measuring the change in quality of life over time, from anticipation until death, might be a good way to capture the processual character of this development. Nevertheless, the timing of each measurement makes it difficult to interpret results.

There is also a problem with the different temporalities of QALY in comparison to the temporalities of the feeding tube in everyday life. The specific temporality of QALY is that it correlates lived life years to the quality of this time. If one has, say, five years left to live but only with harsh treatments that severely reduce one's quality of life, the number five (representing the years lived) can be corrected with a factor between one (full health) and zero (death).[36] The temporality of this particular quality of life is marked by a clear start (the intervention) and end (the end of biological life). The *quality* of this time period is conceptualised as static once the intervention takes effect. It is a single score that represents a stable *outcome*, effect or end result of a particular treatment over time. Transient inconveniences of the treatment and fluctuations of one's illness are hence not included in the measurement of outcomes unless these measurements are repeated over time.

This focus on end results is part of a general orientation in medical research that studies interventions that *cure* particular conditions.[37] A relatively short period of suffering – resulting from the administration of the treatment itself – is accepted to measure the eventual outcome, which is either 'a return to health' or a loss of quality of life when this is not achieved. This particular framing and shaping of the term 'quality' does not apply well to chronic or terminal conditions. These diseases cannot be cured – the feeding tube, for example, will remain inserted in patients' bodies as a prosthesis – and patients will eventually deteriorate further rather than regain 'health'. They will need constant support and treatment, which increases the impact of medical interventions on their lives and substantially changes their level of quality in different ways.[38] But this also means that the functions and identity of the feeding tube keep changing.

The temporal shift of the feeding tube's identity is very difficult to capture in quantitative research on quality of life even when such measurements explicitly seek to gauge 'quality'. A longitudinal ethnographic perspective can, however, identify and assess such shifts and thus provide relevant information to clinicians. This is not done by measuring 'general effects' on groups of people but by pointing towards the different sets of specificities that are at stake for *this* particular patient or in *that* particular situation. But there is one last obstacle to discuss.

Unequal values: the sensuous body or the facts of life

While studying the feeding tube, we observed that there were profound differences between how patients valued the tube. Some valuations of similar events differed remarkably among patients. This was especially clear in valuations of 'having a plastic tube protruding from one's belly'. Some patients had strong reasons for objecting to having a feeding tube inserted.

> Sarah: So, it's preventive, but you'd like to postpone it as long as possible.
>
> Harry: Yes, obviously, it's terrible to have a plastic tube sticking out of your belly.
>
> Sarah: What exactly is so bad about that?
>
> Harry: Well, it's plastic, where you don't expect it. Or want it.
>
> Lene [spouse]: Like you [ethicists] all say, it damages your physical integrity [the meaning of integrity refers simultaneously to the wholeness/intactness of the body and to its violation].

> Harry: The first invasive thing is the breathing device. But that's on the outside of your body. And if you take off the mask, after 10 minutes it's as if you never wore it. But the tube will always be there [you cannot take it off]. And unfortunately you can have a button[39] only after three months. Honestly, I thought that I could have it [the button] right away. So that's a bit of a disappointment.

The patient's reluctance to have a tube inserted was informed by the way in which the tube disrupted the sensual qualities of their body. This surprised the gastroenterologist, who saw maintaining physical fitness and prolonging survival as the ultimate goals and the feeding tube as a means towards these ends ('It's your lifeline!'). Patients, however, considered the social, erotic and aesthetic meanings of the body. The gastroenterologist found this hard to understand in the face of death, but it points to the more sensual ways in which people use and live their body. Having one's bodily integrity threatened by a disfiguring tube – made out of a plastic that contrasts starkly with the skin and that protrudes so that others can see it – could be a major problem. Some would rather live and die without the tube.[40]

To some, such sensual concerns were very strong and important, but others were completely indifferent to the feeding tube in this regard.

> Jeannette: How do you feel about the way that the feeding tube sticks out?
>
> Jenita: [Waves hand dismissively]. It's not important. The benefits are what's important. It's not that I particularly like it, but it's not an issue.

Obviously, the feeding tube is not the same thing in Harry or Jenita's life. Once again, the identity of the feeding tube changes. Yet this time the change is not due to the characteristics of the environment from which the tube derives its function but due to a different sensual appreciation. For those who highly value the sensuality and appearance of their body, the feeding tube is a source of misery. Where once they suffered from dysphagia, fear of choking and weight loss, they now suffer from having a deformed and less desirable and playful body. For those who cared less about this type of aesthetics, the tube did not add to their suffering.

Jenita's indifference to such concerns reveals something else, too. Apparently, people accept some qualities as 'facts of life' and take them as givens. These characteristics accompany the feeding tube, but Jenita does not judge them as detracting from the value of her life. Something comparable seems to be at stake in the case of the disability paradox. People do not compare their life as a handicapped person to a life without impediments. These disabilities have become a fact of life to them. They form the 'givens' from which everything else follows.

Quality-of-life measurements presuppose that the physiologies and values of people are distributed on a Gaussian curve. This presumption suggests that there is a general response to treatments that can be modelled on a shared human physiology in which human bodies respond comparably even if these responses differ in intensity. An example of this is the various degrees of 'increased fatigue' resulting from treatment that patients within the sample report. Individual differences among patients are evened out and made invisible by calculating average responses. If, say, five people were unhappy with their feeding tube because it merely changed the nature of their misery and 10 people were happy because the tube allowed them to do meaningful things, this would result in the reporting of a slight positive effect. Individual differences – such as taking issue with being disfigured by the feeding tube, which is crucial to some yet trivial to others – are aggregated into an average score. The outcome of this process is signified by large standard deviations and unclear overall outcomes, as is the situation today. It is also likely that people with aesthetic concerns are under-represented in a trial because they may opt to not get a tube. What is deemed crucial for quality of life by one person (for example, an intact body) may detract from quality of life for another (who fears choking to death) or horrify an outsider who has not (yet) been confronted with problems that demand drastic solutions (the freshly diagnosed).[41]

Different types of value

The analysis presented in this chapter shows that approaches to studying quality of life – both in how they relate to patients as well as how they practically shape values through employing methods such as QALYs and questionnaires – make certain objects visible that are quite different from the values and arrangements that were observed during the ethnographic study. This chapter also shows that there is a long list of concerns about quality-of-life research. We saw that the meaning of the term itself is unclear, and that it is dubious whether 'functioning' can serve as an outcome variable denoting quality of life because it does not refer to normative and subjective understandings but to a state of the art. The people in our study did not weigh up the goods and bads that were present in their lives and then calculate an overall result. Instead, they preferred to list the positive aspects of their lives.

Acknowledging the temporality of the arrangements that patients with the feeding tube live in is important for understanding their shifting appreciation of the tube. It is hard to imagine how quantitative researchers can study such shifts within existing research designs, other than dismissing them as measurement errors or referring to them as 'response shift' issues. The feeding tube not only changed character depending on the evolving situations of individuals, but also played an active part in influencing these situations and arrangements. Rather than only being an intervention in a patient's *body*, the feeding tube was also an intervention in people's lives and circumstances, which, in turn, influenced what the effects of the feeding tube could be for patients. For instance, the presence of informal carers who could help with administering liquid food could make a big difference between spending one's time waiting for a nurse to come and spending one's time in a more purposeful manner.

Quality-of-life research has shown the problem of averaging values that are important to some but meaningless to others. This issue is sometimes solved on a technical level in questionnaires by adding a question on whether something is important to the respondent or not. Finally, this chapter noted that the research practice of randomisation makes quality-of-life research more difficult. Patients did not want to cede control over their treatment and wanted to decide things for themselves.

This is a long list of issues that highlights one of the points of this book, namely that state-of-the-art biomedical research is unable to address the facts and values of everyday life. Ethnographic methods are far more suited for this. But the analysis also demonstrates that the organisation of research practices, and this includes the 'methods' of research, shapes the object of research and how it can be articulated. Both the ethnographic study and the quantitative studies sought to acknowledge the values that are important to patients, but both did so in very different ways and hence articulated very different types of values, namely specific values of everyday life versus generalised evaluations or judgements. Research practices and methods create a voice for some things rather than for others.

This voicing of quality can be about functioning or about everyday-life values, about average likings or about contextualised appreciations. The values articulated in the ethnographic study are important to the everyday life of patients, but learning about these values is not merely a matter of asking individual subjects about their authentic experiences. In Chapter 6, it was the socio-material network that supported a good life. In this chapter, it is a voice that is created in interactions between researchers, concepts, methods, shifting conditions and so on. Methods and research practices mediate what can be articulated in research or not. This is not a matter of the subjectivity of the researcher getting in the way of objective research, but a matter of the subtle normativities that are embedded in research practices, methods and concepts as well as how these shape what we can learn about the world. Research practices, methods and concepts provide different ways of re-scribing or re-presenting the world.

Putting knowledge about specificities into practice

There is a bitter irony in this analysis. The ethnographic approach attends closely to practices and is therefore highly relevant to clinical and everyday-life concerns, but it has difficulty in making its results heard in clinical practice. The difference between the research traditions of doctors and those of ethnographers is a gap that is hard to bridge. Ethnographic work theorises about the specificity of everyday clinical care and everyday life by articulating their everyday ethics and values as well as their shifting truths. And it does this without generalising or providing guidelines that must be followed. Instead, ethnographic work provides insight into what might be at stake by exploring a variety of possibilities that are not necessarily exhaustive.

The next step is to reflect on the question of whether the identified values and variables are relevant to *this* patient or situation, here and now, and in what ways this might be the case. It is not a matter of 'applying what is best for most'. The irony may well be a double one: that is to say, the interpretation of specific situations is also necessary for drawing connections between general guidelines or findings and a specific patient's situation. However, this tacit work is rarely articulated explicitly, and suspicions about the relatively small sample size in qualitative studies make doctors hesitant to acknowledge what such studies might have to offer. Clinical work is understudied as a form of care work, and epidemiological instruments provide few opportunities for asking open questions about the various values that may be at stake in care practices.

But what exactly does ethnographic research makes visible? Do we create 'a voice' for patients or do we do something else? And how might this work for patients who, literally or metaphorically, cannot speak? How might we address the values that are important to them, in their everyday life while living with a disease? This is the topic of Chapter 12, the last chapter of Part III. If different arrangements and relationships articulate different subject-positions, values and truths, how might we address the facts and values of everyday life?

Notes

1. This chapter draws on: Pols & Limburg, 2016; Pols, 2019b; and Limburg et al., 2018.
2. Willems, 2010b.
3. The limitations of quantitative research styles led Greenhalgh and colleagues (2014) to proclaim a crisis in research. See Timmermans & Berg, 2003, for an analysis on evidence-based medicine.
4. See Stavroulakis et al., 2013, for a more detailed description.
5. Katzberg & Benatar, 2011; Langmore et al., 2006.
6. Vesey et al., 2008; Goyal & Mozaffar, 2014; Shintani 2013; Greenwood, 2013.
7. Vesey, 2013; Todd et al., 2005; Aparanji & Dharmarajan, 2010.
8. Martin et al., 2012.
9. Hossein et al., 2011.
10. Mazzini et al., 1995.
11. Todd et al., 2005; Angus & Burakoff, 2003; Pennington, 2002.
12. Kaufman, 2015.
13. Rabeneck et al., 1997.
14. Interviewing ALS patients required a lot of patience from both the interviewee and the interviewer. Talking could be difficult for informants due to weakened muscles. Partners and children supported them by explaining things to the interviewer. Some informants used a speech computer. Others could not speak at all and delivered their story to us in writing or via their spouse. According to Dutch law and research codes we did not need the approval of an ethics committee for this study, but because this is a particularly vulnerable patient group we took special precautions and let people know they could always opt out of an interview or cancel an appointment, which they sometimes did.
15. WHOQOL, 1995.
16. Pais-Ribeiro, 2004.
17. Balestroni & Bertolotti, 2012.
18. The DALY focuses on (loss of) functioning rather than quality. See Moreira, 2013.
19. See Hunt, 1997a; 1997b.
20. Car-Hill, 1991; Carr & Higginson, 2001. For a critical overview of the meanings of quality of life in quantitative science, see Gill & Feinstein, 1994; Moreira, 2013; Warren & Manderson, 2013.
21. Albrecht & DeVlieger 1999; Lacey et al., 2011; Gauthier et al., 2007.
22. Albrecht & DeVlieger, 1999.
23. Hoppe, 2013.
24. Limburg et al., 2018.
25. Struhkamp et al., 2009.
26. Sprangers & Schwartz, 2010, Ubel et al., 2010; Eton, 2010.
27. Sprangers & Schwartz, 1999, p. 1507.
28. Sprangers & Schwartz, 2010, p. 930.
29. See also Stavroulakis et al., 2013.
30. I reconstructed this from the methods section in Stavroulakis et al., 2013, and this confirmed that participants in the study who received a tube did so at the end of their trajectory. Twenty-seven patients volunteered to be interviewed about their tube three months after its placement. Five of them died before the interview could be conducted, and the condition of eight other patients deteriorated so severely that they had to withdraw from the study. It is a small sample, but it is nonetheless significant that nearly half of the patients dropped out within three months after the tube's placement. This highlights the urgency of considering who benefits from a feeding tube and who does not. Patients described the placement procedure as very burdensome because of the hospital stay that leaves almost all their home-based technological aids literally out of reach. The question whether this procedure is justified by the potential benefits is an important one (Pols & Limburg, 2016).
31. Seeber et al., 2016.

32 This is a possibility in the Netherlands. Veldink et al., 2002, show that 17 per cent of ALS patients resort to euthanasia in the final stages of the disease. It was clear to all participants that these were provisory statements, and the rehabilitation doctor warned people that they might change their mind along the way, and also added that this was perfectly fine (Seeber et al., 2016).
33 Pols & Limburg, 2016.
34 See also Vesey et al., 2008.
35 See also Warren & Manderson, 2013; Warren et al., 2009.
36 Hypothetically, there could be a negative score to represent a situation that is 'worse than death', but I have never seen this being reported in medical research.
37 Weisz, 2014, calls this the infection model of disease.
38 See Pols, 2013c.
39 A button is a flat plastic disc that closes the tube and hides the hole in the stomach. It requires agility to remove this button and to connect a syringe to the extension of the tube, but this produces a better aesthetic effect than the roll of plastic tubing taped to the patient's trunk.
40 See Sakellariou, 2013, who reports on this.
41 Prosthetic and technological aids are likely candidates for this category of interventions, which are shaped over time and through interaction with their users (Winance, 2006; Pols, 2012; 2017a; 2017b; Hoogsteyns & Van Der Horst, 2013; 2015), but local circumstances can also make a difference. Medical anthropologists have been witness to this. If disturbed sleep is caused by local spirits, for example, people will not take sleep medication because this will weaken their strength to fight these spirits (Bonelli, 2012). Sleeping pills will hence have no effect. More research is needed to explore the limits of the model that postulates a generalised physiological response, also within Western biomedical traditions. For example, 'personalised medicine' is a very different biomedical model for predicting individual responses to treatment that ties these responses to the particular genetic make-up of various individuals as well as how these make-ups qualitatively differ from each other.

11
Petrarch's practice of letter writing: the good life in research

In Chapter 10, I analysed how the organisation of research practices and methods co-creates the object of research, and how this process might enable researchers to examine the values of everyday life. Measurements of the quality of life were thought to facilitate research on what patients valued. Such measurements did not, however, provide much insight into the (aesthetic, practical, medical and other) values that are involved in everyday life with a feeding tube or how these values shifted over time on the life trajectories of patients. Ethnographic methods proved better suited for examining such values.

Yet another line of social scientific research seeks to involve patients in research, most notably as co-researchers. This is supposedly done to equalise power differences. However, it is also clear that people with dementia, learning disabilities or severe and long-term psychiatric problems are often not particularly interested in being co-researchers, and that they cannot be disciplined into acting as conventional research subjects who fill out questionnaires. But researchers can – and do – involve them in research as informants. How to do that well? I address this question in the final analytical chapter of this book, where I suggest that our research practices and methods *themselves* can be better geared towards collaborating in research and achieving the good life for research subjects. It is not just a matter of letting people participate on the terms of researchers and their methods. These terms and methods will have to shift to be able to address the facts and values of everyday life and to see what they hold dear.

In this chapter I discuss the philosophical practices of Petrarch (1304–1374) and other Renaissance humanists interested in philosophy as a way of living to further develop and frame the question about the relationship between research methods and research subjects. These philosophical practices are helpful for determining which methods are suitable for learning about the values of everyday life that arise in the interaction between patients and researchers.

Form and content in practices of inquiry

In this chapter, I explore how the organisation of research practices and methods may influence the content of what can be learned. How do practical ways of doing science shape the content of what we seek to understand? And more specifically, how might we create research practices that are sensitive to the values of everyday life? To address these questions, I will analyse a text by the philosopher Nancy Struever on the practices of the good life as conceptualised by Petrarch and his colleagues.[1] Petrarch purposefully and explicitly broke with the academic conventions of his time, which he found obscure and irrelevant to learning about the concerns of everyday life. Petrarch and his colleagues left academia to create a new philosophical practice, one that allowed them to develop ways of knowing that could help answer the question that Petrarch deemed central to philosophy, namely, 'How should one live?' Writing letters central was to this new academic practice. Letter writing allowed for the kind of intimate and open-ended exchange between friends that Petrarch was after.

Reading Petrarch with Struever

In her analysis of Petrarch's philosophical practice of the good life, Nancy Struever discusses how his practice was conducted in response to medieval academic philosophy. Petrarch and his fellow thinkers disapproved of the academic practices of their day. Universities had recently emerged as a new type of institution for the production of knowledge. Petrarch and his allies, however, considered academia formalistic, obscure and self-congratulating. Academic philosophers, they argued, wrote long, opaque and unreadable books about problems in which nobody was really interested. Petrarch and his colleagues turned their backs on these practices, which they accused of being vain and existing only for the pride and joy of certain established scholars. And these practices, moreover, had nothing to say about or contribute to the question of how to live (*vivere*). They developed a new philosophical practice outside academia that was more relevant to the concerns they wanted to address. Their relocation of philosophical inquiry was directly connected to what they wished to study. They created a space for addressing the problems that were relevant to everyday life.

Struever discusses, on the one hand, the *results* of various types of philosophical inquiry. Academic philosophy was concerned with developing general and systematic theories. On the other hand, Struever also discusses the *practices* involved in conducting philosophical inquiry. She shows how form and content influence each other. Practices shape ways of knowing because practices dictate the *forms* of knowledge that can be produced (for example, big books by academic philosophers, or letters by Petrarch). These practices dictate the *methods* and *styles of writing* (logical deduction on the one hand, and dialogical examination on the other) as well as the *audiences* that are addressed (fellow academic philosophers or literate elites). Struever argues that Petrarch and his colleagues were not interested in moralising or creating moral theory, but that they were 'doing moral work' by practising the philosophically informed life that they advocated for rather than developing a theory about the good life. One could say that they practised rather than that they preached by putting the good life into practice as 'men of letters' rather than as writers of treatises. This is an echo of the exemplary lives led by the Cynics and Socrates. The humanist practice of philosophy as a way of living was a means as well as an end. It was simultaneously the product of and condition for this way of 'doing philosophy'; it *enacted* the good philosophical practice.

Struever argues that this commitment to practice is one reason why philologists and philosophers have been puzzled over the meagre contribution of Renaissance humanists, such as Petrarch and Montaigne, to the philosophical canon. Humanist texts frequently engage in conversation with ancient Greek authors, but their collective writings have contributed few new ideas to philosophy.[2] There are even humanists who were well respected in their time but who have left *nothing at all* in writing. Struever argues that their philosophical practice is precisely what they contributed to philosophy. Rather than engaging with philosophers who were already familiar with ancient Greek theory, Petrarch sought to develop new practices of knowing. Petrarch's approach was not unlike that of Socrates, another philosopher who did not write books. It is in their *living* of these practices that the contribution of Renaissance humanists can be found. Their novel counter-academic practices re-localised and reshaped intellectual life. Struever shows that the subversive practices of inquiry that the Renaissance humanists employed are what make them most interesting and still relevant today.

The relocation of philosophical inquiry and the establishment of a new intellectual practice outside the university makes Renaissance humanists surprisingly relevant to contemporary studies of practice, such as those that are the focus of this book. Renaissance humanism can teach us about the workings of research practices. This is a folding of time that the Renaissance humanists would have appreciated. They engaged in time folding practices themselves by conversing with the ancient Greeks as if they were contemporaries. In the next section, I summarise Struever's chapter on Petrarch's work at some length to draw out parallels with the questions that are central to this part of the book, and specifically those that seek to understand how research methods can make the values of everyday life visible. Petrarch's practice of writing letters and engaging in dialogues is a relevant method for achieving this goal. Struever has a different interest and uses different words than I do, but I read her writing on Petrarch as a theoretically informed ethnography on the knowledge practices of Renaissance humanists that is comparable to how Foucault analysed the ancient Greeks in his final lectures. I will quote from Petrarch's letters in English translation by way of illustration.

Struever's reading of Petrarch's intellectual practice

What did Petrarch's new philosophical practice look like? It was a practice that foregrounded the relationship between philosophers and the receivers of their knowledge. This relationship was characterised by *friendship*. It assumed a community of readers (*amicitia*) who wanted to develop ethical insights while living in a world of ignorance. Conversing with this community of friends through letters, however, required discipline and solitude:

> On my return, since I experienced a deep-seated and innate repugnance to town life, especially in that disgusting city of Avignon which I heartily abhorred, I sought some means of escape. I fortunately discovered, about fifteen miles from Avignon, a delightful valley, narrow and secluded, called Vaucluse, where the Sorgue, the prince of streams, takes its rise. Captivated by the charms of the place, I transferred thither myself and my books. Were I to describe what I did there during many years, it would prove a long story. Indeed, almost every bit of writing which I have

put forth was either accomplished or begun, or at least conceived, there, and my undertakings have been so numerous that they still continue to vex and weary me.[3]

Solitude also brought silence with it, which allowed for reading as well as hearing the 'soft sounds' of writers:

> Let us establish an honourable goal for our studies and not the vainglory of the multitude that derives from the witticisms of a windy argument. Let that goal be achieved through the effect of truth and virtue. Believe me it is possible to know something without noisy quarrels. It is not noise that makes the learned man, but contemplation. Therefore, unless we are determined to appear rather than to be, we will enjoy not the applause of the foolish multitude but rather truth and silence. And we shall be happy at the soft sound brought to us sometimes by words of genuine writers. Thus the fields will resound not with sharp noise but with a soft murmur.[4]

This quiet solitude was, however, not a lonely solitude. It was a *generative* solitude that was filled with books and real and imaginary friends who could be engaged in conversation. Petrarch considered his books as friends. Lonesome letter writers needed solitude to engage in constant conversation with their addressees, the authors and ideas they found important, and the friends with whom they engaged in discussion.

Writing letters, even if these were eventually read by a larger audience, enabled a conversation that was characterised by an intimate tone and atmosphere. The intimacy of the letter was an intimacy between friends. The literary form of the letter demanded a certain equality between reader and writer because it was a non-authoritative relationship that was oriented towards the exchange of ideas.

> What Seneca might feel about Cicero's letters is a personal matter. As for me, I must confess, I find them delightful reading; for such reading is a change from having to deal with difficult matters, and is a source of delight if done intermittently but a source of unpleasantness if done continuously.[5]

> In the collection [of *Letters of Familiar Things*] you will find very few letters that can be called masterpieces, and many others written on a variety of personal matters in a rather simple and unstudied manner, tough sometimes, when the subject matter so requires,

seasoned with interspersed moral considerations, an approach observed by Cicero himself.[6]

According to Petrarch, freedom was the condition for achieving truth. There could be no authoritative logical reasoning or dogmatism, but only the 'sweetness' of gaining insight while living in liberty. Both conversation partners could write frankly and openly, which allowed them to address sensitive issues – such as illness or death, friendship or beauty – and express doubts, worries and concerns.[7] The familiarity of the writer with the addressee – and the desire to examine and speak the truth about everyday life – created a particular style of inquiry in which ancient Greek philosophers were argued with as if they were contemporary friends. He calls, for instance, Seneca to account to grill him about his services to Nero who was a cruel prosecutor of Christians. Here Petrarch rebukes Cicero:

> Allow me to say, O Cicero, that you lived as a man, you spoke as an orator, wrote as a philosopher; and it was your life that I censured, not your intellect and your tongue since I admire the former and am astounded by the latter. Moreover, nothing was lacking but constancy in your personal life, a desire for the tranquillity necessary for the practice of philosophy, and withdrawal from civil strife, once liberty was spent and the Republic buried and mourned.[8]

Note that Petrarch does not criticise Cicero's ideas (nor did he criticise Seneca's work), but rather his life and actions. He speaks to the ancient Greek directly, as to contemporary friends. Here he explains this:

> Cicero revealed himself so weak that while I take pleasure in his style I often feel offended by his attitude. I feel the same about his contentious letters and the many quarrels and abuses that he directs against famous men upon whom he had not long before lavished praise. And I feel the same about the casualness with which he does all this. When I read his letters I feel as offended as I feel enticed. Indeed, beside myself, in a fit of anger I wrote to him as if he were a friend living in my time with an intimacy that I consider proper because of my deep and immediate acquaintance with his thought. I thus reminded him of those things he had written that had offended me, forgetting, as it were, the gap of time. This idea became the beginning of something that made me do the same thing with Seneca after rereading after many years his tragedy entitled *Octavia*. Him I also reproached, and thereafter, as the occasion arose, I similarly wrote to Varro, Virgil and others.[9]

This emphasis on everyday life was new at the time, and foregrounded discourse concerning the question of how to live. These letters were conversations, exchanges between friends who are not in each other's presence. Letters could make such absent others present again, and this allowed readers and writers to spend time together and to build and extend their friendship. Rather than the grandiloquence that his contemporaries strove for, Petrarch preferred 'sweetness' in his letters, an aesthetic qualification of the pleasure of gaining wisdom.[10] This allowed him to discuss intimate subjects in a gentle style, and thus to edify both the reader and writer. The letters were public documents that were read and referred to by other readers and writers. The letters were quoted ('In the sixth letter from Petrarch to Y'), collected and printed. They decorated the houses of the literate elites of the time. It is for this reason that these letters addressed an audience that was far broader than a single addressee. Petrarch and his contemporaries sought to include people who wanted to reflect on everyday-life issues by creating an accessible philosophical practice that was concerned with everyday-life problems. The form of the letter enabled the inclusion of far more readers than the philosophical books written at that time.[11]

To Petrarch, letter writing was a social obligation, but it also provided moral and intellectual fulfilment. Petrarch described these intimate obligations as *compulsions* that needed to be acted on or as *moral rages* that needed to run their course. This may sound uninviting, but letter writing was an act instigated by motivation and affect rather than by will, reason or calculation. Petrarch also used the word *lust* (*voluptas*) to explain his motivation to lead a good life. *Voluptas* was an aesthetic, sensuous and relational kind of enjoyment. This type of pleasurable knowledge needs to be generously passed on, and finds its fulfilment when it is received and responded to by others. It was the affection for his friends, and the concerns that were at stake, that inspired the Petrarchan subject to give his very best. Such motivations, again, resonate with ancient Greek ideas about 'being called' by a concern for the good life as a form of 'care for the self'. The topic or the world 'pull' at the thinking subject rather than that the subject is defined by their autonomy, free will, good intentions or ability to reason. Petrarch's subject is a relational subject. His philosophical practice implies a subject who is not the master or the object of their intentions and activities but who finds value in and through its relationships with others.

> If any of these pieces are appealing to you I must say that they are so not because of me but because of you. They are all testimonials of your friendship rather than samples of my talent. Indeed nothing

> among them required great power of speech; this I do not possess and if I did, to speak honestly, I would not use it with this style. Cicero himself did not use such a style in his letters although he was most distinguished in it, nor in those books that required an "equable" style, as he called it, and a "temperate type of speech." And so in his orations we find him using that unique kind of power and a lucid, rapid, and almost torrential kind of eloquence.[12]

The motivation of friendship, as a combination of drive and affect, is crucial to understanding Petrarch's practices. His letters were not about trivial personal details but sought to foster intimacy between him and his friends. The letters enacted a fictional familiarity with his readers. The private character of the letter, regardless of its broader role in social life, invited a careful formulation of matters of interest by both reader and writer. Struever considers Petrarch's relational practice of selfhood as his main contribution to philosophy. Petrarch created a particular form of subjectivity and authenticity through these relationships of friendship and exchange. The moral, confessional style of Petrarch's letter writing as well as his conversations gain meaning by creating and maintaining genuinely friendly relationships. Morality and relationships were hence both the object and the outcome of Petrarch's letter writing. The self of the writer flourished in its moral relationship with others.

The position of the reader

The humanists' relational understanding of knowledge creation through practices of friendship implies an active role for the reader. Freedom, for Petrarch, is an essential condition for truth to emerge as well as for being able to write good letters. Petrarch's conceptualisation of freedom required being untethered from the academic conventions of the day but also the withdrawal of the writing subject into solitude. The writer finds freedom in solitude; it is the condition for being able to live freely. Petrarch finds freedom in his solitude because it allows him to think in conversation with others. Solitude assures that both writer and reader are free to engage with thinking.

> Without question a great number of subjects will present themselves but I welcome this because for me writing and living are the same thing and I hope will be so to the very end. But although all things must have their boundaries or are expected to, the affection of

> friends will allow no end to this work which was begun haphazardly in my earliest years and which now I gather together again in a more advanced age and reduce to the form of a book. For I feel impelled to answer and to correspond with them constantly, nor does that fact that I am so terribly busy serve as an excuse for avoiding this responsibility. Only then will I no longer feel this obligation and will have to consider this work ended when you hear that I am dead and that I am freed from all the labors of life. In the meantime I shall continue along the path I have been following, and shall avoid any exits so long as there is light. And the sweet labor will serve for me almost as a place of rest.[13]

The task of the *reader* was to authenticate and validate what was written, that is, the writing had to be meaningful to him or her. The reader was obliged to respond to the letter by writing back or offering reflections or by raising questions, freely and spontaneously, so that the writer could be enlightened in turn. A letter was useless if it did not have a reader who could respond. Hence, friendship was *lived* (rather than theorised) by Petrarch and his fellows. It formed the basis for developing their ethical insights. Knowledge was developed by exchanging thoughts between dedicated friends who talked and wrote to examine and discover the truth. In this way, Struever argues, friendship was linked to virtue; it is good to treat friends well and to care for them. Friendship was both the facilitator and the source of discovery and insight.

> And so, as there is almost nothing rarer, so there is nothing dearer than true friendship, which as a gift of heaven becomes the one anchor of a stormy life, the one respite from toil that can make happiness sweeter and sadness more bearable. In short, a friend is another self, the support of our condition, the light of our soul, guide of our mind, torch of our studies, pacifier of all dissensions, partner in our troubles and tasks, companion in our travels, and a consolation to our households, present not only at home but also in the country and in war, on land and on sea, an enduring and immortal solace not only during one's lifetime but also beyond the grave. Indeed, whoever dies leaving friends behind seems to live especially after he has died. Since this is so, however great a friend's generosity and kindness, if he clings too tenaciously to this rare boon, if he is similar to that man who either through his fault or, as Juvenal says, 'through the fault of his people never shares a friend and keeps him only for himself', he does not deserve the full glory of friendship.[14]

Petrarch argued that the letter was a form of writing that signified modesty, simplicity, openness, variety and directness. Letter writing is unsuitable for showing off like his contemporaries did with their thick volumes. Reading a letter did not require a lot of time or the assistance of piles of philosophical dictionaries. The first-person perspective was more important than lists of duties or hierarchies of virtues. In this quote, Petrarch rages about logicians' formalistic ways of reasoning, which would lead to absurdities rather than truth:

> So why do these dialecticians depart so radically from their leader? Why I ask do they enjoy being called Aristotelians and are not rather ashamed to be called so? Nothing is more unlike that great philosopher than a man who writes nothing, understands little and proclaims many things uselessly. Who would not laugh at those sophisms with which those learned men weary themselves and others, and in which they waste their entire life, and which are indeed useless to others and harmful to their own lives? Theirs are the sophisms that were frequently ridiculed by Cicero and Seneca. And we may see them in that story about Diogenes who was attacked by an abusive dialectician[15] who said: 'What I am, you are not.' When Diogenes agreed, the dialectician confirmed, 'I am a man.' When Diogenes did not deny that, the clown added, 'Therefore you are not a man.' Then Diogenes answered, 'Your conclusion is in fact false, and if you wish to make it true you must begin your syllogism with me.' There are many such kinds of ridiculous activities in which they indulge. They perhaps know what they are seeking – whether fame or amusement or a plan for a good and blessed life. I certainly do not.[16]

The letter was neither a linear text nor a form of hermetic or logical reasoning that led to a single irrefutable conclusion. It could raise questions rather than answer them and open up alternative conclusions. The letter allowed one to alternate between different styles of writing, to employ fictional elements, to use other forms than linear ones and to evoke multiple contexts in one piece of writing. Letters were also characterised by their informal tone as well as their open-endedness and suggestiveness. They were an accessible form of writing characterised by the generosity and readability of their insights. Letters were also light, mobile and easy to share. The rules of the genre of letter writing set the rules for the type of philosophical inquiry that they facilitated and vice versa:

> Therefore you will find many things in these letters written in a friendly style to a number of friends including yourself. At times they will deal with public and private affairs, at times they will touch upon our griefs which supply plenty of subject matter, or still other matters that happened to come along. In fact I did almost nothing more than to speak about my state of mind or any other matter of interest which I though my friends would like to know.[17]

The role of the reader was hence formative of this philosophical practice. The solitude that was required for writing, and hence the physical distance from one's conversation partner, ensured that morality was not thrust upon the reader as a rule or norm. Morality could only emerge from the dialogue between the reader and writer of the letter. This made the *reception* of the ideas that letters contained relatively more important than the act of writing itself. It was neither *what* the writer said nor the advice given that mattered. Instead, it was the *insights* that the letter provided to the reader, even if these insights differed from those of the writer, that allowed the letter to fulfil its purpose. The reader could become a writer herself because of these insights.

> An imitator must take care to write something similar yet not identical to the original, and that similarity must not be like the image to its original in painting where the greater the similarity the greater the praise for the artist, but rather like that of a son to his father. While often very different in their individual features, they have a certain something our painters call an 'air', especially noticeable about the face and eyes, that produces a resemblance; seeing the son's face, we are reminded of the father's, although if it came to measurement, the features would all be different, but there is something subtle that creates this effect. We must thus see to it that if there is something similar, there is also a great deal that is dissimilar, and that the similar be elusive and unable to be extricated except in silent meditation, for the resemblance is to be felt rather than expressed. Thus we may appropriate another's ideas as well as his coloring but we must abstain from his actual words; for, with the former, resemblance remains hidden, and with the latter it is glaring, the former creates poets, the second apes. It may all be summarized by saying with Seneca, and Flaccus before him, that we must write as the bees make honey, not gathering flowers but turning them into honeycombs, thereby blending them into a oneness that is unlike them all, and better.[18]

Here, once again, we see a conceptualisation of the thinking subject as a relational being rather than an individual and intentional being.

Interestingly, Petrarch described the term 'insight' as an aesthetic sensation. He claimed that insight is sweetness, 'what pleases you'. As in Foucault's analysis of the practices of the Cynics, intellect is not a disinterested form of reason but an embodied, melodic, seductive and, according to Petrarch, even lustful pleasure. The letter was supposed to engender feelings of happiness. Intellectual insights were therefore not only particular forms of truth but also sensuous events. As with the care for the self as practised by the Cynics, the motivation and pleasure of the subject was needed to validate the relevance of their insights. It is not financial gain or political influence that motivate the subject, indeed far from it. Petrarch and his colleagues gave up their well-paid jobs. It was a passion for truth that is created through dialogue that motivated their intellectual practice. The *ethos* of the subjects engaged in these knowledge practices is a specific one. The moral subject seeks knowledge to help others navigate their everyday life, and hence gains knowledge herself. Similar to the case discussed in Chapter 3 in which caregivers tried to uphold dignity, here morality had to be cultivated and nurtured rather than regulated.

The performativity of the letter is hence not enacted in the form of prescriptions ('Thou shalt'). Struever lists various forms, or 'speech acts', that can be found in letters: exhortations, inspirations, reprimands, praises, accusations, evocations, discussions about what is proper and so on. These could only be deemed successful if they brought about a change in the reader by way of providing new as well as pleasant insights. In this way, moral reflection became a practice of dialogue. The person addressed needed to recognise the moral point and its applicability to his or her own life. A philosopher or scientist could not 'add' morality from an external place or standpoint that was beyond someone else's life. Objectivity was not an intended goal. The aim was to reach agreement and share insights. The inherent drive to live a good life pushed – or pulled – these philosophers towards a particular ethical and aesthetic practice of truth that could be conducted in different and direct encounters between friends.

On a more critical note, Struever also discusses the lack of self-deprecation and irony in Renaissance practices of letter writing. The somewhat vain and sometimes self-celebratory style of Petrarch's letters has been noted before. Struever argues that it was difficult for letter writers to distance themselves from what they were writing because of their 'aestheticism' and serious engagement with their own feelings.

> Having learned the reason of my coming, the King seemed mightily pleased. He was gratified, doubtless, by my youthful faith in him, and felt, perhaps, that he shared in a way the glory of my coronation, since I had chosen him from all others as the only suitable critic. After talking over a great many things, I showed him my Africa, which so delighted him that he asked that it might be dedicated to him in consideration of a handsome reward. This was a request that I could not well refuse, nor, indeed, would I have wished to refuse it, had it been in my power. He then fixed a day upon which we could consider the object of my visit. This occupied us from noon until evening, and the time proving too short, on account of the many matters which arose for discussion, we passed the two following days in the same manner. Having thus tested my poor attainments for three days, the King at last pronounced me worthy of the laurel.[19] He offered to bestow that honour upon me at Naples, and urged me to consent to receive it there, but my veneration for Rome prevailed over the insistence of even so great a monarch as Robert. At length, seeing that I was inflexible in my purpose, he sent me on my way accompanied by royal messengers and letters to the Roman Senate, in which he gave enthusiastic expression to his flattering opinion of me. This royal estimate was, indeed, quite in accord with that of many others, and especially with my own, but today I cannot approve either his or my own verdict. In his case, affection and the natural partiality to youth were stronger than his devotion to truth.[20]

This *aesthesis* (in contrast to *ascesis*) was lived rather than argued for. Sociality was created through intimacy because familiarity is necessary to discuss matters of truth in everyday life. The personal style of writing could, however, stray into self-indulgence and prolixity.

Conversing with Struever's Petrarch

In the introduction to her book, Struever remarks that she does not want to treat the thinkers that she studies as mere antiquities. She is taken by the idea of the humanist conversation in the sense that she wants these old thinkers to speak to us and provide relevant ideas. In this sense she herself practises the Renaissance art of humanist conversation even if she does not employ its intimate and self-disclosing style. Quite the contrary, her work is analytically rigorous, heavily footnoted and laced with Latin quotations. It is certainly not as accessible as a letter. Nonetheless, in her discussion of

Petrarch – as I interpret it here in my book – she provides opportunities for developing an approach to studying practices, one that seeks to trace and situate aesthetic and moral values in everyday life and care work.

The question that Struever raises does not concern the development of a substantial philosophy of the good life. As she remarked, the Renaissance humanists certainly had their merits, but these were not their development of new or grand philosophical ideas. It was rather their reshaping and re-representation of the classical works. The humanists founded a new kind of practice that allowed particular groups of people to speak or read about and relate to the values that are pertinent to everyday life. For Petrarch, intimacy was a condition for having interesting conversations about issues that concern someone. Intimacy between friends, and people's motivation or desire to enact the good life, provide a drive for actively developing this practice. Friendship is the condition for meaningful inquiry.

The humanist practice of philosophical inquiry provided a particular answer to the question of 'how to live together'. Petrarch's semi-private conversations emphasised certain goods that differed greatly from the goods that were institutionalised in the universities of his time:

> Among the many subjects which interested me, I dwelt especially upon antiquity, for our own age has always repelled me, so that, had it not been for the love of those dear to me, I should have preferred to have been born in any other period than our own. In order to forget my own time, I have constantly striven to place myself in spirit in other ages, and consequently I delighted in history; not that the conflicting statements did not offend me, but when in doubt I accepted what appeared to me most probable, or yielded to the authority of the writer.[21]

The goods that he valued were also in sharp contrast to the ideas about free, transparent and open public debate that would emerge centuries later. Petrarch's practice, as a pastime of the literate and well-educated classes, was better suited for the subversive literary salons than the public sphere of new citizens. Struever also points to the incipient modernist characteristics of the humanists' letters, which relished intimacy, spontaneity and self-disclosure. I would argue, however, that the letters have rather more pre-modern characteristics in how they reference the ancient Greeks and their practices of the good life. The notion of ethics, for instance, is quite remote from rules-based Kantian perspectives or utilitarian ideas about the greatest gain for the largest number of people.

It would still take several centuries for this type of ethics to emerge during the Enlightenment, which is why humanist ethics are closer to the Greek practices of the good life that Foucault discussed than to modernist, abstract forms of reasoning.[22]

Good life in research

The analysis of Petrarchan practices of letter writing nicely shows how the conditions that are created by a practice also shape the issues that can be discussed. These conditions afford different ways of speaking, writing and living together. Petrarch's letter writing can be seen as an aesthetic (moral, truth-finding) practice pertaining to the good life that was new for his time, at least in relation to academic philosophy. This shows again how the aesthetic and moral values of everyday life informed certain forms of motivated social action that were directed by a desire for truth. This form of social action implied a politics of *relocation*, of grounding a new form of (intellectual) life outside academia. The aesthetic desire or lust for the truth of the good life compelled people like Petrarch to go and 'do something else, somewhere else' rather than to *argue* about the desirability of certain styles of reasoning. By creating a new practice, they avoided a direct confrontation with established institutionalised philosophical discourses, which was a confrontation they could never win. Their emphasis on *motivation* and *pleasure* is generative and constructive. They abandoned authoritative reasoning or deductive logic and chose a style of writing and talking that allowed different participants to join the discussion as well as different topics to be addressed in different ways.

The reason for living this good life, which again includes claims about morality (to address and discuss issues that concerned others), truth (insights pertaining to the daily life of the literate elite) and aesthetics (an aesthetic of 'sweetness', intimacy and dialogue), was that people found truth and hence pleasure in the good life. This motivated attempts at doing good rather than enforcing a common good through the establishment and conformation to certain norms. Instead of *knowing* what is good, readers and writers had to *examine* what is good by probing and *feeling*. Morality and truth take shape through enjoyment, and even through a lust for living the good life. Lust (or motivation) signifies an ability to value things, to act in ways that display care for certain values, and to put them into practice. The humanists were driven by lust to instigate the doing of (this particular form of) good and the cultivation of (this particular form of) knowledge.

This presents us with a quite different conceptualisation of the individual than the conceptualisations that emerged later, in which individuals are compulsively driven by self-enrichment and striving for self-governance. The humanist approach proposed a style that one could cultivate and practise rather than a guideline that dictates how one should live or a psychological framework from which one cannot escape. Renaissance humanism encouraged examinations as well as the use of open and dialogical methods, rather than prescriptions and methods that can only lead to a single authoritative conclusion. Its accessible forms invited others to join.

Valuable research practices

Petrarch's rebellious philosophical practices illustrate how the content of knowledge is dependent on the type of practices through which research is crafted. The creation of knowledge is informed by the socio-material environments (in- or outside the academy) in which knowledge is sought, but also by the concrete forms and methods with which 'publications' or exchanges are made. Socio-material practices co-shape what can be addressed but also to whom this may be addressed. The topic of a letter will be different to that of a book, even if the author intends both to be about the values of everyday life.

What can we learn from Petrarch vis-à-vis the question about research practices that might shed light on everyday care for people with chronic disease or disability? A first conclusion is to recognise that research *itself* is a practice of everyday life. Research practices are aesthetic and moral practices that aim to articulate some form of truth. Conducting research is done in a particular style. For instance, attempts may be made to banish 'observer bias' by using objectifying methods, or one may carefully spell out various possible interpretations so that a reader can evaluate which steps were taken and which rationales were followed. One can formulate elaborate systems that attempt to explain everything, as Petrarch's contemporaries did, or try to bring philosophy back to everyday-life concerns, as Petrarch and his colleagues wanted. These approaches each articulate different objects of research and they therefore generate different 'findings'. They enact different forms of 'good inquiry' that each have their own set of rules. An example of this can be found when studying what scientists *do* and how they shape 'good research' in their everyday work.[23] Although the quest for 'truth' is generally recognised as a central value in various academic genres, their everyday research practices are always characterised by different values and stylistic preferences.[24] These different practices generate different forms of truth.

Audiences, co-researchers and informants

Petrarch believed that good philosophy involved the transmission of insights from intellectuals or academics to various audiences, who in turn would be motivated to make changes in their own lives. 'Effective' practices of creating knowledge are those that generate insights for readers. This creates a very particular relationship between scientists, their 'field' and their informants. The ability or 'productivity of the reader' and conversation partner to generate and validate insights caused Petrarch's philosophical practice to have a clearly defined relationship with his audience because this audience contributed to his inquiries. The reader (and the same is true for the author) is both means and end; the good life is lived by examining it as a writer and reader, or as a researcher and informant. As an aesthetic moral practice geared towards finding truth, humanist research practices did not seek to give advice or provide recommendations, but instead sought to motivate conversation partners and even to awaken in them a 'lust' for what is good and true.

It follows that if an inquiry aims to provide pleasure and foster insight in an audience that is reflecting on what the good life might be, such an inquiry simultaneously makes the lives it wants to affect its object of study. Hence, research practices have to appeal and be accessible to research subjects, too. Research practices should not only avoid violating the values of the research subjects but may also attempt to *accommodate* their values. If we follow Petrarch, the double role of research subjects as the informant and validator of research demands that we acknowledge their values. The practice of doing research itself is also a practice of everyday life in which everyday values emerge for researchers as well as informants. The question is now how research may be designed to allow research subjects to participate in ways that are of value to them, thus allowing them to demonstrate what these values might be.

Research practices themselves, then, can be thought of as practices of the good life. In research, informants are asked to participate in interviews, fill out lengthy questionnaires, donate blood samples and so on. But when one's research object is the everyday-life values of informants, the first step in studying these values is to allow them to be reshaped and to re-emerge through the very practice of inquiry. How might we design research practices that allow researchers to learn about the everyday-life values of informants while also allowing researchers to practice these values together with their informants? What can the term 'pleasantness' – and the methods employed to study this term – tell us about what people value in the various situations occurring in their life? This would demand a practice of the good life, as well as an interpretative analysis of the values that are hence constituted, much like Struever's analysis of Petrarch's letters can be understood as signifiers of his philosophical programme. These are the pointers for Chapter 12.

Notes

1. Struever, 1992.
2. But see Nauta, 2009 on the work of Lorenzo Valla.
3. Robinson, 1898.
4. Bernardo, 2005, vol. 1, Letter I-8, p. 45.
5. Bernardo, 2005, vol. 1, Letter I-1, p. 10.
6. Bernardo, 2005, vol. 1, Letter I-1, p. 11.
7. There are letters reporting on journeys, inventiveness and talent, solitude, drunkenness, relationships with servants, style and even the faithfulness of dogs, to name a few topics.
8. Bernardo, 2005, vol. 3, Letter XXIV-4, p. 319.
9. Bernardo, 2005, vol. 1, Letter I-1, pp. 12–13.
10. See also the chapter on Foucault and the Cynics on *melos* and *melei moi*.
11. Struever does not say much about this, but we know that women were also part of the literate elite of that time. Petrarch's dedication to his beloved Laura is well documented, mostly because Petrarch wrote more than 200 sonnets for her. It is important to acknowledge that women were part of the dialogical practices of Petrarch and his colleagues. There are many pictures showing women in dialogue with Petrarch. It seems that class played a larger role than gender in elite practices of talking and reading.
12. Bernardo, 2005, vol. 1, Letter I-1, p. 6.
13. Bernardo, 2005, vol. 1, Letter I-1, p. 13.
14. Bernardo, 2005, vol. 2, Letter IX-9, pp. 27–8.
15. Dialecticians are logicians, scholars specialised in formal logic.
16. Bernardo, 2005, vol. 1, Letter I-7, pp. 38–9.
17. Bernardo, 2005, vol. 1, Letter I-1, pp. 10–11.
18. Bernardo, 2005, vol. 3, Letter XXIII-19, pp. 301–2.
19. Petrarch was awarded the laureate of poetry, and his laurels are often shown in depictions of him.
20. Robinson, 1898.
21. Robinson, 1898.
22. Pierre Hadot (2004) did not link *writing style* as much to philosophy as a way of living as I do in this book. For this reason I make a different distinction between philosophy-as-practice and modern philosophy, where the former engaged in practical philosophy in dialogue with the situation at hand (and therefore did not strive for coherence, or even putting things down in writing), and the latter wrote coherent, all-encompassing philosophical systems. See the introduction of this book on Hadot, and Chapter 4, where I located Adam Smith in the first tradition; his books do not form a coherent theory, and this was not a concern to him.
23. See Jerak-Zuiderent et al., 2021. Science and technology studies take this as their mission. But so far the focus has been on knowledge rather than on morality and aesthetics.
24. See Banks et al., 2013, and Banks & Brydon-Miller, 2018.

12
Reinventing research practices for studying the values of everyday life

Methods, technologies and concepts inform how an object of research is presented and represented. Petrarch's dialogues and letter-writing practices, and the juxtaposition of quality-of-life studies with ethnographic descriptions of the values found in everyday life, show how 'giving a voice' can better be understood as a practical (moral, aesthetic, truthful) matter of 'making a voice'.[1] In this chapter I explore *how* subjects are allowed to speak or are represented by researchers in their writings as a consequence of the methods and practices that are used to make or let subjects speak.[2]

Research practices craft particular objects and influence how subjects are shaped and positioned.[3] I am looking to find new representations of life and care for people with chronic disease or enduring handicaps. I look for re-scriptions, that is, ways of making the subjects of everyday life and care present again by describing them in a new way. But this is not a search for the individuality or selfhood of patients per se. In Chapters 7 and 9 I analysed individuality and selfhood as valued states, and I conceptualised selfhood as something that is crafted through socio-material practices rather than as referring to a fixed and given subject. Attending to this creativity raises the question of how individuality is made, either by crafting selves by linking these to social forms, or through the creative workings of research methods. The question is, then, not how an individual can be made to speak truthfully or authentically. Articulating how the events and values of everyday life emerge requires that everyday lives are generatively linked to different forms of the social.

'Better hanging out'

My question for this chapter is foremost a practical one, namely what kinds of research practices ('methods', one might say) can support the articulation of the everyday-life values of people living with chronic diseases or other persistent problems or disabilities. The chapters on care practices showed that ethnographic methods are suitable for this endeavour. I examined ethnographic methods in depth during the first Covid-19 lockdown by discussing fieldwork cases with three younger colleagues. We eventually welcomed more colleagues to join our discussions.[4] We all had similar questions and we tried to articulate them in productive ways. The lockdown – a bizarre and involuntary experiment with social life – presented a clear case of the important role of the social. We met in online sessions in which we brought our cases and insights about the use of ethnographic methods together. In textbooks such cases and methods would be discussed under the header of 'participant observation', which is an approach that allows ethnographers to spend time in the field and observe everyday practices. The challenge is to ask open questions.[5] We discussed our methodological approaches, under the working title of 'hanging out better', to analyse how we practised our methods, particularly as we had all conducted research with subjects who were not 'easy talkers' or who could not express themselves verbally in ways that were easy to understand for us researchers. Our little group formed a proper example of research-as-a-practice. We looked for forms of 'doing the everyday' with our research subjects while also reinventing and adapting our discussion practices to an online setting.

'Hanging out' is a way of spending time together that is valued by and pleasant for those participating. It seeks to facilitate learning about what is of value to research subjects. Analysing the *pleasantness* of the time spent hanging out together during research is an important way of determining what pleasantness might mean for our particular research subjects. Analysing this in a research context, then, gives rise to the question how we might live well together in light of the differences between us.

The notion of 'hanging out better' is a reference to Clifford Geertz. He propelled the use of the term 'deep hanging out' to denote the informal and enduring relationships that emerge when ethnographers 'immerse' themselves in the lives of their interlocutors *out there* and how they thus become part of their everyday practices.[6] But rather than the metaphor of *depth* – involving processes of immersion and resurfacing, after which the researcher writes up their findings – we want to specify the *quality* and temporality of relationships, which may continue even after the fieldwork has been completed, for instance because our research subjects[7] live close to us or because we have developed a friendship with them. What is it that we engage in when we attempt to build relationships that are pleasant to both researcher and research subject? What kind of *method* could this form of hanging out be? And if there is no 'immersion' from which to resurface and return to academia, how do these relationships develop or end after fieldwork has been completed?

Our working title suggests that hanging out can be done in better or worse ways, as I will discuss in this chapter. The notion of hanging out also allows us to see things that 'surface', or dare I say, even acknowledge the many superficialities that are an actual part of everyday life rather than the depth that is presumably gained by 'deep reflection'. Ethnographic hanging out explicitly includes 'what can be sensed'. Our working title is, again, a case of 'pointing in action'; it does not involve a clear-cut and final definition but it directs the process of trying to articulate and substantiate the open concept of hanging out. We aim to put research into new words by relating it to the specific circumstances of subjects who cannot easily speak in research practices.[8] In contrast to the academic convention of presenting a newly coined term at the beginning of a text, or of using a term as if it had always existed, I initially wanted to reveal my new concept at the end of this chapter. In this way, the reader would be able to follow us on our quest and trace the process through which we developed the concept. But the tradition of giving away the point at the very start also has benefits because it can guide the reader's focus. That is to say, it is a way of pointing.[9] I will therefore simply tell you right now that the new term is *generative hanging out*, which signifies that research situations are productive of the kinds of knowledge that they are able to provide. The term allows us to ask researchers precisely what their work practices generate and why their approach or methods are appropriate for addressing certain kinds of problems.[10]

The relationship between researcher and research subjects

Immersing oneself in the field is a particular way of creating relationships with one's research subjects. How to do this well is, of course, an anthropological question that is much discussed.[11] Anthropologists have long pondered the relationships they have with their interlocutors. Ever since *Writing Culture* shook up the discipline of anthropology and reminded practitioners of their role in colonialism, anthropologists have wondered whether their relationship with research subjects is good or exploitative.[12] Anthropologists write about their subjects, and this is always both a risk and a responsibility. How does one represent those who are not (or who are also[13]) writing about themselves? How does one represent people who are disenfranchised, and how does one write about problems that are difficult to put into words? The act of immersion suggests a dip as well as a withdrawal. How might we think about the relationship with research subjects as continuing through our writings? Rather than *a priori* moralising the anthropological relationship with interlocutors, I want to practically explore the specific forms of this relationship, much like Marcus himself as well as others did in the slipstream of the self-reflection that followed the publication of *Writing Culture*.[14]

Specifically, I will juxtapose 'hanging out better' with other methods employed in social scientific research, most notably the semi-structured interview.[15] This is a technique I am very fond of (when suitable, of course), and that I teach students who are new to doing fieldwork. I therefore try to learn from my own teaching practices by keeping these new questions in mind. Compared to open interviews, I will argue, 'hanging out better' provides an even more promising approach to learning about the values and truths that are important in the everyday lives of people for whom speaking up is difficult.

Studying 'hanging out better'

Starting from the beginning of the global Covid-19 lockdown, we discussed 'better hanging out' over the internet with three researchers living in Amsterdam and one in Perth, Australia. We all shared an interest in fieldwork methods, and we had all developed creative ways of hanging out with (some of) our interlocutors. We had learned that semi-structured interviews, even when conducted as openly and empathetically as possible, can nonetheless make it difficult to catch a glimpse of what really matters to our research subjects. Maja wanted to think about how her Aboriginal Australian interlocutors with type I diabetes were not really subjects who performed 'as expected' in interviews and in clinical settings. They could verbally represent themselves with clarity, but not in ways that allowed them to be *heard* by healthcare practitioners. Clément wanted to learn how Ghanaian people in the Netherlands manage to live with a disease that is surrounded by taboo, namely sickle cell disease. In Ghanaian everyday life, openly addressing sickle cell disease is not *done*. The task Leonie had set herself was to design practices and methods for involving people with learning disabilities in her research on labelling, diagnosis and access to health care. Maja wanted to explore a particular form of interaction among her interlocutors called 'yarning' or 'having a yarn'. This is a form of conversing and being together that follows a particular linguistic structure but that seems – to an uninitiated listener – to meander in all directions with participants speaking their mind in whichever way they want. Clément learned from his Ghanaian interlocutor, Gladys, how she cared for her children with sickle cell disease by observing how she prepared their meals and by chatting with her about this form of caring for her children while she was working in the kitchen. Leonie experimented in a spectacular way by making a science fiction film about aliens and UFOs together with her research subject, as an alternative to making him a 'co-researcher'. In what follows, I will draw on these examples and on other examples from my own research as well as reflect on the things that I teach students about qualitative interview methods.

The structuring workings of open interviews

The semi-structured interview is a method that is often used by social scientists who are interested in learning how their research subjects see and engage with the world. This approach did not work well in the situations that we discussed in our little group. One-on-one conversations, even when conducted with a very flexible, kind and 'soft' approach, frequently failed to deliver what was hoped for. Maja's interlocutors persistently wanted 'to talk about something else' when she asked them about their diabetes practices. Clément's formal interview with Gladys failed during its first attempt. And Leonie learned that her interlocutors were unwilling to discuss the label of 'mild intellectual impairment', with her or anyone else, because they felt that this label was stigmatising and that it did not address their actual problems.[16]

These accounts resonated with my observations while conducting interviews in long-term psychiatric wards.[17] The interviews I attempted to conduct with people in these wards did not deliver what I had hoped for. I was looking for insights into their experience with their new living environments and the care that they were receiving. After getting over my embarrassment about failing to succeed, I was able to analyse the interviews for what they *did* tell me. Here is what I wrote about this in 2005:

I kept returning to the interviews and discovering that they do contain messages. The clearest one concerns the unease of my respondents during the interview. Some clearly feared one-to-one interaction, and started the interview by asking if they would have to move again or by making a specific request not to tell anybody about what was said during the interview. Others used the interviews to talk without interruption about their psychiatric history; some were glad to have company but disliked the tape recorder; others spoke five lines in half an hour; still others tried to escape the interview after just 15 minutes. One man tried to make a deal with me, namely that I would put his freshly washed shirts in the closet, and then he would answer one of my questions. But it soon became clear that he did not plan to keep his end of the bargain. What this exercise taught me, eventually, was that the problem was neither the respondents nor the interviewer, but rather the interviewing situation that failed to produce a 'perspective'. I was asking my respondents to participate in a situation that they considered unpleasant. It appeared dangerous to them to have an opinion or to speak during the rather formal one-to-one interview... The situation of the interview has specific characteristics and demands; these were made apparent when the patients 'breached' them.[18]

This problem was very similar to the other cases discussed in our little group. Maja's research subjects had suffered for generations through oppression and colonisation, and their yarning practices provided a way to 'educate' newcomers about who they were and what had happened to them. It was not that they were unable to talk about themselves, but the type of problems they grappled with were difficult to articulate. Clément learned that verbal one-on-one exchanges are an important part of professional care settings in which doctors and nurses discuss 'the bad things' of disease and maintain authority over them. Members of the Ghanaian community, on the contrary, were careful *not to speak about the disease* directly. Leonie's interlocutors preferred informal conversations over interviews because they feared they would be unable to answer the questions being asked. Discussing these issues allowed us to reflect on the limitations that even very open and friendly interview situations can create, such as the establishment of hierarchies, associations with hierarchies in other one-on-one conversations in which our research subjects were vulnerable, worries about the competence to articulate concerns, and raising particular taboos that are difficult to talk about.

These analyses taught us a thing or two about conducting interviews. We noted that semi-structured interviews – as open as they may be – are, first, still *goal-oriented* in the sense that a goal is set by the researcher or that a list of topics for discussion is prepared by the researcher.[19] Second, interviews are *hierarchical* – that is to say, they are informed by the idea that the researcher determines what the conversation is about. The interview is, third, *reflexive* because an interview is a conversation about *something*, which suggests a subject–object relationship not just between researcher and researched but also between the researcher–interlocutor dyad and the topic of discussion. Because of this reflexive character, the conversation is always more or less abstract, namely about 'a topic' rather than about events in the here and now. Last, interviews are normative in the sense that the conversation is directed by the interviewer, and this can potentially be experienced as evaluative, critical or disempowering depending on the speech-situations that inform the experiences of the research subjects.

I will discuss these various concerns, and then show how research can be conducted quite differently if one practises 'better hanging out'. Each method has its own virtues and problems.

The goal-directedness of the semi-structured interview

Semi-structured interviews are goal-oriented, or so I teach students in my class on research interviews. They focus on certain topics and exclude others, which was a goal that was difficult to uphold in the yarning practices that Maja observed. This goal-orientedness also has to do with the researcher being 'well prepared', namely with a topic list or set of questions that can be discussed in any order or tentatively used to set the agenda of the conversation. You want to have *all* your topics addressed by every interlocutor if that is at all possible. The topic or question list makes clear to a researcher when the conversation is drifting away from its goal. In my class on interviewing, I teach students to gently but firmly direct the conversation back to the topic at hand if that happens. Research subjects do not mind this, I reassure the students, because they expect the interviewer to guide them through what they need to say. But despite such guidance, interviewers should nevertheless remain friendly and allow time for their interlocutors' hobby-horses. But there is always the transcript to worry about!

The direction that the conversation takes, and I underscore this point in my teaching, is the responsibility of the researcher. This is also what interviewees, particularly professionals, expect. It is also the reason why you must be well prepared, if only to make sure that you provide interviewees with the opportunity to give interesting answers ('Ask open questions, my dear Watson!' Prepare these well!).[20] Respondents *constantly* check if their answers are what the researcher is looking for, because they themselves are not *entirely* sure what the researcher is after. It is the researcher's task to reassure and encourage interviewees, and also to protect them from losing face. Even if your respondents make it difficult for the interview to unfold according to plan (as happened to all of us with our particular interviewees), the researcher is still responsible for looking after their interviewees.

It is very clear that the surplus value of a conversation (the value that remains after the interview situation and that extends beyond the conversation itself) is the *transcript* that will be used for analyses and publications, and that this value accrues to the researcher, not the interlocutor. It is for this reason that researchers have discussed whether interviewees should be *paid* for giving interviews and sharing their experiences.

This belief that research subjects are doing a favour to researchers is even clearer in biomedical research where research subjects *donate*, say, their blood in addition to their story. There is 'nothing in it' for them in any direct way except for the feeling of having done something altruistic, of having made a small sacrifice for the benefit of future generations. In contrast to, for instance, the people who received Petrarch's letters, researchers have little to offer to interlocutors other than their attention, although it must also be said that ethnographers can offer a good conversation.[21]

The descriptions (I should say, of course, re-scriptions) that I have selected from my class on interviewing can be compared to the concept of 'hanging out better'. Such a comparison draws out how even the most open of semi-structured interviews are clear and overt examples of directivity. In my interview class, I also teach students that interviews are, in addition to being goal-oriented, also always relationship-oriented. An interview is a sensitive situation. Interviewees are keenly aware that their answers are being appreciated or not, and will instantly pick up if an interviewer gives dismissive feedback. Even in a role-playing situation you can dramatically see this dynamic unfolding; the conversation is *over* when dismissive feedback is given.[22] Trust has been breached. Good 'rapport', as anthropologists call it, is a necessary condition for conducting good interviews. A relationship of trust needs to be established in quite a short period of time. Allowing an interview to develop into an open and explorative conversation is one of the main challenges, but also one of the greatest rewards if it succeeds.[23]

Averting the eyes

My analysis of the semi-structured interview underscores the critical role that language plays in interviews. Interviewer and interviewee should be willing and able to talk at the same 'level', that is, to tune into each other's ways of understanding the world and to contribute to its mutual understanding. But this is not always possible. The examples provided in our little discussion group illustrate this. The situation in 'hanging out better' is very different. Rather than being goal-oriented, hanging out is foremost relationship-oriented. It is about engaging in an activity together (or not much of an activity, if it only involves chatting) in a relaxed and pleasant way. Hanging out means 'doing something (or not so much) together'. When going for a walk, for instance, walking rather than researching is the main activity. The topic of conversation can evolve freely. In one moment it can be about the activity itself, the next it can be about something that is happening around you ('Hey was that a squirrel/ Brazilian porcupine/ice cream van over there?!'). Or one can talk about an anecdote from a past event, tell a joke, make a random association or even sing a song. Such chats can be used to offer good advice and consolation or to celebrate. And occasionally, chats can be about the research topic that the researcher is interested in. But if and how this is the case can often only gradually be learned or indeed found out later during the analysis.

An example from my very first fieldwork experience can clarify this. I prepared for conducting fieldwork during my master's degree in philosophy and psychology by reading up, under the guidance of a literature professor, on the semiotic approach of C. S. Peirce. I was about to start studying the use of signs by people suffering from dementia in a nursing home. At that time (at the end of the 1990s), dementia was not a topic that had received much attention. The nursing home I went to was unpretentious and located in a sleepy town. With my backpack full of texts about firsts, seconds and thirds, symbols, rhemes and dicents, qualisigns, arguments and semiotic triangles, I went to the nursing home to meet its residents and learn about their world.

One of the first things I had to do was to get rid of all my theory. It was useless for thinking about my life in the nursing home. I did not encounter many 'signs' at first, but I did learn to engage in small talk, which allowed me to spend time together with the residents. Such talk was not about exchanging information but about being together with them. The type of conversation that they were good at involved using general words to describe general situations, which were often pleasantries that could be shared with non-specific others.[24] I, the academic nerd, had to learn how to hold conversations about the weather, about nice new dresses or hairdos, about domestic things, and how good it is to see you today. I learned to hold conversations in which the content did not matter very much, but these conversations were a way of *relating* to others – that is, they allowed me to 'hang out' with the residents.[25] I learned that intonation is far more important than substance when engaging in such general conversations.[26] It was only when I was safely back at my desk, physically removed from life in the nursing home, that I could again pose my questions to C. S. Peirce. An analysis followed that I could never have imagined as being possible. My life as a dedicated ethnographer had started. But this is another story.

The topics can drift and shift when hanging out. Even performative modes of talking by subjects with dementia can change over time. This makes 'hanging out' less goal-directed than the interview. Hanging out focuses less on the research topic and instead engages with the present situation. This demands a completely different mindset from the researcher. You must move from your own analytical questions towards the question of how to participate in the world of your research subjects. Your questions then become: What is going on here? What is this practice about? What holds it together? What is important here? How can participation allow me to learn about this?[27] This is the ethnographer's job in doing fieldwork, and clear answers to these questions are continuously postponed as situations are questioned again and again. Yet this is difficult for novice researchers (What am I doing here? What is all this about?! I have no function within this practice. How can I handle being an outsider in the field? I don't have a clue what is going on!). One should maybe not talk about this in too much detail with research funding agencies. But, as I always say to novice field researchers, the golden rule of this type of research is to accept that you do not know what is going on. This is what you are there for – to learn. Learn to live with not-knowing, allow it to be just that. Eventually you will find things out, and these things are the hidden treasures, ones you may not have known where to look for but that you will find nonetheless.[28] This happens by probing, asking questions, observing and collecting different views. It is acceptable to not-know because you can anticipate that, at some point, a story will develop, something will dawn on you, and you will be able to develop an analysis (maybe with a little help from, say, C. S. Peirce). The result will roughly show what matters to research participants, and this will more or less relate, for better or for worse, to your initial research questions.

So, this is a way of learning about something by looking at something else, or one might also say, a way of learning by averting one's eyes. The different research practices that were discussed in our little group show how a turn towards 'hanging out better' can allow one to learn about the good life with chronic disease. Clément's interlocutor Gladys used the metaphor of 'looking, not talking', which her family uses when caring for sickle cell disease. The phrase denotes the implicit and non-verbal ways that one can employ to relate with someone who has this disease by way of 'hanging in' with someone. Talking, in this instance, meant something like 'speaking about bad fortune', whereas 'to look' meant not closing one's eyes to another person's difficulties and looking after them.[29] To 'stay with the trouble', Donna Haraway might say.[30] Not talking about disease – and instead participating in cooking and caring activities – provided a way for Clément to learn about life with and care for sickle cell disease in a way that respected the values and taboos of the interlocutor.

'Yarning' or 'having a yarn' is a way of talking that avoids addressing topics in a direct way or only focusing on one subject at a time. Rather, yarning is a type of conversation with shifting topics to which everybody who is present can contribute.[31] Maja learned that yarning presented a challenge to her interview approach because she wanted to address the topic of diabetes much too directly. In yarning it is important to respect one's conversation partners by letting them add whatever they want to the conversation, even if this might seem off-topic. By understanding yarning in this way, Maja could provide clues to clinicians for engaging with their Aboriginal Australian patients in a more respectful way.

Leonie's experiences with making a science fiction movie allowed her to learn how her interlocutor was living in the world. This life was mediated by both the *story* (or images) of the movie and the *practice of making it together*.[32] For instance, the videography as well as the story performed his life as an outsider. He was often sent away or rejected by others, and he often filmed feet and ceilings rather than faces. He quarrelled with Leonie about how his problems might be solved if Leonie just gave him some clear assignments. But Leonie did not want to be authoritarian and wanted to give him space. Because of these paradoxical dynamics it took them a while to adjust to working together. Ultimately, one could say, the aim of 'hanging out better' is to (temporarily) find ways of living well together by accommodating each other's preferred ways of doing things.

During the study that I conducted in psychiatric hospitals, I learned much about what people appreciated, not by having them tell me but by observing how they took pleasure in certain things. Participants thus *enacted* the particular things they liked rather than told me. The role of the material environment was important in these enactments.[33]

> Morning coffee is a moment of conviviality on this ward in the residential home, and indeed, there is a lot of talking going on. Mrs Jansen asks for an ashtray; Mrs Jones hands one over to her. There is a lively discussion about yesterday's football match. Dora does not join the conversation. She sits just around the corner, knitting with admirable speed. She is having her cup of coffee there. I can see from where I am sitting that she is listening to the conversation and occasionally smiling at what is being said while never stopping with her knitting. When coffee time is over, she collects the coffee cups and washes them. She then returns to her spot and continues her knitting.

Although somewhat removed from the social situation, Dora was nonetheless able to join and enjoy it. For her, a good social life is to be at a short distance from the centre of activity.

The approach of 'averting the eyes' from one's research goal has its own specific problems to which there are no general solutions. The surplus meaning of what researcher and interlocutor do together may not be all that clear to the interlocutor, or at least not right away. Fieldnotes are often written up when the research subjects are out of the sight. And researchers' concerns with publications may not be very clear to them. Rather than emphasising 'informed consent' – as happens in biomedical research, which formalises an interlocutor's willingness to 'donate' their surplus value – 'hanging out' creates an ethically ambiguous space. Sarah Banks calls this the 'everyday ethics' of research through which everyday negotiations between researchers and research subjects take place. Everyday ethics in research remain an ongoing concern that is reconsidered again and again as relationships unfold. Everyday research ethics do not stop 'when consent is given' but remain part of the relationship. Yet it is hard to predict how exactly this process will unfold or what the stakes might be. This is not an issue that informed consent forms can solve. Nothing discrete is 'given' to researchers, and anthropologists often argue that their research materials are not owned by them but are co-produced with their interlocutors.[34]

An overly moralistic stance can, however, be problematic as well. I received criticism for the paper I quoted earlier. An anthropologist colleague pointed out that I did not obtain consent from the subjects in long-term psychiatry that I had written about, and that I had not received their permission for using my descriptions of them or for demonstrating some of their non-verbal exchanges, which I had done in a presentation. I was unable to obtain their consent because I could not discuss consent with my research subjects.[35] I was simply demonstrating how I was able to make implicit yet indirect contact with one of my research subjects. I had consent from the institution as well as the family members who represented these patients to conduct participant observation and hang out on the ward. I do not remember whether my critic used the words 'colonising the Other', but this is the kind of concern that is at stake here. Writing about powerless subjects was exactly one of the concerns in the *writing culture* debate mentioned earlier. My reply was that if I did not write about them, then nobody would have *any* idea about their situation or way of being in the world apart from the people who took care of them. Nobody was looking over the caregivers' shoulders to see how they were 'hanging in'. I was making a voice for these patients by finding out what it might mean to live with them in a good way. This may be a noble aim, but it is also clear that there is no firm ethical ground to stand on here. It can only be done by trying out how to establish relationships and by critically discussing descriptions.

The conclusion here is that 'hanging out better' provides a research tool that allows interactions to be as open and responsive as possible to the ways in which subjects structure the research process through what they do, what they dislike and how they direct (or 'nudge') researchers. The price to pay for this is that researchers must bracket their research questions and engage in a relationship in which it is not crystal clear from the start if and how it will contribute to their research. Uncertainty about how the process of hanging out will unfold is something that researchers must accept in exchange for allowing the capabilities (and responsibilities) of interlocutors to shape the situation in ways that they find acceptable and maybe even pleasant. The main lesson that can be drawn from Petrarch's philosophical practice is that the research situation is a particular episode in the everyday life of research subjects – and this is preferably a *good* everyday life – in which researchers can learn about their worries, likes and dislikes as well as obstacles and matters of fact. It is a radical way of 'giving space' to research subjects while simultaneously allowing them to structure this space as much as is possible and acceptable[36] to both researcher and interlocutor. This requires averting the eyes from one's research questions while focusing on the present situation as well as shaping the situation in a way that is acceptable and pleasant to both parties.

Hierarchy

I return to interviewing again to discuss the issue of hierarchy. The interview situation is not only structured by the relationship between its aims and content, but also by the relationship between interviewer and interviewee. It is generally the interviewer who determines the topics that will be talked about. The interviewer asks questions and the interviewee gives answers. The surplus value of the conversation, namely the transcript and the quotations therein, accrue to the researcher. There is usually a 'common good' to which research is supposed to contribute: that is, it is supposed to be relevant to research on other people in comparable situations. The interviewees might have enjoyed the interview and learned something from the conversation. But the main surplus value is for the researcher who may publish the results and further their career.

In codes of conduct for research, and to a certain extent also in my interview classes, the researcher and the interviewee are seen as independent subjects within the context of the interview. The interviewee is helping the researcher. The researcher, in turn, protects interviewees, namely by informing them, creating a good atmosphere, being sensitive to interviewees' needs and being interested in what they have to say. The researcher also displays care by anonymising accounts and securely storing data. Interviewees are in no way limited in their autonomy: they are not obliged to tell a story or how they want recount it. Informed consent, which is premised on the notion that an interviewee is knowledgeable about what they are agreeing to do, is the procedural token of autonomy and is often formalised with a signed piece of paper.

It is perhaps around the assumption of rationalistic decision-making that opinions start to differ. But before I address this issue by exploring 'hanging out better', I want to point out that the independence of interviewer and interviewee also suggests that there is a power relationship between them. This power can be negotiated or regulated through the clear definition of roles, which is often done with an eye to protecting the autonomy of participants. The interviewee can, at any point in time, withdraw from the interview and the research project. This option is tacitly assumed for in-depth conversations because it is impossible to have a proper conversation with someone who does not want to participate.[37]

All these rules and relationships become muddled when 'hanging out' together. When researchers and interlocutors[38] hang out, roles are not so clearly defined and power imbalances are not always obvious. For instance, Maja's interlocutors engaged her in particular ways. They wanted her to be present in their network but only on certain terms. She initially volunteered to fulfil the task of bringing food, but she was sternly instructed on how to perform this task (and to listen to complaints about her food-serving capacities). Her interlocutors paid specific attention to the serving of cheese. Maja's group of interlocutors policed her relationship with people outside this group. Her interlocutors 'educated' her about who they are and how she should behave towards them. It was clear that Maja's interlocutors set the terms for her presence. Clément's interlocutor Gladys made it very clear that *she* was the expert who did the cooking, not Clément. He was not allowed to cook things in her kitchen. These research subjects defined clear roles for 'their' researchers who wanted to hang out with them, which the researcher had to take or leave or manoeuvre within.

The situation was different for Leonie and her interlocutor-partner in film-making. Because they were engaged in a process that neither of them was familiar with (making a film), they had to learn together and find out who could do what, and who to ask for help. In this way, more symmetry was introduced into their relationship. In my negotiations with an interlocutor in the long-stay ward involving how to put clean shirts in a cupboard, he refused to accept the trade-off for hanging out, thus effectively blocking the interaction by setting his own terms. In all these examples, hanging out allowed both research subjects and researchers to set the terms for acceptable forms of hanging out together. In no way could the researcher simply take the lead. Things were always negotiated. This means that hierarchies could be established along the way. To make it possible to 'live together', each person had to create a liveable space for themselves and others.

This did not mean that researchers had to be passive and totally subject themselves to the demands of their interlocutors. They had to be creative and find ways respond and negotiate. Maja managed to complete some interviews with some interlocutors, even if they were not quite what she had hoped for in terms of content. The yarning continued, so to speak. Clément was never actually allowed to assist with the cooking, but he was permitted to bring a quiche for Gladys and her family as a token of his friendship and as a demonstration of his expertise in cooking. Leonie and her partner divided the tasks. Her primary skill was that she could read, and she eventually also learned to do the editing. Gijs[39] made the story and was the main actor in the movie. In a similar way, I told my story about putting away shirts in a research paper to learn from this process. The researcher is present and active in the interaction, too.

While hanging out, both partners are responsible for what happens, and neither is completely in control. Terms are negotiated between partners. Rather than doing so independently, partners negotiate the extent in which they are willing to *depend* on each other, which means that they are forced to consider each other's wishes, activities and particularities. This also means that both, metaphorically speaking, expose themselves to risk. Refraining from assuming control and defining clear roles might mean that things go wrong. A fight may take place. A social role or a conversation could be deemed unsatisfactory after all. For instance, Leonie was very upset when she was confronted with a dead cat on Gijs's balcony, and she fussed over ways to get his washing machine repaired. All participants in the discussion group struggled to relate these evolving relationships to their original research plans. And we can only guess what our research subjects thought about us, their researchers.[40]

Interdependence

The interdependency of research partners also means that, inherently, 'there is something in it' for the research subject while hanging out. And this is, of course, also true for the interviewer whose research is being supported by the interlocutor, who, in return, receives attention and the pleasure of a good conversation. In research situations, a minimum of two people have to practically achieve something. And, at least temporarily, they have to live together and develop trust by negotiating the terms that allow research to become an acceptable or even pleasant endeavour for both.[41] An interlocutor on the long-stay ward once though it a good idea to try and have sex with me. Rather than discussing this with me, he went about it very directly. I found this very annoying.[42] He was one of the few interlocutors who had been up for a conversation rather than immediately turning their back on me. But holding a conversation was clearly not what he had been hoping for. This became a situation in which no interaction, let alone 'hanging out better', could be achieved. We got stuck during the phase in which we were supposed to negotiate the terms of our interaction.

The interdependency between researcher and researched means that 'pleasantness', or what in previous chapters I called 'motivation' and 'appreciation' – think also of Petrarch's 'lust' for insights – always plays a role in hanging out better. Pleasure is 'something that's in it' for the interlocutor. It can be found in the opportunity to tell one's story, to reflect on one's life, to enact its pleasantries, to borrow a researcher's skills or to have their undivided attention. In our discussion group it became clear that pleasure could also be found in fulfilling the dream of making a science fiction film. If an interlocutor does not accept the terms or appreciate the arrangement, they will, consciously or unconsciously, 'vote with their feet'. They can allow the researcher to be present or close the door on them. There is pleasure to be found for both in the research encounter, even if the interlocutor also must accept a certain amount of the vulnerability in case the attempt at establishing a relationship fails.

And there are pitfalls here as well. A situation can become asymmetrical if the researcher has to play too many roles or if research subjects become overly dependent on them. One of Leonie's interlocutors, for example, started to depend too much on her as a friend, trustee, advocate, advisor and helper. This posed a problem for Leonie. Her role while hanging out was that of a researcher who is free to negotiate the part that she plays in defining the situation and who is free to leave the situation when she wants. The temporality of the relationship was a concern here. The researcher can often easily step away from the situation,[43] but interlocutors cannot, or at least not as easily, because it is their life after all. Another issue is the lack of clarity about the surplus value that accumulates from hanging out, which is particularly the case for the interlocutor. Again, there is an issue with everyday ethics that cannot simply be resolved. Everyday ethics cannot be clearly defined on a consent form and signed away, because they emerge from the process of hanging out and from the contingent negotiations of terms that determine this relationship.

Reflexivity: subject–object relations

In the discussion above, we can see that understandings of interviews or research situations are unstable. One might imagine a continuum in which the semi-structured interview between independent persons is found on one end, and hanging out as a situation that is created by participants as it evolves on the other end. These opposing poles may not exist in reality, because qualitative research situations often involve elements of both types of interviews, and they both rely in similar ways on the use of language or certain activities. Of course, 'talking' is itself an activity that should be considered. We saw, in practice, that asking people to participate and hold conversations is informed by other situations in which one is spoken to.[44] I mentioned examples of Australian colonisers who ordered people out of their homes, or of supposedly intelligent citizens who disenfranchise people with intellectual disabilities. Small talk in the nursing home was informed by the small talk that my interlocutors had been engaging in all their lives. Similarly, my poor ability of engaging in small talk demonstrated that my conversations were also informed by ones I had engaged in before. Questionnaires with closed questions leave less space for historical conversations that enter into one's research than semi-structured interviews, but these conversations *are* part of the ways in which questions are interpreted and answered.[45]

This mixture of structure and unstructuredness (or becoming) compels us to move away from conceptualising researchers and research subjects as independent individuals towards acknowledging them as mutually dependent beings. As interdependent beings, they are given (or take) the time to hang out together in ways they can appreciate, and both researchers and research subjects share the responsibility for the outcome of this process. An interview can also take on the explorative character that 'hanging out' has, but only if the interviewer and interviewees can flourish under the conditions that make up a 'formal' interview and only if the topic is of mutual interest. Interviews are generally asymmetrical because the researcher initiates these conversations, but the interviewee can still be given the space to influence the interview situation on their own terms.

To push the idea of the independent subject a bit further, I would like to underscore that the interview – in comparison to hanging out together – is reflexive, analytical and abstract. The act of interviewing suggests a subject–object relationship, but this relationship is not that between researcher and interlocutor. The interviewee is not the object of the research but their experiences are.[46] Or the object is their expertise in or feelings about something, or whatever the reason was for the interviewer to talk with the interviewee. The subject–object relationship is found between, on the one hand, two subjects – namely interviewer and interviewee – and on the other hand, the topic that they discuss, address or try to evoke.

To put it more technically, the object of study is something that is verbally expressed by the interviewee with support from the probing questions posed by the researcher. The spoken words are recorded or jotted down, transcribed, and subsequently used as quotes in publications. The words produced by interviewer and interviewee are the object of further analysis and articulated as the object of research. In this way, a series of translations is made to create a representation (the text of the transcript) of something (that which the text refers to, the actual conversation). These are not the same things, as conversations are open-ended and transcripts are finished. People can reflect on what is being represented in words.[47]

While hanging out together (but also during the interview), one could say that the two subjects – researcher and interlocutor – are *creating* or constructing an object *together*.[48] This happens in a more overt way than is usually assumed in the case of the interview-that-is-taken-to-be-a-representation-of-something.[49] Researcher and interlocutor negotiate how they may do things together and what these things might look like. It is a concrete, immanent and emerging object that is in the process of being created. This object is underdetermined at every stage of this process and becomes clearer the longer the relationship lasts. But it may also fail to take shape. There is always 'noise', and there will be misunderstandings, sudden dislikes, betrayals or changes of mind. Rather than representing 'something that is already there', hanging out involves the *creation* of something that is *becoming*. This may sound theoretical but it is actually quite practical. It is a process akin to how the women without hair were permanently constructing their selves by using make-up, putting on wigs or scarves and anticipating the gaze of others. The self could never be *fixed* and *given* but was constantly worked on, crafted and sometimes reinvented.[50]

The switch to practices is something that I return to again and again in this book to shift attention from theory to practice, from entities to doings, from representations to creations, or from the conceptualisation of the good life as something with particular characteristics to a conceptualisation of life that is every day in the making. These makings involve negotiations between goods and bads while exploring new situations and inventing new relationships. This can be a completely non-verbal activity. The 'things', technologies, concepts and situations that influence these processes of 'making a living' also play a role in creating its goodness, even if they cannot utter a single word. This makes the method of hanging out particularly suitable for research involving non-fluent speakers as well as animals or plants.[51] But hanging out can also provide a fresh perspective on the situations of those who are verbally fluent. There are always things that people do not notice in their practices (such as particular effects of what they do) as well as things they no longer notice or find too unimportant or self-evident to address. In this way, the interview is a co-creation too, even if its construction is dominated by the framework of the researcher.[52]

Of course, the object that is 'becoming' solidifies only when it is put into writing, and hence into representations. 'Wovon man nicht sprechen kann, darüber muss man', unfortunately, 'schweigen'. That is to say, research cannot but stick to representations.[53] That is one reason why one has to be so careful when constructing representations in research: anything put into words leaves many things unsaid. But the inverse is also true. 'Worüber man spricht' changes something into a thing that can be talked about, and hence gives it a particular shape – that is, a representation of something or a re-scription. Turning to practices, for instance, can be done tacitly, as Petrarch did. He did not oppose his colleagues directly but simply switched 'to do something different'. I think the turn to practice is too important to not elaborate on further. Acknowledging the importance of practices means acknowledging that there is a world in which things and words and people are dependent on one another for their articulation. This acknowledgement also allows us to study how all these entities support or resist these articulations.[54] It is not possible to do research without representation, even though it is possible to temporarily escape its problems by hanging out with others and by engaging them in evolving relationships.

What follows

How to practically shape research practices for studying the everyday values and truths of living with and caring for chronic disease? I have shown how different research practices created different relationships or led to arrangements that allowed for the articulation of selves, values and relevant issues in order to live with disease in different ways. The differences between quantitative and ethnographic approaches to studying how ALS patients consider and live with a feeding tube are a clear example of how various research practices can address the values and concerns of everyday life as well as how they may fail to do so. Petrarch's practice of writing letters led to different results than the books written by his academic contemporaries because dialogues and letters are better at addressing the concerns of everyday life.

A research practice that is geared towards learning about the values of everyday life can attempt to do just that: make visible the role of various arrangements, things and values found in everyday life, and how these shape life with disease and its effects. The kinds of truth that people must live with can be analysed on this practical level: do you have a stigmatised disease? Are you a member of the 'stolen generation' that has lived a history of powerlessness and exploitation? Or are you unable to read? What does it mean to live with such trauma or inability, and what options or suggestions are there to be considered and weighed in order to make life better?

My research on long-term psychiatric wards shows that much can be learned by looking at how people enact rather than talk about their appreciations. In this way, likes and dislikes can become apparent, but also the role of buildings and other material objects. We have learned that living with diabetes is something that may be difficult to individualise and talk about, but we also learned that shared practices of talking (yarning) as well as eating and exercising together are good ways to enact diabetes care. Maja's account shows that the model of improving self-care by providing 'health information' is much less effective than creating shared practices of caring. Clément's study illustrated some of the difficulties in talking about sickle cell disease, and how these could be circumvented by learning about childcare practices. Leonie's film is still in the making, but the endeavour provided insight into how her interlocutor lived in the world and with other people around him through the collaborative process of making the film as well as through its storyline, in which aliens are his friends and humans are much less understanding. We learned about the aesthetic and moral values that are important to the lives of our interlocutors.

Research on the good life for people with chronic disease, then, does not result in a normative prescription for how to live. Instead it provides us with an approach to examining, trying out and learning what 'works' and what gives pleasure, and providing insight or other valued experiences. This is also true for the practice of doing research itself, which unfolds as an everyday practice involving activities, articulations, appreciations and negotiations. Hanging out creates connections between the everyday lives of researchers and interlocutors by folding them together. Research practices often completely determine how research is conducted, such as, for instance, in a laboratory situation where variables are strictly defined and controlled. There, the everyday life of research subjects is determined by researchers.

In this book, research practices were moved in a different direction, away from restrictions set by researchers and towards the everyday practices of interlocutors in homes, clinics and work spaces. Here, completely new and alternative practices of sharing everyday life were invented – for instance, by making a science fiction movie or by serving cheese. Finding the overlaps between the most important truths and values of both research subjects and researchers allows for a new articulation and representation of these truths and values. This may not lead to knowledge about the *perspectives*[55] of research subjects, but it does reveal their positions, preferences and desirable ways of being related to, as well as the effects and workings of certain values, techniques or forms of care. It may also show how people learned about simple remedies such as the bathrobe trick.

The lack of goal-directedness, the creation of more symmetrical relationships and the temporary 'escape' from reflexivity that is inherent to hanging out and collectively attempting to temporarily live a good life, together provide the necessary conditions for research subjects to create acceptable or pleasurable ways of hanging out. There is 'something in it' for the interlocutor, and this applies particularly to the act of hanging out itself. It is the responsibility of the researcher to learn what that 'something' is and to co-shape their research practices accordingly. What are the terms upon which researcher and research subjects can live together? Does living together require wheelchairs, speech computers, food or interesting activities?[56] Kindness or clear tasks? How can we do justice to all this in our writing? And what are the right research questions to ask?

Living a good life can be done in many ways. What is good (true, beautiful) is part of living a good life because it is intrinsic to a practical way of living. What counts as a good life depends on where one was born, what one has lived through and what is of value in the era one lives, as well as one's cultural traditions. In the case of hair loss it became clear that historical events that are deemed relevant can be very random. The good life may be studied empirically – in different settings and for different persons – to learn about everyday life and the role of different care practices as well as the values and knowledges that inform them. Comparisons between practices may bring out suggestions for what may be good or better ways to live everyday life and how to care for it best.[57]

Generative hanging out

I promised to substantiate the discussion of better hanging out as *generative hanging out*. Generative hanging out is generative on two levels. This approach generates, first, a set of practices for living together with and getting to know interlocutors. Generative hanging out is about doing the everyday together and negotiating how to do this well. By creating folds and overlaps, and by taking fieldnotes, the researcher gains experience with the world of their interlocutors, or, alternatively, works to develop a shared practice. Interlocutors can participate actively, but also more passively, by allowing researchers to become part of their world and by showing them around. The ALS patients discussed in Chapter 10, for instance, could not move freely, and some of them could not speak. We were nevertheless able to get a clear idea about their concerns with the feeding tube. Annelieke Driessen has written a beautiful book about the good life for people with dementia by analysing the interactions between caregivers, patients and other people as well as with buildings, bathtubs and dance parties.[58] People with dementia are represented in their active engagements as co-shapers of the good life. But this can only be done by shifting 'the terms' and making these terms relevant to the worlds of our interlocutors.

In addition to producing shared practices, generative hanging out also provides ideas about how one may live with disease and problems that do not go away or that are hard to represent verbally. One can retrospectively decide if hanging out was good (or better) for conducting research by seeing if it did just that, namely generating new ideas and practices as well as allowing lessons to be drawn from specificities. As in Petrarch's approach to doing philosophy, the results of hanging out and what it generates can be returned to the interlocutors. Of course, the development of theory can also be an aim of research, as can the articulation of everyday values in various practices. However, the concrete relevance of care studies to care practice is often obvious to ethnographers even if it remains difficult to apply their insights and therefore improve such practices.[59]

My quest to reinvent the good life ends with these suggestions for how research might address this topic and to what effect. The concluding chapter will reflect on the question how the specific case studies and historical detours presented in this book can help generate knowledge that is based on specificities and the articulation of shared concerns. This is in stark contrast to knowledge that is based on generalisations and the assumption that findings should be universally valid. Shared concerns can be found by hermeneutically linking detailed understandings of specific situations with other situations, and hence transposing findings from one specific place to another. This requires active comparisons rather than passive 'applications'.

Notes

1 Lawy, 2017 shows how speaking always also implies 'listening'. Moser & Law, 2003 show how technologies may assist in 'making a voice'.
2 Note that there is a grim history of abuse of research subjects within research practices in the twentieth century. People have been ruthlessly submitted to research designs that were harmful to them – or even lethal (see e.g. Lederer, 1995), during and after the Second World War (eugenics programmes, see e.g. Proctor, 1988; Weindling, 1989), but also after that, for instance the Tuskegee syphilis trials. See Reverby, 2000; 2009; Brandt, 1978. Today, dubious medical research practices are those that recruit poor people from developing countries as research subjects. See Petryna, 2007; 2009; Petryna et al., 2006; Cooley, 2001; Benatar, 2001.)
3 Much work has been done to conceptualise the expertise of patients: see Epstein, 1996; Callon & Rabeharisoa, 2002; 2003; 2008; Pols, 2014; Pols & Hoogsteyns, 2015; Rabeharisoa et al., 2014; Scott, 1991. This literature is mostly about patients who are able to express themselves verbally, or who even master the skills of scientific research.

4   This led to a proposal for a special issue of *Medical Anthropology*, which is now in preparation (Pols & Krause, forthcoming).
5   Taylor, 2014 writes about hanging out as a way to discover unexpected things. See Schurian-Dąbrowska & Krause, 2023 for what ethnographers may learn when they do not speak the language of their field.
6   Anthropologist Renato Rosaldo is often credited with first using the term 'deep hanging out', in relation to ethnographic research methodology. See Clifford, 1996. Geertz (1998) made the term more widely known (Redman, 2019).
7   The concept of 'research subject' is also starting to fall apart because the relationship between researcher and subject is not only informed by the aims of research. I will still use the term for clarity, but with the addition of the term 'interlocutor', which more clearly signifies the process of exchange that takes place in this relationship.
8   Hirschauer, 2006; Faubion & Marcus, 2009; Fortun et al., 2014; De la Cadena, 2015. See also art-based approaches for including non-verbally fluent subjects in research (Strohm, 2012; McKearny & Zoanni, 2018; Driessen, 2018a; 2018b; 2019; 2023; Hendriks, 2023; Cleeve, 2023; Scholtes, 2023; Carreras & Winthereik, 2023). Some patients experience many problems but do not speak up at all (Habraken et al., 2008).
9   One of the confusions for young researchers learning to write academic articles is that a paper generally does not follow their own pathway from ignorance and imprecisely formulated research questions to insight and discovery. To give away the point at the start can hence feel quite strange to them. Indeed, the idea that methods and results can be strictly separated is an important one in quantitative research traditions, but this is not a virtue in qualitative traditions.
10 See Derksen & Morowski, 2022. They argue for a plurality of methods in order to learn different things about certain phenomena.
11 See for example Ballestero & Winthereik, 2021; De la Cadena, 2015; Lassiter, 2005; Niewöhner, 2016; Fortun et al., 2014; Hastrup, 2018; Pols, 2005; Strohm, 2012.
12 Clifford & Marcus, 2010; Holmes & Marcus, 2008.
13 This is for instance the case when one studies researchers in action.
14 Participation thereby leads to forms of involvement which transgress sheer observation and turn into various forms of more or less active collaboration (Sánchez Criado & Estalella, 2018, p. 8). These collaborations emerge often without these having been a constitutive element or strategic design of the research. They may consist of 'moments' (Hoppe et al., 2019; Hastrup, 2018), field events (Ahlin & Li, 2019), or relationships that grow over time. However, while 'collaborative' methods have become a buzzword in general anthropology and in health-related research (Lassiter, 2005; Niewöhner, 2016; Rappaport, 2008; Goodley, 1996; Gilbert, 2004;), it often remains unclear what forms these collaborations may take.
15 I use this term for all interviews that pose open questions, because interviews are always semi-structured, even in-depth ones. And I will argue below that it is a good thing to understand interviews in this way in order to clarify the role of the researcher. There are, however, also very open forms of interviewing, such as the autobiographical interview. These interviews are still 'on the terms of the researcher' because they involve verbal accounts.
16 These problems involved practical matters, such as bank issues, debts and finding a job, not their intellectual capacities.
17 See Pols, 2005, and Chapter 3, above.
18 Pols, 2005, p. 207.
19 See for the point of restricting one's view Taylor, 2014.
20 See Despret, 2006, 2015 about researchers who pose interesting questions to their animal research subjects.
21 This can be different for cases in which research participation can result in support for patient organisations or lead to visits to conferences, for instance.
22 I always give instruct students not to tell or invent very sensitive stories while practising, because the classroom is a place for making and learning from mistakes. But they can be painful even during a mock interview nonetheless!
23 This certainly is an ideal-type situation, and examples of this in my book are the conversations I had with women who lost their hair.
24 Guess who also studied 'le langage des déments'? Luce Irigaray, while working on her PhD thesis. She counted words to discover that individual words disappear and general ones stay.
25 Needless to say, there is a lot of semiotics to be found in these conversations!

26 Even people who could not really talk could often still sing or use certain phrases. The musicality of language comes with a strong syntax that apparently sticks even to brains that are 'worn thin'. One of my interlocutors conducted all her conversations using the same words, which were ostensibly describing a flower bush in her garden and a visit by the queen to her village. The tone of her voice informed us what she was actually engaging with (having an argument with a fellow resident, having a conversation about the weather, responding to others or taking a turn in the conversation), and this worked surprisingly well for addressing staff. But this did not work very well for her fellow residents, who were distracted by the strange words and accused her of 'uttering lies'.

27 Famously, Harold Garfinkel (1967) taught how one can learn about norms through breaching experiments. Such breaches can be purposefully staged, but also always lead to awkward situations and concerns about 'deceiving' research subjects. When one starts participating in a practice one is not familiar with, however, one can be fairly sure there will be such breaches. And these are excellent moments to learn how 'things are done' or ought to be done in this practice.

28 Taylor, 2014.
29 Dréano, forthcoming.
30 Haraway, 2018.
31 De Langen, forthcoming.
32 Dronkert, 2023.
33 Pols, 2005.
34 Pels et al., 2018; De Koning et al., 2019; Dilger et al., 2019.
35 This demanded that I negotiated consent for the research with the family representatives of the patients, an example of formal ethical demands that would not solve the problems of everyday ethics I address here, such as how to talk to people in a way that would be acceptable to them.
36 Remember that we are still talking about 'living together' – that is to say, the researcher has preferences and limitations that are to be respected as well.
37 Although people can still withdraw from the research, of course.
38 I use the notion of interlocutors for the research subject in the situation of participant observation or hanging out.
39 He would not have liked that I use a pseudonym for him. Like in the movie they made about his holidays, 'things had to be as they are', true to reality. Using a pseudonym is an example of a trade-off that researchers and interlocutors often think is a good research practice.
40 There are some ways to find this out. I always insist on the importance of a goodbye ritual when leaving the field. This is the moment when you learn how your research subjects felt about your presence. I once overheard a conversation while conducting fieldwork in a residential home for older people with psychiatric problems and dementia. 'Who is that, she doesn't do anything all day!' 'Oh, no, she is the psychologist, she supervises what happens here.'
41 This also underscores the dubiousness of 'undercover' research, which might, for instance, be done to study criminal gangs. Research is dependent on the trust that research subjects have in the researcher, but this trust can be broken by a researcher's unrevealed intentions and possibly harmful publications.
42 It was in no way intimidating. I was clearly more powerful than him even in terms of physical strength. Creating relationships and forging productive encounters are key ingredients to ethnographic fieldwork. This can be inspiring, but fieldwork encounters are not always pleasant. Fieldwork often involves establishing relationships with individuals we would avoid or not come across in our everyday lives. This comes with risks of mental health problems or sexual harassment (Berry et al., 2017; Schneider, 2020; Williams, 2017. Fieldworkers should prepare for this. See Hopmans et al., 2022).
43 This was different for Maja in her engagements with the Aboriginal community, because the community demanded you show up also when the research is done. See also the next note on Clément.
44 And the same is of course true for situations in which one hangs out. In Clément's case, for instance, this involved minor obligations, such as being a kind of family member who supported the family with particular things, such as a language course or other lessons.
45 I once presented an elderly lady with a 'psychiatric symptoms checklist'. I asked questions about one bizarre or terrible symptom after the other (Are you having sombre feelings? Is it difficult to get out of bed in the mornings? Do you see things that are not there? Are you

hearing voices?). The answers given had to be classified as no, a little, often, always. The lady smilingly answered all the questions with, 'Oh, you can put down "a little".' I used this occasion to triumphantly argue to my quantitative colleagues that their methods had some flaws and that they did not function as mere 'thermometers'. Needless to say, they were not impressed. Such strange answers could be 'averaged out' by large quantities, or the list could simply be taken out of the database. I would also like to make a strong point about establishing a research ethics that does not force people to answer *all* the questions on a questionnaire. It is an abuse of power and leads to unreliable results.

46 Interestingly, for novice qualitative interviewers who have been trained in a quantitative tradition, it is difficult to discriminate between experiences and opinions. To them these appear to be the same things, but drawing a distinction between the two makes a large difference for what one can get out of an interview.
47 In practice it is mainly researchers and their colleagues who do this.
48 See Pels et al., 2018.
49 Of course, an object is also constructed by its representation in the researcher's fieldnotes, in this case representations of the experiences of the researcher.
50 See also Foucault's work on practices of the self (Foucault, 1983, 1986).
51 Fox Keller, 2000; D'Hoop, 2021b; Despret, 2006, 2015.
52 Ask any novice writer how words sometimes play with them and make them say things they did not fully intend! I remember my first paper in English. The sentences sounded *so* good, but what did they actually mean?! We are always caught up in orderings, even if we try to escape them. We cannot step out of the horizons of possibility that our era and its circumstances impose on us. But we can try to make friends who can help us, by discussing with others and probing new theories or reading ever more books.
53 Note that this famous quotation from Wittgenstein (1976) utters a truth rather than a prescription.
54 This is Latour's move, namely to turn things into 'actants' that steer people (1993).
55 See Pols, 2005.
56 Hoppe et al., 2019 argue for the important role of soup in academia, which they consider a metaphor for how one may bridge academia and the world beyond this. Ironically, providing food to research subjects was explicitly disallowed by the European grant we received for studying the use of telecare technologies.
57 See Pols, forthcoming, b; and Pols, 2019a, on aesthetic values.
58 Driessen, 2019; see also Driessen 2018a, 2018b.
59 The achievement of improvements is a theme for another book, which will address a particular issue, namely that it often seems clear what is good to do but that actually *doing* this is very difficult. This is a topic that is neglected in ethics as well as in social science. However, writing a book demands a certain practice of writing that appears to be vanishing from academia unless one can get a grant for it. See on the issue of 'improvement' Pols, forthcoming, b.

13
Conclusions: reinventing the good life, grasping specificities

Generative concepts

To end the book, I am again faced with the challenge of linking theory with empirical findings, this time to account for what my exercises in pointing and folding have delivered. My aim in writing this book was to generate concepts for studying specific situations in everyday life and care, and particularly the values of everyday life. I wanted to generate re-scriptions of practices that are useful for learning how we may study care as a practice in which everyday-life values take shape and are shaped with the aim of doing something good for those living with chronic disease or other problems that do not go away. Everyday life practices always involve combinations of good things as well as bad things. These bad things cannot be eradicated or cured.

To generate these re-scriptions, I observed care practices, unfolded historical concepts and refolded them into my empirical findings, thus combining theoretical and empirical approaches. The generative hermeneutic work that is necessitated by the ethnographic study of care practices always involves observations but also questions about how to put such observations into words. Care studies – the branch of science and technology studies and empirical ethics developed during research on health care – are concerned with the study of values, or forms of the good that point to things that are (made) important in healthcare practices.[1] Care studies hence articulate how people, things and words together give shape to forms of the good that seek to improve specific situations or make them more bearable. My particular focus was on situations involving chronic patients or people with disabilities that do not go away. Here, it is unclear what kind of care might be considered good. This is in contrast with care practices that seek to achieve a cure and that therefore strive to reach a clear endpoint. There is clarity about what needs to be done even if this goal is not achieved. I employed the notion of aesthetic values of everyday life to ask about what is appropriate, nice or even beautiful in everyday concerns. This notion was also used as a pointer in my quest to learn about what is good in chronic care. Aesthetic values are present in practices, but they lack theoretical development as to what type of values they are and how people act on them. How may we study the values of everyday life? Which historical, theoretical and empirical approaches can be folded together to do so? What does a regaining of a sense of the role that aesthetic values of everyday life play allow us to see that might otherwise be overlooked?

What are everyday-life values?

I start by outlining the kind of object that the values of everyday life have become in the context of this analysis. I argued that it is crucial to approach this question as an empirical issue, which is to say, as a question that is posed in specific situations. This must be done because neither generalising research methods nor prescriptive ethics can provide a vocabulary for learning about the values of everyday life. What values emerge in everyday situations, how do they emerge and to what effect? The analyses presented in this book illustrate that myriad values emerge in myriad forms. Values might have an aesthetic character, are informed by conventions and culturally specific notions of appropriateness, emerge from local conceptualisations of morality, be embedded in scientific results – in the form of parameters of efficiency – and introduced into care practices as ethical principles, practical decisions and so on. Everyday-life values are highly varied in nature and they are not only relevant to people; they can also be embedded in words and things as well as research methods. Values can play an active role by seducing, evoking, motivating, translating or preventing certain activities or feelings. An active-passive subject fits with this understanding of values. The values of everyday life act upon people or make them act.

My ethnographic case studies showed that there is a difference between everyday values and their partner concept in the theoretical domain, namely principles. Everyday-life values are different, first, in that they overflow the domain of ethics as it is demarcated by modern philosophy. Everyday-life values can have multiple characteristics and these may shift from one situation to another, such as, for example, when good blood pressure becomes a matter of 'behaving well'. Everyday values depend on their material-semiotic relationships with other entities. Principles, in contrast, are theoretical in nature. They are abstract as well as true and good in themselves. They are used to create a modernist approach to ethics by universalising and hence decontextualising values. Principles are the same for everyone everywhere. There are no exceptions to who should be treated with dignity or not. Principles were formulated in response to pre-modern philosophies of the good-life-as-practice, such as those proposed by Adam Smith and the humanist philosophers who drew on the work of the ancient Greeks. Social theory abolished the concept of individual morality as a way of understanding societies and governing individuals or for making them govern themselves. Turning religion into a private matter was another way to alleviate fears about idiosyncratic or even violent passions and to move these beyond the purview of the state.

One could say that, historically speaking, the universal truth and goodness of principles as well as their role in undergirding general norms were a way to rescue individual morality from the irrationality of individuals. Principles make it more difficult for people to act on idiosyncratic whims, which would merely lead to dissensus. Principles are meant to be the same for every rational person, everywhere, and provide similar guidelines for all human activities. Consequently, through the unity that principles provided, a peaceful nation could be envisioned. Morality became a concern on the level of managing the nation state. Eventually psychology took the place of morality, and this further enhanced efforts towards social engineering. During this era there were thinkers, such as Adam Smith, who articulated concerns about the role of public goods, such as art and education, in a rationalised society. Principle- or rule-based ethics are, in our times, often institutionalised in the form of ethics committees that seek to regulate practices using universal principles rather than to teach individuals how they might consider acting in difficult situations as well as how to justify such actions.

Caregivers, as well as others, translated abstract principles into everyday values in their professional practices to be able to put them to use. Such translations resonate with Adam Smith's moral theory that drew connections between everyday moral values and conventions to 'ground' the values of everyday life. The acknowledgement of the embeddedness of everyday values in conventions is similar to what I have argued for in this book. Studying such values calls for *situating* them.

The translation of abstract principles makes their specific workings and effects unpredictable. The principle of autonomy, for instance, led to the unforeseen possibility of patients shutting the door on caregivers. And dignity could, surprisingly, allow patients to be dirty. Principles, once taken out of the realm of abstract theory, were brought into relationship with local conventions rather than universal norms. The various kinds of everyday-life values that principles can be turned into is hence a concrete and specific matter. It depends on how such values are translated and put into practice. Everyday-life values matter in a practical way; they matter *somewhere*. They are empirically substantiated, situated, concrete and put into practice.

Categorising the varieties of everyday-life values has proven to be difficult. Values are not in and of themselves of a specific type but come to matter and function differently in specific practices. Everyday-life values are therefore always relational to things, people, words, norms, conventions and so on. This is why a value such as 'citizenship' can be an aesthetic value in one situation, a principle in another and an economic value in yet another. In particular, my analyses have shown that the difference between aesthetics and morality may be difficult to pinpoint. Does dignity, for example, relate to morality or aesthetics? To obligation or motivation? *Humanitas* or *dignitas*? There are different traditions in thinking about dignity in either register.

Ethics and etiquette, similar to other repertoires of valuing (justice, economy, medicine and so on),[2] both provide answers to the question 'what to do?' even if they apply different criteria for evaluating certain situations. But everyday *moral* or ethical values are not good and true in themselves, even if they may be good and true *somewhere*. Ethical and moral values in everyday life resemble aesthetic values in that they share a relationship with conventions and concrete historical situations. They are all informed by cultural, artistic and contingent historical events because they each are socially rooted and embedded phenomena. Everyday values were included under the header of morality in pre-modern philosophy. In everyday life, the question is, 'What to do *here and now*?' This question can be answered in different ways by reference to different repertoires of valuing.

Classifying and demarcating values is, however, difficult even though it is a matter of political importance. My chapters about women who lost their hair due to chemotherapy as well as the chapter on long-term psychiatry showed how aesthetic values could lead to breaches in conventions or be creatively used to reshape such conventions. The use of images of conventional femininity could prevent the attribution of unwelcome valuings, such as 'being a cancer patient'. Human rights or democratic principles are considered pertinent in some places yet valued differently in others.[3] How, say, 'speaking one's mind freely' is labelled and governed is crucial for what people can or cannot say and do. How one is capable of valuing various things greatly determines how one is able to live.[4]

Ideally, the aesthetic values of everyday life are permissive and motivating rather than prohibitive and demotivating. In contrast, one could say that etiquette is a form of rule-based aesthetics that requires knowledge of those rules in order to be able to follow them. Moving between different types of etiquette may be difficult; see Bourdieu, who describes knowing how to behave as 'cultural capital'. Etiquette was not, for example, simply a matter of entering the salons at will or invitation, one also had to know the proper codes of conduct. The idea that aesthetic values can be motivating values is related to how ancient Greek philosophers understood the good-life-as-practice, but also to how later humanists drew a connection between motivation and the pleasure of gaining wisdom about the good life. In this understanding, aesthetic values may generate new forms of social life – for example, by providing the possibility of wearing scarves rather than wigs on a bald female head.

Aesthetic values and particular styles of living may seduce individuals and hence act on them rather than rationally convince them. One may feel inspired by a flower-power style or instead by a more managerial style. Aesthetic values appeal to people and motivate or influence their activities. Aesthetic values actively, but also passively, affect people on the level of their motivations and appreciations.[5] The motivational character of aesthetic values points to their subversive potential; they may organise people through shared passions that relate to different rationalities, rather than through arguments that fit the rationality of the opponents. Hence aesthetic values may change social and cultural forms in unforeseen ways. Such motivated forms of sociality are often overlooked in social and political theory, where social coherence is often interpreted as a matter of governance, regulation or pre-given distinctions such as class, gender, age or race. Motivated socialities are important for understanding the ways in which people organise themselves.[6] Motivations are crucial drivers for the emergence of social forms.[7]

The analyses presented in my book underscore that it is crucial for social and political theory to address everyday-life values. If these are ignored, no sense can be made of care practices or of any other practices in which values are negotiated in order to orient specific situations towards something good. Without an acknowledgement and understanding of the role of everyday-life values, the work of caregivers remains a mystery. Why would caregivers – who are not doctors and who receive low wages as well as little support for dealing with varied and difficult situations – do this work at all if they did not think it would lead to anything good? There is a dearth of tools for supporting such practices and evaluating them 'on their own terms',[8] which is the current and sad situation in contemporary societies governed by neoliberal policies. When efficiency and affordability are the sole guidelines for organising care practices, other values disappear from view, as they are thought of as private and as replaceable by efficiency values or general rules. When the orientation towards everyday values that is inherent to care practices (as well as to other parts of the public sector) disappears, it will ultimately have an effect on policy as well. This limited conceptualisation of care explains why caregivers complain that they are being swamped by bureaucracy, which can be summed up as a lack of recognition by policymakers as well as a frustration with not being able to do what they know is best for their patients.[9] It is not only *what* people value but *that* people value that is key to understanding and supporting (governing) care practices.

It is important to note that methods for providing evaluation and support are still necessary; an orientation towards something good does not automatically result in good outcomes. All cases in this book clearly illustrate this point. Upholding autonomy in care for people with learning disabilities had unexpected effects, and this was also the case for citizenship in mental healthcare, for quality-of-life measurements in care for people with ALS, and for the curative orientation in cancer care. The shared space that is provided for negotiating the contingent and specific values of everyday life, and how this space is secured and sustained within care settings (in the relationships between caregivers, managers, financers and so on), is an important concern for evaluating care practices for problems that do not go away.[10]

Aesthetic values, goodness and truth

Everyday aesthetic values proved to be great pointers for tracing values-in-practice because they are empirically situated: that is, they exist in practice and not so much in theory. Everyday aesthetic values are informed by the senses, namely the ability to appreciate something as nice, appropriate or beautiful or to evaluate it as the opposite. Aesthetic values can move or seduce those who are summoned by them, or they can be more actively strived for by inspiring different kinds of activities. This is obvious in the case of the arts, but it is also true for everyday events. One may want to treat a nasty cough, strive for a good death, aspire to a beautiful goal, work hard to articulate an elegant argument, consider whether a feeding tube might provide more time for pleasurable activities in light of one's particular living conditions, and hence try to shape a state of worth. My book aimed to open an intellectual space for studying, discussing and understanding aesthetic values and other forms of everyday-life values.

In their modernist guise, aesthetic values were seen as private tastes that were of public concern only in the sense that they were supposed to motivate economic activity; each individual could buy what they preferred or craved. Pre-modern and humanist traditions of scholarship (re-)established the connection between truth, goodness and beauty. Each good thing has a particular truth as well as a particular beauty or aesthetic style. And these terms can be interchanged. Each true thing has a particular relation to goodness and a particular style or form of beauty to match. And each beautiful (or appropriate) thing relates to a particular truth and to a particular suggestion for what is good to do.

I re-articulated this 'mixture' of the concrete interrelations between truth, beauty and goodness to make sense of everyday-life values. I was inspired to do so by pre-modern philosophies of the good-life-as-practice. Rather than drawing connections between the good and the true through a prescriptive (if explorative and practical) exemplarity ('this is how one should live the good life') as these philosophers did, I sought to describe how the good, the true and the beautiful are connected locally, without judging these a priori as good or not. My reinvention of this interrelatedness suggests how we might move away from various problematic modernist distinctions, such as between facts and values, is and ought, subject and object, nature and culture. Modernist ethics and epidemiology employ very different repertoires of knowledge production, but they share the assumption that facts and values belong to different realms and that they can (and should!) be separated. In modern science, methods are designed to enforce this separation. Good methods result in objective facts. In modern ethics, this task is achieved by referring to universal principles and norms rather than to private sentiments. Academic ethics is about formulating a mode of reasoning on values, not about stating or studying (or re-scribing) facts. Academic ethics is often seen as a non-empirical philosophical endeavour.

In the study of everyday practices, however, such a separation does not hold. To understand everyday-life values and their workings, one needs to attend to the particular truths that are inscribed (how is the situation understood or treated?) as well as to the particular notions of goodness that these imply (what do the actors show in their activities as to what is good to do in a certain situation? How do they think they can do this well?). Truth and goodness come together 'as a package'. Consequently, scientific approaches contain notions of goodness (such as objectivity, reliability, generalisability or specificity) as well as notions of truth, which is visible in the concepts and methods that are used (what is the specific situation, how many variables should be included, how are their relationships operationalised, how may ethnographic methods be improved to learn about the values of everyday life?). Chapter 6 on Habermas and the new citizens showed how universality could also be seen as an aesthetic style that belongs to a particular practice and that enacts a certain understanding of truth and goodness. The same goes for styles of research that rest on assumptions about specific forms of 'appropriateness' (should objectification outweigh the preferences of the research subjects or should this be the other way around?). I referred to this entanglement as the creativity of methods.

The creativity of methods

The creativity of methods emerged clearly in the example of the feeding tube. Here, research on quality of life could not re-scribe everyday life in ways that did justice to what patients valued. Ethnography could, in contrast, make the values of everyday life visible and illustrate the shifting concerns involved with having or anticipating a feeding tube. And ethnographic research was more helpful than conducting interviews, particularly when patients had difficulties with representing themselves as the chapter on generative hanging out showed. Ethnography set the stage for 'doing things together' and could create situations that were acceptable, or even pleasant, to all participants. This approach relied less on verbal capacities and self-representations and more on observations of activities and attempts to create a suitable research practice.

Although boundaries may be fluid, the inseparability of goodness, truth and beauty empirically and practically re-scribes knowledge claims no matter how theoretical these may be. Theories always fold together empirical situations and concepts. This is not in itself problematic. However, it implies that there is a need to describe and explain the practical or technical ways in which *any* knowledge claim comes into being. Researchers need to be open about their concepts and methods, and indeed this is common scientific practice.[11] But rather than discussions about 'proper methods' that rely on shared assumptions in research communities, the more urgent question is how different methods shape the object of research and whether this object is appropriate for dealing with the concerns at hand.

What is problematic, then, is denying or mystifying the creative character of methods, and hence the folded nature of knowledge, because this always involves the folding together of empirical situations and theories. This can be problematic because researchers might think that they are simply describing the truth 'out there', which means they fail to acknowledge how their methodologies and concepts play a role in *creating* this truth. Or alternatively, if one claims to be reasoning in the realm of 'pure theory', this does not account for the generative effects that result from the folding of particular empirical situations into theories. There are many examples of the conflation of truth and representation, such as how the goal of ending civil wars influenced how social theorists understood the social, and how the rising class of rich, bourgeois and trading citizens was inscribed in theories about citizenship. Another example is the ongoing debate about the 'Western' character of human rights. Human rights are criticised for upholding the pretence that they 'come from nowhere' while failing to consider that situations may vary greatly in different parts of the world.[12]

If the creativity of methods is not acknowledged and the world is perceived as a singular and coherent entity, one can all too easily believe that there are no variations in scientific approaches or that different approaches will eventually provide 'the whole picture'. Such a 'totalitarian' epistemology silences different registers for understanding the world, and therefore also hinders the employment of such repertoires for acting in the world. These may be silenced for good reasons, although, of course, the reasons for doing so are always debatable. Silencing is a risky strategy in that it may systematically exclude certain voices without giving them the space to justify their truth, beauty and goodness. Academic knowledge claims can be similarly problematic if they are totalising.[13]

Debating methods can be complex because it is impossible to gain knowledge without employing demarcations and epistemological or methodological frameworks. The best option therefore is to analyse the various limitations and possibilities that certain methods may have, as was exemplified in the chapters on quality of life and Petrarch's philosophical practice. Metaphors for correspondence and discovery abound in the positivist sciences. My discussion of aesthetic values, however, showed how methods can work in a creative manner, and therefore, how descriptions are always re-scriptions. Such re-scriptions are true statements, yet they are also folded together with various situations and concepts. The world is not 'made up' or 'discovered' by methods but different worlds are 're-scribed' by them.

Another example of form-creating-content that the book discussed was how neoliberalist frameworks hinder an understanding of care practices as involving negotiations about the values of everyday life. Neoliberalism is not a formal theory of knowledge, but it nevertheless works locally in a similar manner, namely by framing policies in a particular manner and by foregrounding some things (efficiency, the market, independent actors) while leaving out other things (the orientation of care practices towards socially shared values, the importance of art and education, the 'evils of capitalism').[14] The neoliberal framework privileges particular ways of acting and governing ('do whatever you want as long as you pay for it with private money') rather than others (such as, say, worrying about the exhaustion of the planet or other common goods). Acknowledging the creativity of methods focuses attention on the kinds of research objects that are created, how strong their claims to truth are, and how useful these objects are for understanding the concerns one wants to address.

Creativity in everyday life

Paying attention to and rehabilitating aesthetic values and creativity as well as their connections to goodness and truth also shows that creativity is a central notion for understanding individuals, their social lives and related collectives. Creativity in everyday life, as I showed in the case of women who have lost their hair, already starts with brushing one's teeth and getting dressed. These women were actively reinventing their everyday selves to create a state of worth for themselves. This involved playing with or adapting social conventions and trying to put these to good use. Such reinventions could be active and intentional efforts towards a state of worth. For example, ALS patients experimented with various ways of eating and using the feeding tube, and tried to integrate these activities into their practices of tasting food as well as their negotiations of the social dimensions of eating. But creativity could also create states of worth that were less intentional and sometimes also less aesthetically pleasing. For example, this was the case for people with learning disabilities who tried to combine smoking pot with holding a job, and who sometimes overindulged in the former when on the dole. A self was created that gave rise to concerns among caregivers who did not see a life shrouded in clouds of smoke as a valued state of worth. In a similar vein, in the long-stay ward the possibility of *not* being creative could lead to patients being dirty. This was less clearly articulated as a goal, but it was nevertheless informed by what patients and caregivers valued, and therefore resulted in a particular aesthetic outcome. Aesthetic values linked certain motivated socialities together. The role of creativity was also apparent in the notion of 'making a voice' for patients. Rather than conceptualising patients as speaking in authentic individual voices, my cases showed how voices are always created through sociomaterial collectives.

Creativity is central to how people lead their daily lives, construct scientific truth and imagine a just and good society. Social theory decided to discard the aesthetic values of everyday life to achieve a greater good (an *ordered* society), but the everyday life values have proven to be of much greater influence than their dismissal, privatisation or individualisation justifies. Aesthetic values influence mundane forms of culture and suggest new possibilities for living together with others.[15] A creative orientation to the things that people value is evident in many value-oriented activities, such as work done in the public sector concerning care, education, art and even law enforcement. These are all value-oriented practices and they are not 'productive' in the sense that they aim for monetary gain. They are attempts at doing something good (true, beautiful) because we have decided as a society to value these things. Moreover, we continue doing them even if it is forbidden, the ultimate good will never be achieved and even if it continues to cost a great deal of public money.

It is important to note that creativity is a descriptive term here, rather than a judgement. Creativity can also be exhausting or confusing. Creating and reinventing oneself may be constantly required within a liberal framework, because individuals are deemed responsible for the making and blossoming of their own life. Technologists and proponents of innovation call for the constant recreation of practices, of course with the use of the particular technology they have on offer.[16] For instance, in secularising societies, rituals for burial and mourning have become increasingly individualised, which means that people have to reinvent such practices and adapt them to their particular situation.[17] This provides welcome opportunities in some ways, but lacks the ease of habits and routines that were previously informed by religion and social convention. Creativity is an important concept to keep in mind when attempting to understand human activity.

Everyday ethics, aesthetics and veridiction

The term 'everyday ethics', as developed in this book, is a descriptive notion for practices in which values – or forms of the good – are actively addressed (strived for, cherished, proposed, achieved) and that actively shape what happens and what participants (people, words, things) do in certain situations. The notion of ethics here denotes an open conceptualisation of the good rather than a particular category of (moral) values. It mimics pre-modern understandings of morality that were open to different types of values. Everyday ethics may hence not be an ideal concept, given its association with a set of values that can be labelled as moral. I nonetheless wish to retain this concept in order to fold it together with historical and present-day writings on everyday ethics.[18] A more precise description would therefore be, 'Everyday ethics refers to forms of doing good-in-practice that include everyday forms of truth, beauty and other kinds of values'. This description emphasises what is done *here*, *now*, and what this implies for certain conceptualisations of the good in certain practices. These are neither prescriptive notions of the good, nor do they automatically lead to good practices.

Practices of the good life – or one could more precisely say *a* good life – are practices in which an observer can discern particular understandings of what this good life is and how such a life is embedded in technologies, words or habits. One may want to stick to a doctor's advice, for instance, or instead interpret such advice a bit more loosely in order to enjoy life more.[19] Technologies may be chosen for their capacity to enhance professional control even if they were intended to encourage patients' self-management.[20] I call this the intra-normativity of practices.[21] Intra-normative goods may be in tension with each other, and they will always be accompanied by bads, such as is the case for people living with a chronic disease or disability. Chronic disease represents a bad that may change its shape but that will never be resolved.[22] This does not suggest giving up, because there will still be efforts to improve one's situation for the better, or at least for a little bit better. It is precisely such entanglements of the good and the bad that I was particularly interested in exploring for this book.

Determining or judging if a certain practice of the good life can be evaluated as good or not is a question of secondary importance. 'Evaluating' may be done by comparing the specificities of various situations, and there are different methods or practices for carrying out such comparisons as well as different ways for actually improving things.

Practices towards improvement merit a separate book.[23] For now, the point is to change our normative perspective on the good life and to make this useful for present-day care practices. Such a normativity is not about prescribing how people should live, but about learning what forms of the good are pertinent to particular everyday-life practices and the forms of everyday ethics they motivate. Normativity, here, is about the terms, methods and techniques that are used to describe (and hence re-scribe) everyday lives as well as what they can or cannot articulate.

Normativity: from exemplary to exemplar

In considering the good life of 'ordinary people', the meaning of the term 'exemplary' – as employed by philosophers of the good-life-as-practice (and I argued that caregivers can in some ways be seen as their present-day counterparts) – shifts from an ideal-typical or prescriptive exemplarity, which serves as a model for others to replicate or learn from, towards a more *descriptive* exemplarity, namely one that denotes an exemplar of which something (a case, a situation) is an example.[24] The practices of people living with chronic disease or problems that do not go away resemble the less than perfect practices of ancient Greek citizens rather than the prescriptive and ideal-type models proposed by philosophers exemplifying how to live the good life. Citizens and patients are similar in their striving for certain forms of the good, but differ in which goods they find important, in the strictness of the 'methodology' employed to examine and achieve a good life, and in their conviction about the necessity of teaching others. People with chronic disease are an exemplar of 'ordinary people' leading imperfect lives. They grapple with deciding what is good to do and how to do this in circumstances that may be not so good. The type of goodness they pursue may not be wisdom and virtue, and may be contestable or even considered wrong. For example, eating a lot of cake at a birthday party may be wrong from the perspective of diabetes management, but it may be the right thing to do to let off steam while accepting that one will have to face the consequences later. These actions are forms of the good for actors even if they are not good in all respects.

I hence use the notion of the exemplar, not in the way that examples can be demonstrations of a certain generalisation or universalisation, or of a model type of exemplarity, but instead as a way to link different situations and to learn from their (emerging) specificities and complexities.[25] I do this, for instance, by comparing the workings of certain principles or technologies, or by contrasting the styles of normativity in thinking about the good life. Principles, technologies or a good life are, then, the exemplar that links empirical examples. The exemplar is an open analytical concept that can be used to identify variations and specificities while simultaneously narrowing the analytical scope by pointing to certain phenomena and not others. In this way, it is possible to transfer knowledge from one specific situation to another or from one imperfect good life to another.

The generative ability of the exemplar is not dependent on ideal types, typicality or typologies of which some situation is an example. The exemplar is generative because it can be used to draw connections between situations and all their specificities to identify their differences and similarities, and hence to order them in specific ways. The exemplar, then, is a generative hermeneutic concept and strategy for folding words and situations together, and therefore also for re-scribing and analysing a certain situation.[26] The situation that becomes an example of a certain exemplar links goodness, beauty and truth not in prescriptive but in descriptive ways: *this* is thought of or enacted as good, true and appropriate, in specific ways, *here*.

The notion of the exemplar that can be used to link examples has other methodological resonances. The analyses presented in this book suggest a shift away from *persons* as exemplars (as in clinical case studies) to *situations*, *things* or *concepts* as exemplars. A situation can be an example of different exemplars. For instance, situations may be linked by the working of certain values (autonomy, dignity), the use of certain things (feeding tubes, wigs, washcloths), ways of 'making a voice' for patients, or by the methods used to produce knowledge (through epidemiological research, academic ethics, ethnography). This shift in using the exemplar to make situations relevant to other situations suggests taking the *social character* of situations and lives more seriously. For example, the bathrobe trick mentioned in the introductory chapter was analysed as an exemplar of everyday techniques for living well with COPD. Mrs Jacobs's situation presented one particular way of putting this exemplary technique into practice and of learning about its effects. This is an example of the exemplar 'techniques that are of value to everyday life practices of people with chronic disease'. The specificities of various cases and situations are brought into relationship through the lens of the exemplar – that is, the phenomenon of which these situations are a specific example. Exemplars are hence analytical tools to make re-scriptions of situations by organising comparisons between different situations. Choosing the exemplar to analyse a situation is a way of paying attention to the formulation of one's research question.

What can one learn from specific situations?

Clearly, everyday-life values are not universal or general phenomena, but neither are they individual matters of taste. Values appeared in my analyses as social things that are created by linking conventions to experiences or by resisting certain conventions. Values could be informed by motivations, appreciations and effects that are historically and culturally situated. The chapters on women who lost their hair due to chemotherapy as well as the chapter on long-term psychiatry showed how aesthetic values played a role in breaching conventions, but also how aesthetic values could creatively reshape conventions. The relationship between aesthetic values and conventions could be traced back to Adam Smith's major work on morality. It makes little sense to speak of individual (or idiosyncratic) morality or aesthetics; individuals are always situated in a mosaic of social conventions, historical events and contingent appreciations.

The study of specificities did not lead to general or universal understandings. The re-scription of specifications by linking them through the use of an exemplar allows one to draw out lessons from one situation that are relevant to another. The detailedness of ethnographic descriptions makes it possible for readers or listeners to intimately understand a situation. A situation becomes known in all its intricacies. This level of detail makes it possible to compare insights from one intimately known practice to another, namely by being attentive to the similarities and differences between them. In practice A the effects of using dignity as an orienting value are different than in practice B. These comparisons are focused by the exemplar of which both situations are a specification.

Specificity

Situations are specific as well as complex, but not in the sense of being unique, completely individual, original or idiosyncratic. Any concrete situation in linear time-space may be understood as a unique point in history. However, folding time-space – or relating specific situations to exemplars – allows one to analyse certain situations by linking them to other situations. Like this they become examples that can be compared to each other. Think again of the women who lost their hair. I analysed their situation as an exemplar of the meanings and practices that are attached to feminine baldness. We needed to learn about conventions, historical events and cultural contexts to understand how they as well as others perceived baldness. Why was feminine baldness deemed so bad even if these women themselves were not so bothered by this? This question was answered by tracing the social meanings of baldness for women, which included varied and often gruesome imaginaries of social exclusion, dehumanisation and punishment.

Specificities hence involve details that are made relevant through the lens of the exemplar. Determining which situations are selected as examples, and of what situation they are exemplary, depends on the aim of the study and influences the salience of the analysis. Clinical case reports are used to learn about rare physiologies or diseases. An individual case is an example of a disease that may be relevant to other cases elsewhere. This book, I hope, can be used to learn about the everyday-life values for people with chronic problems, whom I turned into an exemplar of 'ordinary people' who must juggle with the goods and bads that occur in their lives. But the good life is also an exemplar of problems that do not go away and cannot be solved.

Seeking to learn from specificities leads to a double complexity: that is to say, it involves relating at least two elements as an exemplar (say, the use of technology of which X and Y are examples) from two different situations (hospital Z and A). Each element (that is, each technology) relates to its own socio-material context in specific ways. Differences and similarities can then be explored. What is different in situation Z in comparison to situation A? The creativity of methods becomes visible again; the exemplar (technology use) shapes the context (hospital Z or A) of both elements (technology X and Y). The re-scription of a practice changes depending on the choice of the exemplar. If an ethnographer is conducting fieldwork in a hospital, it matters analytically if care practices on the ward are linked to exemplars like, say, software for enhancing accountability, to transmural collaborations or to certain notions of good care. This is a decision that determines how a situation can be turned into a specification of something else (the exemplar).

Specific situations can also be linked across time and space. Think about folding together the Greek notions of *bios*, *ethos* and *parrhesia* with contemporary concerns about everyday life. I was able to connect these concepts – and move away from other concepts – which carried my analysis forward, and the corroboration of this approach by early modern humanists extended my analysis even further. Petrarch's practice of writing letters and engaging in dialogue provided an example of thinking about the good life as an imperfect and ongoing everyday practice, and exemplified how the form of interactions influences how concerns that are relevant to everyday life might be addressed. Adam Smith's example of the impartial spectator helped to connect everyday-life values to conventions (rather than to abstract principles), and the example of the salons illustrated the importance of style and appearance in determining who is allowed to participate in public life. These are all specific situations that are connected through an analytical exemplar.

The question how to learn from specific situations is hence also the question how to learn from variations in situations that are linked by an exemplar. Drawing such a connection generates interpretations that overflow one particular situation or practice. Truth claims can be made through an analysis of differences and similarities – and hence variations – between situations. The usefulness of such claims is again relational. Others, elsewhere, may also use an exemplar to generate an understanding of their own situation by comparing or weighing differences and similarities as well as by considering various options for how to act or which technology to try out. The question if interpretations generate useful ways of understanding and improving other situations is ultimately about practices rather than about theories. Are the situations similar enough? Are the differences relevant? Interpretations must be (made) useful *somewhere*.

Discontinuities and coherences

Different situations embed different coherences (tacit theories, logically related terms, genres of activities).[27] The cases in this book cannot simply be added up to present one coherent narrative or to create a single theory that 'connects all the dots' and that provides a logical framework in which all specificities are simultaneously linked together. The cases in the book, like any exploration of everyday life, show how specificities related to various theoretical concerns and empirical contingencies. The open concepts that were employed to link them are generative for learning from specificities. Abstract notions of autonomy or dignity cannot encompass a complete philosophy of care; everyday values keep reappearing and messing up any attempt at establishing an orderly theory of dignity. One coherent framework cannot include *all* the variables that are relevant to a practice.[28] It is for this reason that differences and varieties are averaged out in statistical research, or not explored at all. Coherences are formed by defining what x and y axes represent and what questions are posed in questionnaires. This means one has to select one's concepts and exemplars carefully because they re-scribe practices in certain ways and may frame one coherence rather than another.[29]

In a study on self-quantification and self-measurement we managed to show very clearly how (here: quantitatively constructed) coherences could become a problem in everyday life. This issue occurred because quantitative approaches created singular logical coherences that clashed with the multitude of concerns and coherences in everyday life that do not mesh well with such logical equations. Here is a quote from that paper:[30]

> Here is Melanie, a self-tracker. She worked on her health by attempting to lose weight. In doing so, she was confronted with the difficulty of such an aim.
>
> I think that's the problem with focusing on weight loss. Because if I am exercising regularly and eating well, then I feel okay. That's why I don't like making weight loss a goal. Because if I say, 'I want to be this number by a certain time,' then I panic. And there shouldn't be panic. I should be enjoying things. And that's why I don't make a number goal. So, it is my goal, my motive is to lose weight, but I just think that for overall mental health, there needs to be more than that . . . It's kind of a weird game. Because if I cheat, or if I go out drinking all weekend, and I don't see any weight loss, I think: 'Well I expected that!' But if I am working really hard [and there's no weight loss], then it sucks. If I have been working out and eating well and my weight doesn't change, then that feels really bad. And that's when I start binging. I have gotten better, but I used to binge when I would behave really well all week and I didn't lose weight.

Melanie set off with a grand good: she wanted to achieve good health. Her health apps translated this grand good into the specific acts of exercising, dieting and tracking her weight. Yet the grand goods and these specific ones could not be aligned so easily. This provided Melanie with a different concern: that of getting into a panic and starting binge eating. In order to make sense of the situation, she had to invoke the category of 'mental health' to make her grand good of 'health' feasible again, and to be able to deal with the un-calculability of her body. Hence, she could reshape the practices in which she wanted to achieve health.

In the example the health app technology is a co-shaper of what is a problem of health (weight that is too high) and what to do about it (sports and reduced calorie intake). Weight loss could be measured very precisely. The scales related Melanie's health practices of dieting and exercising and evaluated the results of these actions: good or not good. This was particularly troublesome when the calculations led to unexpected results; she dieted and ran (she worked very hard on the calculations, and 'behaved well'), but gained weight anyway. The logic of the device did not emerge in practice. Her body behaved differently. The logic embedded in the technology clashed with an as yet unknown logic of Melanie's body and mind.

The example shows how calculating weight loss creates a coherence. Exercise minus food intake equals weight loss. Different concerns interfered with this logic and invalidated the calculation. There was the notion of mental health, the moralising effect of numbers, and the unpredictability of the body. This particular quantified logic (weight loss equals caloric intake minus exercise) proved to be just one among various possible coherences in everyday life, and moreover, one that did not hold up very well.[31] One could say that this logic of weight loss links the functioning of an individual body to a generalised notion of how *any* body is expected to function. Melanie's body, however, is a specific body living in specific circumstances. The generalisations embedded in the quantitative logics of the weight-loss app were made concrete in practice and did not neatly correspond with her life.

A clash of coherences may happen in individual lives, but something similar happened in the chapter on life in the French salons. Universalist language had a different relationship with the situation of citizens compared to that of *salonnières*. Universalising characterised the aesthetic style of private citizens who aspired to establish a common good, but such an aesthetic did not match that of salon visitors who indulged in particular – and exclusive – pleasures. Ethical principles were specified in practice, and hence characterised a specific rather than a general theory.

A key task for researchers seeking to re-scribe a practice, then, is to juggle with and negotiate various coherences (modes of ordering or modes of doing good, narratives, imaginaries, language games, repertoires, genres, paradigms), and to point out which ones can contribute to or reinvent certain understandings. What are meaningful re-scriptions for a particular purpose or audience? Is truth foregrounded, or are aesthetic values central, or are the moral relationships with others more important?

This is much more difficult than arguing about the differences found *within* one coherence, as is common in research that is strongly oriented towards one paradigm and set of methods or between people who understand the world in the same terms. The activity of folding implies that there is a possibility to relate findings to *different* frameworks rather than just one. It matters if one studies the good life in a prescriptive or a descriptive way. This means that researchers must consider the pros and cons of the terms and methods they use to create their object of research, and that researchers must be aware how these terms or techniques creatively re-scribe their object. This is not an easy task. The folded character of concepts illustrates how language and concepts are needed for communicating, but also that concepts can speak for the one who is talking, often without the speaker being aware of this. Using a concept from a certain language game evokes a particular coherence.[32] It makes, for example, a big difference if people's appreciations are considered as private tastes or as formative of social orderings. Concepts obtain their meaning in the ways they are used and related to other concepts, things and ways of acting. Juggling coherences also makes the task of governing differences more difficult because different contexts for understanding things have to be brought together.

What is an individual? What is the social?

I will illustrate the argument above by showing how the exemplars generated in this book can be used to link various specificities that each imply different coherences. This will also demonstrate how the creativity of methods shapes the understanding of an object of research. To do so, I will list the various conceptualisations of the individual that played a role in the analyses presented in this book as well as how these co-constitute a particular notion of the social. This shows how the coherences of 'the social' and the individuals that constitute this phenomenon are not a 'given'. For instance, linking individuals to populations through statistical analysis is very different compared to analysing individuals through the lens of ethnography, and hence, practices. In social theory, there are many different concepts for describing the social, such as networks, dynamic relations between actors, conventions, regions, fluids, rules, aesthetic genres and so on. Each coherence implies that its constituents are understood in particular ways, and vice versa, each notion of the individual comes with a certain understanding of the social. Neither the social nor its constituents are a given.

I present a variety of possible individuals, a variety of psychologies, moralities and socialities. This analysis is, on the one hand, an antidote to the idea that there is a singular individual that stands in relation to a singular sociality. On the other, this analysis is also an antidote to the neoliberal worldviews that govern contemporary care practices. Neoliberalism conceptualises the individual as a rational being who calculates maximum gain and effect while cherishing private pleasures that they seek to fulfil by earning money. In the neoliberal logic, wealthy societies are created by individuals who pursue private gains.[33]

My analysis of key historical texts shows that there are many varieties of the 'modernist' individual. In the exemplars described below, many variables have also been left out. I present a theoretical abstraction, but one that explicitly folds in different empirical situations to exemplify this abstraction. These are historical characters, but we can also find them in present-day practices. This provides the reader with the possibility of reinventing their own approach to thinking about what a good life is and how we might study this. I hope to have created more space for generating different re-scriptions that can help to identify and deal with the problems of our here and now, and that can help sustain the possibility of living as well as possible under difficult circumstances.

The intelligent emotions of individuals in Greek good-life-as-practice

A first character is found in the Greek stories that presented everyday life as a practical exemplar. The ancient Greeks presented individuals as gaining pleasure and motivation from doing something good, or of being able to be seduced to do good. Individuals could be seduced by wisdom, goodness and a willingness to take care of friends or fellow citizens. Or, as Petrarch called it, some philosophers even *lusted* after wisdom. The achievement of wisdom was their reward. Although these individuals strived for different forms of the good, their feelings and values were seen as good things because they motivated people to achieve truth and goodness. Feelings and values acted upon these individuals, which meant they did not master their motivations but were instead moved by them. Feelings and people were both active and passive. Such feelings and values also led philosophers of the good life to examine the goodness of their own lives, and to put the lives of others to the test by speaking the truth about them.

The Greek philosophers regarded the good life as a practice rather than as a prescription or doctrine on how one should live. Preaching the good life came *after* examining its practical consequences. One had to put things to the test and undertake things to learn what truth and goodness might entail. Theories about practices of the good life could be formulated in support of such practices, as 'technologies of the self' or as ways to practise one's ethos. The devotion of these philosophers to the task of leading a good and true life made them exemplary characters that others could learn from. They functioned as ideal types of the good life.

There is another character that can be found in these stories. The good philosophers were different from the Athenian citizens who lived vain and often failing lives. These imperfect lives were a prominent topic in discussions about Petrarch's practices. The reader or discussion partner was crucial for making knowledge about everyday life relevant. Failing to reach or move the addressees and to engage them in dialogue invalidated the process of examining everyday life. Good life practices were *relational* practices. Care for the self was also care for others. The conversation partner was also a less than perfect character. The role of the conversation partner is closer to the ordinary lives of people with chronic disease than to exemplary lives of the philosophers. I used the notion of ordinary lives as exemplar, of which concrete lives were examples that showed attempts to live as well as possible while acknowledging that things do not always turn out well.

The necessity, appreciation and goodness of motivations was a way to make everyday-life values central to the lives of Greek philosophers of the good-life-as-practice. In Greek practices of the good life, knowledge about the good life was very much attuned to the practices of everyday life and the examinations that took place therein. Knowledge of the good life entailed a particular mode of speaking the truth and of knowing through dialogue. The good-life-as-practice can be seen as a knowledge practice of its own. And as Foucault argued, it generates knowledge to improve individual lives.

The philosophers of the good-life-as-practice frequently referred to Greek society with its vertical organisation of women, children and slaves in the household, and its citizens who were ruled and sent out to fight in endless wars by their governors or *demos*. Outside the city-states there were foreigners to combat. The philosophers of the good-life-as-practice were linked to the citizenry as their critics, healers and educators. In Greek society, what we would now call 'vagrancy' was possible, as the practices of the Cynics testified. There were different forms of the good life, such as Stoicism, and these were all involved in organising a particular form of sociality. Petrarch explicitly addressed women through his practices of writing letters and engaging in dialogue. In addition to literary writings and poems, accessible forms of writing and speaking about the good life were tied to social and artistic forms for the generation of knowledge about everyday life. Petrarch wrote many sonnets that celebrated courtly yet unattainable love.[34] Petrarch's practice is an example of how the good-life-as-practice is a notion that I could refold with different kinds of sociality. In Petrarch's days, class was a major distinctive demarcation. All these forms of the good life share a connection to truth, goodness and beauty: that is, they are oriented towards practice rather than theory.[35]

Dangerous passions

A different characterisation of individuals is the conceptualisation of the individual that took place during the transition from pre-modernity to modernity. In this period the characterisation of motivations moved away from them being seen as benign and helpful to judge situations towards them being seen as unruly and dangerous passions. The historical background to this transition is the European civil wars of the seventeenth century. These wars were fought, it was argued, because of the desires of noble or religious people and their lust for fame. This resulted in widespread bloodshed, which was seen by social theorists as caused by the derailment of honourability or religious whims. However, republicans of that era believed in an ideal of 'the good life as a practice of going to war'.[36] The amount of bloodshed could not be justified from a modern (or what Foucault calls 'humanist') perspective. Besides warfare, another social setting in which ideas about individuals as driven by passions emerged was the shift from pre-modern feudal societies to new nation states that sought to establish a republic or benevolent monarchy for governing the emancipated citizens.[37] These new nations desired peace in order to conduct trade. New forms of government were sought to replace the reign of courts and nobility.

These soon-to-be modern individuals obtained a universal nature that predisposed them to engaging in certain behaviours rather than being driven or seduced by moral and aesthetic motivations for doing good. The wide variety in individual efforts towards achieving the good were seen in a bad light because this variety was thought to lead to dissensus and war rather than peaceful civilisation. Generalisations for understanding individuals were developed, which often relied on assumptions about natural evolution. These generalisations were thought to be the key to pacifying differences. Individual preferences or passions were increasingly disconnected from the expression of power (the royal court as a theatre) and religion, which were increasingly understood as private matters of taste. These tastes were subsequently tamed by reconceptualising them as drivers of self-interest. This development made the *particular* substances of individual cravings irrelevant. What people valued was translated into 'what drives people' – that is, into a psychological, third-person explanatory category rather than a moral or aesthetic first-person category. As a general force, individual preferences and tastes found there use again, namely as drives that could be channelled by the market and through (rational) governance. Central regulation and trade became exemplars of the social for these psychologically driven subjects. Understanding people as psychological beings was also a result of the new forms of knowledge that were provided by the sciences. These increasingly prevailed over cultural beliefs or rules that were determined by the churches.

Fragile sentiments and stern reason

The advent of modernity brought with it the emergence of the Romantic, sentimental individual (labelled as 'effeminate' by republicans around the time of the French Revolution). Romantic individuals read novels, thought about their inner world and conversed with their intimate circle of friends and family. There were social, semi-public circles where a sensitivity to literature became the most important form of life, such as the salons. The counterpart to the Romantic individual was the thinking human subject who was capable of independent reasoning and emancipation by turning to deliberative procedures to achieve universal rationality or incontestable norms and principles. This private individual could become a public figure and citizen by leaving individual feelings and overly specific motivations at home, as well as by publicly striving for the common good through a 'rational' universal ethics.

The notion of humans as being equal and possessing a general humanity suited these modern characters, and the term equality – for understanding human nature as well as the rights of citizens within the state – became the cornerstone for thinking about a just society – but not for *practising* it. Universal humanity or human nature provided the possibility for creating a state that could unite different interests, and even of finding such a thing as a common good. However, this state did not include women, poor people, slaves, peasants or colonial subjects. Concerns about an imaginary or future nation state linked these 'humans' together, but also the civil wars and fears about strife discussed above.

How to design new forms of government without relying on religion or the dubious capacity of individuals to steer their behaviour in a moral manner? Order and predictability had to be implemented by other means so that a society could be created in which trade could flourish. The emancipating citizens or bourgeoisie, who were often traders, served as the exemplar for individuals that were supposed to become universal humans. The emergence of 'the human' came with a form of strict reasoning that could guide rationality and provide orientation towards the (indeed *the*!) common good. Exactly *what* the new state would look like and how to implement procedures for ensuring its goodness was a matter of concern for these individuals. Social theory had to provide pathways for wealthy traders towards peace and political influence. Early understandings of parliament and the market were the primary social forms that were relevant to these individuals.[38] A particular form of private and sentimental literature, which allowed for the most individual expression of the most individual emotions, was similarly important.

Calculated men

Another character that appeared during this age is the scientific or statistical individual. The statistical individual emerged alongside the budding science of economics (which then still encompassed what only in the beginning of the nineteenth century would come to be known as 'psychology'). Quantitative models were designed to have as few relevant variables as possible. This approach allowed for the testing of models to predict the behaviour of *all* individuals, and hence to make it possible to socially engineer them.[39] The statistical individual is a general individual in the sense that private feelings and preferences are not considered relevant for understanding or explaining this individual. Statistics is all about the characteristics that individuals share to some quantifiable degree.

The aggregation and calculation of individual scores reveals how certain characteristics are divided over a given population, and, much later, how probable effects are determined in the treatment of a majority of patients. To study the latter, a general model of human physiology was assumed necessary. This model was eventually criticised when researchers found that differences in physiology were related to sex or to ethnic background. Subgroup diversity is a problem for generalisations because this suggests that the statistical population needs to be redefined.[40] Large and non-homogeneous populations lead to tendencies 'towards the mean' rather than differentiations.

Another problem is the influence of context, culture and environment. Psychological premises in the field of economics were used to model individuals as a universal entity by drawing on general assumptions about how 'people behave' and how their activities are determined. This was done, presumably, without taking context or situation into account. People all around the globe are assumed to respond in the same way. It is still rarely questioned that knowledge in contemporary psychology is almost exclusively based on experiments with Western psychology students.[41]

The statistical individual is still dominant in many academic traditions, but this concept tells us nothing, even when subgroups are specified, about the contingent values of everyday life and how these are negotiated. Statistics are not very suitable for studying care practices for people with chronic conditions because these practices are too complex (that is, they contain too many variables), too unstable and too specific. Statistical man is mirrored by the 'universal human' in ethics, who, interestingly, hides his own situatedness behind a veil of ignorance in order to assess particular problems.[42] These are exemplars of what I called *modernist* individuals who share certain characteristics and to whom differences in terms of individual morality or aesthetics are distracting, trivial or simply of no use. Statistical man is an amoral or value-free being at heart. In Chapter 10 on quality of life, I showed how the statistical individual – the aggregated, calculated and generalised scores of many individuals – did not provide tools for thinking about the everyday values that are involved with using a feeding tube. These values were 'averaged out', which led to the privileging of the functional body over the sensuous body. Alternatively, measurements of quality of life can result in a general score with an unclear or mystical origin, and they often denote a general idea of 'functioning' that is only retrospectively labelled as pertaining to quality of life. Statistics can measure the prevalence of certain values (or other phenomena), but not their nature, variation of appearance, negotiation, or the patterns in which they emerge. Specification hence always *precedes* quantification because it is necessary to delineate exactly *what* will be counted. In quantitative approaches, sociality is generalisable human nature and this can be practically delineated by selecting particular populations and samples.

The good life reinvented, and reinventing it everyday

A final character is the empirical-theoretical reinvention presented in this book. My analyses of care practices and everyday-life values showed how individuals are the result of their relationships and interactions with the material-semiotic environment. Here, things and values are acting upon individuals, making them both an active as well as a passive entities, which resonates with ancient Greek understandings of motivated individuals that strive for a good and true life. Individuals are presented as leading lives that are always in the making, and this process starts the moment they get up and get dressed. They creatively reshape themselves on a daily basis to achieve a state of worth by negotiating with the conventions of the world they live in. This is certainly a different type of individual than the ones that neoliberalism foregrounds. Individuals become someone by pursuing something good that they hold to be true or appropriate in order to create a state of worth. Individuality or selfhood, then, becomes a value to strive for. It is created in concrete everyday situations. The caregiver can be considered an exemplary character of this particular approach to understanding of individuals.

The good life is not simply the life of an individual. Individuals are connected to others and to practices. They have no voice of their own in or of themselves. Analysing the aesthetic values of everyday life shows that individuals are linked to or disconnected from one another and their environment in very different ways. In particular, I explored how people value situations through their activities, and how they are motivated to work towards achieving states of worth. Even if people do not know each other personally, they can share an appreciation for, say, the difficulties of being a bald woman, for care practices that are oriented towards cleanliness or for the appropriateness of activities such as working or smoking pot.

These connections can fold people together into 'motivated collectives' if these collectives are formed by appreciations, desires or motivations, which can happen through actively articulated passions or through more passive cultural habits and forms of good taste. Such emergent motivated collectives can be (re-)introduced into social theory, and thus their variations and mechanisms can be studied further. Motivated sociality concerns what people like, what makes them happy, and what they find important or convenient to do. These are lives and collectives that emerge through ubiquitous but varied activities of valuing things that people undertake in relation to the problems they encounter on their path. This striving for the good that cannot resolve the bad has taken on a more global dimension in relation to climate change, migration and the exhaustion of natural resources. The lives of people with chronic disease are exemplars for problems that do not go away.

This understanding of the good life conceptualises individual lives not as unique or idiosyncratic but as shaped and connected through shared socialities and environments. The individual as a fleshy historical body might be unique, but this body is folded together with various older or newer socialities and is simultaneously capable of creating new socialities. The exemplar of this messy, underdetermined individual points social theorists towards practices through which social and material traditions overlap and are reinvented. This is a challenge for

> social scientists and philosophers who are interested in understanding different forms of life. These forms are local, social, specific and emerging.
>
> In the everyday life and practices of individuals, striving for or orienting towards something good, beautiful or appropriate turns individuality itself into a value or state of worth that needs to be achieved. On a day-to-day basis individuals recreate and shape who they are, with varying degrees of originality and success. The social nature of contemporary values of everyday life and their embeddedness in conventions marks their link to pre-modern 'philosophies' of the good-life-as-practice. Adam Smith proposed the concept of the impartial spectator which, in late Foucauldian terms, can be considered a technology of the self, namely a practice to become a better or worthier self. These are states of worth that are not about authenticity or inner truth. These states of worth are achieved through generative processes that attempt to create something good: leading a good life as much as possible, caring for others as much as possible, and seeking truth by learning from everyday practice. More often than not, such attempts will fail, and some problems will merely morph into different problems rather than be resolved. But Pierre Hadot's account of the philosophers of the good-life-as-practice shows that giving up is hardly ever an option or even a solution. It is with these methods and concepts that practices for living with chronic disease may be studied, and that knowledge about variations in specific situations may be generated.

To conclude: the good-life-as-practice

This book has combined approaches from material semiotics and care studies to analyse empirical studies of everyday-life values and attempts at doing good. Empirical research on forms of the good can be done in health care but also in other practices that are oriented towards something good.[43] This kind of research entails a shift from a prescriptive normativity towards learning about existing normativities and towards examining how a problem is defined and created through the methods and concepts that make this problem visible as well as how this structures possibilities for acting. Lung-function tests cannot teach about bathrobe tricks even though the latter might be crucial for leading a good life with chronic disease. The epistemological promise of care studies is to provide generative theories for analysing specific situations. This endeavour is helpful for thinking about methods that can include specific subjects in research and thus enable researchers to learn about the goods and bads in the lives of these subjects as well as about the terms and conditions under which very different people can live together.[44] These practices can be analysed as examples of the social phenomenon that one wants to study.

The creativity that is required for living with problems that do not go away was foregrounded by using ethnographic methods. Curative medical discourse is oriented towards curing and solving problems. But this is often not feasible, and scientific medical vocabularies have little to say about caring for patients who cannot be cured but who nonetheless must live with their problems. In Dutch health insurance, there is a trend towards only financing health care that is 'effective' – that is, care that eradicates problems. But what does this imply for care for problems that will not disappear? Will it become impossible to provide care in these instances, or will there be only care of which the goodness cannot be established? These are important questions in times when populations in the Global North are ageing and global health problems continue to emerge. The current emphasis on preventing health issues should not allow policymakers to forget that there are many people with chronic conditions who are forced to lead a life that is as good as possible, even if this life cannot be free from disease or health problems. The discourse on prevention, with its promise of stopping disease from occurring, runs the risk of glossing over this important issue. At some point we will all die, and this will not be from good health. Different forms of research can make the concerns with chronic disease visible.[45]

Ideals, technologies, historical resonances: these all provide ever so many possibilities for renewing the clinical case history by carefully selecting exemplars and using them to link relevant examples. The challenge will be to learn not just about individuals with rare conditions but also about situations with shared characteristics, such as the use of certain technologies, principles, problems, techniques and so on. These situations can be made relevant by choosing interesting exemplars, which can then generate interpretations that will help with understanding the problems we are facing today. The promotion and development of healthcare technologies is one such problem.[46] Another issue is the lack of infrastructure for supporting local care practice in exchanging, discussing and feeding into the situated expertise of caregivers. Such practices serve to support the negotiation of *specific* problems and values in day-to-day care practices. This can only be done by taking the values of everyday life seriously. After all, to care is to create relationships that seek to achieve something good, *here, now*.

Notes

1. See for examples Mol et al., 2010; Moser, 2008; Winance, 2007; 2010; Mol, 2010; Willems, 2010c; Winthereik & Langstrup, 2010; Taylor, 2010; Pols, 2011; 2015; Van Hout et al., 2015.
2. See Boltanski & Thévenot, 2006.
3. Dányi, 2020a, 2020b.
4. It is for these reasons that aesthetic and religious values are protected as individual liberties in liberal states.
5. See also Gomart & Hennion, 1999, for more on this subject.
6. But see Hennion, 2003; DeNora, 2000; and Appiah, 2008.
7. See also the work of Johan Huizinga (2008 [1938]), who proposed the term 'homo ludens' or 'playing man'. And see Meyer, 2009 on aesthetic formations.
8. See Mol, 2006; Moser, 2010.
9. This is also called moral distress: see Jameton, 2013.
10. See Moser, 2010; Mesman et al., 2019, present examples of how specificities may be handled to improve care practices.
11. Note that transparency in terms of methods and concepts is a methodological problem in big data research, because the relationship between data and the ways in which these are constructed becomes invisible.
12. See Pollis et al., 2006.
13. See Pols et al., forthcoming.
14. The term is from Hirschman & Rothschild, 1973.
15. That aesthetic values are formative of socialities and societies also highlights the important role of the arts in helping to shape new forms of living together. A vivid example is post-apartheid South Africa, where a torn country had to deal with its violent past. Art was used to do that, and the committees of truth and reconciliation are examples of new forms designed for re-creating collectivities (Buikema, 2020). See also Nauta (1987) for relationships between culture and Culture.
16. See Pols & Moser, 2009.
17. RVS, 2021.
18. Banks, 2020; Banks & Brydon Miller, 2018; Banks et al., 2013; Brodwin, 2013; Pols 2023.
19. Piras & Miele, 2017, describe how this works out in diabetes care.
20. Pols, 2015.
21. Pols, 2015.
22. Some nuance is in order here. Diseases and handicaps may not always be bad. Deaf people stress that they live a good live in 'deaf culture'. People who are blind have other senses that are enhanced. Experiences with illness may make people realise what they value in life or make doctors understand what their patients are going through. The goodness of something that is bad deserves careful further study.
23. But see Pols, forthcoming, b, for some general contours.
24. It is for this reason that philosopher Lolle Nauta coined the term 'exemplary situation', in his lectures from 1987, to indicate a situation that is inscribed in seemingly abstract theory. See Mol, 2000, for an explanation in Dutch, and Mol, 2021, for an English one.

    Lolle Nauta was, by the way, and without ever claiming such a title himself, an exemplary contemporary philosopher of the good-life-as-practice. He hardly ever wrote in English (which is the *lingua franca* in Dutch academia today) but taught formidable classes on social philosophy, usually by starting with a single sentence, such as, for instance, 'Aufklärung ist der Austritt des Menschen aus seiner selbstverschuldeten Unmündigkeit.' (Kant, 1996) and then lecturing about its meaning in the two following hours. He demonstrated to his students what attitudes and techniques he deemed appropriate for practicing a philosophical life by enacting them: trust, curiosity, precision, healthy scepticism of 'great philosophers' (as well as himself), which should be argued with rather than slavishly followed, and upholding equality between conversation partners by only focusing on the argument. I also fondly remember him not wearing the black robe (toga) during academic celebrations and events because he did not want to present himself as being of a 'higher rank' than anybody else. Such acts of 'aesthetic subversiveness' are now rarely seen in academia.

25 Linking situations in a certain ways highlights some things and not others. Hence, the meaning of a situation shifts when juxtaposed with one exemplar or another. This method affects what object can be made. See, for a practical way of doing this, Vogel, 2021.
26 In the analysis of qualitative materials the question is often, 'Why is this particular fragment relevant or interesting to me?' This demonstrates again how research questions inform the way in which exemplars are selected. It also shows that, contrary to students' hopes, categories do not simply 'emerge' from the material, and that these do not require the 'application of theory' or emerge from the stroke of genius ('abduction'). Linking specific situations with each other is hard work, but it can be done by experimenting with and further developing the particular exemplar that allows for the most interesting reading of the material. Concerns about 'coding' one's material are therefore not a matter of doing this 'reliably' but of doing this in a way that generates a useful, responsible and truthful understanding of specific situations.
27 The notion of 'modes of ordering' is helpful here (Moser, 2005; Pols, 2006b). Modes of ordering form the coherences that come together in 'messy' practices (Law, 2004). See also Pols et al. 2019.
28 See for this point Pols, 2003.
29 Remember that an 'open concept' makes it possible to empirically study the possible coherences that are folded into that concept.
30 Pols et al., 2019.
31 See also De Laet, 2017, and Vogel, 2017.
32 Or sets of coherences, such as seen with the concept of dignity that is embedded in different theories.
33 Among other things, this erases the informal economy of unpaid labour and care. See Folbre, 2009.
34 Marriage was a formal and practical affair, and sexual adventures were not seen as relating to love. Hence the character of the distant and unattainable lover. See Verstegen, 2021.
35 Hadot, 2004.
36 Wars certainly set a stage for displaying the courage of leading characters, even if these sent innumerable 'ordinary people' to their death. This became problematic during the emancipation of traders (and hence non-nobility) and the emergence of early forms of humanism.
37 There are many discussions about the pros and cons of the monarchy (for Hobbes only a single person could guarantee the unity of a country) and the value of safe spaces where dissensus was allowed, for instance in experimental science. See Shapin & Schaffer, 1985.
38 See Nauta, 1984.
39 For readers who desire theories about discipline and governance, see Burchel et al. 1991; Lemke 2015, on the use of statistics by governments.
40 See for instance M'charek, 2005.
41 But there is discussion about this in social psychology. See for example Gergen, 2015; Derksen, 2019.
42 The veil is from Rawls, 1971.
43 See for, instance, our research on 'good science' (Pols et al., forthcoming), which describes how scientists are oriented towards accomplishing good science, what their values are and how these may be problematic in practice.
44 See Pols, 2008 on relational citizenship.
45 See Cohn, 2014.
46 The promotion of technologies in health care is one area where words are not specific enough. The term 'technology' in policy discourse is used to refer to any technology, as if all technologies have the same goal and the same effect. What is missing here is detailed observations that examine how technologies are handled in practice as well as what problems they address and what values they achieve, and then to ask if these are desirable. The development of health technologies is a big industry where lots of money goes around, but where answers to emerging health care problems will not be found if critical studies are not conducted. This is but one example of how studies of specific practices can be informed by studies of other specific practices. See Pols, 2012.

Acknowledgements: a letter to Laura, who will be born soon

Thank you!

I write this Petrarchan letter to you to tell you that I have finished writing the book! I suppose that by the time you finish reading it, you will have become immersed in relational understandings of people and things. The metaphor of friendship was used several times to characterise the relationship between philosophers of the good-life-as-practice and their audience. Although I did not elaborate much on the notion of friendship and its many forms, it was clear that friendship has aesthetic connotations of sweetness, courage and honesty, and that it describes the quality of a relationship that was cherished by the philosophers of the good-life-as-practice. For Petrarch, friendship was both the subject and object in the search for wisdom. Friends are capable of telling each other things that are true, even if doing this is sometimes difficult. But friends are also the imagined receivers of Petrarchan wisdom. Without readers his work would have been useless.

I have also learned that friendship is an ethical relationship. Friends are there to help their friends. Without friends we would not be able to go on adventures, think up and try out new ideas, and listen to or tell stories that are true, good, and maybe even beautiful. Kristine and I always try our best to create a friendly environment for our students, because we both think this is the best way to learn things. Would you not say that finding the bad in the good, and maybe also the good in the bad, can best be done through an open and friendly exchange, one that creates space for things that are difficult to tell? All too clear or overly critical standpoints do not encourage agile and imaginative thinking.

Kristine Krause

But Laura, the reason I write to you with a heart full of the sweetness of friendship is that I want to describe to you the practical ways in which I wrote this book. Looking at the practice of writing reveals all these friends, including those who will never read this book! At the same time, I discovered that this notion can stretch across many different relationships that I had never considered as friendships before!

Collecting and ordering

The book as a project started in 2018, when it was nothing more than a set of ideas that refused to come together in a coherent manner. That the theorisation of aesthetic values would play a role in this book was clear, but it long remained opaque how exactly this would be the case as well as how aesthetic values might relate to care practices and forms of everyday life that stubbornly refuse to be characterised as heroic. I tortured dear Amade with numerous outlines that never stuck.

Amade M'charek

The process of assembling, ordering and removing passages and chapters, changing them once again, making lists of new ingredients, and then shuffling for a final time, came to a temporary end when I arrived at the Ca' Foscari University in Venice in April 2019 on a scholarship. I had just recovered from a debilitating concussion and was full of energy to kickstart my life again and see if I could do it all over: organising everyday life.

Barbara da Roit

Taking one's time

My first friend in Venice was time. Time is the necessary companion of the writer of books. Time was kind and generous to the author. It is a scarce resource in contemporary academia, at least in the Netherlands. My scholarship in Venice provided me with seemingly limitless clock and calendar time. I got up at 6.00 or so and started my day by greeting the city and the 20 or so churches I could see from my roof terrace. Then to my desk with just my computer, books, papers and a cup of tea as companions. This was rare and exciting, delicious and intimate, adventurous as well as monotonous. Petrarch again: solitude is the necessary condition for engaging in conversation with one's friends.

Time and friendship I also found at the Socrates Foundation. You will remember that I held the chair named 'social theory, humanism and materialities' at the behest of this foundation. My hope is that my book will feed into discussions about humanism and humanist theory, but maybe most of all, that it will contribute to discussions on contemporary humanist practices. I fondly remember the discussions I had with the other Socrates professors as well as representatives of the Humanistisch Verbond that hosts the Socrates Foundation. I do believe that the work on the good life-as-practice by early humanists can provide us with inspiration for the future, particularly at a time when 'Enlightenment humanism' or humanism as a secular religion is losing its appeal among young people. Friendship can be a great basis for humanist activities, as the early humanists such as Petrarch showed so clearly and incisively.

Stichting Socrates, its board, and the Socrates professors:
Yolande Jansen, Cor van der Weele, Erik Rietveld, Lieteke van Vucht-Tijssen, Heleen Pott, Neelke Doorn, Maureen Sie, Marc Davidson, Harro van Lente

Inspiration

Next to time, beauty was my second friend in Venice. Venice is probably the most beautiful city in the world, filled with art of all times, from its narrow, winding and disorienting alleys to its bridges, stairs and tangle of canals. It was sometimes too much. Art is found in Venice's innumerable churches and imposing palazzi as well as on its scattered islands and inside the humblest of chapels. I could not have wished for a more inspiring environment to write in, alternating between working on a chapter and exploring the city, discovering its art and history, alone or in the company of friends. I am grateful to the Italian sociology team for hosting me without swamping me in work, which is a rare gift. I am grateful to my fellow students in the language course for their company. While the writing distracted me from too much art, I had visitors who distracted me from too

Irma Roose and Robert Jan Both, Gaby Berken Mersmann, Lon Goedewagen and Marjo Smit, Ingrid Geesink, Frank Pols and Robert Wurzer and their friends from Munich

Piëtro Girardi for teaching me my very

much writing. They joined me on my journey through the treasures of Venice, its Biennale and the tastes of the Italian cuisine; everything we ate was truly delicious!

First readers

But Laura, the most precious friends while writing a book are one's first readers and responders. Stern and dazzlingly lucid, Anne and Ariane commanded me to drastically change the order of the chapters I had crafted while in Venice. They pointed out that, even though I argue against the idea that 'theory comes first', I had ordered the chapters of the book just like that: by starting with the theory and having the empirical chapters follow after. They urged me to 'practise what I preached', just as the philosophers of the good-life-as-a-practice would have done! I dedicate the book to them.

Living with chronic disease

But Laura, something else happened too that I cannot so easily connect to friendship. The Covid-19 pandemic, its lockdowns, the facemasks and all sorts of social restrictions made their mark while I was writing this book. In early 2020 my lungs were infected, but only in January 2021 did the doctor send me home to recover from 'long Covid'. I now had a chronic disease myself! Looking back, I would say that I have been to hell and back, tortured by my own body, which seemed to think that it needed to get rid of itself rather than of some virus living within it. Like so many others, at first I could not work more than half an hour each day. But this precious half hour I spent on rewriting and polishing up the book. I tried, oh irony, to live a better life with this disease.

Although nobody knew exactly what the virus had done to us, many people helped me to learn how to live with the effects that I was experiencing. I learned so much from these 'professional friends' who have left such a big mark on my life. I think that many of them, in one way or another, also

first jazz piano lessons in Venice!

Annekatrin Skeide and Ariane d'Hoop

Thanks to all the caregivers and patients who have participated in my research!

Tamara Weis, Vincent Komen, Ab Dijkman,

suggested that I had to become friends with, or at least a bit more friendly towards, my tortured and torturing body as well as my derailed life. I am not so sure if I managed to follow this advice well, but I certainly learned a thing or two about the simultaneous presence of good and bad things in one's life as well as the necessity of having to deal with problems that do not go away. My friends who also happened to be doctors helped me to reason about what was going on through this disease unknown, and helped me to consider what to do.	Debbie Schreuder, and Antje Stapert HanneLore Modderkolk, Annemarie Mol

More arts

One particularly deep yet complex friendship that supported me in these days of illness, lockdown and minimal writing is with a very particular object and the worlds it represents, namely that of the piano and music. I started learning how to play the piano only a couple of years ago. My passion for its sounds came into full swing when I started to learn jazz piano. I am immensely grateful to my piano teacher, a most awesome piano player and composer, who has made this adventure possible. Writing can be exhausting and overly ambitious, but early morning dialogues with the piano are as unassuming as they are spectacularly comforting. Engaging with playing music has taught me a thing or two about the question 'how to live', or why this could be a question.	My piano, inherited from 'tante An'. Philipp Rüttgers

More readers!

Then there was the second round of friends and readers who served as guinea pigs for this book. They did not demand reorderings. They critically read the second draft and helped me dot the Is and cross the Ts. I was delighted as well as humbled by their inspiration and enthusiasm, and I tremendously enjoyed the sheer pleasure of thinking, discussing and hanging out together!	Kristine Krause, Annelieke Driessen, Sonja Jerak-Zuiderent, Dick Willems, Myrthe Lenselink, Suzanne Metselaar, Christine Ceci, Holly Symonds, Harkeert Judge, and again Ariane and Annekatrin

Language

But my language editor was less pleased with my conversational and informal 'Dutchy' English. He was used to more formal language in academic writing, where author and readers are put at more of a distance from one another. Our different approaches juxtaposed an epistemology of distanced reasoning with Petrarch's notion of friendship. I feel that our collaboration resulted in the befriending of the best of both worlds in order to find the most fitting tone. It is another great example of how 'voice' is not something that is 'liberated' by taking away obstacles but instead co-shaped through mutual relationships and techniques.

Chris Hesselbein

The first and the last words

I got help with the stylistic experiments that form the preface of the book and these last words. One of the reviewers of the manuscript wished to hear more about the life history and positioning of the author and the questions that led to the emergence of this book. They even suggested that these reflections would be written in the form of a letter! These experiments were certainly the most difficult parts to write. Yet another thing was the title. What you read first was created last: a generous gift from Annemarie.

Anne, Ariane and Ruth Benschop

The anonymous reviewers

Annemarie Mol

Dedicated friendship

But Laura, my long-time companion in life was my most dedicated friend. Bertus has dragged me through two very long periods of illness in these last six years, always matter of fact, generous with his support and cheer, always with great humour, and always minding the cats and cooking the meals for whoever happens to pass by. He did all this while also helping the penniless and speechless people who are trapped by the Dutch bureaucracy. If I had not written this Big Book to argue that it is not particularly fruitful to

Bertus Eskes

approach everyday lives as exemplary lives, I would have to nominate him for 'being a good person'.

Awesome colleagues and family members

I could never have functioned as a researcher without the support of many great colleagues: Muriël Kiesel, Leonie Dronkert, Maja de Langen, Clément Dréano, Annemarie van Hout, Anja Hiddinga, Christien Muusse, Bram Gootjes, Bagas Wicaksono, Kurt Cassar, Ellen Algera, Tanja Ahlin, Ildikó Plájás, Natashe Lemos-Dekker, Roos Buikema, Brit Ross Winthereik, Dixi Strand, Estrid Sörensen, Juan Carlos Aceros, Daniël López, Miquel Domenech, Mary Ellen Purkis, Kristin Björnsdottir, Janelle Taylor, Mette Nordahl Svendsen, Henriette Langstrup, Griet Roets, Helen Kohlen, Maartje Hoogsteyns, Lisette de Jong, Jonna Brenninkmeijer, Stephanie Meirmans, Maarten Derksen, Marieke Bak, Ben de Bock, Maartje Schermer, Kasper Kruithof, Marga Nieuwenhuizen, Danny de Vries, Bregje de Kok, Oskar Verkaaik, Annette Kamp, Yolande Voskes, Mariëtte van den Hoven, Bert Molewijk, Petra Verdonk, Christine Dedding, Niels Mulder, Hans Kroon, Kasturi Sen, Laura Hartman, Hanna Horvath, Trudie Gerrits, my RVS colleagues, and my family Jan, Ruud, Hans and Steph, Frank and Robert, Auke, Marijke, Leendert and Thijmen.

Farewell!

Sources used in the book

Chapter 3 builds on analyses made in:
1. Pols, J. (2013) Through the looking glass. Good looks and dignity in care. *Medicine, Health Care and Philosophy*. DOI 10.1007/s11019-013-9483-3.
2. Pols, J. (2013) Washing the patient. Dignity and aesthetic values in nursing care. *Nursing Philosophy*. https://doi.org/10.1111/nup.12014.
3. Pols, J., Pasveer, B., & Willems, D. (2018). The particularity of dignity: relational engagement in care at the end of life. *Medicine, Health Care and Philosophy*, 21(1), 89–100. https://doi.org/10.1007/s11019-017-9787-9.

Chapter 5 is based on analyses made in:
Pols, A. J., Althoff, B., & Bransen, E. (2017) The limits of autonomy: Ideals in care for people with learning disabilities. *Medical Anthropology*, 36(8), 772–85. DOI 10.1080/01459740.2017.1367776.

Chapter 7 develops the analysis made in:
Pols, J. (2013) Through the looking glass: Good looks and dignity in care. *Medicine, Health Care and Philosophy*. DOI 10.1007/s11019-013-9483-3.

Chapter 10 develops the analyses made in:
1. Pols, J. & Limburg, S. (2015) A matter of taste? Quality of life in day-to-day living with ALS and a feeding tube. *Culture, Medicine and Psychiatry*, 40(3). https://doi.org/10.1007/s11013-015-9479-y.
2. Pols, J. (2019) The quality of time and its quantifications: Negotiations about the feeding tube at the end of life. *European Journal for Nursing History and Ethics 1*, 87–105, https://www.enhe.eu/archive/2019/4839.

References

Abrahamsson, S., Bertoni, F., Mol, A., & Martín, R. I. (2015). Living with omega-3: New materialism and enduring concerns. *Environment and Planning D: Society and Space, 33*(1), 4–19.

Adler, P. A., Adler, P., & Fontana, A. (1987). Everyday life sociology. *Annual Review of Sociology, 13*(1), 217–23.

Ahlin, T., & Li, F. (2019). From field sites to field events: Creating the field with information and communication technologies (ICTs). *Medicine Anthropology Theory, 6*, 1–24.

Albrecht, G. L., & DeVlieger, P. J. (1999). The disability paradox: High quality of life against all odds. *Social Science & Medicine, 48*(8), 977–88.

Alenichev, A. (2020). Ethics and etiquette in an emergency vaccine trial: The orchestration of compliance. *Global Bioethics, 31*(1), 13–28.

Althoff, B. (2014). *Spelen verboden? Een zoektocht naar de balans tussen zorg en autonomie in de ambulante zorg voor volwassen clienten met een licht verstandelijke beperking die alcohol en/of drugs gebruiken* [Master's thesis, University of Amsterdam].

Angus, F., & Burakoff, R. (2003). The percutaneous endoscopic gastrostomy tube: Medical and ethical issues in placement. *American Journal of gastroenterology, 98*(2), 272–7.

Aparanji, K. P., & Dharmarajan, T. (2010). Pause before a PEG: A feeding tube may not be necessary in every candidate! *Journal of the American Medical Directors Association, 11*(6), 453–456.

Appiah, K. A. (2008). *Experiments in Ethics*. Harvard University Press.

Appiah, K. A. (2010). *The Honor Code: How moral revolutions happen*. Norton.

Arendt, H. (1958). *The Human Condition*. Chicago: University of Chicago Press.

Back, L. (2015). Why everyday life matters: Class, community and making life livable. *Sociology, 49*(5), 820–36.

Balestroni, G., & Bertolotti, G. (2012). EuroQol-5D (EQ-5D): An instrument for measuring quality of life. *Monaldi Archives for Chest Disease, 78*(3).

Ballestero, A., & Winthereik, B. R. (Eds.). (2021). *Experimenting with Ethnography: A companion to analysis*. Duke University Press.

Banks, S. (2016). Everyday ethics in professional life: Social work as ethics work. *Ethics and Social Welfare, 10*(1), 35–52.

Banks, S. (2020). *Ethics and Values in Social Work*. Bloomsbury.

Banks, S., Armstrong, A., Carter, K., Graham, H., Hayward, P., Henry, A., & Strachan, A. (2013). Everyday ethics in community-based participatory research. *Contemporary Social Science, 8*(3), 263–77.

Banks, S., & Brydon-Miller, M. (Eds.). (2018). *Ethics in Participatory Research for Health and Social Well-being: Cases and commentaries*. Routledge.

Barilan, Y. M. (2012). *Human Dignity, Human Rights, and Responsibility: The new language of global bioethics and biolaw*. MIT Press.

Barry, A. (2002). Reporting and visualising. In C. Jenks (Ed.), *Visual Culture* (pp. 43–57). Routledge.

Bartlett, R., & O'Connor, D. (2007). From personhood to citizenship: Broadening the lens for dementia practice and research. *Journal of Aging Studies, 21*, 107–18.

Beauchamp, T. L., & Childress, J. F. (2001). *Principles of Biomedical Ethics* (5th ed.). Oxford University Press.

Benatar, S. R. (2001). Distributive justice and clinical trials in the Third World. *Theoretical Medicine, 22*, 169–76.

Berg, M., & Mol, A. (Eds.) (1998). *Differences in Medicine: Unraveling practices, techniques and bodies*. Duke University Press.

Berlin, I. (1958). *Two Concepts of Liberty: An inaugural lecture delivered before the University of Oxford on 31 October 1958*. Clarendon Press.
Bernardo, A. S. (Trans.) (2005). *Francesco Petrarca: Letters on familiar matters* (Vols 1-3). Italica Press.
Berry, M. J., Argüelles, C. C., Cordis, S., Ihmoud, S., & Estrada, E. V. (2017). Toward a fugitive anthropology: Gender, race, and violence in the field. *Cultural Anthropology, 32*(4), 537-65.
Bijsterveld, K. T. (1995). *Geen kwestie van leeftijd: Verzorgingsstaat, wetenschap en discussies rond ouderen in Nederland, 1945-1982*. Van Gennep.
Blumer, H. (1954). What is wrong with social theory? *American Sociological Review, 18*, 3-10.
Boltanski, L., & Thévenot, L. (1999). The sociology of critical capacity. *European Journal of Social Theory, 2*(3), 359-77.
Boltanski, L., & Thévenot, L. (2006). *On Justification: Economies of worth*. Princeton University Press.
Bonelli, C. (2012). Ontological disorders: Nightmares, psychotropic drugs and evil spirits in southern Chile. *Anthropological Theory, 12*(4), 407-26.
Boschma, G. (1997). *Creating nursing care for the mentally ill: Mental health nursing in Dutch asylums, 1890-1920*. University of Pennsylvania Press.
Bourdieu, P. (1977). *Outline of a Theory of Practice* (Trans. Richard Nice). Cambridge University Press.
Bourdieu, P. (1984). *Distinction: A social critique of the judgement of taste* (Trans. Richard Nice). Harvard University Press.
Brandt, A. M. (1978). Racism and Research: The case of the Tuskegee syphilis study. *Hastings Center Report, 8*(6), 21-9.
Bransen, E., Althoff, B., & Pols, J. (2015). *Waar bemoei ik me mee? Handreiking voor begeleiders van mensen met een lichte verstandelijke beperking die alcohol of drugs gebruiken*. Trimbos-instituut.
Brodwin, P. (2013). *Everyday Ethics: Voices from the front line of community psychiatry*. University of California Press.
Buikema, R. (2020). *Revolts in Cultural Critique*. Rowman & Littlefield International.
Burchell, G., Godon, C. & Miller, P. (1991). *The Foucault Effect: Studies in governmentality*. University of Chicago Press.
Buse, C., & Twigg, J. (2018). Dressing disrupted: Negotiating care through the materiality of dress in the context of dementia. *Sociology of Health & Illness, 40*(2), 340-52.
Butler, J. (2012). Can one lead a good life in a bad life? Adorno Prize Lecture. *Radical Philosophy, 176*.
Butler, J. (2015). *Notes toward a Performative Theory of Assembly*. Harvard University Press.
Byers, P. (2016). Dependence and a Kantian conception of dignity as a value. *Theoretical Medicine and Bioethics, 37*(1), 61-9.
Callon, M., & Rabeharisoa, V. (2002). The involvement of patients' associations in research. *International Social Science Journal, 54*(171), 57-65.
Callon, M., & Rabeharisoa, V. (2003). Research 'in the wild' and the shaping of new social identities. *Technology in Society: Studies in Science, Technology, and Society (STS) North and South, 25*(2), 193-204.
Callon, M., & Rabeharisoa, V. (2008). The growing engagement of emergent concerned groups in political and economic life: Lessons from the French Association of Neuromuscular Disease Patients. *Science, Technology, & Human Values, 33*(2), 230-61.
Canguilhem, G. (1989). *On the Normal and the Pathological*. Zone Books.
Carey, A. C. (2009). *On the Margins of Citizenship: Intellectual disability and civil rights in twentieth-century America*. Temple University Press.
Carr, A. J., & Higginson, I. J. (2001). Measuring quality of life: Are quality of life measures patient centred? *British Medical Journal, 322*(7298), 1357.
Carreras, N., & Winthereik, B. R. (forthcoming). Making ethnographic comics with alt-narratives as collective forms of analysis.
Carr-Hill, R. A. (1991). Allocating resources to health care: Is the QALY (Quality Adjusted Life Year) a technical solution to a political problem? *International Journal of Health Services, 21*(2), 351-63.
Cato (2016). Dokter, én patiënt. https://www.kanker.nl/ervaringen-van-anderen/blogs/dokter-en-patient (accessed 21 July 2023).

Ceci, C., Pols, J., & Purkis, M. E. (2017). Privileging practices: Manifesto for 'new nursing studies'. In T. Foth, D. Holmes, M. Hülsken-Giessler, S. Kreutzer, & H. Remmers (Eds.), *Critical Approaches in Nursing Theory and Nursing Research: Implications for nursing practice* (pp. 51–68). V&R unipress.

Ceci, C., & Purkis, M. E. (2021). *Care at Home for People Living with Dementia: Delaying institutionalization, sustaining families*. Bristol University Press.

Chochinov, H. M., Hack, T., Hassard, T., Kristjanson, L. J., McClement, S., & Harlos, M. (2002). Dignity in the terminally ill: A cross-sectional, cohort study. *The Lancet*, *360*(9350), 2026–30.

Clarke, J., & Wilson, D. (1999). Alcohol problems and intellectual disability. *Journal of Intellectual Disability Research*, *43*(2), 135–9.

Cleeve, H. (2023). Drawing in ethnography: Seeing and unseeing everyday life with dementia. *Medical Anthropology*.

Clifford, J. & Marcus, G. E. (Eds.) (2010). *Writing Culture: The poetics and politics of ethnography*. University of California Press.

Clifford, J. (1996). Anthropology and/as travel. *Etnofoor*, *9*(2), 5–15.

Cohn, S. (2008). Making objective facts from intimate relations: The case of neuroscience and its entanglements with volunteers. *History of the Human Sciences*, *21*(4), 86–103.

Cohn, S. (2014). From health behaviours to health practices: An introduction. *Sociology of Health & Illness*, *36*(2), 157–62.

Cooley, D. R. (2001a). Distributive justice and clinical trials in the Third World. *Theoretical Medicine*, *22*, 151–67.

Cubellis, L., and Lester, R. (Eds.). (forthcoming). *Traces of Care: Discernment and the work of recognition*. Duke University Press.

Derksen, M., & Morawski, J. (2022). Kinds of replication: Examining the meanings of 'conceptual replication' and 'direct replication'. *Perspectives on Psychological Science*, *17*(5), 1490–1505.

d'Hoop, A. (2021a). On the Potentialities of Spaces of Care: Openness, Enticement, and Variability in a Psychiatric Center. *Science, Technology, & Human Values*, *46*(3), 577–599.

d'Hoop, A. (2021b). 'Making buildings hospitable with swifts'. In *Winged Geographies: Birds in space and imagination*. https://dial.uclouvain.be/pr/boreal/object/boreal:238707.

d'Hoop, A. (2023). *The Slightest Attachment: When psychiatric spaces enact affinities*. transcript Verlag.

d'Hoop, A., & Pols, J. (2022). 'The game is on!' Eventness at a distance at a livestream concert during lockdown. *Ethnography*. https://doi.org/10.1177/14661381221124502.

Dancy, J. (2017). Moral particularism. *Stanford Encyclopedia of Philosophy* (winter 2017 Edition). https://plato.stanford.edu/archives/win2017/entries/moral-particularism (accessed 21 July 2023).

Danholt, P., & Langstrup, H. (2012). Medication as infrastructure: Decentring self-care. *Culture Unbound: Journal of Current Cultural Research*, *4*(3), 513–32.

Dányi, E. (2020a). The insides and outsides of parliamentary politics. *Social Studies of Science*, *50*(2), 245–51.

Dányi, E. (2020b). Búskomor politics: Practising critique in the ruins of liberal democracy. *Sociological Review*, *68*(2), 356–68.

Daston, L., & Galison, P. (2007). *Objectivity*. Zone Books.

De Certeau, M. (2011). *The Practice of Everyday Life*. University of California Press.

De Koning, M., Meyer, B., Moors, A., & Pels, P. (2019). Guidelines for anthropological research: Data management, ethics, and integrity. *Ethnography*, *20*(2), 170–4.

de la Bellacasa, M. P. (2011). Matters of care in technoscience: Assembling neglected things. *Social Studies of Science*, *41*(1), 85–106.

de la Bellacasa, M. P. (2017). *Matters of Care: Speculative ethics in more than human worlds*. University of Minnesota Press.

De la Cadena, M. (2015). *Earth Beings: Ecologies of practice across Andean worlds*. Duke University Press.

De Laet, M. (2017). Personal metrics: Methodological considerations of a praxiographical approach. In M. Jonas, Littig, B., & Wroblewski, A. (Eds.), *Methodological Reflections on Practice Oriented Theories* (pp. 107–23). Springer.

De Laet, M., Driessen, A., & Vogel, E. (2021). Thinking with attachments: Appreciating a generative analytic. *Social Studies of Science*, *51*(6), 799–819.

De Langen, M. (forthcoming). Giving into the field: Non-research roles in an ethnography of Aboriginal Australian diabetes care.

Dehue, T. (1995). *Changing the Rules: Psychology in the Netherlands 1900–1985*. Cambridge University Press.
Dehue, T. (2001). Establishing the experimenting society: The historical origin of social experimentation according to the randomized controlled design. *American Journal of Psychology, 114*(2), 283.
Dehue, T. (2002). A Dutch treat: Randomized controlled experimentation and the case of heroin-maintenance in the Netherlands. *History of the Human Sciences, 15*(2), 75–98.
Dekkers, W. (1999). The lived body as aesthetic object in anthropological medicine. *Medicine, Health Care and Philosophy, 2*(2), 117–28.
DeNora, T. (2000). *Music in Everyday Life*. Cambridge University Press.
Depla, M. F., Pols, J., de Lange, J., Smits, C. H., de Graaf, R., & Heeren, T. J. (2003). Integrating mental health care into residential homes for the elderly: An analysis of six Dutch programs for older people with severe and persistent mental illness. *Journal of the American Geriatric Society, 51*(9), 1275–9.
Derksen, M. (2019). Putting Popper to work. *Theory & Psychology, 29*(4), 449–65.
Despret, V. (2006). Sheep do have opinions. In B. Latour and P. Weibel (Eds.), *Making Things Public: Atmospheres of democracy* (pp. 360–70). MIT Press.
Despret, V. (2015). Thinking like a rat. *Angelaki, 20*(2), 121–34.
Diederichs, M. (2005). Stigma and silence: Dutch women, German soldiers and their children. In K. Ericsson & E. Simonsen (Eds.), *Children of World War II: The hidden enemy legacy* (pp. 151–64). Berg.
Dilger, H., Pels, P., & Sleeboom-Faulkner, M. (2019). Guidelines for data management and scientific integrity in ethnography. *Ethnography, 20*(1), 3–7.
Dohmen, J. (2003). Philosophers on the 'art-of-living'. *Journal of Happiness Studies, 4*(4), 351–71.
Draaisma, D. (1992) (Ed.). Special issue on Serres. *Kennis en Methode, 3*.
Draaisma, D. (2000). *Metaphors of Memory: A history of ideas about the mind*. Cambridge University Press.
Dréano, C. (forthcoming). Exploring complexities in care through cooking.
Driessen, A. (2018a). Pleasure and dementia: On becoming an appreciating subject. *Cambridge Journal of Anthropology, 36*(1), 23–39.
Driessen, A. (2018b). Sociomaterial will-work: Aligning daily wanting in Dutch dementia care. In F. Krause & J. Boldt (Eds.), *Care in Healthcare: Reflections on theory and practice* (pp. 111–33). Palgrave Macmillan.
Driessen, A. E. (2019). *A Good Life with Dementia: Ethnographic articulations of everyday life and care in Dutch nursing homes* [PhD thesis, University of Amsterdam].
Driessen, A. (2023). Articulating interesting subject positions for people with dementia: On hanging out in nursing homes. *Medical Anthropology*.
Dronkert, L. (2018). *Access Denied: How diagnostic categories work in negotiating care for people with learning disability* [Grant proposal].
Dronkert, L. (2023). Cripped collaborations: Science fiction and the access to disability worlds. *Medical Anthropology*.
Dussauge, I., Helgesson, C.-F., & Lee, F. (2015). *Value Practices in the Life Sciences and Medicine*. Oxford University Press.
Düwell, M. (1999). Aesthetic experience, medical practice, and moral judgement: Critical remarks on possibilities to understand a complex relationship. *Medicine, Health Care and Philosophy, 2*(2), 161–8.
Edgar, A. (2004). A response to Nordenfelt's 'The varieties of dignity'. *Health Care Analysis, 12*(2), 83–9.
Ehn, B., Löfgren, O., & Wilk, R. (2015). *Exploring Everyday Life: Strategies for ethnography and cultural analysis*. Rowman & Littlefield.
Elias, N. (1978). *The Civilizing Process: Sociogenetic and psychogenetic investigations* (Trans. E. Jephcott). Blackwell.
Emanuel, E., & Emanuel, L. (1992). Four models of the physician-patient relationship. *Journal of the American Medical Association, 267*, 2221–6.
Epstein, S. (1996). *Impure Science: Aids, activism and the politics of knowledge*. University of California Press.
Epstein, S. (2008). Patient groups and health movements. In *The Handbook of Science and Technology Studies*, edited by E. J. Hacket et al. (pp. 499–539). MIT Press.

Eton, D. T. (2010). Why we need response shift: An appeal to functionalism. *Quality of Life Research*, 19(6), 929–30.
Fassin, D. (2014). *A Companion to Moral Anthropology*. Wiley.
Faubion, J. D., & Marcus, G. E. (2009). *Fieldwork Is Not What It Used to Be: Learning anthropology's method in a time of transition*. Cornell University Press.
Faubion, J. D., & Rabinow, P. (2000). *Aesthetics, Method, and Epistemology*. Penguin Books.
Flynn, E., & Arstein-Kerslake, A. (2014). Legislating personhood: Realising the right to support in exercising legal capacity. *International Journal of Law in Context*, 10(1), 81–104.
Folbre, N. (2009). *Greed, Lust and Gender: A history of economic ideas*. Oxford University Press.
Fortun, K., Fortun, M., Bigras, E., Saheb, T., Costelloe-Kuehn, B., Crowder, J., ... & Kenner, A. (2014). Experimental ethnography online: The asthma files. *Cultural Studies*, 28(4), 632–42.
Foucault, M. (1972). *The Archaeology of Knowledge*. Tavistock Publications.
Foucault, M. (1975). *The Birth of the Clinic: An archaeology of medical perception*. Vintage Books.
Foucault, M. (1978). *The History of Sexuality*. Pantheon Books.
Foucault, M. (1983). *Discourse and Truth: The problematization of parrhesia*. University of California.
Foucault, M. (1986). *The Care of the Self: The history of sexuality 3* (Trans. Robert Hurley). Pantheon. Books.
Foucault, M. (2011). *The Courage of the Truth (The Government of Self and Others): Lectures at the Collège de France, 1983–1984*. Picador.
Foucault, M., (2000). *Ethics, Subjectivity and Truth: The essential works of Michael Foucault, 1954–1984* (Ed. Paul Rabinow). Penguin Classics.
Fox Keller, E. (2000). *The Century of the Gene*. Harvard University Press.
Frederiks, B., van Hooren, R. H., & Moonen, X. (2009). Nieuwe kansen voor het burgerschapsparadigma: een pedagogische, ethische en juridische beschouwing. *NTZ*, 35(1), 3–30.
Frost-Hartwig, C. (2022). 'A noble act: Care and belonging through shared moral experience in an island community'. Unpublished thesis, Copenhagen University.
Gabriela Arguedas, R., & Lynn, M. M. (2017). The reproductive rights counteroffensive in Mexico and Central America. *Feminist Studies*, 43(2), 423–37.
Gallagher, A. (2004). Dignity and respect for dignity – two key health professional values: Implications for nursing practice. *Nursing Ethics*, 11(6), 587–99.
Garfinkel, H. (1967). *Studies in Ethnomethodology*. Prentice-Hall.
Gauthier, A., Vignola, A., Calvo, A., Cavallo, E., Moglia, C., Sellitti, L., Mutani, R., & Chió, A. (2007). A longitudinal study on quality of life and depression in ALS patient–caregiver couples. *Neurology*, 68, 923–6.
Geertz, C. (1998). Deep hanging out. *New York Review of Books*, 45(16), 69–72.
Gennep, A. T. G. (1997). Paradigma-verschuiving in de zorg voor mensen met een verstandelijke handicap. *Tijdschrift voor orthopedagogiek*, 36(5), 189–201.
Gergen, K. J. (2015). Culturally inclusive psychology from a constructionist standpoint. *Journal for the Theory of Social Behaviour*, 45(1), 95–107.
Giddens, A. (1984). *The Constitution of Society*. University of California Press.
Gilbert, T. (2004). Involving people with learning disabilities in research: Issues and possibilities. *Health & Social Care in the Community*, 12(4), 298–308.
Gill, T. M., & Feinstein, A. R. (1994). A critical appraisal of the quality of quality-of-life measurements. *Jama*, 272(8), 619–26.
Gilligan, C. (1982). *In a Different Voice*. Harvard University Press.
Goffman, E. (1956). *The Presentation of Self in Everyday Life*. University of Edinburgh Press.
Goffman, E. (1963). *Stigma: Notes on the management of spoiled identity*. Simon & Schuster.
Goffman, E. (1990). *Asylums: Essays on the social situation of mental patients and other inmates*. Doubleday.
Gomart, E., & Hennion, A. (1999). A sociology of attachment: Music amateurs, drug users. *Sociological Review*, 47(S1), 220–47.
Goodley, D. (1996). Tales of hidden lives: A critical examination of life history research with people who have learning difficulties. *Disability & Society*, 11(3), 333–48.
Goyal, N. A., & Mozaffar, T. (2014). Respiratory and nutritional support in amyotrophic lateral sclerosis. *Current Treatment Options in Neurology*, 16(2), 270.
Greenhalgh, T., Howick, J., & Maskrey, N. (2014). Evidence based medicine: A movement in crisis? *BMJ*, 348, g3725.
Greenwood, D. I. (2013). Nutrition management of amyotrophic lateral sclerosis. *Nutrition in Clinical Practice*, 28(3), 392–9.

Griswold, J. C. (1998). *Adam Smith and the Virtues of Enlightenment*. Cambridge University Press.

Habermas, J. (1962). *Strukturwandel der Öffentlichkeit: Untersuchungen zu einer Kategorie der bürgerlichen Gesellschaft*. Luchterhand Neuwied.

Habermas, J. (1981). *The Theory of Communicative Action*. Beacon Press.

Habraken, J. M., Pols, J., Bindels, P. J., & Willems, D. L. (2008). The silence of patients with end-stage COPD: A qualitative study. *British Journal of General Practice, 58*(557), 844–9.

Hadot, P. (2004). *Filosofie als een manier van leven*. Ambo.

Hanley, R. P. (2009). *Adam Smith and the Character of Virtue*. Cambridge University Press.

Haraway, D. (1988). Situated knowledges: The science question in feminism and the privilege of partial perspective. *Feminist Studies, 14*(3), 575–99.

Haraway, D. (2018). Staying with the trouble for multispecies environmental justice. *Dialogues in Human Geography, 8*(1), 102–5.

Harbers, H. (2005). *Inside the Politics of Technology: Agency and normativity in the co-production of technology and society*. Amsterdam University Press.

Harding, S. G. (2004). *The Feminist Standpoint Theory Reader: Intellectual and political controversies*. Routledge.

Hartsock, N. C. M. (1983). The feminist standpoint: Developing the ground for a specifically feminist historical materialism. In S. Harding & M. B. Hintikka (Eds.), *Discovering Reality: Feminist perspectives on epistemology, metaphysics, methodology, and philosophy of science* (pp. 283–310). Springer.

Hastrup, K. (2018). Collaborative moments: Expanding the anthropological field through cross-disciplinary practice. *Ethnos, 83*(2), 316–34.

Heilbroner, R. L. (1982). The socialization of the individual in Adam Smith. *History of Political Economy, 14*(3), 427–39.

Hendricks, A. (2007). UN Convention on the Rights of Persons with Disabilities. *European Journal of Health Law, 14*(3), 273–80.

Hendriks, R. (2023). Clothing the clown: Creative dressing in a day-centre for people with dementia. *Medical Anthropology*.

Hennion, A. (2003). Music and mediation: Towards a new sociology of music. In M. Clayton (Ed.), *The Cultural Study of Music: A critical introduction* (pp. 80–91). Routledge.

Hennion, A. (2007). Those things that hold us together: Taste and sociology. *Cultural Sociology, 1*(1), 97–114.

Heyes, C. J. (2007). *Self-Transformations: Foucault, ethics, and normalized bodies*. Oxford University Press.

Hirschauer, S. (2006). Putting things into words: Ethnographic description and the silence of the social. *Human Studies, 29*(4), 413–41.

Hirschman, A. O. (1997). *The Passions and the Interests: Political arguments for capitalism before its triumph*. Princeton University Press.

Hirschman, A. O., & Rothschild, M. (1973). The changing tolerance for income inequality in the course of economic development. *Quarterly Journal of Economics, 87*(4), 544–66.

Hobbes, T. (1968 [1651]). *Leviathan*. Penguin Books.

Hoffmaster, B. (1992). Can ethnography save the life of medical ethics? *Social Science & Medicine, 35*(12), 1421–31.

Hoffmaster, B. (2017). Freedom to choose and freedom to lose: The procurement of cadaver organs for transplantation. In D. Price (Ed.), *Organ and Tissue Transplantation* (pp. 183–9). Routledge.

Holmes, D. R., & Marcus, G. E. (2008). Collaboration today and the re-imagination of the classic scene of fieldwork encounter. *Collaborative Anthropologies, 1*(1), 81–101.

Hoogsteyns, M., & Van Der Horst, H. (2013). Wearing the arm (or not): Reconceptualising notions of in- and exclusion in disability studies. *Scandinavian Journal of Disability Research, 15*(1), 58–69.

Hoogsteyns, M., & van der Horst, H. (2015). How to live with a taboo instead of 'breaking it': Alternative empowerment strategies of people with incontinence. *Health Sociology Review, 24*(1), 38–47.

Hopmans, J., Tasneem Anonnya, N., & De Kok, B. (2022). Guidance document, prepared for the masters in medical anthropology and the masters in cultural and social anthropology, Department of Anthropology, University of Amsterdam.

Hoppe, S. (2013). Chronic illness as a source of happiness: Paradox or perfectly normal? *Health, Culture and Society, 5*(1), 265–78.

Hoppe, S., Vermeulen, L., Driessen, A., Roding, E., de Groot, M., & Krause, K. (2019). Learning in collaborative moments: Practising relating differently with dementia in dialogue meetings. *Anthropology in Action*, 26(3), 10–22.

Hossein, S. M., Leili, M., & Hossein, A. M. (2011). Acceptability and outcomes of percutaneous endoscopic gastrostomy (PEG) tube placement and patient quality of life. *Turkish Journal of Gastroenterology*, 22(2), 128–33.

Huizinga, J. (2008 [1938]). *Homo Ludens: Proeve eener bepaling van het spel-element der cultuur*. Amsterdam University Press.

Hume, D. (1978 [1739–40]). *Treatise of Human Nature* (Vol. 3). Oxford University Press.

Hunt, S. (1997a). The problem of quality of life. *Quality of life Research*, 6(3), 205–12.

Hunt, S. (1997b). Quality of life claims in trials of anti-hypertensive therapy. *Quality of Life Research*, 6(2), 185–91.

Jacobs, N. (2022). *Ethics by Committee: A history of reasoning together about medicine, science, society, and the state*. University of Chicago Press.

Jacobson, N. (2009). A taxonomy of dignity: A grounded theory study. *BMC International Health and Human Rights*, 9(1), 3.

James, W. (2010). *The Will to Believe: And other essays in popular philosophy*. Harvard University Press.

Jameton, A. (2013). A reflection on moral distress in nursing together with a current application of the concept. *Journal of Bioethical Inquiry*, 10(3), 297–308.

Jerak-Zuiderent, S., Brenninkmeijer, J., M'charek, A., & Pols, J. (2021). Goede wetenschap: Een visie van binnenuit. https://pure.uva.nl/ws/files/63928368/2021_sept_Goede_wetenschap_visie_van_binnenuit_ZonMw_project.pdf.

Jonsen, A. R., & Toulmin, S. (1988). *The Abuse of Casuistry: A history of moral reasoning*. University of California Press.

Kahneman, D., & Tversky, A. (1979). Prospect theory: An analysis of decision under risk. *Econometrica*, 47(2), 99–127.

Kant, I. (1996 [1784]). An answer to the question: What is enlightenment? In M. Gregor (Ed.), *Practical Philosophy* (*The Cambridge Edition of the Works of Immanuel Kant*) (pp. 11–22). Cambridge University Press.

Kant, I., (2007 [1764]). *Opmerkingen over het gevoel van het schone en het verhevene* [*Observations on the Feeling of the Beautiful and Sublime*] (Trans. I. Kamphof). Damon.

Kant, I. (2009 [1790]). *Kritiek van het oordeelsvermogen* [*Critique of Judgment*] (Trans. W. Visser and J. Veenbaas). Boom.

Kateb, G. (2014). *Human Dignity*. Belknap Press of Harvard University Press.

Katzberg, H. D., & Benatar, M. (2011). Enteral tube feeding for amyotrophic lateral sclerosis/motor neuron disease. Cochrane Library. DOI: 10.1002/14651858.CD004030.pub3.

Kaufman, S. (2015). *Ordinary Medicine: Extraordinary treatments, longer lives, and where to draw the line*. Duke University Press.

Knorr Cetina, K., Schatzki, T. R., & von Savigny, E. (2000). *The Practice Turn in Contemporary Theory*. Routledge.

Kohlberg, L. (1981). *The Philosophy of Moral Development: Moral stages and the idea of justice*. Harper & Row.

Kohlen, H. (2009). *Conflicts of Care: Hospital ethics committees in the USA and Germany*. Campus Verlag.

Lacey, C., Huria, T., Beckert, L., Gilles, M., & Pitama, S. (2011). The hui process: A framework to enhance the doctor-patient relationship with Māori. *New Zealand Medical Journal*, 124, 72–8.

Lamont, M., & Thévenot, L. (2010). *Rethinking Comparative Cultural Sociology: Repertoires of evaluation in France and the United States*. Cambridge University Press.

Landes, J. B. (1988). *Women and the Public Sphere in the Age of the French Revolution*. Cornell University Press.

Landeweer, M. (2014). Radeloze Joop (81): Soms loopt urine langs haar enkels. *AD NL*. https://www.ad.nl/gezond/radeloze-joop-81-soms-loopt-urine-langs-haar-enkels~af8145d5.

Langmore, S. E., Kasarskis, E. J., Manca, M. L., & Olney, R. K. (2006). Enteral tube feeding for amyotrophic lateral sclerosis/motor neuron disease. *Cochrane Database Systematic Review*, 4, CD004030.

Langstrup, H. (2013). Chronic care infrastructures and the home. *Sociology of Health & Illness*, 35(7), 1008–22.

Larrabee, M. J. (1993). *An Ethic of Care: Feminist and interdisciplinary perspectives*. Psychology Press.

Lassiter, L. (2005). Collaborative ethnography and public anthropology. *Current Anthropology*, 46(1), 83–106.

Latour, B., & Woolgar, S. (1979). *Laboratory Life: The construction of scientific facts*. SAGE Publications.

Latour, B. (1987a). *The Pasteurization of French Society*. MIT Press.

Latour, B. (1987b). *Science in Action: How to follow scientists and engineers through society*. Harvard University Press.

Latour, B. (1992). Where are the missing masses? The sociology of a few mundane artifacts. In J. Law & W.E. Bijker (Eds.), *Shaping Technology/Building Society: Studies in sociotechnical change* (pp. 225–58). MIT Press.

Latour, B. (1993). *We Have Never Been Modern*. Harvard University Press.

Latour, B. (2004). Why has critique run out of steam? From matters of fact to matters of concern. *Critical Inquiry*, 30(2), 225–48.

Latour, B., & Girard Stark, M. (1999). Factures/fractures: From the concept of network to the concept of attachment. *RES: Anthropology and Aesthetics*, 36, 20–31.

Law, J. (1994). *Organizing Modernity*. Blackwell.

Law, J. (1997). Traduction/trahison: Notes on ANT. *Convergencia*, 13(42), 47–72.

Law, J. (1999). After ANT: Complexity, naming and topology. In J. Law & J. Hassard (Eds.), *Actor Network Theory and After* (pp. 1–14). Blackwell.

Law, J. (2004). *After Method: Mess in social science research*. Routledge.

Law, J., & Hassard, J. (Eds.). *Actor Network Theory and After*. Blackwell.

Law, J., & Mol, A. (2020). Words to think with: An introduction. *Sociological Review*, 68(2), 263–82.

Law, J., & Ruppert, E. (2013). The social life of methods: Devices. *Journal of Cultural Economy*, 6(3), 229–40.

Law, J., Ruppert, E., & Savage, M. (2011). The double social life of methods. CRESC Working Paper Series, No. 95. Open University.

Lawton, J. (1998). Contemporary hospice care: The sequestration of the unbounded body and 'dirty dying'. *Sociology of Health & Illness*, 20(2), 121–43.

Lawy, J. R. (2017). Theorizing voice: Performativity, politics and listening. *Anthropological Theory*, 17(2), 192–215.

Lederer, S. E. (1995). *Subjected to Science: Human experimentation in America before the Second World War*. Johns Hopkins University Press.

Lefebvre, H. (1991). *Critique of Everyday Life*. Verso Books.

Leget, C. (2013). Analyzing dignity: A perspective from the ethics of care. *Medicine, Health Care and Philosophy*, 16(4), 945–52.

Lemke, T. (2015). *Foucault, Governmentality, and Critique*. Routledge.

Limburg, S. D., Pols, J., & Limburg, M. (2018). Kwaliteit van leven bij locked-in-syndroom: Kan dat? *Nederlands Tijdschrift voor Geneeskunde*, 162:D2048.

Liszka, J. (2009). Re-thinking the pragmatic theory of meaning: Repensando a teoria pragmática do significado. *Cognitio*, 10(1), 61–79.

Liszka, J. J. (2013). New directions in pragmatic ethics. *Cognitio*, 14(1), 51–61.

Liszka, J. J. (2014). 2014 Presidential Address: Peirce's idea of ethics as a normative science. *Transactions of the Charles S. Peirce Society*, 50(4), 459–79. https://doi.org/10.2979/trancharpeirsoc.50.4.459.

Liszka, J. (2021). *Pragmatist Ethics: A problem-based approach to what matters*. State University of New York Press.

López-Gómez, D. (2015). Little arrangements that matter: Rethinking autonomy-enabling innovations for later life. *Technological Forecasting and Social Change*, 93, 91–101.

Lord, J., & Hutchison, P. (2003). Individualised support and funding: Building blocks for capacity building and inclusion. *Disability & Society*, 18(1), 71–86.

Lutz, S. (2011). The history of hospice and palliative care. *Current Problems in Cancer*, 35(6), 304–9.

Macfie, A. L. (1967). *The Individual in Society: Papers on Adam Smith*. Routledge.

MacIntyre, A. C. (1969). Hume on 'is' and 'ought'. In W. D. Hudson (Ed.), *The Is-Ought Question: Controversies in philosophy* (pp. 35–50). Palgrave Macmillan.

Mahmood, S. (2001). Feminist theory, embodiment, and the docile agent: Some reflections on the Egyptian Islamic revival. *Cultural Anthropology*, 16(2), 202–36.

Mahmood, S. (2011). The subject of freedom. In S. Mahmood, *Politics of Piety: The Islamic revival and the feminist subject* (pp. 1–39). Princeton University Press.

Maio, G. (1999). Is etiquette relevant to medical ethics? Ethics and aesthetics in the works of John Gregory (1724–1773). *Medicine, Health Care and Philosophy, 2*(2), 181–7.

Malpas, J., & Lickiss, N. (2007). *Perspectives on Human Dignity: A conversation*. Springer Science & Business Media.

Margalit, A. (1998). *The Decent Society*. Harvard University Press.

Markula, P. (2003). The technologies of the self: Sport, feminism, and Foucault. *Sociology of Sport Journal, 20*(2), 87–107.

Markula, P. (2004). 'Tuning into oneself': Foucault's technologies of the self and mindful fitness. *Sociology of Sport Journal, 21*(3), 302–21.

Martin, L., Blomberg, J., & Lagergren, P. (2012). Patients' perspectives of living with a percutaneous endoscopic gastrostomy (PEG). *BMC Gastroenterology, 12*(1), 1–8.

Martin, L. H., Gutman, H., & Hutton, P. H. (1988). *Technologies of the Self: A seminar with Michel Foucault*. University of Massachusetts Press.

Masson, J. D. (2002). Non-professional perceptions of 'good death': A study of the views of hospice care patients and relatives of deceased hospice care patients. *Mortality, 7*(2), 191–209.

Matiti, M. R., & Trorey, G. M. (2008). Patients' expectations of the maintenance of their dignity. *Journal of Clinical Nursing, 17*(20), 2709–17.

Mattingly, C. (2012). Two virtue ethics and the anthropology of morality. *Anthropological Theory, 12*(2), 161–84.

Mazzini, L., Corra, T., Zaccala, M., Mora, G., Del Piano, M., & Galante, M. (1995). Percutaneous endoscopic gastrostomy and enteral nutrition in amyotrophic lateral sclerosis. *Journal of Neurology, 242*(10), 695–8.

McCloskey, D. (2010). *The Bourgeois Virtues: Ethics for an age of commerce*. University of Chicago Press.

McCrudden, C. (2008). Human dignity and judicial interpretation of human rights. *European Journal of International Law, 19*(4), 655–724.

M'charek, A. (2005). *The Human Genome Diversity Project: An ethnography of scientific practice*. Cambridge University Press.

M'charek, A. (2010). Fragile differences, relational effects: Stories about the materiality of race and sex. *European Journal of Women's Studies, 17*(4), 307–22.

M'charek, A. (2013). Beyond fact or fiction: On the materiality of race in practice. *Cultural Anthropology, 28*(3), 420–42.

M'charek, A. (2014). Race, time and folded objects: The HeLa error. *Theory, Culture & Society, 31*(6), 29–56.

M'charek, A., & Casartelli, S. (2019). Identifying dead migrants: Forensic care work and relational citizenship. *Citizenship Studies, 23*(7), 738–757.

M'charek, A., & van Oorschot, I. (2019). What about race? In A. Blok, I. Farias & C. Roberts (Eds.), *The Routledge Companion to Actor-Network Theory* (pp. 235–45). Taylor & Francis.

McKearney, P., & Zoanni, T. (2018). Introduction: For an anthropology of cognitive disability. *Cambridge Journal of Anthropology, 36*(1), 1–22.

Mead, G. H. (2009). *Mind, Self, and Society: From the standpoint of a social behaviorist* (Vol. 1). University of Chicago Press.

Meininger, H. (2001). Autonomy and professional responsibility in care for persons with intellectual disabilities. *Nursing Philosophy, 2*, 240–50.

Mesman, J., Walsh, K., Kinsman, L., Ford, K., & Bywaters, D. (2019). Blending video-reflexive ethnography with solution-focused approach: A strengths-based approach to practice improvement in health care. *International Journal of Qualitative Methods, 18*, 1609406919875277.

Metselaar, S. (2011). The structural similarity between the *Itinerarium mentis in Deum* and the *Collationes in Hexaemeron* with regard to Bonaventure's doctrine of God as first known. *American Catholic Philosophical Quarterly, 85*(1), 43–75.

Metselaar, S. (2015). *God as First Known* [PhD thesis, Vrije Universiteit Amsterdam].

Meyer, B. (2009). *Aesthetic Formations*. Palgrave Macmillan.

Meyer, B., & Verrips, J. (2008). Aesthetics. In D. Morgan (Ed.), *Key Words in Religion, Media, Culture* (pp. 2–30). Routledge.

Meyers, P. A. (1998). The 'ethic of care' and the problem of power. *Journal of Political Philosophy, 6*(2), 142–70.

Mol, A. (1998). Missing links, making links: The performance of some atheroscleroses. In M. Berg & A. Mol (Eds.), *Differences in Medicine: Unravelling practices, techniques and bodies* (pp. 144–65). Duke University Press.
Mol, A. (2000). Dit is geen programma: Over empirische filosofie. *Krisis: Tijdschrift Voor Filosofie*, *1*(1), 6–26.
Mol, A. (2002). *The Body Multiple: Ontology in medical practice*. Duke University Press.
Mol, A. (2006). Proving or improving: On health care research as a form of self-reflection. *Qualitative Health Research*, *16*(3), 405–14.
Mol, A. (2008). *The Logic of Care: Health and the problem of patient choice*. Routledge.
Mol, A. (2010). Care and its values: Good food in the nursing home. In A. Mol, I. Moser & J. Pols (Eds.), *Care in Practice: On tinkering in clinics, homes and farms* (pp. 215–34). transcript Verlag.
Mol, A. (2015). Who knows what a woman is. *Medicine Anthropology Theory*, *2*(1), 57–75.
Mol, A. (2021). *Eating in Theory*. Duke University Press.
Mol, A., & Berg, M. (1994). Principles and practices of medicine: The co-existence of various anemias. *Culture, Medicine, and Psychiatry*, *18*(2), 247–65.
Mol, A., & Hardon, A. (2020). What COVID-19 may teach us about interdisciplinarity. *BMJ Global Health*, *5*(12), e004375.
Mol, A., & Law, J. (1994). Regions, networks and fluids: Anaemia and social topology. *Social Studies of Science*, *24*(4), 641–71.
Mol, A., Moser, I., & Pols, J. (2010). Care: Putting practice into theory. In A. Mol, I. Moser & J. Pols (Eds.), *Care in Practice: On tinkering in clinics, homes and farms* (pp. 7–27). transcript Verlag.
Moonen, X. (2015). Is inclusie van mensen met een verstandelijke beperking vanzelfsprekend? Lecture. https://www.zuyd.nl/binaries/content/assets/zuyd/onderzoek/inaugurele-redes/inclusie-mensen-verstandelijke-beperking---lectorale-rede-xavier-moonen.pdf.
Moreira, T. (2013). *The Transformation of Contemporary Health Care: The market, the laboratory, and the forum*. Routledge.
Moser, I. (2005). On becoming disabled and articulating alternatives: The multiple modes of ordering disability and their interferences. *Cultural Studies*, *19*(6), 667–700.
Moser, I. (2006). Disability and the promises of technology: Technology, subjectivity and embodiment within an order of the normal. *Information, Communication & Society*, *9*(3), 373–95.
Moser, I. (2008). Making Alzheimer's disease matter: Enacting, interfering and doing politics of nature. *Geoforum*, *39*(1), 98–110.
Moser, I. (2010). Perhaps tears should not be counted but wiped away: On quality and improvement in dementia care. In A. Mol, I. Moser & J. Pols (Eds.), *Care in Practice: On tinkering in clinics, homes and farms* (pp. 277–300). transcript Verlag.
Moser, I., & Law, J. (2003). Making voices: New media technologies, disabilities, and articulation. In G. Liestol et al. (Eds.), *Innovation: Media, methods and theories* (pp. 491–520). MIT Press.
Muusse, C., Kroon, H., Mulder, C., & Pols, J. (2020). Working on and with relationships: Relational work and spatial understandings of good care in community mental healthcare in Trieste. *Culture, Medicine, and Psychiatry*, *44*, 544–64.
Nauta, L. W. (1984). Historical roots of the concept of autonomy in Western philosophy. *Praxis International*, *4*, 363–77.
Nauta, L. W. (1987). *De factor van de kleine c: Essays over culturele armoede en politieke cultuur*. Van Gennep.
Nauta, L. W. (2009). *Philosophy in Defense of Common Sense: Lorenzo Valla's humanist critique of scholastic philosophy*. Harvard University Press.
Nicolini, D. (2012). *Practice Theory, Work, and Organization: An introduction*. Oxford University Press.
Niewöhner, J. (2016). Co-laborative anthropology: Crafting reflexivities experimentally. *Ethnos*, 81–125.
Nordenfelt, L. (2003a). Dignity and the care of the elderly. *Medicine, Health Care and Philosophy*, *6*(2), 103–10.
Nordenfelt, L. (2003b). Dignity of the elderly: An introduction. *Medicine, Health Care, and Philosophy*, *6*, 99–101.
Nordenfelt, L. (2004). The varieties of dignity. *Health Care Analysis*, *12*(2), 69–81.
Norman, J. (2018). *Adam Smith: What he thought and why it matters*. Penguin Books.
NOS Nieuws. (2014). *Van pyjamadagen tot de vader van Van Rijn*. https://nos.nl/artikel/2004427-van-pyjamadagen-tot-de-vader-van-van-rijn.

Nunes, F., & Fitzpatrick, G. (2018). Understanding the mundane nature of self-care: Ethnographic accounts of people living with Parkinson's. In *Proceedings of the 2018 CHI Conference on Human Factors in Computing Systems* (pp. 1–15). Association for Computing Machinery.

Nussbaum, M. C. (2001). *The Fragility of Goodness: Luck and ethics in Greek tragedy and philosophy* (Vol. 2). Cambridge University Press.

Oosterveld–Vlug, M. G., Pasman, H. R. W., Gennip, I. E., Muller, M. T., Willems, D. L., & Onwuteaka–Philipsen, B. D. (2014). Dignity and the factors that influence it according to nursing home residents: A qualitative interview study. *Journal of Advanced Nursing, 70*(1), 97–106.

Ootes, S., Pols, A., Tonkens, E., & Willems, D. (2010). Bridging boundaries: The concept of 'citizenship' as a boundary object in mental healthcare. *Medische Antropologie, 22*(2), 375–88.

Osborne, T. (1992). Medicine and epistemology: Michel Foucault and the liberality of clinical reason. *History of the Human Sciences, 5*(2), 63–93.

Pais-Ribeiro, J. (2004). Quality of life is a primary end-point in clinical settings. *Clinical Nutrition, 23*(1), 121–30.

Pels, P., Boog, I., Henrike Florusbosch, J., Kripe, Z., Minter, T., Postma, M., Sleeboom–Faulkner, M., Simpson, B., Dilger, H., & Schönhuth, M. (2018). Data management in anthropology: The next phase in ethics governance? *Social Anthropology, 26*(3), 391–413.

Pennington, C. (2002). To PEG or not to PEG. *Clinical Medicine, 2*(3), 250.

Petryna, A. (2007). Clinical trials offshored: On private sector science and public health. *BioSocieties, 2*, 21–40.

Petryna, A. (2009). *When Experiments Travel: Clinical trials and the global search for human subjects*. Princeton University Press.

Petryna, A., Lakoff, A., & Kleinman, A. (Eds.) (2006). *Global Pharmaceuticals: Ethics, markets, practices*. Duke University Press.

Phillips, C. J. (2016). The taste machine: Sense, subjectivity, and statistics in the California wine world. *Social Studies of Science, 46*(3), 461–81.

Pickering, A. (Ed.). (1992). *Science as Practice and Culture*. University of Chicago Press.

Pink, S. (2012). *Situating Everyday Life: Practices and places*. SAGE.

Pinker, S. (2008). The stupidity of dignity. *New Republic, 28*(5), 28–31.

Piras, E. M., & Miele, F. (2017). Clinical self-tracking and monitoring technologies: Negotiations in the ICT-mediated patient–provider relationship. *Health Sociology Review, 26*(1), 38–53.

Pitkin, H. F. (1967). *The Concept of Representation*. University of California Press.

Pocock, J. G. A. (2003). *The Machiavellian Moment: Florentine political thought and the Atlantic republican tradition*. Princeton University Press.

Pollis, A., Schwab, P., & Koggel, C. M. (2006). Human rights: A western construct with limited applicability. In C. Koggel (Ed.), *Moral Issues in Global Perspective* (Vol. 1) (pp. 60–71). Broadview Press.

Pols, J. (2003). Enforcing patient rights or improving care? The interference of two modes of doing good in mental health care. *Sociology of Health & Illness, 25*(4), 320–47.

Pols, J. (2004). *Good Care: Enacting a complex ideal in long-term psychiatry*. Trimbos-instituut.

Pols, J. (2005). Enacting appreciations: Beyond the patient perspective. *Health Care Analysis, 13*(3), 203–21.

Pols, J. (2006a). Accounting and washing: Good care in long-term psychiatry. *Science, Technology & Human Values, 31*(4), 409–30.

Pols, J. (2006b). Washing the citizen: Washing, cleanliness and citizenship in mental health care. *Culture, Medicine, and Psychiatry, 30*(1), 77–104.

Pols, J. (2008). Which empirical research, whose ethics? Articulating ideals in long-term mental health care. In G. Widdershoven, T. Hope, J. McMillan, & L. Van der Scheer (Eds.), *Empirical Ethics in Psychiatry* (pp. 51–68). Oxford University Press.

Pols, J. (2011). Breathtaking practicalities: A politics of embodied patient positions. *Scandinavian Journal of Disability Research, 13*(3), 189–206.

Pols, J. (2012). *Care at a Distance: On the closeness of technology*. Amsterdam University Press.

Pols, J. (2013a). Washing the patient: Dignity and aesthetic values in nursing care. *Nursing Philosophy, 14*(3), 186–200.

Pols, J. (2013b). Through the looking glass: Good looks and dignity in care. *Medicine, Health Care & Philosophy, 16*(4), 953–66.

Pols, J. (2013c). *The Chronification of Illness: An empirical ethics in care*. https://pure.uva.nl/ws/files/2680465/171876_PDF_7682Weboratie_Pols_DEF.pdf.

Pols, J. (2014). Knowing patients: Turning patient knowledge into science. *Science, Technology & Human Values*, *39*(1), 73–97.

Pols, J. (2015). Towards an empirical ethics in care: Relations with technologies in health care. *Medicine, Health Care and Philosophy*, *18*(1), 81–90.

Pols, J. (2016). Analyzing social spaces: Relational citizenship for patients leaving mental health care institutions. *Medical Anthropology*, *35*(2), 177–92.

Pols, J. (2017a). How to make your relationship work? Aesthetic relations with technology. *Foundations of Science*, *22*(2), 4214.

Pols, J. (2017b). Good relations with technology: Empirical ethics and aesthetics in care. *Nursing Philosophy*, *18*(1), e1254.

Pols, J. (2019a). Care, everyday life and aesthetic values. In J. Brouwer & S. van Tuinen (Eds.), *To Mind Is to Care* (pp. 42–61). V2_Publishing.

Pols, J. (2019b). The quality of time and its quantifications: Negotiations about the feeding tube at the end of life. *European Journal for Nursing History and Ethics*, *1*(1), 87–105.

Pols, J. (2023). Inzoomen, scherpstellen: Naar een antropologie van alledaagse ethiek in de gezondheidszorg. Inaugural lecture. https://pure.uva.nl/ws/files/131373253/Oratietekst.pdf.

Pols, J. (forthcoming, a). Care as an attempt to do something good: Studying normativity in practices of health care and research. In L. Cubellis & R. Lester (Eds.), *Traces of Care: Discernment and the work of recognition*. Duke University Press.

Pols, J. (forthcoming, b). Introduction to the special issue: Generative hanging out: Developing research practices for subjects' creative engagements in research. *Medical Anthropology*.

Pols, J., Althoff, B., & Bransen, E. (2017). The limits of autonomy: Ideals in care for people with learning disabilities. *Medical Anthropology*, *36*(8), 772–785.

Pols, J., Depla, M., & De Lange, J. (1998). Gewoon oud en chronisch: Mogelijkheden en beperkingen in de zorg voor ouderen met een psychiatrische achtergrond in het verzorgingshuis. Trimbos-reeks.

Pols, J., & Hoogsteyns, M. (2015) Shaping the subject of incontinence: Relating experience to knowledge. *ALTER: European Journal of Disability Research*, *10*(1), 40–53.

Pols, J., & Limburg, S. (2016). A matter of taste? Quality of life in day-to-day living with ALS and a feeding tube. *Culture, Medicine, and Psychiatry*, *40*(3), 361–82.

Pols, J., M'charek, A. A., Jerak-Zuiderent, S. J., & Brenninkmeijer, J. (forthcoming). Achieving good science: The integrity of scientific institutions. *Learning and Teaching*.

Pols, J., Michon, H., Depla, M., & Kroon, H. (2001). Rehabilitatie als praktijk: Een etnografisch onderzoek in twee psychiatrische ziekenhuizen. Trimbos-reeks.

Pols, J., & Moser, I. (2009). Cold technologies versus warm care? On affective and social relations with and through care technologies. *Alter*, *3*(2), 159–78.

Pols, J., Pasveer, B., & Willems, D. (2018). The particularity of dignity: Relational engagement in care at the end of life. *Medicine, Health Care and Philosophy*, *21*(1), 89–100.

Pols, J., Willems, D., & Aanestad, M. (2019). Making sense with numbers: Unravelling ethico-psychological subjects in practices of self-quantification. *Sociology of Health & Illness*, *41*(s1), 98–115.

Poster, M. (2002). Everyday (virtual) life. *New Literary History*, *33*(4), 743–60.

Proctor, R. (1988). *Racial Hygiene: Medicine under the Nazis*. Harvard University Press.

Pullman, D. (2002). Human dignity and the ethics and aesthetics of pain and suffering. *Theoretical Medicine and Bioethics*, *23*(1), 75–94.

Rabeharisoa, V., Moreira, T., & Akrich, M. (2014). Evidence-based activism: Patients', users' and activists' groups in knowledge society. *BioSocieties*, *9*, 111–28.

Rabeneck, L., McCullough, L. B., & Wray, N. P. (1997). Ethically justified, clinically comprehensive guidelines for percutaneous endoscopic gastrostomy tube placement. *Lancet*, *349*(9050), 496–8.

Rapp, R. (2004). *Testing Women, Testing the Fetus: The social impact of amniocentesis in America*. Routledge.

Rappaport, J. (2008). Beyond participant observation: Collaborative ethnography as theoretical innovation. *Collaborative Anthropologies*, *1*(1), 1–31.

Rawls, J. (1971). *A Theory of Justice*. Belknap Press of Harvard University Press.

Redman, S. J. (2019). Deep hanging out as historical research methodology: The National Anthropological Archives at the Smithsonian Institution. *History of Anthropology Review*. https://histanthro.org/bibliography/archives/deep-hanging-out-as-historical-research-methodology (accessed 21 July 2023).

Renders, F. A., & Meininger, H. P. (2011). Afscheid van het burgerschapsparadigma? *Nederlands tijdschrift voor de zorg aan mensen met verstandelijke beperkingen*, *37*(3), 147–67.

Reverby, S. M. (2000). *Examining Tuskegee: The infamous syphilis study and its legacy*. University of North Carolina Press.

Reverby, S. M. (Ed.) (2009). *Tuskegee's Truths: Rethinking the Tuskegee syphilis study*. University of North Carolina Press.

Rietveld, E. (2019). *The Affordances of Art for Making Technologies*. University of Twente.

Robinson, J. H. (Ed. and Trans.) (1898) *Francesco Petrarch: The first modern scholar and man of letters. Selections from his Correspondences*. https://history.hanover.edu/texts/petrarch.html (accessed 21 July 2023).

Rorty, R. (1979). *Philosophy and the Mirror of Nature*. Princeton University Press.

Rosen, M. (2012). *Dignity: Its history and meaning*. Harvard University Press.

Rousseau, J. (1979 [1762]). *Emile: Or, On education* (Trans. Alan Bloom). Basic Books.

Ruppert, E., Law, J., & Savage, M. (2013). Reassembling social science methods: The challenge of digital devices. *Theory, Culture & Society*, *30*(4), 22–46.

RVS. (2019). Advise Intensieve vrijwillige hulp-Heldere grenzen aan drang in de jeugdzorg. https://www.raadrvs.nl/documenten/publicaties/2019/11/25/intensieve-vrijwllige-hulp---heldere-grenzen-aan-drang-in-de-jeugdzorg (accessed 21 July 2023).

RVS (2021). Stervelingen: Beter samenleven met de dood. https://www.raadrvs.nl/stervelingen/documenten/publicaties/2021/12/9/stervelingen---beter-samenleven-met-de-dood (accessed 21 July 2023).

Sakellariou, D. (2013). 'As You Can See We Plod Along': Narratives of living with motor neurone disease in Wales [PhD thesis, Cardiff University].

Sánchez Criado, T., & Estalella, A. (2018). Introduction. In A. Estalella & T. Sánchez Criado (Eds.), *Experimental Collaborations: Ethnography through fieldwork devices* (pp. 1–30). Berghahn.

Scarry, E. (1985). *The Body in Pain: The making and unmaking of the world*. Oxford University Press.

Schama, S. (1988). *The Embarrassment of Riches: An interpretation of Dutch culture in the Golden Age*. Fontana.

Schneider, L. T. (2020). Sexual violence during research: How the unpredictability of field work and the right to risk collide with academic bureaucracy and expectations. *Critique of Anthropology*, *40*(2), 173–93.

Scholtes, U. (forthcoming). Drawing techniques for feeling bodies: Exploring drawing as a methodological tool for finding words.

Schurian-Dąbrowska, L., & Krause, K. (2023). Researching words without speaking them: Language as care practice. *Medical Anthropology*.

Scott, J. W. (1991). The evidence of experience. *Critical Inquiry*, *17*(4), 773–97.

Searle, J. R. (1969). How to derive 'ought' from 'is'. In W. D. Hudson (Ed.), *The Is-Ought Question: Controversies in philosophy* (pp. 120–34). Palgrave Macmillan.

Seeber, A. A., Pols, A. J., Hijdra, A., Grupstra, H. F., Willems, D. L., & de Visser, M. (2016). Experiences and reflections of patients with motor neuron disease on breaking the news in a two-tiered appointment: A qualitative study. *BMJ Supportive & Palliative Care*. bmjspcare-2015-000977 (accessed 21 July 2023).

Serres, M. (1995). *Conversations on Science, Culture, and Time: Michel Serres with Bruno Latour* (Trans. R. Lapidus). University of Michigan Press.

Shapin, S. (2011). *Changing Tastes: How foods tasted in the early modern period and how they taste now*. Uppsala University.

Shapin, S. (2016). A taste of science: Making the subjective objective in the California wine world. *Social Studies of Science*, *46*(3), 436–60.

Shapin, S., & Schaffer, S. (1985). *Leviathan and the Air-pump*. British Society for the Philosophy Science.

Sharon, T. (2015). Healthy citizenship beyond autonomy and discipline: Tactical engagements with genetic testing. *BioSocieties*, *10*(3), 295–316.

Shintani, S. (2013). Efficacy and ethics of artificial nutrition in patients with neurologic impairments in home care. *Journal of Clinical Neuroscience*, *20*(2), 220–3.

Singer, P. (1995). *Animal Liberation*. Pimlico.

Skeide, A. (2021). Experiences as actors: Labor pains in childbirth care in Germany. *Medical Anthropology*, *40*(5), 446–57.

Skeide, A. (2022). Music to my ears: A material-semiotic analysis of fetal heart sounds in midwifery prenatal care. *Science, Technology & Human Values*, *47*(3), 517–43.

Smith, A. (1937). *An Inquiry into the Nature and Causes of the Wealth of Nations*. Modern Library.

Smith, A. (2010 [1776]). *The Theory of Moral Sentiments*. Penguin.

Spiegelberg, H. (1970). Human dignity: A challenge to contemporary philosophy. In R. Gotesky & E. Laszlo (Eds.), *Human Dignity: This century and the next. An interdisciplinary inquiry into human rights, technology, war, and the ideal society* (pp. 39–64). Gordon & Breach.

Sprangers, M. A. G., & Schwartz, C. E. (1999). Integrating response shift into health-related quality of life research: A theoretical model. *Social Science & Medicine*, *48*(11), 1507–15.

Sprangers, M. A., & Schwartz, C. E. (2010). Do not throw out the baby with the bath water: Build on current approaches to realize conceptual clarity. Response to Ubel, Peeters, and Smith. *Quality of Life Research*, *19*(4), 477–49.

Stavroulakis, T., Walsh, T., Shaw, P. J., & McDermott, C. J. (2013). Gastrostomy use in motor neurone disease (MND): A review, meta-analysis and survey of current practice. *Amyotrophic Lateral Sclerosis and Frontotemporal Degeneration*, *14*(2), 96–104.

Strathern, M. (1991). *Partial Connections*. Rowman & Littlefield.

Strathern, M. (1996). Cutting the network. *Journal of the Royal Anthropological Institute*, *2*(3), 517–35.

Strohm, K. (2012). When anthropology meets contemporary art: Notes for a politics of collaboration. *Collaborative Anthropologies*, *5*(1), 98–124.

Struever, N. S. (1992). *Theory as Practice: Ethical Inquiry in the Renaissance*. University of Chicago Press.

Struhkamp, R., Mol, A., & Swierstra, T. (2009). Dealing with in/dependence: Doctoring in physical rehabilitation practice. *Science, Technology & Human Values*, *34*(1), 55–76.

Swierstra, T. (2013). Nanotechnology and technomoral change. *Etica e Politica*, *15*(1), 200–19.

Sztompka, P. (2008). The focus on everyday life: A new turn in sociology. *European Review*, *16*(1), 23–37.

Tadd, W., Bayer, A., & Dieppe, P. (2002). Dignity in health care: Reality or rhetoric. *Reviews in Clinical Gerontology*, *12*, 1–4.

Taylor, D., & Vintges, K. (2004). *Feminism and the Final Foucault*. University of Illinois Press.

Taylor, J. (2010). On recognition, caring and dementia. In A. Mol, J. Moser & J. Pols (Eds.), *Care in Practice: On tinkering in clinics, homes and farms* (pp. 17–56). transcript Verlag.

Taylor, J. S. (2014). The demise of the bumbler and the crock: From experience to accountability in medical education and ethnography. *American Anthropologist*, *116*(3), 523–34.

Thévenot, L. (2001). Pragmatic regimes governing the engagement with the world. In T. R. Schatzki, K. Knorr-Cetina & E. von Savigny (Eds.), *The Practice Turn in Contemporary Theory* (pp. 56–73). Routledge.

Thévenot, L. (2002). Which road to follow? The moral complexity of an 'equipped' humanity. In J. Law & A. Mol (Eds.), *Complexities: Social studies of knowledge practices* (pp. 53–87). Duke University Press.

Thévenot, L., Moody, M., & Lafaye, C. (2000). Forms of valuing nature: Arguments and modes of justification in French and American environmental disputes. In L. Lamont & L. Thévenot (Eds.), *Rethinking Comparative Cultural Sociology: Repertoires of evaluation in France and the United States* (pp. 229–72). Cambridge University Press.

Thomas, W. (1928). *The Child in America: Behavior problems and programs*. Alfred A. Knopf.

Thygesen, H., & Moser, I. (2010). Technology and good dementia care: An argument for an ethics-in-practice approach. In S. D. Schillmaier (Ed.), *New Technologies and Emerging Spaces of Care* (pp. 129–47). Ashgate.

Timmermans, S., & Berg, M. (2003). *The Gold Standard: The challenge of evidence-based medicine and standardization in health care*. Temple University Press.

Todd, V., Rosendaal, G. V., Duregon, K., & Verhoef, M. (2005). Percutaneous endoscopic gastrostomy (PEG): The role and perspective of nurses. *Journal of Clinical Nursing*, *14*(2), 187–94.

Tonkens, E. H. D. (1999). *Het zelfontplooiingsregime: De actualiteit van Dennendal en de jaren zestig*. Bakker.

Tonkens, E., & Weijers, I. (1999). Autonomy, solidarity, and self-realization: Policy views of Dutch service providers. *Mental Retardation*, *37*(6), 468–76.

Toulmin, S. (1976). On the nature of the physician's understanding. *Journal of Medicine and Philosophy, 1*(1), 32–50.
Tronto, J. C. (1993). *Moral Boundaries: A political argument for an ethic of care*. Psychology Press.
Ubel, P. A., Peeters, Y., & Smith, D. (2010). Abandoning the language of 'response shift': A plea for conceptual clarity in distinguishing scale recalibration from true changes in quality of life. *Quality of Life Research, 19*(4), 465–71.
United Nations (2006). *Convention on the Rights of Persons with Disabilities*. https://social.desa.un.org/issues/disability/crpd/convention-on-the-rights-of-persons-with-disabilities-crpd (accessed 21 July 2023).
Van de Bovenkamp, H. M., & Trappenburg, M. J. (2009). Reconsidering patient participation in guideline development. *Health Care Analysis, 17*(3), 198–216.
Van der Stap, S. (2006). *Meisje met Negen Pruiken*. Prometheus.
Van der Weele, S., Bredewold, F., Leget, C., & Tonkens, E. (2021). The group home as moral laboratory: Tracing the ethic of autonomy in Dutch intellectual disability care. *Medicine, Health Care and Philosophy, 24*, 11325.
Van Gennep, A. (2000). *Emancipatie van de zwaksten in de samenleving: over paradigma's van verstandelijke handicap*. Boom Koninklijke Uitgevers.
Van Gennip, I. E., Pasman, H. R. W., Oosterveld-Vlug, M. G., Willems, D. L., & Onwuteaka-Philipsen, B. D. (2013). The development of a model of dignity in illness based on qualitative interviews with seriously ill patients. *International Journal of Nursing Studies, 50*(8), 1080–9.
Van Hout, A., Pols, J., & Willems, D. (2015). Shining trinkets and unkempt gardens: On the materiality of care. *Sociology of Health & Illness, 37*(8), 1206–17.
Veldink, J. H., Wokke, J. H., van der Wal, G., Vianney de Jong, J., & van den Berg, L. H. (2002). Euthanasia and physician-assisted suicide among patients with amyotrophic lateral sclerosis in the Netherlands. *New England Journal of Medicine, 346*(21), 1638–44.
Verstegen, P. (2021). Voorwoord. In: F. Petrarca, *Het liedboek*. Atheneum.
Vesey, S. (2013). Dysphagia and quality of life. *British Journal of Community Nursing, 18*(Sup5), 14-19.
Vesey, S., Leslie, P., & Exley, C. (2008). A pilot study exploring the factors that influence the decision to have PEG feeding in patients with progressive conditions. *Dysphagia, 23*(3), 310–16.
VGN [Vereniging Gehandicaptenzorg Nederland]. (2007). Kwaliteitskader gehandicaptenzorg: Visiedocument. VGN.
VGN [Vereniging Gehandicaptenzorg Nederland]. (2022). Kwaliteitskader Gehandicaptenzorg 2017–2022, https://www.vgn.nl/kwaliteitskader-gehandicaptenzorg-2017–2022. Retrieved 3-4-2022
Viner, J. (1927). Adam Smith and laissez faire. *Journal of Political Economy, 35*(2), 198–232.
Vintges, K. (2001). 'Must we burn Foucault?' Ethics as art of living: Simone de Beauvoir and Michel Foucault. *Continental Philosophy Review, 34*(2), 165–81.
Vintges, K. (2012). Muslim women in the Western media: Foucault, agency, governmentality and ethics. *European Journal of Women's Studies, 19*(3), 283–98.
Vogel, E. (2016). *Subjects of Care: Living with overweight in the Netherland* [PhD thesis, University of Amsterdam].
Vogel, E. (2017). Hungers that need feeding: On the normativity of mindful nourishment. *Anthropology & Medicine, 24*(2), 159–73.
Vogel, E. (2021). Juxtaposition: Differences that matter. In A. Ballestero & B. R. Winthereik (Eds.), *Experimenting with Ethnography: A companion to analysis*. Duke University Press.
Vos, R., Willems, D., & Houtepen, R. (2005). Coordinating the norms and values of medical research, medical practice and patient worlds: The ethics of evidence-based medicine in 'boundary fields of medicine'. In Ruud ter Meulen et al. (Eds.), *Evidence-Based Practice in Medicine and Health Care: A discussion of the ethical issues* (pp. 87–95). Springer.
Waldron, J. (2012). *Dignity, Rank, and Rights*. Oxford University Press.
Walker, M. U. (1998). *Moral Understandings: A feminist study in ethics*. Cambridge University Press.
Warren, N., & Manderson, L. (2013). *Reframing Disability and Quality of Life: A global perspective*. Springer.
Warren, N., Manderson, L., & Misajon, R. (2009). More than SF-36? Using narratives to elaborate health and well-being data in recent lower-limb amputees. In V. Møller & D. Huschka (Eds.), *Quality of Life and the Millennium Challenge* (pp. 59–80). Springer.
Weindling, P. (1989) *Health, Race and German Politics between National Unification and Nazism, 1870–1945*. Cambridge University Press.

Weisz, G. (2014). *Chronic Disease in the Twentieth Century: A history*. JHU Press.
Welch, E. (2009). Art on the edge: Hair and hands in Renaissance Italy. *Renaissance Studies, 23*(3), 241–68.
WHOQOL. (1995). The World Health Organization quality of life assessment (WHOQOL): Position paper from the World Health Organization. *Social Science & Medicine, 41*(10), 1403–9.
Wilde, M. (2015). *Brave New Neighbourhood: Affective citizenship in Dutch territorial governance* [PhD thesis, University of Amsterdam].
Willems, D. (2010a). Hoe een onwaardige laatste levensfase te voorkomen. https://projecten.zonmw.nl/nl/project/hoe-een-onwaardige-laatste-levensfase-te-voorkomen.
Willems, D. (2010b). Quality of life: Measure or listen. A reflection for disability studies. *Medische Antropologie, 22*(2), 289.
Willems, D. (2010c). Varieties of goodness in high-tech home care. In A. Mol, I. Moser & J. Pols (Eds.), *Care in Practice: On tinkering in clinics, homes and farms*. transcript Verlag.
Willems, D., & Pols, J. (2010). Goodness! The empirical turn in health care ethics. *Medische Antropologie, 22*(1), 161–70.
Williams, B. C. (2017). #MeToo: A crescendo in the discourse about sexual harassment, field work, and the academy (part 2). *Savage Minds*. https://savageminds.org/tag/fieldwork (accessed 21 July 2023).
Winance, M. (2006). Trying out the wheelchair: The mutual shaping of people and devices through adjustment. *Science, Technology, & Human Values, 31*(1), 52–72.
Winance, M. (2007). Being normally different? Changes to normalization processes: From alignment to work on the norm. *Disability & Society, 22*(6), 625–38.
Winance, M. (2010). Care and disability. Practices of experimenting, tinkering with, and arranging people and technical aids. In A. Mol, I. Moser & J. Pols (Eds.) *Care in practice: On tinkering in clinics, homes and farms* (pp. 93–117). transcript Verlag.
Winch, D. (1968). Review: *The Individual in Society: Papers on Adam Smith*. By A. L. Macfie. *Economic Journal, 78*(311), 666–7.
Winthereik, B. R., & Langstrup, H. (2010). When patients care (too much) for information. In A. Mol, I. Moser & J. Pols (Eds.), *Care in Practice: On tinkering in clinics, homes and farms* (pp. 195–213). transcript Verlag.
Wittgenstein, L. (1921). Logisch-philosophische Abhandlung. *Annalen der Naturphilosophie, 14*, 185–262.
Wittgenstein, L. (1976). *Tractatus logico-philosophicus: Logisch-philosophische Abhandlung*. Suhrkamp.
Woittiez, I. B., Putman, L. S., Eggink, E., Ras, M., & Ross, J. A. (2014). *Zorg beter begrepen: Verklaringen voor de groeiende vraag naar zorg voor mensen met een verstandelijke beperking*. Sociaal en Cultureel Planbureau.
Wolpe, P. R. (1998). The triumph of autonomy in American medical ethics: A sociological view. In R. De Vries & J. Subedi (Eds.), *Bioethics and Society: Sociological investigations of the enterprise of bioethics* (pp. 38–59). Prentice Hall.
Woolhead, G., Calnan, M., Dieppe, P., & Tadd, W. (2004). Dignity in older age: What do older people in the United Kingdom think? *Age and Ageing, 33*(2), 165–70.
Zigon, J. (2007). Moral breakdown and the ethical demand: A theoretical framework for an anthropology of moralities. *Anthropological Theory, 7*(2), 131–50.
Zigon, J. (2008). *Morality: An anthropological perspective*. Berg.
Zizzo, N., Bell, E., Lafontaine, A. L., & Racine, E. (2017). Examining chronic care patient preferences for involvement in health-care decision making: The case of Parkinson's disease patients in a patient-centred clinic. *Health Expect, 20*(4), 655–64.
Zuiderent-Jerak, T. (2015). *Situated Intervention: Sociological experiments in health care*. MIT Press.

Index

Notes are denoted by the use of 'n'.

abstract reasoning 32, 55n13, 86n3
Adorno, Theodor, *Dialektik der Aufklärung* 26n21, 140
aesthesis 27n41, 277
aesthetic depreciation 69, 87n21
aesthetic motivations 17, 61, 69, 162–3, 203, 204–5, 331
aesthetic socialities 17, 163, 178, 219, 323–4
    changing social conventions 21, 26n30, 11, 13–15, 17, 68, 82, 85–6, 99, 163, 184, 214, 318, 333, 223
    the self as a practice of worth 219–35
aesthetic values
    citizens against 137–59
    creativity and 319
    cultural differences 65
    dignity and 52–4
    everyday-life 13–14, 35, 64–5, 312–13
    genres 14–15, 16–17, 25n8, 27n42, 158–9
    goodness and truth 194–6, 213–16, 314–18
    individual liberties 338n4
    modes of ordering 86n5
    motivations 61
    parrhesia and 203–4
    particularities 137–59
    of politics 151–2
    questions on 20–1
    rights and 69
    scientific methods 65
    social values 15–17, 161–2, 165–86
    styles of 14–15
    true, the beautiful and the good 162, 194–8, 298, 315, 330
    what are 11–12
aesthetics and veridiction 320–1
agency, distribution of 131–3, 232–3
Albrecht, G. 247, 248
alcohol and drug use
    learning disabilities 122, 125–6, 129, 131–3, 136n20, 318–19
Alexander the Great 198
ALS, living with (case study) 241–61, 262n14, 263n32, 302, 304, 318
ALS Tertiary Care Centre 244
Althoff, Brigitte 122, 123, 133
ancien régime 92, 141, 146–7, 151
Anderson sequence (DNA) 44–5
anthropology 4, 14, 26, 122, 285, 306, 306n14
anthropologists 285–6

anthropology of the good, sociology and 14–15
Appiah, Kwame Anthony 69, 159n5
appreciating things 167, 215, 231–2
archaeological readings, Foucault's 189–216
Arendt, Hannah 159n6
aristocracy 109, 117n45, 147
art 147, 153, 338n15
artfulness 13–14, 26n32
articulations 55n1
artworks 87n30, 207, 216n18
authenticity 153–4
    to artificiality 225–6, 236n14–15
autonomy, principle of 119–35
    autonomy and learning disabilities 120–1
    in everyday life 123–4
    flipside of 126–8
    and institutions 121–2
    upholding 314
'average man' category 109–10
averting the eyes 291–5

baldness, female 166–72
    aesthetic socialities 219–20, 323–4
    facing the facts 168–71
    looking bad, good or beautiful 172–5
    nothingness, illness and death 175–6
    protecting others and managing responses 171–2, 212–13
    subject–object relations 301
    workshops 168, 175, 222–31
baldness, male 186n1
Banks, Sarah 294
'bathrobe trick' 3, 4, 7, 9–19, 303, 322, 336
Beck Depression Inventory 245–6
'bedsore case' 48–50, 51–3, 66, 78
'behavioural economics 116n19
Bios (everyday life) 118n52, 162, 191, 192, 196, 203–17, 234, 324
blind people 338n22
Boltanski, Luc 14, 36, 56n30
Bourdieu, Pierre 16, 313
bourgeoisie 110, 141, 142, 147, 153, 332
Boyle, Robert 94
Bransen, Els 122
breaching experiments. 307n27

cancer
    diagnosis 173, 187n9
    hair loss due to chemotherapy 161, 163, 165–86, 219–35

Canguilhem, Georges 186n7, 216n19
capitalism
   everyday-life values in early capitalist thinking 91, 92, 111–14, 116n9, 118n53
   evils of 110–11
   promoting 116n9
care for the self (*epimeleia/melei moi*) 55n5, 162, 192, 204–5, 271
care studies 4, 9, 25n5, 26n16, 61, 305, 309–10, 336
caregivers
   'bedsore case' 48–50
   dignity in long-term psychiatry 63–86
   how they do good 32
   morality regained 82–4
   philosophy of care 123–6, 127, 129, 131–3
Casartelli, Sara 69
Catherine (naked body) 178
Catholic Church 51–2
Cato the Younger 7
Ceci, Christine 160n21
'chemo head' 175–6
chemotherapy 161, 163, 165–86, 219–35, 226–7
children
   with cancer 236n19
   childcare practices (sickle cell disease) 286, 287, 288, 293, 297, 303
   parents massaging their 227–8
Christianity 201
chronic diseases 3, 5, 186n2, 210–11, 213–15, 303, 320, 322
   See also individual diseases
Cicero 269–70, 274
'Cicero approach' 50–1, 52
citizens/citizenship
   against aesthetics 137–59
   or cleanliness 75–8
   concepts 312
   emergence of 139
   individuals in the community 157–9
   paradigm 121–2, 123–4
   patient-citizens 135n9, 157–8
   political emancipation of 142, 143, 151, 159n8, 160n9
   relational 27n44, 86n19, 136n29
   sick citizens and the normativity of a good life 72, 210–11
   subject-positions 211–13, 217n23
   values 51–2, 69
civil society 141, 149
civil wars 93–5, 331, 339n36
class socialisation 16
classicism 7, 147, 148
cleanliness, hygiene and 27n42, 36, 71, 73–8, 87n27, 187n10
Clifford, J., *Writing Culture* 285
clinical gaze 167, 184
coercion 127
coherence 61–2, 104, 116n18, 138, 150, 156, 159, 162, 190, 220, 313, 339n27,n29, n32
coherences, discontinuities and 325–8
commerce 107, 108–9, 141
community, individuals in the 124, 157–9
concentration camps 177–8, 187n13

concepts, historical and theoretical 30
consent 119, 120, 123, 294–5, 299, 307n35
COPD (chronic obstructive pulmonary disease) 1–2, 322
'countervailing passions' 106
courage 167, 182
court, French royal 146–7
creativity
   in everyday life 318–19
   of methods 33–4, 42, 238, 316–18, 324, 328, 338n11
'critical awareness' 234
'cultural capital' 313
culture 27n34, 65, 166
Cynicism 189–216, 267, 276, 330
   true life of the Cynics 196–9

DALYs (Disability Adjusted Life Years) 246, 262n18
Dányi, Endre 69
deaf people 338n22
death, facing 177, 201–2
death, threat of 165–7
Delphi, oracle of 202–3, 216n15
dementia 48, 60, 71, 136n30, 160n21, 291
democracy 68, 117n45, 119, 138, 140, 152, 201
deontological ethics 61, 117n26
depreciation, aesthetic 69, 87n21
descriptions, object 43–4, 45–7
descriptive utterings 153
deterioration, symbols of 250–1, 262n30
DeVlieger, P. 247, 248
d'Hoop, Ariane 15
diabetes 125–6, 286, 287, 288, 293, 297, 303
Dialektik der Aufklärung (*Dialectic of Enlightenment*) (Horkheimer and Adorno) 140
dietitians 125–6
dignitas values 52–4, 66–7, 68–9, 70, 75, 82
dignity 48–54
   in care 70
   categories of 12
   concepts 48, 57n54, 57n60, 66–7
   dirt and 71
   in end-of-life care 79–81
   as engagement 81–2
   hair loss due to chemotherapy 165
   pointing and folding 54
   refolding 52–3
   refolding words with practices 53–4
   tales about 78–9, 225
   unfolding in literature 50–2
Diogenes 193, 197, 204, 274
dirt and dignity 71
dirty wards 72–3
discontinuities and coherences: *see* coherences
DNA reference sequence 44–5
dog metaphor 197–8, 204
domestic world 36
Down's syndrome 133
Draaisma, Douwe 43, 44
Driessen, Annelieke 136n30
drug use, alcohol and
   learning disabilities 122, 125, 126, 129, 131–3, 136n20, 318–19

Dumézil, Georges 204
dysphagia (difficulty swallowing) 243, 244

eating, ALS and 241–61
economy, morality versus 95–6
Elias, Norbert 15, 236n15
emancipation, political 142, 143, 151, 159n8, 160n9
empathy 25n8, 97
empirical study
　different care practices 36–7, 38
　ethics 55n6, 100
　　how caregivers do good 32, 55n11–12, 56n14
　　open concepts 31–2
empirical-theoretical reinvention 334–6
end-of-life care, dignity in 78, 79–81
engagement, dignity as 81–2
Engels, Friedrich 107
Enlightenment 14, 91, 116n2, 142–3, 159n7, 216n1, 236n6, 279
　Scottish 93, 108
Epictetus 194
epidemiological research 5–6, 11, 261, 315, 322
equality 51, 53, 68, 69, 75, 84, 108, 142–3, 148, 152, 155–6, 157, 216n1, 269, 332, 338n24
ethics
　deontological 61, 117n26
　empirical 55n6, 61, 100, 309
　ethical discourse 3
　ethical principles 59–61, 63–86, 312
　medical 64, 119
　modernist 11, 32, 209
　pragmatic 117n35–6
　reinvention of 61
　'universal human' 334
ethnographic research/studies 37, 38, 39
　quality of life 241–61
ethnography (definition) 56n28
ethos (exemplary life) 162, 192, 195, 201, 203–8, 211, 214, 216n12, 219, 267, 329
etiquette 15, 77, 103, 192, 313
Eton, D. T. 250
EuroQol Group 245
'everyday ethics' (aesthetics and veridiction) 25n7, 35, 158, 261, 294, 299, 307n35, 320–1
everyday life (*bios*) 118n52, 162, 192, 203–9, 214
everyday-life values 64–5, 111–14, 118n53
　creativity in 318–19
　definitions 310–14
　empirical-theoretical reinvention 334–6
　good care: creating relations 128–31
　as a good life 213–15
　reinventing research practices for studying 283–305
everyday-life values, principles and
　living with ALS and a feeding tube 241–61
　theory versus practice 152–5
evidence-based medicine (EBM) 33–4
evidence-based practice 6, 25n14
exemplary life (*ethos*) 162, 192, 195, 201, 203–8, 211, 214, 216n12, 219, 267, 329

exemplary to exemplar, normativity: from 321–2
'experiences' (opinions) 144
expressive utterings 153–4
external values 33
eyebrows, disappearing (after chemo) 175

facts, facing the 168–71
false news/fake facts 216n13
fame 105, 192, 331
family members, patients and 76, 79–81, 307n35
farmers 109, 116n3
feeding tubes
　ALS and 241–61, 263n39, 302, 304, 316, 318
　definition 242–3
　of deterioration 250–1
　different 256–7
　as facilitator of happy events 253–4
　as a solution 251–3
　as a transformer of misery 255
femininity 150, 223, 236n12, 312
feminism 220, 235n2, 235n5
Ferguson, Adam 110
Flaccus 275
'flower power' goodness 68
focus groups 78–9
folded objects 44–5, 46–7
foldedness (concept) 18, 19, 29–54
folding approach 40–2, 46, 206, 216n17, 268, 322, 324
　See also refolding approach; unfolding approach
folding metaphor 39–40
Foucault, Michel
　archaeological readings 189–216
　clinical gaze 167, 184
　Enlightenment 'humanism' 236n6
　experimental gay practices 234
　'game of truth' 216n5, 216n7
　good-life-as-practice 8, 162, 163, 201, 330
　humanism 116n2
　lectures on the good life 190–4
　normal and deviations 186n7
　notion of discourse 36, 209, 217n21
　parrhesia 55n5
　'technologies of the self' 220
fragile sentiments 332–3
France 92, 94, 139, 141, 146–7
Frankfurter Schule 26n21, 139–40
freedom 193, 231, 232, 234, 270
French Revolution 94, 143
friendship 40, 56n39, 268–72
Frost-Hartwig, Christine 236n19

game, playing the game (distribution of agency) 131–3
Garfinkel, Harold 307n27
gastroenterologists 250, 254
Gaussian curves 259
gay men 234
Geertz, Clifford 284
general practitioners (GPs) 79–81
generalising, modes of 5–6
generative hanging out 285, 304–5

INDEX　　367

geneticists 44–5
geriatric assistants 48–50, 52, 71, 74–5, 77
Gilligan, Carol 26n15
Goffman, Erving 236n7, 236n12, 236n14
good-life-as-practice 220–1, 336–7, 339n43
  in ancient Greece 195, 329–30
  evaluation of 62, 320–1
  Foucault and 8, 162, 163, 201, 330
  friendship 40, 56n39
  good lives that are not so good 211–13
  Hadot and 336
  reinvented, and reinventing it everyday 334–6
'good science' 18, 34, 55n11, 339n43
goodness and truth, aesthetic values 26n30, 68, 194–6, 213–16, 314–18
goods, a variety of 34–5
governance 65, 92, 93–5, 201, 332
Greece, ancient
  the Cynics in 189–216
  Foucault and 162
  good life in 30
  intelligent emotions 329–30
  schools of thought 95, 163, 267, 269–70
  slaves and women in 217n22
  true, the beautiful and the good 194–6, 219
greed 103, 104, 106, 117n43

Habermas, Jürgen 139–46, 149–54
  on madness 160n18
  rationality 160n9, 208
  Strukturwandel der Öffentlichkeit (*The Structural Change of the Public Sphere*) 140, 145
  Theorie des kommunikativen Handelns (*Theory of Communicative Action*) 140, 144–5, 153
Hadot, Pierre 7, 26n17, 8, 282n22, 336, 339n35
hair loss *see* baldness, female
hairdresser, hospital 53–4
'hanging out' (research practice) 284–5, 295–301, 306n5, 307n36–8
  averting the eyes 291–5
  'deep hanging out' 284, 306n6
  generative 285, 304–5
  small talk 291–2, 306n24
  studying 'hanging out better' 286–7, 290
Haraway, Donna 55n1, 293
harnessing passions 106
Hawking, Stephen 217n24, 242
Heinz (ethical dilemma) 6, 26n15
HeLa cell line 44, 57n47
Hennion, Antoine 15, 27n37
hermeneutics
  double 190, 57n51
  generative 30, 47, 48–54, 309, 322
hierarchy, in interviews 296–8
hippy goodness 68
Hirschauer, Stefan 45–6
Hirschman, Albert 93–4, 101–2, 104–8, 109, 110, 111
historical descriptions/texts 39, 40–1, 41–2
Hobbes, Thomas 94, 105, 107, 109, 117n45, 339n37
Hoppe, S. 308n56

Horkheimer, Max, *Dialektik der Aufklärung* 140
human psyche 43
human rights 51, 53, 66, 69, 313, 317
human, the 189
humanism 116n2, 209, 216n1, 236n6, 265–82
humanitas values 52, 53, 54, 67, 68–9, 70, 75, 82
Hume, David 106–7, 117n31
hygiene and cleanliness 27n42, 36, 71, 73–8, 87n27, 187n10

imaginaries 166, 187n11
impartial spectator, morality and the 96–100, 336
imperfect life, as a good life 8–9
inauthentic utterings 154
independent life 122, 196–7, 249
individuality
  analysing 162, 283
  dangerous passions 331–2
  individual liberties 338n4
  individual morality 89–115
  individuals in the community 157–9
  statistical individual 333–4
  what is an individual 328–9
inductive morality 98
innovative practices of the self 226–31
  massage in the hospital 226–8
  workshop as a technology of the self 228–31
inquiry, form and content in practices of 266
institutions, autonomy and 121–2
intellectual
  disabilities label 135n6
  insights 276
  practice 268–72
intelligent emotions 329–30
interdependence (of research partners) 298–9
interviews, open
  averting the eyes 291–5
  goal-oriented 289
  hierarchy 296–8
  one-on-one conversations 287–8
  relationship-oriented 290
  semi-structured 287, 299, 306n15
  structuring workings of 287–9
invisible hand trope 100–1, 103, 104, 113, 144
Irigaray, Luce 306n24
irony and mockery 141, 159n5

James, William 87n32
Juvenal 273

Kahneman, Daniel 116n19
Kant, Immanuel 8, 159n8
'knowing' 167, 183, 191–2, 216n5, 231, 266–7, 230

knowledge, clinical 216n19
Kohlberg–Gilligan debate 6, 26n15
Kohlberg, Lawrence 26n15

labour, division of 61
Lacks, Henrietta 44, 57n47

Landes, Joan, *Women and the Public Sphere in the Age of the French Revolution* 139, 145–56, 160n10
language, Dutch 166
Latour, Bruno 308n54
Laura (Petrarch's love) 282n11
Law, John 42
Lawy, J. R. 305n1
learning disabilities 119–35
  alcohol and drug use 122, 125, 126, 129, 131–3, 136n20, 318–19
  distribution of agency 131–3
  medical professionals caring for those with 125–6
  practical matters 306n16
legal principles 65
letter writing, Petrarch's practice of 265–82, 282n7
liberalism 65, 116n2
'life-saving' discourse 166
Limburg, Sarah 244, 248, 252, 255, 257
Linguet, Simon-Nicholas Henri 109
Lisa (philosophy of care) 131
Lisa (scarves/wigs) 180–1
listening skills 38
literary sphere 142, 147, 149–50, 333
locked-in syndrome 248–9
looking bad 172–5, 184, 186n8
looking beautiful 179–81
looking good 172–5, 181–3, 228
lung diseases 1–2, 79–81, 322
lust (voluptas) 271, 279

McCloskey, Deirdre 116n9
Macfie, A. L. 96–104, 117n23, 117n26
madness 160n18
Mahmood, Saba 235n2
make-up 171, 176, 182, 224, 230
Mandeville, Bernard 92, 95, 106
Marcus, G. E., *Writing Culture* 285
Marcuse, Herbert 140
marriage 194, 339n34
Martin (distribution of agency) 131
Marx, Karl 107, 110
massage, hospital 226–8, 234
material semiotics 10, 35–6, 44, 45–6, 80, 311, 334
material trace 45–7
materiality 9, 215
M'charek, Amade 44–5, 46, 69
Mead, G. H. 234
mechanistic thinking 97, 109, 116n21
medical
  discourse 3
  ethics 64, 119
  paternalism 119
  professional understanding 125–6
medieval academic philosophy 266–7
melody (*melos*) 204–5
mental health 70–1, 245, 307n42, 326, 327
'mere opinions' 144, 145, 153
methods, creativity of 33–4, 316–18, 338n11
Meyer, Birgit 16, 17, 27n41
Middle Ages 201
middle class 90, 93, 107, 108
Mill, John Stuart 145

Millar, John 108
Mirabeau 109
mirror, seeing in the 167, 169
mockery, irony and 141, 159n5
modern philosophy 8, 282n22
modernist ethics 11, 32, 209
  principles 63–86
'modes of ordering' 27n42, 36, 56n30, 86n5, 138, 159, 327, 339n27
Montaigne, Michel de 267
Montesquieu 108
Moonen, Xavier 122
morality
  debates 86n3
  versus economy 95–6
  end of 89–115
  and the impartial spectator 96–100, 336
  Petrarch and 267, 270–2, 275, 276
  regained 82–4
  Smith's work on 96–100
  social 100–2
  truth and 279
  See also aesthetic values
motivation(s)
  aesthetic 61, 69, 204–5
  'motivated collectives' 335
  motivated social organisation 137, 159n1
  motivated socialities 221, 279, 313, 319, 335
  truth and 209–10
motor neurone disease 241–61
moveable goods 108, 109
musicality of language 307n26

natural affections 107–8
Nauta, Lolle 55n5, 338n24
Nazi Germany 26n21, 140, 160n12, 177–8
negotiations, everyday 60, 89
neoliberalism 89, 318, 328
Nero 270
neurology nurses 49
newspapers 141, 149
Norman, Jesse 95–6, 99, 116n19, 117n42
normativity
  concepts and methods 27n47, 33–4, 214
  from exemplary to exemplar 321–2
  Foucault 186n7
  'man as he really is' 105
  normative and descriptive qualifications 247–9
  normative utterings 153
  sick citizens and 72, 210–11
North, John 55n5
nurses
  different care practices 36–7
  psychiatric 49, 52, 70–3, 75–7
  nursing homes 60, 66–7, 291–2
Nussbaum, Martha 26n30

obesity 29, 55n2
object–subject relations (reflexivity) 299–302
observation, participant 38–9
O'Connor, Sinead 179, 223
open concepts 31–2, 55n7, 216n4, 339n29
ordering, modes of *see* 'modes of ordering'

INDEX   **369**

ordinary lives 172, 174, 190, 212–16, 321–2, 330
oxygen supplies 255

pain, being in 226–7, 236n18
palliative oncology care 170
parrhesia (speaking the truth) 162, 192, 198, 199–204, 205, 209–11
participant observation 38–9, 56n28, 284, 295
particularist style 86n3, 137–59, 148
passions
    calculating work of the interests 104–8
    dangerous 331–2
    reducing the 109
    taming of the 89–115
peasants 116n3
Peirce, C. S. 291, 292
people and things 9–10
percutaneous endoscopic gastrostomy (PEG) 242–3
performative workings 42
'personal-public' sphere 150
'personalised medicine' 263n41
Petrarch 40, 265–82, 282n7, 282n11, 302, 324, 329–30
philosophers 7–8, 60
philosophy, as good life practice 7–8, 282n22
pointing and folding 46, 54
political emancipation 142, 143, 151, 159n8, 160n9
politics 118n53
    aesthetics of 151–2
    parrhesia 201–3
    and possessions 108–10
    technologies of the self 220, 231
Pols, Jeannette 177, 180–1, 258
'possible freedom' 231, 232, 234
'post-literary opinions' 144
poverty, living in 197
power-free discussion 153
practice (definition) 55n10
pragmatic ethics 117n35–6
pre-modern philosophy 8, 9, 42, 60–2, 100, 104, 117n31, 189, 234, 278, 311, 315, 320, 331, 336
pride 67, 101, 103
principles
    autonomy 119–35, 314
    ethical 59–61, 63–86, 312
    legal 65
    and the values of everyday life 77–8, 152–5, 310–14, 322
print media 149–50
private to public (public sphere citizen structure) 142–3
proper love (*amour propre*) 109
prophecy (mode of veridiction) 200–1
prophet (speaking the truth) 199
'propriety' 26n30, 98, 101
psukhe ('the soul') 191–2
psychiatric hospitals 48–50, 114–15, 287–8, 293–4
    dignity in long-term 63–86, 86n19
    long-term wards 298, 302, 307n26, 319
    relational citizenship 86n19, 136n29
psychiatric nurses
    citizenship and 75–6
    on cleanliness 76–7
    dignity and 49, 52, 70–1
    dirty wards and 72–3
public opinion 142, 144–5, 149–50, 208
public sphere
    changing structure of 139–43
    different 149–50
    individual differences 154–5
    from private to public 142–3
    from representation to deliberation 141
Purkis, Mary Ellen 160n21
'pyjama days' example 66

QALYs (Quality Adjusted Life Years) 246, 247, 256
quality of life
    dysphagia and 244
    key values 135n14, 259–61
    living with ALS and a feeding tube 241–61
    locked-in syndrome 248–9
    normative and descriptive qualifications 247–9
    statistical individual 334
    temporality 250–3
    understanding 245–6
Quesnay, François 109
questionnaires 238, 246, 249, 250, 260, 265, 300, 325

radiologically inserted gastrostomy (RIG) 242–3
rationality 101–6, 114, 116n19, 137–59, 160n9, 160n12, 208
Rawls, John 67
re-scription 29–30, 145, 302, 309–10, 317–18, 322–4, 327–8
    concept 167, 216n17, 283
    use of term 55n3, 56n17
reader, position of the (Petrarch's letters) 272–7
reality, empirical study and 33
reasoning
    abstract 32, 55n13, 86n3
    mathematical 94
    stern 332–3
    styles of 156, 274, 279
reduction concept (metaphors) 42
reflexivity (subject–object relations) 299–302
refolding approach 206
    new dignities 52–3
    words with practices 53–4
refugees 69, 80
rehabilitation coaches 72
reinterpreting concepts 32
relational
    citizenship 27n44, 86n19, 136n29
    perceptions 223–4
    practice 128–31, 330
religious practices 16, 17, 65, 338n4
Renaissance humanism 265–82
representation, new forms of 149–50
representation to deliberation (public sphere citizen structure) 141
repressing passions 106
republicanism 139, 146, 148

research practices, valuable 280–1
 audiences, co-researchers and informants 281–2
 reinventing for studying the values of everyday life 283–305
 young researchers/students 306n9, 306n22, 308n46
research subjects
 concept 306n7
 expertise of 305n3
 relationship between researcher and 285–6, 306n14, 307n42, 308n49
 researcher and goodbye ritual 307n40
residential homes 36–7, 48–50, 70–7, 87n27, 294, 307n40
response shift (temporality) 250, 253, 260
'right to support' 122
Rights of Persons with Disabilities, Convention on the 122
Robinson Crusoe (character) 98–9
'role models' 217n24
Romanticism 159n7, 332
Rome, ancient 189
Rosaldo, Renato 306n6
Rosen, Michael 51
Rousseau, Jean-Jacques 109, 150, 159n7

salons, life in the 137–59
 public sphere of the 145–6
 the salons 147
 salons under fire 148–9
Scarry, Elaine 236n18
scarves 168, 174, 179–80, 228, 230, 313
Schaffer, Simon 94
science and technology studies (STS) 9, 26n16, 27n45–6, 33, 56n14–17, 65
Scottish Enlightenment 93, 108
Second World War 26n21, 69, 119, 177–8, 187n13, 236n10, 305n2
Seeber, A. A. 251
self-disclosure 149–50
self-interest 94–5, 96, 116n4, 117n42
self-love 101, 105, 109
self-measurement 326–7
self-quantification 326–7
self-worth 318
 on imminent aesthetic socialities 219–35
 innovative practices of the self 226–31, 233–4
 maintaining 52
 social life and 74
selfhood 176–7, 183, 221–2, 225–7, 229, 231–4, 272, 283
semiotics, material 10, 35–6, 44, 45–6, 80, 311, 334
Seneca 269, 270, 274, 275
sentiments, fragile 332–3
Serres, Michel 39, 40
service users 47
settings, care 63, 70–1, 134, 288, 314
sexual harassment 307n42
Shapin, Steven 94
shaping the self 184, 193, 221–2
shaping the social 221–2
showering 1–2
silence 269

situated and relational perceptions 223–4
situated spectator 98
situations, as exemplar 322
 specific situations 321, 323–5, 339n25–6
slaves 69, 217n22, 330
sleep medication 263n41
Smith, Adam
 'Adam Smith problem' 91–2, 95–6, 103
 'great mob of mankind' 109
 on the impartial spectator 324–5
 on luxury 109
 Macfie and 117n23, 117n26
 moral theory as a theory of the good life 82, 99–100, 311
 morality and the impartial spectator 96–9
 'propriety' 26n30, 98, 117n35
 and the taming of the passions 89–115
 on the ward 114–15
 writing style 116n18
 The Theory of Moral Sentiments 95–7
 The Wealth of Nations 95–6, 100
smoking 87n21
social
 death 185
 morality 100–2
 shaping the 221–2
 theorists 39, 41–2, 60–1, 89–115, 117n31, 137–8
 what is the 328–9
social life, changing 231–4
social values, aesthetic values as 15–17, 161–2, 165–86
socialities, aesthetic
 changing social conventions 163
 female baldness 219–20, 323–4
 the self as a practice of worth 219–35
socialities, motivated 221, 279, 313, 319, 335
socio-economic status 80
sociology, and anthropology of the good 14–15
Socrates, *Apology* 192, 194, 201–3, 205, 216n15, 267
solitude 268–9
soup metaphor 308n56
sovereign life 196, 198
sovereign power 108, 141, 146, 151, 339n37
specific situations 321, 323–5, 339n25–6
specificities
 comparing 30, 36–7, 56n33, 56n36
 generative concepts 309–10
 grasping 309–37
 putting knowledge into practice 261
 what are everyday-life values 310–14
spectator
 impartial 96–100, 336
 situated 98
spinal cord injuries 249
'standpoint feminism' 235n5
state of worth 36, 87n30, 162, 176–7, 183–4
 women and 219–35, 318
statistical individual 333–4
Stengers, Isabelle 159, 160n21
stern reason 332–3
Steuart, Sir James 108
Steven (smokes cannabis) 129–30, 131
Stoicism 117n23, 194
straight life 196–7

Strathern, Marilyn 55n10
Struever, Nancy 266–73, 276–8, 282, 282n11
Struhkamp, Rita 249
'sub-literary opinions' 144
subject–object relations (reflexivity) 299–302
subjectification (definition) 209
Sugar Lee Hooper 179, 223
suicide, assisted 82
suicide bombers 216n12
sympathy, and the impartial spectator 96–100
syphilis trials, Tuskegee 119, 135n1, 305n2

tarnishing (*ontluistering*) 47, 67
teacher/technician (speaking the truth) 200
techne (mode of veridiction) 200–1, 216n5
technological metaphors 43
technologies, healthcare 339n46
technologies of the self 195, 220–1, 223–31, 233, 320, 322, 329
    workshop as 228–31
technology, good in 38–9
temporality 250–3, 256–7, 260 285, 299
theory vs practice 27n47, 152–5
thermometer example 34
Thévenot, Laurent 14, 36, 56n30
things
    appreciating 167
    people and 9–10
    valuing 167
    words and 45–7
Thomas, William 57n45
Tocqueville, Alexis de 110, 144–5
tranquillity 102, 270
transparency 278, 338n11
true, good and beautiful 205
truth
    Cynics and 196–9
    morality and 279
    and motivation 209–10
    open concept 160n16, 216n4
    speaking the 162, 192, 198, 199–203
tubes, feeding
    ALS and 241–61, 263n39, 302, 304, 316, 318
    definition 242–3
    of deterioration 250–1
    different 256–7
    as facilitator of happy events 253–4
    quality of life and 243–4
    as a solution 251–3
    as a transformer of misery 255
Tuskegee syphilis trials 119, 135n1, 305n2
type I diabetes 286, 287, 288, 293, 297, 303

unconcealed life 196–7, 204
'undercover' research 307n41
unfolding approach 50–2, 206, 216n17
'universal human' 334
universalising, modes of 6
universalism, life in the salons, or citizens against aesthetics 137–59
unmoveable goods 108
unnatural affections 108
utilitarianism 61, 97, 99, 111, 116n19
utterings 153–4

values
    different types of 259–61
    dignity in long-term psychiatry 63–86, 86n3
    everyday patient values in care for people with learning disabilities 119–35
    how they work 64–6
    quality of life key 135n14, 259–61
    the sensuous body or the facts of life 257–9, 263n41
    valuing things 167, 231–2
    what are 11–12, 153–4
    'what drives people' 331–2
Van der Stap, Sophie, *Girl With Nine Wigs* 181, 223
vanity 101, 103
'veil of ignorance' metaphor 67
veridiction, modes of 200–1, 202–3, 216n5, 320–1
Verrips, Jojada 17
vice(s) 92, 95, 101, 104, 108, 198
voice, giving or making 119–35, 260–1, 305n1

walkers (self-worth) 225–6
washing practice 27n42, 36, 76–7, 187n10
wealth 93–4, 102, 108, 111, 192, 328
weight loss 243, 252, 326–7
wellness practices 3
wigs 53–4, 168–70, 174, 178–83, 222, 224–5, 228, 236n7
'will-work' 136n30
wisdom (mode of veridiction) 200–1
wise (speaking the truth) 199–200
witches, burning of witches 177–8
witness/witnessing 168–9
Wittgenstein, Ludwig 57n42, 308n52
women
    ancient Greek 217n22
    in different relationships 186n5
    femininity 150, 223, 236n12, 312
    feminism 220, 235n2, 235n5
    hair loss due to chemotherapy 161, 163, 165–86, 212–13, 219–35
    'Look good, feel better' workshops 168–86, 222–31
    as mothers 146, 148, 152
    and the public sphere 139, 142, 143, 145–6
    Renaissance humanists and 282n11
    self-worth 219–35, 318
words and things 45–7
World Health Organization Quality of Life (WHOQOL) Group 245
worth *see* self-worth
worthlessness 224, 226–7, 229, 232, 234

'yarning' practices 287–9, 297, 303